VARIABLE QUALITY IN CONSUMER THEORY

VARIABLE

QUALITY

IN

CONSUMER

THEORY

TOWARD A DYNAMIC
MICROECONOMIC THEORY
OF THE CONSUMER

WILLIAM M. WADMAN

M.E. Sharpe
Armonk, New York
London, England

Library of Congress Cataloging-in-Publication Data

Wadman, William M.
Variable quality in consumer theory : toward a dynamic microeconomic theory of the
consumer / William M. Wadman.
p.   cm.
Includes bibliographical references and index.
ISBN 0-7656-0464-7 (hc. : alk. paper) ISBN 0-7656-0465-5 (pbk. : alk. paper)
1. Consumption (Economics) I. Title.
HB801.W225   1999
339.4′7—dc21   99–29525
CIP

Printed in the United States of America

The paper used in this publication meets the minimum requirements of
American National Standard for Information Sciences
Permanence of Paper for Printed Library Materials,
ANSI Z 39.48-1984.

BM	(c)	10	9	8	7	6	5	4	3	2	1
BM	(p)	10	9	8	7	6	5	4	3	2	1

Dedication

This book is dedicated to economists, past and present, who have devoted time to the research of variable quality. Among authors in this field, I would like to acknowledge Hendrik S. Houthakker, Franklin M. Fisher, Karl Shell, John Muellbauer, and Duncan S. Ironmonger.

For their patience, encouragement, and love, this work is also dedicated to the members of my family: to my wife, Linda, and to our children, Jeffrey, Bethany, Chris, Bert, and Jennifer.

Authors know that books are not easily written. This one has been no exception. Yet writing a scientific book can be like writing a novel. Ideas, like characters, once loose upon a page harbor their own lives, follow their own unsuspected paths, mature in unforeseen ways, and mingle with their own logic. If useful, they have progeny.

Stuart A. Kauffman
The Origins of Order

Contents

List of Figures

Acknowledgments

A work of this sort is never the accomplishment of a single person. Many people have been of assistance to me, either in terms of encouragement, exchange of ideas, or simply through their friendship. Within the Cameron School of Business and the larger community of the University of North Carolina at Wilmington (UNCW), I would like to thank the following friends, colleagues, and students: Sheila Adams, Arvid Anderson, John Anderson, Ravija Badarinathi, Jack Baker, Robert Burrus, Cem Canel, David Carter, Denis Carter, Steve Christophe, Chris Dumas, Fara Elikai, Claude Farrell III, Bill Goffe, Dan Golden, William Hall, P.J. Lapaire and Elizabeth Adams-Lapaire, Luther Lawson, Chancellor James Leutze, Gabriel Lugo, Allan McDowell, Jim and Babette McNab, Kevin Ross, Peter Schuhmann, Charles West, and Amy Zeng.

For interesting conversations and exchange of ideas during the time I spent in the Fulbright program at ILADES/Georgetown in Santiago, Chile, I would like to thank Jorge Marshall, Felipe Morandé, Jorge Rodriguez, Aristites Torché, and Marcel Claude.

For their willingness to take of their time to review my manuscript, I owe a special debt of gratitude to Professors Richard H. Day, Franklin M. Fisher, Hendrik S. Houthakker, Duncan S. Ironmonger, John Muellbauer, and Karl Shell. I also appreciate the words of encouragement extended by Simon P. Anderson, Robert Axelrod, and Michael D. Cohen. In addition, although his field is neurobiology, I truly appreciate the exchange of ideas provided generously by Professor Jean-Pierre Changeux of the Institut Pasteur.

As any researcher knows, little progress is made without the assistance of highly qualified secretaries. In this regard, I would like to acknowledge Janet M. McGee, Karen W. Shannon, Patricia M. Geiser, and Rebecca A. Chilcote. I would also like to thank the fine staff of the William Madison Randall Library at UNCW, especially the staff of the Office of Interlibrary Loans.

Last, but by no means least, I appreciate the standards of scholarship and technical support provided by the editors and staff of M.E. Sharpe. I especially want to acknowledge and extend my thanks to Sean M. Culhane, Esther L. Clark, and Eileen Maass. I would also like to thank Lucille Sutton, of Irwin/McGraw-Hill, for her encouragement and suggestions at an earlier stage in this project. As always, any remaining errors in this work are my responsibility.

W.M.W.

University of North Carolina at Wilmington

Part 1

Evolution of Variable Quality in Economic Thought

Antecedents to a New Theory of Consumption

Chapter 1

Introduction

When I began this project I was simply interested in presenting a brief history of the manner in which economists addressed the topic of variable quality. That was over fifteen years ago.

My interest in the theoretical issues of variable quality arose initially from my work as a health economist in the California State Department of Health. During that time I became acutely aware of the need to understand better the relationship of quality to efficiency, specifically as these concepts applied to health care service. Efforts to reduce health care costs of the California Medicaid program, known as MediCal at that time, were intended to save taxpayers' money, while at the same time having no adverse effects on Medicaid recipients. As continues to this day, the critical issue was whether the quality of publicly funded health care programs was maintained, while efficiency of the programs improved. In other words, did "savings" generated by the MediCal Reform Program arise from improved efficiency of the state's Medicaid program, or did "savings" arise from a deterioration in the quality and quantity of health care services rendered to Medicaid recipients?

In an effort to understand these issues, I began to examine how economists defined and measured quality. I sought a similar understanding of the definitions and measures of quality employed by physicians and other health care professionals. What I found was considerable variation and obtuseness in the theory, definitions, and measurement techniques of both groups.

The present work does not address the issues of quality and efficiency in the health care sector. My approach is much more limited. As it turns out, however, even the more limited topic is extensive. What I set out to do was gain a better understanding of how economists define and measure quality—specifically, the quality of goods and services transacted in retail markets. As with the case of physicians, economists have many different interpretations, or points of view, regarding what constitutes quality. I am no exception.

In the process of trying to understand the contributions to variable quality made by earlier economists, and in an effort to synthesize those contributions, I began to realize that a new, dynamic version of consumer theory was gradually unfolding. It grows out of those earlier works on variable quality.

In part 1, the contributions of economists, from the classical period to the work of John Muellbauer, are presented. Many of the ideas that form the basis of the new theory evolve in this early stage. As the reader will discover, many contemporary ideas regarding "quality" are, in fact, quite old. In similar fashion, many of the current debates, or alternative interpretations of "quality," are not new. The book builds throughout part 1 in preparation for part 2.

A rather large portion of part 1 is devoted to the contribution of Hendrik Houthakker.

Many authors in the field of variable quality view Houthakker's work as the foundation for the hedonic technique and for other theoretical issues associated with quality. Part 1 compares the contributions of Hendrik Houthakker and Henri Theil. Most important, chapter 4 identifies a problem within the Houthakker constraint, when the model is forced away from its initial solution—that is, away from Houthakker's *basic price system*. Comparison of Houthakker and Theil reveals that unless the Houthakker model can function away from its initial basic solution, it becomes, in effect, the same model as that developed by Theil.

As is well known, Houthakker is credited with one of the first applications of indirect utility. Interestingly, he also provided a technique to identify the "quantity" unit of measure of a product or service (i.e., to separate quantity from the numerous dimensions of quality). Separation of quantity from quality is essential to any theory of variable quality, and to the ability to compare and rank-order levels of quality. Not all economists are in agreement on this point, however.

Part 1 concludes with the works of John Muellbauer, Franklin Fisher, Karl Shell, Zvi Griliches, Jack Triplett, and others. Inasmuch as the characteristics approach to consumer theory frequently is linked to issues of variable quality, part 1 also covers the works of two authors in this field: Kelvin Lancaster and Duncan Ironmonger.

In part 2 the nature of the Houthakker constraint is examined at length. In the effort to understand better his constraint, an entirely new approach to variable quality is developed. The new model, which is a variation on the original work by Houthakker, takes a consumer approach. The model incorporates material from fields outside economics. Research findings from neuroscience and psychology, specifically on the topics of perception, cognition, generation of self, and self-awareness, are included. Mathematical

developments in nonlinear dynamics, particularly the theory of attractors, are utilized. A Feigenbaum model of human decision making is presented. The model is based on a phase space that examines the interaction of human perception and expectation with experience and learning.

In the revised model, consumer perception of quality is assumed unique to each consumer. Like beauty, quality is assumed to exist in the eye of the beholder. A consumer's concept and perception of self are seen as playing a central role in the processes of perception and evaluation of the quality of products and services purchased and consumed. From a consumer perspective, quality is defined and measured in terms of a product or service's ability to enhance consumer self-image and/or to protect that self-image. As self-image changes over the life span of a consumer, so does the perception, evaluation, and ranking of quality. The relationship of a consumer's consumption technology to his or her self-image is discussed.

Within this context, the existence of a single ranking of quality across all consumers is unlikely. In fact, the maintenance of a single "theory of the consumer" is viewed as unrealistic and impractical. With the perception of quality based on, and influenced by, individual consumer perception of self, the aggregation of consumers to create quality indices becomes more difficult, but not impossible. Issues of separability and aggregation likewise become more complex.

Because of the heavy emphasis on the individualistic and subjective nature of quality, the new model argues that sampling techniques utilized to investigate consumer behavior should be restricted to stratified-clustered samples drawn on numerous cohorts of consumers. In other words, there is no single "Representative Consumer," but rather a representative consumer for each cohort of consumers under examination. The tighter the stratification and clustering of characteristics of a cohort population, the greater the ability to control for and study the effects of variable quality.

To the extent possible, consumers should be subdivided into cohorts based on age, sex, income, geographical location, level of education, occupation or profession, worldview, culture, religion, and so forth. Under conditions of variable quality, the application of a general theory of the consumer may lead to statistical results that obfuscate the impact of quality or generate mixed results. The model identifies circumstances wherein such conditions might arise.

A particularly unusual feature of the new model is the assumption that consumer decision making regarding variable quality requires consumer participation in both the objective function and the constraint, both of which operate in a more complex consumption space. Participation in the constraint is based on a new interpretation of the parameters in the original Houthakker constraint. Specifically, the new theory posits the existence of willingness-to-pay components within that constraint. One of the willingness-to-pay components is based on a redefinition of Houthakker's b_i. In the new model, b_i reflects consumer expectation of quality (from a specific product or service) and consumer consumption experience (learning) derived from consumption of that product or service. Several different forms of learning and interaction with willingness-to-pay are examined.

Consumption experience is assumed to be unique to each consumer, interpreted by each consumer within the context of the consumer's self-image, and his or her expectation of quality. A gap or inconsistency between the consumer's expectation of quality and the interpreted consumption experience of quality is assumed possible. A loopy system of human perception, based on an interaction of expectation and experience, is assumed capable of explaining the existence of such inconsistencies and of finding possible solutions. This approach is similar to the C-D gap of Ronald Heiner, yet with significant differences.

In the world of variable quality it is furthermore assumed that the constraint and objective function may become truncated, that consumer decision making might occur only within neighborhoods along a spectrum of variable quality, and that the constraint and objective function may be dynamic (e.g., the constraint may vibrate in $x_i x_j$ consumption space). The dynamic behavior of objective function and constraint arises from learning processes within the consumer. Learning reduces inconsistencies between consumer expectation and consumption experience. The implications for individual consumer demand curves are correspondingly unusual. The model assumes that consumers do not "know" the entire length of their individual demand curves. Only neighborhoods, where consumers have consumption experience, may be known. Individual consumer demand curves, therefore, may be truncated—that is, exist only in segments over demand space. The concept of a window within quality-quantity space is developed and holds implications of $x_i x_j$ consumption space and for demand space. Windows are also assumed possible in demand space. Finally, under variable quality, the concept of a demand reservation price is expanded. The obverse of a reservation price is introduced.

In the new model the concept of consumer surplus is expanded, as are the concepts of compensated and equivalent variation. Under conditions of variable quality, findings from psychology—based on human experiments regarding consumer willingness-to-pay and the framing of decisions—acquire new importance and applicability. Targeting, discrete choice, and lexicographic ordering are included within consumer decision making, as they apply both to quality and to quantity.

Learning from experience also applies to consumer decision making regarding the household budget and subbudgets. Decentralization of subbudgets within total consumer income is required and introduces new perspectives on consumer decision making regarding substitution across subbudgets. The standard presumption that an increase in quality will induce an increase in demand is examined under the requirements of decentralized subbudgets. At the level of an individual consumer, unless the consumer is willing to allocate additional funds to the appropriate subbudget, higher quality will not induce higher demand. This issue has implications for the definition and measurement of inflation and for quality-adjusted price indices. Income compensation for quality-induced higher prices is evaluated, and refinements on the methods of compensation are introduced.

Involvement of the consumer in both the objective function and the constraint results in a consumer theory that is indeterminate, at least until consumers interact with producers and transactions occur. Interaction between consumers and producers, however, may only reduce indeterminacy, but not necessarily eliminate it. Interaction between these two groups occurs at several levels in the model. Interaction begins at the level of quality-quantity consumption space, extends to $x_i x_j$ consumption space, and then to demand space. At all levels, the interaction of consumers and producers is argued to be better understood in terms of hunter-prey models, other applications of dynamic game theory, and through various models of mathematical biology. The likelihood of nonequilibrium market solutions is increased, either as shortside solutions on the demand or supply surface. The model assumes firm behavior analogous to first-degree price discriminating monopoly or other forms of price discrimination by oligopolists. The importance of discrete choice models is underscored.

Early Attempts to Introduce Variable Quality

1. Introduction

It is debatable whether there ever was a time in the history of economic thought when variable quality went unrecognized. Introduction of the assumption of homogeneous goods and services, however, resulted in reduced emphasis on quality and led to a general presumption, usually unstated, that quality was constant. In this book we do not utilize the homogeneity assumption, but refer instead directly to the assumption of constant quality. This assumption is labeled the "isoquality" assumption.

In chapter 2 we review some of the early work on quality, from the classical period to the early 1950s. Our coverage does not include all contributions to the field, for it is only a partial history of thought. It does, however, provide a sample of major trends of thought during the period.

2. Classical Contributions

Economists have long recognized the existence of variable quality. Adam Smith, for example, made reference to variation in the quality of labor:

> It is often difficult to ascertain the proportion between two quantities of labour. The time spent in different sorts of work will not always alone determine this proportion. The different degrees of hardship endured, and the ingenuity exercised must likewise be taken into account. There may be more labour in one hour's hard work than in two hours' easy business; or in an hour's application to a trade which costs ten years' labour to learn, than in a month's industry in an ordinary and obvious employment. But it is not easy to find any accurate measure, either of hardship or ingenuity. In exchanging, indeed, the different productions of different sorts of labour for one another, some allowance is commonly made for both. It is adjusted, however, not by any accurate measure, but by the higgling and bargaining of the market, according to that rough equality, which, though not exact, is sufficient for carrying on the business of common life. (Smith 1776/1952, p. 13)

Although not explicit, Smith revealed an awareness of variation in the quality of labor by his comments on "hardship endured" and "ingenuity exercised." He is the first author to suggest that variation in quality could be accounted for via bargaining processes of the market (i.e., "by the higgling and bargaining of the market"). Smith was the first to assume that competitively negotiated price could serve as a measure of quality. Smith was also pragmatic and recognized that there are many difficulties in the measurement of quality, namely, that "it is not easy to find any accurate measure, either of hardship or ingenuity."

Another early attempt to include variable quality in economics was the theory of land rent developed by David Ricardo (1817/1969). In an illustration given by Ricardo, the productivity of various grades of land was used to demonstrate how, as the price of wheat (corn) increased, less productive land was cultivated, and the rent premium grew for the top grades of land. Difference in the productivity of land is essentially the same concept as difference in the grades of labor discussed by Adam Smith. Both examples illustrate an awareness of variable quality.

The first author to employ the assumption of constant quality was William Stanley Jevons. In *The Theory of Political Economy*, Jevons (1871) introduced constant quality in his definition of a market:

> A market, then, is theoretically perfect only when all traders have perfect knowledge of the conditions of supply and demand, and the consequent rates of exchange, and in such a market, as we shall see, there can be only one ratio of exchange of one *uniform commodity* at any moment. (Jevons, chapter 4, emphasis added)

A careful reading of the "theories of value" of most economists of this period reveals similar assumptions of constant quality. Most authors, however, were not explicit on the topic. In fact, the brevity with which the subject was treated suggests the assumption of constant quality was taken for granted, the implications of the assumption were presumed to be insignificant, and/or quality differences were assumed captured in market prices.

In 1883, Henry Sidgwick began to address some of the measurement problems that arise when quality is not constant. In particular, he studied bias in price comparisons when the quality of a product has changed or when new products are introduced. Sidgwick believed that such bias could be eliminated through the use of utility theory:

> Here again there seems to be no means of attaining more than a rough and approximate solution of the problem proposed; and to reach even this we have to abandon the prima facie exact method of comparing prices, and to substitute the essentially looser procedure of comparing amounts of utility or satisfaction. (Sidgwick 1883, p. 68)[1]

And we have to deal similarly with a further source of inexactness introduced into this calculation by the progress of the industrial arts. The products of industry keep changing in quality; and before we can say whether any kind of thing—for example, cloth—has really grown cheaper or dearer, we must compare the quality—that is, the degree of utility—of the article produced at the beginning of the period with that of the more recent ware. This source of difficulty reaches its maximum in the case where entirely new kinds of things have been produced or brought into the country by trade. To leave them out altogether might clearly vitiate the result. . . .

> So far we have been considering the difficulty of carrying a standard of value from one time to another. But precisely similar obstacles stand in the way of our obtaining definite results, when we compare the different values of gold (or any other ware) in different places at the same time. (Sidgwick 1901, p. 73)

Alfred Marshall was interested in the problems that variable quality and the introduction of new products can impose on price indices.[2] Marshall is generally credited with introduction of the constant quality, or homogeneity assumption.[3] On this matter he was preceded by Jevons, although Marshall was more thorough and explicit regarding the assumption.

Like Adam Smith, Marshall recognized the variability of labor quality.[4] He also addressed the idea of constant quality of output. In his work on consumer demand and market equilibrium, Marshall stated his constant-quality assumption as follows:

> Now let us translate this law of diminishing utility into terms of price. Let us take an illustration from the case of a commodity such as tea, which is in constant demand and which can be purchased in small quantities. Suppose, for instance, that tea *of a certain quality* is to be had at 2 s. per lb. (Marshall 1916, p. 94, emphasis added)

> Let us then turn to the ordinary dealings of modern life; and take an illustration from a corn-market in a country town, and let us assume for the sake of simplicity that all the corn in the market is *of the same quality*. (Marshall 1916, p. 332, emphasis added)

In addition to Smith, Ricardo, Jevons, Sidgwick, and Marshall, other writers who made reference to variable quality include Knut Wicksell, Richard Ely, and Thomas Carver, among others.

In his *Lectures on Political Economy*, first published in 1901, Knut Wicksell devoted a section to "Objections against the Theory of Marginal Utility—Exceptions to the Theory." In this material he considered the implications of variable quality for the theory of marginal utility:

> In reality, however, there is one circumstance which, even in these cases, imparts to the law of marginal utility a wider and more individual application than one would at first sight suppose, namely that most goods on the market are supplied in a number of different qualities. At a horse fair, for example, there is usually not merely one kind of horse, but horses of the most varied kinds as regards age, strength, swiftness, endurance, etc. For example, suppose a buyer has to choose between three horses, at 500, 550, and 575 shillings. At these prices he may prefer the second horse to both the cheaper and the dearer one: in other words he values the difference in quality between the first and the second at more than 50 s., but that between the second and third at less than 25 s. If every conceivable price and quality were to be found in the market, every buyer would certainly extend his demand up to the point at which a further addition in quality would exactly correspond to the additional price asked. If we conceive this difference of quality (looked at subjectively) as being the marginal utility of the commodity "horse" (which would be in full accordance with the genesis of the concept) then, here also, the marginal utility, at least for buyers, would be approximately the same as the price or, at any rate, proportional to it. (Wicksell 1901/1934, pp. 69–70)*

His comment, "If we conceive this difference of quality (looked at subjectively) as being the marginal utility of the commodity 'horse' (which would be in full accordance with the genesis of the concept)," suggests that

Wicksell viewed the quality of a product or service as closely related to, if not identical with, the utility the consumer derives from the product or service (similar to Sidgwick). To be sure, most authors assumed that an increase in quality would evoke an outward shift in the demand curve, but Wicksell appears to go beyond that when he assumed that the difference between two levels of quality is the marginal utility of the commodity. It also appears that he viewed "quality" as a subjective concept—that is, "quality" is in the eye of the beholder, in this case, the consumer.

Wicksell was aware that the value of a firm's output could change as a result of a change in the quality of its output. He emphasized this possibility when he assumed, "that the price of the matured wine, which is definitely fixed in the world market, is such that, when sold for consumption abroad, 3-year wine commands a wholesale price of 90 s. per hl., 4-year wine 100 s., and 5-year wine 110 s." (Wicksell 1901/1934, p. 174). Hans Brems suggested that "Wicksell's treatment of maturing wine may well be the first treatment of product quality as a variable in economic theory" (Brems 1959, p. 206). Clearly, earlier authors had been aware of product quality, and Ricardo's theory of rent would antedate Wicksell's contribution.[5]

In addition to the quality of consumer goods, Wicksell was aware of variable quality in land and labor. Examples of each, respectively, are presented in the following quotes from his *Lectures*:

> After the payment of the wages so determined . . . there remains, as a rule, a surplus for the landlord, which is greater or less according to the quality and size of his holding. (Wicksell 1901/1934, p. 113)

> All the labourers are regarded as possessing the same skill and strength. A merely

---

*From *Lectures on Political Economy,* vol. 1, by Knut Wicksell. Copyright © 1934 Lund Humphries Publications. Reprinted by permission of the publisher.

quantitative difference in physical strength, however, can easily be taken into account, if we treat a particular labourer as equal to 1.1, 1.2, etc., or 0.9, 0.8, etc., of the average labourer. On the other hand, a higher quality of labour cannot, as was once supposed, be reduced to terms of simple unskilled labour; in fact, at least at any given moment, the different classes of workers represent distinct groups, each of which is paid according to its own marginal productivity. (Wicksell 1901/1934, p. 113)

Wicksell's reference to physical strength in relationship to an average worker illustrates two important concepts in the development of quality as a variable in economics. First, that the concept of "quality" can be subdivided or broken down into subcomponents or characteristics, some of which may be measurable. And second, the concept of a quality numeraire—the average laborer—against which other levels of quality (workers) are compared. Wicksell's point that a higher-quality worker "cannot, as was once supposed, be reduced to terms of simple unskilled labour" is a bit perplexing. He is aware that a "merely quantitative difference in physical strength . . . can easily be taken into account," but he indicates that high-quality labor cannot be compared with ("be reduced to") unskilled labor. This set of conclusions suggests that Wicksell did not recognize physical strength as a quality characteristic; had he done so, his two conclusions would be inconsistent. However, Wicksell's earlier reference to the age, strength, swiftness, and endurance of horses suggests an awareness on his part of the characteristics approach to quality.

Richard Ely also provided an example of a characteristics approach to the subdivision and measurement of quality. In his chapter on the concepts of marginal utility and subjective value, Ely states, "Even in the case of an indivisible good—an automobile, for example—one may choose between having more or less of certain desirable qualities,

such as size, or power, or attractive finish" (Ely 1923, p. 131). Ely, however, did not pursue the concept further.

In the early 1920s, Thomas Carver considered the impact of variable quality on the market behavior of consumers. According to Carver,

> [t]he first law of the market is that things of the same kind and quality tend to have the same value at the same time and place. That is to say, at any given time and place, if there are a large number of units, all exactly alike and equally desirable, they will all tend to sell at the same price and have the same power in exchange. If they are unlike, some of them being more desirable than others, of course some will have more power in exchange than the others. . . . The tendency, however, is towards a uniform price at the same time and place. Where a commodity has become standardized so that there are many units that are equally desirable, it has become customary to buy the article by quantity without taking the trouble to pick out the specific units desired. Wheat, coal, cotton, pig iron, and many other commodities are so graded and standardized as to sell in this way. On the other hand, there are a great many commodities that are not easily standardized. In these cases the purchaser will usually insist on picking out the individual units which he desires. Race horses, dwelling-houses, farms, building-lots, and a multitude of other things will probably always have to be bought and sold in this way. (Carver 1921, pp. 345–346)

The concept of standardized or graded goods represents a level of sophistication above the simple recognition of variable quality or the assumption of constant quality. In the case of graded goods, or goods standardized to certain levels of quality, variation in quality is permitted and assumed measurable through the grading process. Where quality is measurable and grades can be clearly identified, Carver correctly states that consumers reduce the amount of time and resources devoted to collecting information on quality. In the case where goods cannot be standardized, consumer search and information costs are higher.

3. The Contribution of Agricultural Economists

In addition to efforts to adjust for bias in price indices, some of the earliest attempts to measure quality began with agricultural economists in the 1920s.[6] Models developed by these authors to define and measure "quality" contained ideas similar to those advanced by Edward Chamberlin and Kelvin Lancaster. Some of their methods were simple versions of methods developed later under the "hedonic technique."

Of the agricultural economists involved in the study of variable quality, Frederick Waugh was the most outstanding (Waugh 1929). The goals of Waugh's research were (1) "to discover the quality factors—such as size, shape, color, condition, pack, and other physical characteristics—which influence the prices of locally grown vegetables in the Boston wholesale market"; (2) "the development of a statistical method of analyzing market demand for quality"; and (3) "the study of the relationship of such price analyses to economic theory" (Waugh 1929, p. 15).

From his research, Waugh concluded that factors of quality do influence vegetable prices; that many of the dimensions of "quality" can be measured; that price differentials between different grades of a given vegetable decrease as the total supply of the vegetable decreases; and, that it is profitable for firms to adjust production and marketing practices to account for quality factors in consumer demand (Waugh 1929, pp. 21–22).

As an example of the influence of quality on asparagus prices, Waugh studied the following factors and how they related to the unit sale price of asparagus: the relationship of the length of green color (measured in inches); the number of stalks per bunch; and the variation in size (within a bunch). He found that all three factors were statistically significant in their relationship to price. These three factors,

however, did not explain all of the variation in asparagus prices. Other less important factors Waugh identified as contributing to price variation included the compactness and weight of the asparagus bunch, straightness of stalks, the amount of insect and mechanical injury, freshness of the product, the method of tying the bunches, general appearance of the pack, and so on (Waugh 1929, p. 45). He made similar studies of tomatoes and hothouse cucumbers, and in each case he identified statistically significant characteristics of quality.

The statistical technique employed by Waugh was multiple correlation. Although current methods are more powerful, it is worth noting that his approach was essentially the same as the early hedonic technique. Whereas the hedonic method attempts to adjust price indexes for variation in quality, as measured by changes in the characteristics of goods and services, Waugh addressed the influence of variable quality on consumer demand for vegetables.

In addition to his work to define and measure the quality of agricultural products, Waugh recommended that variable quality be more thoroughly studied in all areas of economic theory. Regarding the status of theory in his day, he found the treatment of variable quality to be incomplete and in general to not receive sufficient attention:

> Any theory, in order adequately to explain prices, must, therefore, take quality into consideration. . . . The criticism of economic theories of value presented here is not that they are illogical or incorrect, but that they are not comprehensive enough to explain certain important aspects of market values. . . . The present study makes no pretense of setting up a complete theory of prices. It is concerned primarily with one aspect—that of quality as a determinant of prices—and it is suggested that since quality plays an important part in influencing prices in the actual market that economists should give it more serious attention. This criticism applies equally well to all schools of economic thought. . . . In order to base his theory on the facts of the

market, therefore, the economist should re-examine his assumption of uniform quality and include some consideration of the influence of quality on the market. . . . As a matter of fact, writers of economic theory have not done this. (Waugh 1929, pp. 20, 30–35)*

According to Waugh, the failure of economists to recognize the importance of variable quality was twofold. First, he pointed out that for some schools of thought variable quality was already explained by the theory of substitution and therefore it deserved no further attention. Second, for other economists, variable quality was too insignificant to merit further research (Waugh 1929, p. 35).

Although not expressed in these terms, essentially Waugh argued that, for proponents of the theory of substitution, change in the price of "qualities" could be handled in the same manner as change in the price of "goods." The theory of substitution, consequently, was sufficient; no other theoretical work was necessary. As Waugh pointed out, however, substitution between qualities of the same commodity probably occurs more frequently than substitution between commodities (Waugh 1929, pp. 36–37).

Additionally, Waugh could have pointed out that substitution of one quality for another frequently results in zero consumption of the less preferred quality—that is, the consumer may not simultaneously consume multiple grades of quality of a single commodity.

The second reason behind the failure of economists to study variable quality was, according to Waugh, the assumption that quality variation was insignificant. His response to that point-of-view was that the relationship of quality to commodity price was not as simple as first appeared, and that further study was merited (Waugh 1929, p. 38).

The empirical results and theoretical issues addressed by Waugh are noteworthy. For ex-

ample, in addition to the results already mentioned, Waugh anticipated Hans Brems when he discerned that consumer and producer perceptions of quality may not be identical:

> A good buyer or seller usually recognizes good quality, but is seldom able to state accurately what the most important elements of quality are and their individual influences on prices. (Waugh 1929, p. 17)

> Most of the grades for farm products now in use in the United States have been written largely by producers. . . . This does not mean that dealers and consumers have not been consulted in the matter, nor does it mean that no studies have been made of market requirements for various qualities, but the final decision as to the qualities to be included in grade requirements has usually been left largely to the producers. (Waugh 1929, pp. 69–70)

Waugh identified the difference between the value or price of quality and its cost. As we shall see shortly, Brems was also credited with having noted this difference. Waugh's view on the separation of cost and price was expressed as follows:

> . . . the analysis of market prices gives the farmer only part of the information he needs in order to arrive at the most advantageous production and marketing policies. He needs to know not only the premium [price] paid for quality products but, also, the relative cost of producing the various qualities on his farm. (Waugh 1929, p. 65)

Waugh was aware of the difficulties consumers have in identifying and measuring the quality of the products they purchase, and of the potential for brand-name identification to become a surrogate for quality measurement. In this regard, he was contemporary with Edward Chamberlin and his work on product differentiation. According to Waugh,

---

*From *Quality as a Determinant of Vegetable Process* by Frederick Waugh. Copyright © 1929 Columbia University Press. Reprinted with permission of the publisher.

[t]he factors which have the greatest influence on prices are those which are identified in the minds of the buyers with quality.... It may be true that these factors do not in all cases indicate superior quality.... In general, consumers know little about the varieties of the products they buy. They buy on appearance, but the factors which they consider in making their purchase are those factors which they associate with quality.... This fact has been demonstrated in the study by Benner and Gabriel of the retail price of eggs in Wilmington, Delaware. This study indicated that the important quality factors influencing retail egg prices were first, cleanliness; and, second, size. The interior quality of the eggs had practically no influence on prices in spite of the fact that this factor is undoubtedly more important than all others in the minds of consumers. The consumer has no way of judging the interior quality of the eggs he buys.... [I]f the study had analyzed the variation in the prices of eggs sold at retail under various brand names which met different quality specifications, it might be found that the consumer pays a premium for quality, but that the quality is judged by the brand of trade mark, which has established a certain reputation for quality. (Waugh 1929, pp. 87–89)

Finally, Waugh recommended that market location, regional consumer preferences, snob effects, and supply factors for each grade of quality should be considered in any effort to measure the influence of quality on price (Waugh 1929, p. 96).

4. Variable Quality and Product Differentiation: The Contribution of Edward Chamberlin

Edward Chamberlin's doctoral dissertation, completed in 1927, introduced the concepts of monopolistic competition and product differentiation. Both concepts built upon the phenomenon of variable quality, but also included activities tangentially related to quality. In the evolution of economic thought, his approach represented a new direction and was one of the first widely accepted economic models that directly included "quality" as an explanatory variable.

Chamberlin's principal point of interest was the firm, not the consumer. He assumed that consumers prefer higher to lower quality and that firms adjust quality to attract consumers. He provided examples of product changes that might attract consumers. He did not, however, believe that product differentiation could be quantified. To the contrary, Chamberlin considered product variation, which includes quality variation, as essentially immeasurable:

> Another peculiarity is that "product" variations are in their essence qualitive, rather than quantitative; they cannot, therefore, be measured along an axis and displayed in a single diagram. Resort must be had, instead, to the somewhat clumsy expedient of imagining a series of diagrams, one for each variety of "product." (Chamberlin 1933, pp. 78–79)

In a subsequent publication he changed his view on the measurability of product variation (Chamberlin 1953).

Chamberlin was unclear on the difference between quality variation and product variation. Similarly, he did not specify how product variation relates to the concept of a "commodity." For the agricultural economists, in their research on variable quality, the commodity was easily identified as a particular fruit or vegetable. In the case of services and industrial products, however, the range of quality variation is much larger, as are the complexities involved in identifying the boundaries of the commodity. In other words, when does variation of the product become of sufficient magnitude that the product crosses a threshold and becomes another commodity? The limited information Chamberlin provided on the concept of a commodity suggests he viewed the group of differentiated products for a specific market and/or industry as the commodity set:

> Let us turn now to what we may call the group problem, or the adjustment of prices and "products" of a number of producers whose

goods are close substitutes for each other. The group contemplated is one which would ordinarily be regarded as composing one imperfectly competitive market: a number of automobile manufacturers, of producers of pots and pans, of magazine publishers, or of retail shoe dealers. From our point of view, each producer within the group is a monopolist, yet his market is interwoven with those of his competitors, and he is no longer to be isolated from them. (Chamberlin 1933, p. 81)

Chamberlin's emphasis on the differentiation of products may have deterred him from consideration of how differentiated products could be combined into commodity groups. He was emphasizing differences between products and probably did not wish to point out similarities or grouping. Nonetheless, he was aware, for example, that differentiated products of the automobile market are to be grouped differently, somehow, from differentiated products of the retail shoe market. His use of markets and industries as grouping criteria is essentially a producer or supply-side approach to the definition of a commodity. In any case, he does not define the limits of product differentiation; that is, he does not identify when the differentiation of a product is such that the product ceases to belong to the original commodity group, and has instead joined a new group.[7]

In retrospect, the major contribution of Edward Chamberlin, in terms of a theory that permits variable quality, lies in the identification of a motive for producers to foster product variation. The motive, of course, was profit, and the mechanism was attraction of consumers through differentiated products. To the extent that the objective of Chamberlin's work was construction of the monopolistically competitive model, and product differentiation served as the vehicle to accomplish that goal, then variable quality should be viewed as a side

issue, or as simply an additional tool to assist in accomplishing the main objective. Clearly, variable quality did not receive the same degree of direct emphasis by Chamberlin as it did, for example, by Frederick Waugh.

5. The Contribution of Hans Brems

The models of variable quality constructed by Hans Brems were within the framework of monopolistic competition.[8] Similar to Chamberlin, Brems focused on profit-maximizing firms in markets and industries where product quality is variable. He extended his analysis beyond the firm, however, and considered the effect of variable quality on consumer behavior. He also considered the impact of variable quality within macroeconomic models.

For his definition of quality, Brems initially adopted the product differentiation approach of Chamberlin. In fact, he was sufficiently satisfied with Chamberlin's definition that he quotes him, instead of producing a definition of his own:

> By "product quality" or just "product" we mean the same thing as Chamberlin. Speaking about the "product" he says: "Its 'variation' may refer to an alteration in the quality of the product itself—technical changes, a new design, or better materials; it may mean more prompt or courteous service, a different way of doing business, or perhaps a different location." (Brems 1951, p. 9*)

In his book *Product Equilibrium under Monopolistic Competition*, Brems separated the concept of "selling effort" from that of "product quality," and although he adopted Chamberlin's definition of product differentiation, throughout most of his book Brems spoke of product quality, or simply "quality" (Brems 1951, chapters 3 and 4).

Similar to Waugh, Brems concluded that

quality has two meanings or interpretations: the quality perceived by consumers, and the quality manufactured into a product by firms. This divergence of views was, and is, an important issue, one that introduces alternative value judgments, as well as problems of exchange and market equilibrium. According to Brems,

> we shall have to make up our mind as to the meaning of the term "quality," for two quite different meanings are possible. First, one might describe what the consumer gets from the product. Second, one might describe what the producer puts into it. (Brems 1951, pp. 18–19)

The producer's criteria were described by Brems as the "blueprints" of the product (Brems 1951, p. 19). They are essentially the physical characteristics of the product.

The potential difference in opinion between consumers and producers, or the potential divergence of quality criteria between the two groups, was a problem that received considerable attention from Brems. He believed that rarely do producer's and consumer's criteria for quality coincide. Ultimately, in order to resolve the problem, Brems sided with producers:

> At this point we must answer the question: If quality of product should be included among the parameters of action, should "quality" be taken in the meaning of consumer's criteria or the meaning of producer's criteria? The answer is easy. A number of consumer's criteria are often interrelated through one and the same producer's criterion. . . . Producer's criteria are perhaps more likely to be independent of each other than are consumer's criteria, and are, consequently, more usable for parameters of action. (Brems 1951, p. 20)

Although Brems discussed the consumer's criteria at length, he nevertheless decided in favor of producers as the arbitrators of quality. This point is further clarified in a subsequent chapter on production costs, where he stated, "Whenever in this volume criteria appear as parameters of action, be it in the cost equation or in the demand equation, the word criteria means producer's criteria" (Brems 1951, p. 57). As we shall see later, however, this issue is not resolved, and other authors have adopted consumer's criteria as the measure of quality.

In his chapter on consumer demand, Brems explained quantity demanded as a function of price, selling effort, and product quality (Brems 1951, pp. 26–27). To analyze demand, two steps are necessary, namely:

> The demand equation must tell us how price and all the various quality and selling-effort criteria affect the time rate of quantity sold. There are two steps to be taken by anyone who tries to find the demand equation in real life. First, one must tell how producer's criteria affect consumer's criteria, next one must tell how those consumer's criteria affect the time rate of quantity sold. (Brems 1951, p. 28)

Brems did not provide solutions to either step. Interestingly, he found the first step to be an issue of little importance to economists; it is, instead, a matter to be handled by engineers:

> Fortunately, the first step in demand analysis, that is, the translation of variations of producer's criteria into variations of consumer's criteria, in many cases can be left to the engineers, and should be. (Brems 1951, p. 28)

In this area, Brems appears to have been heavily influenced by the automotive industry and the role of engineers in the manufacture and styling of automobiles (Brems 1951; see his chapters on consumer demand and cost).

Although most previous authors assumed that an improvement in quality would bring about an increase in demand, Brems suggested we do not know how consumers will respond to changes in quality (Brems 1951, pp. 29–30). He was also one of the first economists to analyze consumer demand for durable goods under the conditions of variable quality. His model for such demand assumed that consumers purchase new consumer durables when the cost of replacement is less than the cost of maintenance, and that the quality of a durable good is measured, among other things, by the length of time before replacement (Brems 1951; see his chapter on consumer demand).

In his analysis of cost, Brems assumed that cost was a function of the quantity sold, plus the expenditure on selling effort and product quality (Brems 1951, p. 56). He also assumed that firms have sufficient knowledge of the cost-quality relationship to attain the least-cost optimum in the production of a given level of quality; thus,

> [i]t is important that the "right" factors are used in the "right" time rates of quantity. Otherwise the time rate costs will be higher than necessary. We shall always assume that the problem of minimizing c [cost] has been solved in the sense that for any given set of values of q [quantity sold] and $\alpha_1 \ldots \alpha_m$ [characteristics of quality and selling effort], c is at its minimum. (Brems 1951, p. 56)

By this assumption, of course, he ignored one of the major problems confronting quality-control engineers and others.

In his analysis of demand and cost, Brems considered both the quantifiable and nonquantifiable aspects of quality (Brems 1951, pp. 23–25, 27–28, 56–57). He provided some examples of each, again drawn mostly from the automotive industry, and he suggested a methodology for applying mathematical analysis to problems where "variables" are nonquantitative. Briefly, his procedure was to specify a given configuration of the non-quantitative aspects of quality, while permitting variation in the quantifiable aspects of quality. In the case of consumer demand, one would analyze variation in quantity sold that results from changes in price and other quantifiable aspects of selling effort and product quality, while all nonquantitative aspects of quality and selling effort were assumed constant. Once this analysis was completed for a given configuration of nonquantitative "variables," a different configuration was se-

lected and the analysis repeated (Brems 1951, chapters 2–4). The weakness in the procedure, of course, lies in the assumption that nonquantitative aspects of quality will not vary as one changes the quantifiable variables.

As stated earlier, Brems also considered the possibility that the quality of a product manufactured by a firm will not be the quality of product desired by consumers (Brems 1951, chapter 5). This possibility arises from the divergence of quality criteria between consumers and producers. Unless engineers, previously referred to by Brems, can "adequately" estimate the relationship of producer and consumer quality criteria, the possibility of divergence introduces the prospect of disequilibrium in markets. Brems suggested further that, as a result of the nonquantitative aspects of quality, demand and cost curves could be discontinuous (Brems 1951, p. 64). Later, he worked around these difficulties by assuming his functions became continuous (Brems 1951, p. 69), for example, by assuming a process of iterative quality adjustments, combined with iterative selling efforts and other strategies vis-à-vis consumers and rival firms, such that producers and consumers tended toward market equilibrium.

Related to the problem of divergence of consumer and producer criteria for quality is the need to define the limits of variable quality for "products." Brems was aware of this necessity. In his book *Product Equilibrium under Monopolistic Competition*, he considered market equilibrium in price-quantity space, and he stated, "One will look in vain for any common physical unit throughout the q-axis. There is none" (Brems 1951, p. 76). The symbol q represents quantity. He cited examples of variable quality from a mechanical clock, to an electric clock, to a clock-radio, to a stereo-radio-clock combination, etc. To establish a boundary to such product variation, Brems assumed the $\alpha_1 \ldots \alpha_m$ (the quality characteristics) defined the product

(Brems 1951, p. 75). This approach, however, did not answer the question, for the real need is to provide a set of criteria for the determination of the $\alpha_1 \ldots \alpha_m$. As we shall see later, other authors have taken this same approach. In subsequent books and articles, Brems did not attempt any further improvement on this explanation.

Because Brems did not focus on the problem of boundaries to quality variation, he did not realize the problems associated with separating quality variation from quantity variation. Consequently, he employed the concept of quantity as if "quantity" could always be easily separated from the complex dimensions of quality. In the development of monopolistically competitive models, he was not alone in this oversimplification.

On the subject of "quality criteria," or what today would be called "quality characteristics," Brems anticipated some of the problems associated with the Lancaster approach to consumer theory (Lancaster 1966a). Briefly, both for producers and consumers, Brems considered the possibility that some criteria, or characteristics, might be complementary, while others are "counteracting" (Brems 1951, pp. 70–74). In the case of two counteracting criteria, an increase in one criterion reduces the desirability of the other. In the case of two complementary criteria, an increase in one criterion increases the consumer's interest in obtaining the other.

The concept of counteracting, or competing, quality criteria was a refinement on the general notion that "quality" could be broken down into criteria or characteristics. The measurement of quality, particularly the weighting process utilized in aggregating numerous characteristics into a single index of quality, becomes more complex when it can no longer be assumed that all characteristics are complementary. The existence of trade-offs between characteristics creates problems in the ranking and measurement of quality.

For most investigators of this period, the theory of monopolistic competition had generated interest in selling costs and the marketing activities of firms. Brems was no exception. He developed an input-output model that utilized the a_{ij} to represent product quality and selling effort (Brems 1957). From the model he hoped it would be possible to determine the relationship between the quantity of the product sold and the numerical value of the a_{ij}, the optimum unit cost in relationship to the quality elasticity of demand, and the optimum price given various price elasticities of demand.

In addition to his work in microeconomics, Brems was one of the first economists to analyze the impact of variable quality on macroeconomic models. (See, for example, his chapter "Nonprice Competition and National Output," Brems 1959.) In contemporary terms, the relationship of variable quality to macroeconomic phenomena is restricted primarily to the influence of variable quality on price indices.

In the field of investment and capital theory, Brems developed a model to explain the effect of variable quality of durable goods on the capital-labor ratio (Brems 1959, chapter 19). The quality of producer durables was measured in terms of three performance characteristics: first, the direct labor input, which was defined as "the number of man-hours of direct labor required per annum to cooperate with one physical unit of producers' goods" (Brems 1959, p. 214); second, the productivity of producers' goods, which was defined "as the output of consumers' goods per annum per physical unit of producers' goods" (Brems 1959, p. 214); and third, "the useful life of one physical unit of producers' goods" (Brems 1959, p. 214). Brems found that an increase in labor's wage would result in the production of producers' goods that were more labor-saving, more productive in terms of consumer goods produced, and more durable (Brems 1959, p. 223). In terms of capital intensity, he found that the lower the wage rate, the less capital-intensive the economy. The opposite held for high wage rates (Brems 1959, p. 225).

On a separate but related subject, Brems considered the relationship of variable quality to technological change. He noted that, "Not all technological progress is of the kind . . . where less input is required per unit of output of a given product" (Brems 1959, p. 287). He described this first type of technological progress as "process innovation." In addition, he defined an alternative type of technological change, namely, "product innovation":

> Here, the product itself is changed. Product innovation is frequently designed to accelerate obsolescence of durable consumers' goods, automobiles affording an excellent example. But in doing so, product innovation also accelerates obsolescence of the durable producers' goods used to produce the consumers' goods. (Brems 1959, p. 287)

Technological change probably has been the single most important factor contributing to the variable quality of products and services. Brems did not discuss the topic in detail, but his subdivision of technological change into two categories, especially his concept of product innovation, was a valuable contribution.

6. The Contribution of Lawrence Abbott

Lawrence Abbott's approach to variable quality, like that of many other researchers of the period, was within the framework of monopolistic competition. Several unique elements, however, deserve attention. First, Abbott attempted to define quality. Second, he subdivided quality into three categories. And third, he was one of the first economists to utilize consumer criteria to establish commodity groups, or boundaries of product or quality variability.

According to Abbott, the word "quality" may be used

> to describe any or all of the various qualitative characteristics of a physical product or service, or combination of the two, offered for sale. "Quality" thus includes materials, design, style, location of a retail outlet—in short, any and every qualitative attribute. Quality is therefore a multi-dimensional variable—a compound of numerous elements (e.g., in a necktie: size, shape, type of construction, pattern, color scheme, material, texture, durability, resistance to wrinkling, color fastness), each of which is variable. (Abbott 1953, p. 827*; Abbott 1955, pp. 4, 125[†])

It should be noted that Abbott's definition of "quality" was quite similar to Chamberlin's definition of "product differentiation" (Chamberlin 1933, pp. 56, 71–72). By the 1950s, the term "product differentiation" had begun to equate with, and eventually to be replaced by, the term "quality." If the term "quality" included not only characteristics of the good or service produced but also the advertising, sales procedures, retail location, and other factors surrounding transfer of ownership, then "quality" was almost identical with the term "product differentiation." The only remaining difference was the notion that "product differentiation" indicated the product had been deliberately made different (differentiated) so as to attract consumers. Conversely, the term "quality" could be understood to be a term describing the state of the product or service, and nothing else.

Two points should be raised regarding Abbott's definition of "quality." First, he utilized the terms "qualitative characteristics" and "qualitative attribute" without clarification of the terms "qualitative" and "quantitative." Abbott's use of the term "qualitative" implies there may be other characteristics or attributes of the product that are not "qualitative" in nature. If he assumed that some characteristics were quantitative, as contrasted with qualitative, his definition would have been improved had he made a distinction between the two. In effect, Abbott's use of the words "qualitative characteristics" has only pushed the definition of quality back a step—that is, he defines "quality" through use of the word "qualitative," but never defines "qualitative."

The second point regarding Abbott's definition of quality has to do with the phrase "offered for sale." It could be argued that a definition of "product differentiation" requires a statement "offered for sale"; however, the phrase does not seem necessary for a definition of "quality." The quality of a product is not necessarily something associated with it only at the time of sale. Most assuredly, advertising, sales procedures, and location of retail outlet are all capable of influencing the consumer's estimation of the quality of a product. All of that notwithstanding, the product itself also has quality characteristics that exist before, during, and after the time of sale. Goods purchased by a firm and included as inventory are not void of quality characteristics until the time of marketing. It is possible that the quality of a product (in the consumer's eye) can increase, over time, through advertising. It is also possible that quality can deteriorate after purchase as the good wears out. All of this implies that quality varies over time and across individuals, but it does not support the notion that "quality" exists only at the time the product is offered for sale.

Services, in contrast, are different from products in the timing of their production. In many respects, services do not exist until, or

near, the time of sale. As a result of these production and marketing characteristics, Abbott's statement about quality and the phrase "offered for sale" are more applicable to services than to goods. In any case, his definition would not suffer if the statement "offered for sale" were deleted.

After providing a general definition of the word "quality," Abbott went on to subdivide the concept into three categories: vertical, horizontal, and innovational. By vertical quality he meant

> the kind of quality change or comparison which may properly be described in terms of "higher" or "lower." Two things distinguish this kind: (a) the "superior" of any two qualities is considered preferable by virtually all buyers, and (b) it entails greater cost. . . . Vertical differences in quality frequently consist of differences in the quantity of some desired ingredient or attribute. . . . The simplest kind of vertical variation is a change in the size of the unit. (Abbott 1953, p. 828)

Abbott's definition of horizontal quality is

> those differences about which there is no clear-cut agreement. Two things distinguish this type: (a) different people will rank dissimilar qualities in different orders, and (b) cost differences, if any, are purely incidental. The existence of this category depends on the fact that people differ in their circumstances, values, and tastes. With differences of this sort we may properly speak of one quality being "more suitable" or "more appealing" than another, but such a statement is meaningful only if made with reference to a particular buyer or group of buyers. (Abbott 1953, pp. 828–829)

Abbott defines innovational quality as the

> introduction of a novel quality which is judged superior by most or all buyers, and which either costs no more to produce or is well worth whatever additional cost is involved, so that the older quality must eventually become obsolete. This kind of quality change, associated with innovation and progress, leads to "improved" rather than "higher" quality. . . . Here the superiority is not due to better materials or workmanship, nor does the change alter the grade or price class to which a product be-

longs, but rather creates quality differences and improvement within each grade. (Abbott 1953, p. 829)

Abbott concluded his section on definitions with an explanation that it is not necessary to assume that all quality changes will fit neatly into one of the three categories. A hybrid of quality change is possible (Abbott 1953, p. 829).

A few comments are in order regarding each of these definitions. First, as regards vertical quality, the definition suggested that higher vertical quality could exist only at a higher price (cost). Of course, such price (cost) measures should be adjusted for inflation (i.e., measured only in real terms). However, cost-of-living indices are usually adjusted for quality change, which complicates the matter. As we shall see later, monetary measures of quality are not problem-free.

Abbott's statement that "The simplest kind of vertical variation is a change in the size of the unit" leaves unclear the relationship of "quantity" to that of "vertical quality." His statement that vertical quality can be described in terms of higher and lower levels of quality suggests a range of vertical-quality variation. At a later point in his article, Abbott explained the continuous nature of vertical quality:

> Vertical variability will be restricted to a single dimension, and conceived to be of such a character that the possible varieties can be arranged in order, in an "array" or "spectrum." More specifically, it will be assumed that vertical quality is variable in only one respect, is continuously variable, and is such that for every level of quality there is a different, and only one, corresponding cost function. (Abbott 1953, pp. 830–831)

Although he introduced, at least insofar as vertical quality is concerned, the concept of a continuous spectrum of change, in his article (Abbott 1953) he did not provide a criterion to determine the endpoints of the spectrum. Nor did he specify that the spectrum is infinitely continuous in either direction. In his book, published two years later, Abbott addressed the need to establish boundaries to variable quality and avoided the open-ended problems he encountered earlier.

Several aspects of his definition of innovational quality also need clarification. For example, the statement that innovational quality change "leads to 'improved' rather than 'higher' quality" opens several questions. If a level of vertical quality, say at the mid-range of vertical-quality variation, experiences an innovational change, is that level of quality "improved," to use Abbott's term, or is it "higher" on the spectrum of vertical-quality variation? In other words, why cannot "improved" also mean "higher" quality?

On innovational quality, Abbott further stated that innovation did not "alter the grade or price class to which a product belongs, but rather creates quality differences and improvements within each grade." This statement, although intended to be helpful, did not reduce the confusion.[9] Innovation that creates quality differences and improvements cannot simultaneously cause change within a grade and yet not alter the grade. Innovation will either introduce new, higher "super grades," or it will cause a total reordering of the grading scale from the highest to lowest levels. Under such transformation the grading requirements for each grade receive new specifications, all of which reflect the new standards brought about by the innovational change. It is also possible that innovational quality change will create a new grade between two previous grades, for example, a "medium" between a "high" and a "low."

Abbott's concept of horizontal quality was a contribution in the sense that it explicitly introduced consumer "tastes" into the world of variable quality. In fact, it could be argued that his major contribution lies in the ability of his model, through his definitions, to isolate and presumably hold constant the complexities of taste. Admittedly, numerous aspects of quality are subjective; nevertheless, Abbott points out that there are also many aspects of quality that are quantifiable. In this respect, his contrast of vertical and horizontal quality was useful. We should also note that, although the concept of taste can be interpreted more easily within Abbott's definition of horizontal quality, all other aspects of horizontal and vertical quality are essentially the same as the distinction made by Brems between nonquantitative and quantitative quality.

The confusion referred to earlier regarding the relationship of vertical quality and innovational quality was not reduced in any of Abbott's subsequent publications (see, for example, his book *Quality and Competition*, 1955). The definitions provided in that work were identical to those in his original article. In the book, however, Abbott provided an additional paragraph on the relationship of the three types of quality:

> We may thus conceive of three "directions" in which quality may be changed. Quality may be moved upward through vertical variation, resulting in "better" quality, or sideways through horizontal variation, resulting in "more suitable" or "more appealing" quality, or forward through innovational variation, resulting in "improved" or "more efficient" quality. (Abbott 1955, p. 129)

The suggestion of upward, sideways, and forward directions could imply the existence of an intersection or origin (assuming the existence of downward, backward, etc.), but the implications of such a point of origin were not considered. A better approach would have been simply to explain how innovation affects vertical and horizontal quality, and not set apart innovation as a type of quality per se. The concept of innovational quality is essentially the same as that of technological change, and/or the introduction of new goods or services, and as such probably would have been better handled if interpreted in terms of its impact on vertical and/or horizontal quality.

Finally, it is interesting to compare Abbott's three definitions of quality with the characteristics approach of Kelvin Lancaster or with the hedonic price index work of Zvi Griliches and colleagues. In essence, it is vertical quality that is utilized in these fields.[10] Interestingly, as knowledge of consumer psychology has improved, and as information on consumer decision making in markets has grown, it has become possible for many previously non-measurable aspects of quality to be quantified. Or, to use Abbott's terms, over the years consumer research has shifted many goods and services from the category of horizontal quality to the category of vertical quality.

The third contribution of Abbott was his attempt to define the grouping of products according to consumer, instead of producer, quality criteria. Initially, Abbott adopted the same grouping methodology first proposed by Chamberlin, and subsequently refined by Brems. For Chamberlin and Brems, the market was the mechanism that subdivided products into groups, and the groups were usually defined in terms of industry groupings of firms. Brems further increased the bias toward firms by explicitly adopting producer quality criteria, which, as far as the subject of quality was concerned, permitted him to ignore the market grouping mechanism altogether.

In his article on quality, Abbott employed a market criterion to explain the grouping of products. From his definition of a market, however, it was not clear whether he viewed the market as establishing groups of products, which firms produce, or groups of products, which consumers consume. The difference is slight, but it is important. His definition is as follows:

> The market is defined as embracing those products which are competitive in the sense of being substitutable alternatives, each capable of serving some given purpose, or, let us say, performing some given function, or rendering some given service, or enabling its

possessor to engage in some given activity. In other words, products will be considered to belong within the same market or industry if they can be regarded as variable means to some definable common end. (Abbott 1953, p. 828)

The principal weakness with this grouping criterion is the potential divergence of quality criteria of consumers from those of producers, a phenomenon introduced by Brems, and discussed even earlier by Waugh. If we accept the concept that producers and consumers (and outside regulatory bodies such as government) have different sets of quality criteria, the market no longer functions as a grouping mechanism. As suggested, markets can indicate which products are exchanged between producers and consumers, but the exchanged products may represent only a subset of the total products within producer and consumer product groupings. The exchange simply represents the intersection of the two groupings or sets, but the items contained within the consumer set may not match one-for-one with items in the producer set. The possibility, introduced by Brems, that engineers may inaccurately estimate the relationship of producer and consumer criteria opens the door for situations where the two sets are mutually exclusive and no transactions occur. Under such circumstances, the divergent producer and consumer product groupings are not reflected in market transactions, yet the two groupings could still exist. Of course, as described earlier, under market conditions, partial overlap of the sets of criteria is likely.

According to Abbott, if products can be substituted by the consumer to accomplish the same objective, or "definable common end," then such products belong to the same market. Although Abbott did not explicitly stipulate the following assumption, it seems implied: The variable quality of a product is limited to that set of products, identified by substitutability, as belonging to the same

market. In other words, within the group of different yet substitutable products each product would represent a level of quality within the set—the set being defined as the market. Unfortunately, besides the problems already discussed, there are others associated with this approach.

First, it is possible to utilize competition among substitutable products as the definition of a specific market and still continue to assume that quality is constant. In fact, as Waugh pointed out earlier, not only does the theory of substitution operate within the confines of the isoquality model but substitution has also been used in the past to oppose the development of any new theory of variable quality. In effect, Waugh states the proponents of the theory of substitution claim that the theory of substitution eliminates the need for a theory of variable quality. Conversely, Abbott employs the theory of substitution as part of his theory of variable quality.

Second, differences exist between the concepts of variable quality across a commodity and variable quality within a market. Abbott seems to perceive that identifying the products, each of a different level of quality, within a given market is equivalent to defining the limits of variable quality for a commodity. On the one hand, variable quality exists across the commodity set; on the other, variable quality exists across a market. In either case, the theory of substitution would apply—that is, substitution of different "qualities" within a commodity group, or substitution of products (each of a different level of quality) within a market group.

The difficulty that arises is this: In the example of the necktie, employed by Abbott in his definition of quality, it is possible, for example, to include changes in size, shape, material, and texture (all characteristics listed by Abbott) such that the necktie becomes a scarf or cravat. The necessity obviously exists to define the boundaries of characteristics for neckties and those of scarves or cravats.

However, with Abbott's criterion of substitution it is possible to have substitution within the set or group titled neckties, and substitution, under certain circumstances, between neckties and cravats. Using Abbott's criterion of substitutability to establish market groups, we could conclude that neckties and cravats belong to the same market, but do we then conclude that they also belong to the same commodity group? Is substitutability between neckties equivalent to substitutability between neckties and cravats? Do neckties and cravats represent different levels of quality within a given market? Or, does quality variation apply separately to neckties as one group and to cravats as another? With the limited criteria provided by Abbott (in his article), it is not possible to answer such questions.

Another difficulty with the market approach to product grouping is the problem of complementary quality characteristics. As discussed earlier, quality characteristics of products can be divided into counteracting and complementary. The existence of complementary characteristics introduces the possibility that some products, which serve the same "common end," may have a complementary instead of a substitution relationship. Under such circumstances, Abbott's market criterion for product grouping could ignore the complementary products.

Most of the difficulties we have discussed so far regarding Abbott's early work on product grouping were surmounted in his book, which he published two years after his article (Abbott 1955). In his book he stated that products are grouped according to consumers' criteria, which are in turn based on a concept of basic wants or human needs. In what follows, we first present Abbott's explanation of human wants and then show how he related wants to the concept of heterogeneous products. According to Abbott,

> [w]hat people really desire are not products but satisfying experiences. Experiences are attained through activities. In order that ac-

tivities may be carried out, physical objects or the services of human beings are usually needed. Here lies the connecting link between man's inner world and the outer world of economic activity. People want products because they want the experience-bringing services which they hope the products will tender. Two levels of wants are thus distinguishable. The more fundamental kind of want—the desire for an experience—will be termed a basic want; its derivative—the desire for a product which actually or supposedly provides the means to that experience—a derived want. (Abbott 1955, pp. 39–40)

> A "want" for an experience is in truth not a single want but a complex of related, supplementary wants, usually consisting of a major want plus numerous minor wants. . . . I shall employ the term "constellation of wants" to denote such a clustering. (Abbott 1955, p. 42)

After a lengthy discussion regarding the heterogeneity of human wants, Abbott introduced his consumer's criteria for the grouping of products of variable quality. Stated briefly, consumers are assumed to group products according to each product's ability to fulfill a basic want, or constellation of wants:

> A group of heterogeneous products can be viewed as a set of variable means to the satisfaction of some common set of ends—those contained in some specified constellation of basic wants. . . . Products which can serve the wants in the constellation belong within the group; products which cannot possibly serve them lie outside the group. (Abbott 1955, p. 82)

Once products had been grouped by this form of consumers' criteria, Abbott grouped industries according to their production of products that served a given clustering or constellation of wants:[11]

> The industry, then, consists of all those products, any one of which is capable of making a particular type of contribution toward the attainment of some experience or activity. When several products are used jointly in

some activity, all products capable of making one type of contribution form one group or industry. (Abbott 1955, pp. 82–83)

With this criterion for establishing boundaries to groups of products, Abbott could have incorporated his idea of continuous variation of vertical quality, and then applied the concept of boundaries to a continuous range of variable quality. This development did not materialize, however, until the work of Hendrik Houthakker.

Aside from Abbott's definition of quality and his use of consumers' criteria for product grouping, the remainder of his work provided only slight refinements on the monopolistically competitive model. He generally limited his analysis to vertical quality and employed a firm-oriented cost approach to a price-quality-quantity equilibrium. Although Abbott focused more on consumer behavior than, say, Chamberlin or Brems, he generally assumed that the effect of quality on consumer demand could be measured by its impact on cost to the firm. The firm-oriented nature of his approach is seen in the following illustration:

> Let firms now be free to vary quality vertically. Our problem is: what variation will occur? In order to investigate this question, we need further information about demand: namely, the change in quantity demanded associated with each change in the level of quality. This information can be assembled in the form of a schedule, and plotted as a curve; but it will not be the familiar kind of demand curve showing quantity demanded as a function of price. Instead, it will show quantity demanded as a function of quality height, or, more precisely, of the cost uniquely associated with that height of quality at that rate of output. (Abbott 1953, pp. 834–835)

The curve referred to by Abbott was an invention of his titled the "options curve." It provided a methodology for firms to study the effect of variable quality on consumer demand. The author's description of the curve is as follows:

> This curve is sufficiently unconventional to warrant some further comments as to its character. It is, in a sense, a demand curve; for it shows, for each height of quality selected (represented by the cost of supplying that quality), the quantity demanded. But it differs from the ordinary demand curve in that it does not give the demand price but rather the demand cost at each rate of output—that is the cost which the firm must incur in order to induce the purchase of that output, price being held at a predetermined level. (Abbott 1953, p. 835)

One might ask, "Whose demand is it?" Because the curve is based on cost to the firm, instead of consumer behavior in consumption space, the options curve appears to be a locus of equilibrium points where, for given levels of quality, transactions have occurred between producers and consumers. The curve does not isolate the effect of quality on consumer demand, nor does it explain paths toward equilibrium. In essence, the curve represents another attempt to use cost as the measure of quality. The curve did, however, stimulate further research on the relationship between quality and profits of the firm.

7. The Dorfman and Steiner Response to Abbott

A year after the Abbott article, Robert Dorfman and Peter Steiner produced an article on the same subject, that was a response, in part, to the earlier piece by Abbott (Dorfman and Steiner 1954). The Dorfman and Steiner article was also firm-oriented.

Before we consider their model, it is useful to review the Dorfman-Steiner definition of quality. Although they represented their article as an attempt to clarify several points raised by Abbott, they made no reference to his three definitions of quality. It may be presumed, based on their assumptions regarding the measurability of quality, that they limited their model to vertical quality. In the definition that follows, Dorfman and Steiner present several of their assumptions regarding quality and demand, as well as quality and cost:

> By quality we mean any aspect of a product, including the services included in the contract of sales, which influences the demand curve. ... Each conceivable quality will have a definite average cost curve, but there may be several different qualities with the same average cost curve. In this case we may assume that only that quality which has the most favorable demand curve will be given serious consideration. Thus we may assume that quality can be improved only at the expense of operating on a higher average cost curve. By quality improvement we mean any alteration in quality which shifts the demand curve to the right over the relevant range and raises the curve of average variable costs. (Dorfman and Steiner 1954, p. 831)

Several comments are in order regarding this definition. First, by stipulating that quality means "any aspect of a product, including the services included in the contract of sales, which influences the demand curve," the authors have, like many authors before them, permitted the mixing of quality and quantity. As we shall see later, any definition of "quantity" is a relative or arbitrary decision, yet one that must be made if one is to speak of quantity at all, and if one is to be able to compare and rank different levels of quality of the same commodity. In their article, Dorfman and Steiner provide a very general, almost all-inclusive definition of quality, and then in their mathematics introduce quantity as the "rate of sales per unit of time" (Dorfman and Steiner 1954, p. 832). The use of the word "rate" was also adopted by Abbott and Brems, but the word is potentially misleading, for it permits avoidance of a definition of the term "quantity." As with others before them, Dorfman and Steiner do not define quantity—that is, they do not specify "rate of what" (the dollar value of sales is not unique as it is also influenced by

quality), and apparently leave the meaning to intuition.

A careful reading will indicate that Dorfman and Steiner assumed that least-cost optimization in the production of quality always prevails, and that revenue maximization across alternative levels of quality is possible. The necessary information is assumed available to the firm.

With this definition and set of assumptions, the authors provided the following model for optimization of resources in the production of quality:

$$q = f(p,x), \qquad (1)$$

where q is the rate of sales per unit of time, p is price, x is an index of quality, and f is assumed continuous and differentiable (Dorfman and Steiner 1954, pp. 831–832). The cost function is

$$c = c(q,x) \qquad (2)$$

and c is defined to be the average cost of production (Dorfman and Steiner 1954, p. 832). In order to optimize profits in terms of any change in quality and price, the authors first assume the quantity of output is fixed and specify the optimal price-quality relationship for selling that predetermined quantity. This result is accomplished through the total differentials,

$$dq = (\partial f/\partial p)dp + (\partial f/\partial x)dx \qquad (3)$$

$$dc = (\partial c/\partial q)dq + (\partial c/\partial x)dx \qquad (4)$$

which with quantity fixed, or $dq = 0$, gives

$$dp = -[(\partial f/\partial x)/(\partial f/\partial p)]dx \qquad (5)$$

$$dc = (\partial c/\partial x)dx, \qquad (6)$$

and $(\partial x/\partial p) \neq 0$ is assumed. The next step is to allow quality to vary and seek its profit-maximizing optimum. The value of this two-step procedure, according to Dorfman and Steiner, is that costs, other than the cost of quality, are eliminated by the first step.

The net effect on profit that results from a change in quality can now be derived from equations (5) and (6), namely

$$qdp - qdc = -q[(\partial f/\partial x)/(\partial f/\partial p) + \partial c/\partial x]dx. \quad (7)$$

According to the authors, a positive level of quality cannot be optimal unless the bracketed value in equation (7) is zero (Dorfman and Steiner 1954, pp. 827–828). With this information they establish the following necessary conditions for profit maximization at any given level of output (as measured in terms of quantity):

$$(\partial f/\partial x)/(\partial f/\partial p) + \partial c/\partial x = 0 \text{ if } x > 0$$
$$\geq 0 \text{ if } x = 0.$$

Dorfman and Steiner do not consider the case where $x = 0$. In the case where $x > 0$, the condition for profit maximization may be reduced to

$$-(\partial f/\partial p) = [(\partial f/\partial x)/(\partial c/\partial x)]. \quad (8)$$

According to Dorfman and Steiner,

[t]he left-hand side of this equation is the slope of the ordinary demand curve. The right-hand side measures essentially the rate at which sales increase in response to increases in average cost incurred in order to increase quality. (Dorfman and Steiner 1954, p. 832)

If an inequality should exist in equation (8), say the right-hand side is greater than the left, then quality would, for example, increase.

This model shows that the level of quality depends on price, average cost of production, and the previous relative level of quality. Or, in other words, that

[q]uality tends to be higher the greater the sensitivity of consumers to quality variation (measured by $\partial f/\partial x$), the lower the sensitiv-

ity of consumers to price variation (measured by $\partial f/\partial p$), and the lower the effect on average costs of quality changes (measured by $\partial c/\partial x$). (Dorfman and Steiner 1954, pp. 832–833)

Later in their article the authors expand their optimizing condition to include the quality elasticity of demand,

$$\eta_c = (c/q)[(\partial f/\partial x)/(\partial c/\partial x)]. \quad (9)$$

Equation (9) is equivalent to the ordinary elasticity of demand by

$$\eta = (p/c)\eta_c, \quad (10)$$

where, regarding equation (8),

$$\eta = (p/q)(\partial f/\partial p).$$

With this information, Dorfman and Steiner introduce the following theorem:

If the price which a firm can charge is predetermined and if the firm can influence its demand curve by altering its product, it will, in order to maximize its profits, choose the quality such that the ratio of price to average cost multiplied by the elasticity of demand with respect to quality expenditure equals the reciprocal of the mark-up on the marginal unit. (Dorfman and Steiner 1954, p. 835)

In symbols, this condition is given by,

$$(p/c)\eta_c = p/(p-mc). \quad (11)$$

This is the same problem addressed by Abbott, but which he attempted to explain with options curves.

Before we leave Dorfman and Steiner, a few comments are in order regarding their methodology. First, their use of total differentials provided a simpler and clearer construction of the problem. Conversely, their procedure also underscored the importance of clarifying the relationship of quality to quantity. For example, in equation (4) we have the marginal cost of quantity neatly separated from the marginal cost of quality. And, in equation (3) we have the change in quantity completely separate from the change in quality. All of this, of course, is possible given adequate definitions of quantity and quality in equations (1) and (2). These definitions, in turn, rely on the set of assumptions behind the production function and preference map. The nature of these assumptions shall be discussed in subsequent chapters. As we shall see, much depends on the ability to identify and separate quantity and quality.

Chapter 3

Theory of the Consumer and Variable Quality

The Contributions of James Duesenberry and Henri Theil

1. Introduction

In chapter 2 we found that most authors, with the exception of Lawrence Abbott, had a firm-oriented approach to the subject of variable quality. In this chapter we discuss the work of two authors who took a consumer approach. In chapter 4 we review the work of Hendrik Houthakker. To understand and appreciate more fully the contribution of Houthakker, however, we must first discuss the work of James Duesenberry and Henri Theil.

2. The Contribution of James Duesenberry

James Duesenberry is not usually associated with the subject of variable quality, although his reputation is well established in other aspects of consumer theory. In his classic text, *Income, Saving and the Theory of Consumer Behavior* (Duesenberry 1949), he devoted a small but rather important section to the role of variable quality in consumer behavior. In fact, the material of that section was critical to the development of his hypotheses regarding the nature of shifts in the aggregate consumption function.

Duesenberry assumed that people desire goods in order to serve various purposes or needs, and he assumed that some goods are superior to others in their capacity to satisfy needs, namely:

> [W]e can now argue that people do not, for the most part, desire specific goods but desire goods which will serve certain purposes.
> But, of course, people are not indifferent as between the goods which will serve the same purpose. . . . Almost any activity can be carried out in a variety of ways and a variety of goods can be used to implement it. Sometimes the goods which can be substituted for one another for a single purpose go by different names . . . sometimes they are different brands or varieties of the same kind of goods. But the important point is that they are qualitatively different ways of doing the same thing. Even more important they are not just different but some are better than others. (Duesenberry 1949,* p. 20)

Duesenberry was aware of the quantitative and nonquantitative aspects of quality, or the vertical and horizontal to use Abbott's definitions. In the construction of his model, Duesenberry assumed there exists a consensus among consumers regarding the best means of fulfilling any given purpose or need:

---

*From *Income, Saving and the Theory of Consumer Behavior* by James S. Duesenberry. Copyright © 1949 by the President and Fellows of Harvard College, renewed 1977 by James S. Duesenberry. Reprinted by permission of Harvard University Press.

The superiority of one good over another for a specific purpose may be a technical superiority. . . . In other cases it may be an aesthetic superiority or superiority with respect to some criterion such as newness of design. But whatever the basis of the comparison there is likely to be, at one time, a high degree of agreement about the best means of satisfying any particular need. . . . [I]f a large number of people were asked to rank, in order of preference, a number of different types of automobiles, houses, or cuts of meats, the rank correlation would be high. This would be particularly true if the whole range of substitutes from the cheapest to the most expensive were included. (Duesenberry 1949, pp. 20–21)

Duesenberry acknowledged that the degree of uniformity in the ranking of goods might be affected by the homogeneity versus heterogeneity of the population sampled, but he believed that a high degree of uniformity would prevail.

Of course, the correlation obtained in this kind of test would be higher the more homogeneous the group involved. Age differences, regional differences, and differences in social class will reduce the correlation. But the correlation would still be quite high even if a random sample of the whole population were used. The lowest correlation would presumably result from a test of agreement on aesthetic or recreational activities; but these items account for a small part of most budgets, even in high income groups. (Duesenberry 1949, p. 21)

Duesenberry also assumed that the needs of consumers are given for each individual and that the principal economic choice open to an individual consumer is the quality of products to purchase to satisfy his or her needs.

We have already concluded that people use goods and services in order to satisfy certain needs or to carry out certain activities. The physical needs are a given datum and for our purposes most of the activities carried on by an individual can be predicted if we know his age, occupation, social status, and marital status. . . . On the whole then the consumer has only one degree of freedom in making choices about consumption. He can

vary the quality of the goods and services he uses for any purpose. (Duesenberry 1949, p. 23)

Although he did not devote much time to consideration of the relationship of quantity to quality, Duesenberry was aware that complex issues were involved. In the quotations that follow, note that Duesenberry does not provide a clear definition of quantity. As a result, many of his remarks have multiple interpretations.

So far all our emphasis has been upon qualitative differences. But, of course, quantitative variations are also important. Variation in the quantities of goods consumed has a number of different aspects. In some cases quantitative variation is variation in the proportion of times in which one or another of a set of substitutes is used for a given purpose. A man may eat dinner every night, sometimes in an expensive restaurant, sometimes in a cheap one. If he increases the proportion of times in which he eats in the expensive one, then he is, in a sense, improving the average quality of his meals. (Duesenberry 1949, p. 21)

This result obtains, of course, only if one defines quantity to be the quantity of all meals consumed, or if one considers only the average quality of all meals consumed. If quantity were subdivided into the quantity of cheap meals and the quantity of expensive ones, then there are two averages, one for the cheap and one for the expensive meals. Note that one cannot conclude from this example that as quantity increases quality increases. The total quantity of meals consumed in a given time period could remain constant and quality could vary in any desired direction. For example, the consumer could always select to eat at the cheap restaurant, instead of a mixture of the two restaurants, in which case quantity remains the same as before, but average quality is lower. Further note that Duesenberry's use of the words "cheap" and "expensive" implies that cost is an index of quality.

Another type of quantity-quality relationship provided by Duesenberry is the following:

> In a second group of situations quantity differences are essentially differences in variety. The quality of a library depends on the number of books not because more books fill up more space but because the books are different. (Duesenberry 1949, p. 21)

This statement is very similar to his previous one. In this example, instead of comparing two qualities of restaurants across the number of meals consumed, the author compares the quantity of different books to the same quantity of an identical book. In this example, however, as the quantity of different books increases, the quality of the library increases. In the previous case involving meals, an increase in quantity could conceivably leave quality unaltered. In the library example, because the author is more explicit regarding the nature of quantity (i.e., the quantity of different books) a positive relationship exists between quantity and quality. Note, however, that had he permitted the restaurants to vary —not only between cheap and expensive, but among Chinese, Mexican, French, and American cooking, and so on—the same arguments could be made for his first example. As we shall see later, what these two contrasting examples introduce is the difference between the quantity of an item (e.g., a meal) and quantity of an element of the item, or quantity of different elements of the item (e.g., the quantity of different books in a library), both of which constitute the characteristics of quality. Hence, the need to distinguish between quantity and quality.

In still another example, Duesenberry illustrates the confusion that can arise from an unclear definition of quantity. His example also illustrates the arbitrary nature of any definition of quantity.

> There are, of course, cases in which quantity variations are directly important. It is presumably better to have a large steak than a small one. But for our purposes there is no difficulty in looking at this as a special case of quality variation. (Duesenberry 1949, p. 22)

The first and last sentences of this statement could be taken as contradictory, depending on how one defines the term "quantity." For example, if quantity is defined as the number of steaks, then the size of the steak can be considered an element of quality, and the two sentences are consistent. Conversely, if one defines quantity as the number of ounces of steak, then there is a quantity difference between the first set of ounces (the large steak) and the second set of ounces (the small steak). The quality of the two steaks could be assumed equal, but their quantities are different. Number, size, weight, protein content, fat content, age, and so forth—all of these criteria or characteristics could be defined as either a measure of quantity or a measure of quality.

Finally, Duesenberry provides a few thoughts regarding the role of quality in "preference theory or utility theory":

> These approaches emphasize changes in the quantities of a set of goods. . . . [T]hey lead one to think of differences in consumption patterns in terms of differences in the amounts of the same specific goods rather than in terms of the qualities of goods consumed. But it seems clear that psychologically an improvement in the living standard consists in satisfying one's needs in a better way. This may sometimes involve consuming more of something but it very often consists in consuming something different. (Duesenberry 1949, p. 22)

After discussion of human needs and the relationship of quantity to quality, Duesenberry introduced the following four propositions as the basis for his consumption theory:

> (1) [P]hysical needs and the activities required by the culture require the consumption of certain kinds of goods; and (2) each of the needs, whether physically or socially generated, can be satisfied by any of a number of qualitatively different types of goods; (3) these different types of goods, or, in the broader

sense, ways of doing things, are regarded as superior or inferior to one another; (4) there is a generally agreed-upon scale of ranks for the goods which can be used for any specific purpose. (Duesenberry 1949, p. 22)

In addition, Duesenberry assumed that as income increased, the quality of goods and services purchased by consumers would increase (Duesenberry 1949, pp. 23–29). In fact, in light of his earlier statement regarding quality as the only degree of freedom open to consumer choice, he seems to suggest that all consumers have the same basic wants and all strive to satisfy the same wants. Consumers with higher incomes, however, satisfy their wants not with greater quantity, but with higher-quality products and services. Quality appears more important in his model than does quantity—the fuzzy nature of the quantity-quality relationship notwithstanding. The following statements are some examples of his views on income and the consumption of quality. Note that if income cannot be increased, the drive for higher quality may result in reduced savings.

On the consumption side it may be assumed that in choosing consumption goods everyone will always prefer higher quality goods to lower quality goods. But usually superior goods will be more expensive (superiority here being regarded as a subjective not as an objective matter). Inferior goods which are expensive will not be sold and can be eliminated from consideration. That implies that, with a given income, one can improve the quality of one's living standard only by reducing saving. (Duesenberry 1949, p. 23)

Suppose a man suffers a 50 per cent reduction in his income and expects this reduction to be permanent. Immediately after the change he will tend to act in the same way as before . . . but eventually he will learn to reject some expenditures and respond by buying cheap substitutes for the goods formerly purchased. (Ibid., p. 24)

A rising standard of living is one of the major goals of our society. Much of our public policy is directed toward this end. Socie-

ties are compared with one another on the basis of the size of their incomes. In the individual sphere people do not expect to live as their parents did, but more comfortably and conveniently. (Ibid., p. 26)

It seems fairly obvious that improvement in the standard of living is identical with improvement in the quality of goods consumed. (Ibid., p. 29)

To explain why people continually strive for higher living standards, or higher quality, Duesenberry introduced various psychological phenomena—that is, the demonstration effect, maintenance of self-esteem, and the desire for social status (Duesenberry 1949, pp. 25–32). A few examples of the relationship of quality to these phenomena are presented below.

For any particular family the frequency of contact with superior goods will increase primarily as the consumption expenditures of others increase. When that occurs, impulses to increase expenditure will increase in frequency, and strength and resistance to them will be inadequate. The result will be an increase in expenditure at the expense of saving. We might call this the "demonstration effect." People believe that the consumption of high quality goods for any purpose is desirable and important. If they habitually use one set of goods, they can be made dissatisfied with them by a demonstration of the superiority of others. (Duesenberry 1949, p. 27)

In a society in which improvement in the living standard is a social goal, the drive for maintenance of self-esteem will become a drive to get higher quality goods. It can operate quite independently of the desirability of these goods from any other standpoint. (Ibid., p. 29)

Our social goal of a high standard of living, then, converts the drive for self-esteem into a drive to get high quality goods. The possibility of social mobility and recognition of upward mobility as a social goal converts the drive for self-esteem into a desire for high social status. But since high social status requires the maintenance of a high consumption standard, the drive is again converted into a drive to obtain high quality goods. (Ibid., p. 31)

On the basis of his assumptions regarding quality and consumer behavior, Duesenberry went on to build a macroeconomic model of aggregate consumption and national saving patterns. Of importance to our work here, his model introduced additional hypotheses regarding the relationships of consumer income, saving, and the quality of goods and services consumed. As we shall see later, other hypotheses exist: Some are similar to Duesenberry's and some are not.

3. The Contribution of Henri Theil

During the same period that Chamberlin, Brems, and Abbott were analyzing product differentiation and quality variation within the context of monopolistic competition, Henri Theil began to study the constraint and preference map in consumption space under conditions of variable quality. Although previous authors had assumed that an exogenous increase (decrease) in quality would shift outward (inward) the demand schedule, Theil was one of the first to analyze variable quality and demand phenomena from the perspective of consumption space.

4. The Theil Model

In his article "Qualities, Prices and Budget Enquiries" (Theil 1951–52), Henri Theil defined each good within the set of a single commodity to be a "quality" of the commodity. That is, if a good represents a level of quality within the commodity, Theil labels the good a "quality" of the commodity. Theil does not refer to goods as representing levels of quality of a commodity; instead, they *are* the "qualities" of the commodity (Theil 1951–52, p. 129). Theil, however, does not define quality; instead, recalling the distinction outlined above, he defines "a quality": "Let us define a quality as a perfectly homo-

geneous good, at least as a good the heterogeneity of which may be neglected" (Theil 1951–52,* p. 129).

With this approach, Theil comes extremely close to incorporating the assumptions of the isoquality or homogeneous model of pure competition. In effect, he assumed that a quality of a commodity is a good, and each such good (quality) does not vary in any of its characteristics (i.e., it is "perfectly homogeneous"); consequently, all that remains to establish the isoquality model is to declare that only one commodity exists. In such a situation the qualities (goods) of the commodity become the goods in an n-good model of perfect competition under the homogeneous assumption.

According to Theil, we may "define a commodity as a set of qualities; the number of elements of such a set is, of course, to a certain extent arbitrary" (Theil 1951–52, p. 129). And, "Most 'commodities' distinguished in budget enquiries are heterogeneous; often they can be described as 'aggregates' of more perfectly homogeneous 'qualities'" (Theil 1951–52, p. 129). This concept of a commodity is more precise than the earlier market-grouping approach of Edward Chamberlin. It is also more to the point than the sometimes vague statements by Lawrence Abbott and Hans Brems. Unfortunately, like Chamberlin and Brems, Theil encountered difficulty when he endeavored to explain "how" qualities group to form a commodity. What is more, he never did consider "why" they group. Abbott and Duesenberry are better prepared to address this last question.

As stated earlier, Theil's use of "qualities" in a one-commodity model was very close, if not identical, to the isoquality, or constant-quality model of perfect competition. Theil was aware of this possibility, and, by implying that a single commodity is limited in its ability to satisfy all human wants, he estab-

---

*From "Quality, Prices and Budget Enquiries" by Henri Theil, *Review of Economic Studies* 19(3), no. 50 (1951–52): pp. 155–164. Copyright © Review of Economic Studies Ltd. Reprinted by permission of the publisher.

lished a peculiarity to his one-commodity model that separated it from pure competition. In what follows, please note Theil's reference to the small quantity of each quality purchased by consumers of the single commodity. This is his only reference to human wants or needs, and it is derived by implication. Without this interpretation, Theil's one-commodity model is analogous to the purely competitive model, and therefore open to our previous criticism.

> As long as we deal with qualities the traditional theory of consumer's behavior may be regarded as fundamentally correct with respect to the problems considered above [i.e., the problems of variable quality]. However, the number of qualities is usually tremendous, so that the quantity bought of each of these qualities will often be quite small unless the period considered is very long. Hence the difficult problem of indivisibility obtains its greatest importance just in the case when the commodity problem is reduced to a triviality. Moreover, a theory dealing with such a large number of goods (= qualities) cannot be said to be manageable with respect to the usual budget data. (Theil 1951–52, p. 129)

The reduction of the "commodity problem . . . to a triviality" results from (1) the increased significance of substitution between qualities (within and between commodities) instead of substitution between two or more commodities, (2) the greater significance of the marginal utility of qualities instead of commodities (which gets to the indivisibility problem), and (3) the possibility to limit the analysis to a single commodity and simply observe consumer behavior vis-à-vis changes in qualities of the commodity.

It should be noted that Theil's statement regarding homogeneous "qualities" also applies to models that assume that goods and services can be broken down into attributes or characteristics—characteristics that enter the utility function. In such models the characteristics are usually assumed to be of constant quality. In fact, the "quality" of a good

or service, in such models, is usually measured by the "quantity" of isoquality characteristics. Different types and combinations of characteristics are often associated with a single good or service, but within each category of characteristic the quality of the characteristic is assumed constant—only its quantity is allowed to vary.

The attempt to measure quality by breaking down goods and services into characteristics, which in turn can be broken down further into sub-characteristics, is a never-ending nesting process. At some point the decision must be made to stop the nesting and assume that the level of (sub)characteristics is an adequate approximation to some specified level of quality.[1] Finally, statements regarding homogeneous qualities and characteristics apply to quality only in the quantitative or vertical sense. Nonquantifiable or horizontal quality is another problem entirely.[2]

Given his definitions of "a quality" and a commodity, Theil developed one-commodity and n-commodity models of consumer behavior. In the one-commodity model he assumed income, y, and the price of each "quality" were fixed. He also assumed "the consumer is able to vary the quantity of the commodity and the qualities bought" (Theil 1951–52, p. 129). From these assumptions, Theil developed a quantity-quality constraint in consumption space. With reference to the statement that the consumer can vary quantity and quality, he adds, "Of course, these variations are not independent, if his outlays are equal to y" (Theil 1951–52, pp. 129–130).

Note that his statement regarding quantity-quality trade-offs holds only if saving is not permitted or is held constant. If we assume, as Theil did, that there is no saving in the model (specifically, that all income is expended on qualities of the single commodity), then the sum of the quantity of each quality purchased equals the quantity of the commodity purchased. Furthermore, it is not possible to increase the quantity of the commodity without simultaneously reducing its quality, as measured by the purchase of "lower" qualities. Conversely, if saving were possible, then we could define the quantity of the commodity to be the quantity of a single quality (good), and quantity of the commodity (quantity of the good) could vary with no change in quality (i.e., no change in the type of good purchased). A small quantity purchased simply results in increased saving. (Although Theil did not address the issue, the concept of a trade-off between quality and saving was considered by Brems and Duesenberry.)

The principal objective of Theil's article was to develop a model that would explain utility maximization under conditions of variable quality (Theil 1951–52, p. 129). To accomplish this objective he established a quantity-quality space into which he introduced a utility function and a budget constraint, both of which have quality and quantity as arguments. He assumed that quantity, x, was the quantity purchased of the commodity, and that x was the summation of the quantity of all qualities purchased (Theil 1951–52, pp. 129–130). To introduce quality, he assumed that the average price paid for the commodity was a measure of quality:

> [W]e shall use the average price paid (defined as the ratio of the amount spent to the quantity bought) as a "quality indicator" of the set of qualities bought. This procedure may be considered useful even if the consumer buys a number of different qualities in the same period (e.g. butter for Sunday and margarine for the other days), because then the average price paid is an indicator of the "average" quality bought. (Theil 1951–52, p. 130)

Theil represents the average price paid by the symbol p. He further assumed there were no snob effects associated with the use of price as a measure of quality.

> It may be added that the way in which p enters into this function [the utility function] has no necessary relationship with the behaviour of a consumer who reacts according to Veblen's description. Such a consumer attaches value to some commodity because its price is high. In our case the average price paid is only a quality indicator such that, if a consumer prefers some cheap quality to a more expensive one (*ceteris paribus*), the latter quality is left out of consideration. (Theil 1951–52, p. 130)

Note that in this last statement Theil has implicitly assumed that cost can serve as an index of quality. This conclusion can also be drawn from his observation that "a worse quality usually implies a lower price than a better quality (if it does not, we can rule out the worse quality altogether)" (Theil 1951–52, p. 130).

In the one-commodity model, Theil defined the average price paid as "the ratio of the amount spent to the quantity bought" (Theil 1951–52, p. 130). In a footnote to that definition he adds, "Alternatively: the average price paid is a weighted average of the constituent quality prices, the weights being the quantities bought of the individual qualities" (Theil 1951–52, *n*.2, p. 130). He has, in effect, two definitions of average price:

$$p = (\sum_{i=1}^{k} q_i p_i)/x,$$

which is the ratio of the amount spent on the commodity to the quantity purchased of all qualities; and

$$p = \sum_{i=1}^{k} (q_i p_i)/q_i,$$

which is the definition in his footnote. In both expressions, p is the average price paid, q_i is the quantity purchased of the ith quality, p_i is the price of the ith quality, k is the number of "qualities," and x is the quantity of the commodity.

Given y, x, and p, Theil introduced the usual convex utility function, which is maximized against the constraint, $px = y$. In (x, p) space the constraint is a hyperbola instead of the usual linear budget constraint. A graphical example is provided in Figure 3.1, where

Figure 3.1 **Theil's Quantity-Quality Space**

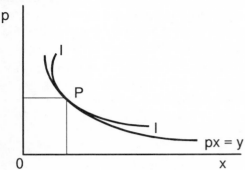

Figure 3.2 **Theil: Quality and an Increase in Income**

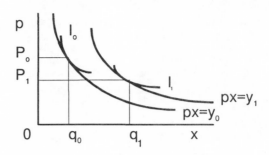

all symbols are as previously defined and I represents an indifference curve. (See diagram 1, Theil 1951–52, p. 130, for Theil's illustration.)

Theil was aware of the special nature of the optimum at P, and explained the conditions required to assure an interior solution: "If equilibrium is stable the second derivative of price with respect to quantity along the budget line [*sic*] [indifference curve] must be larger (at least not smaller) than the same derivative along the budget line" (Theil 1951–52, pp. 130–131).

On the subject of the utility function, Theil ignored the possibility of trade-offs between quantities of different qualities, and he assumed that a single optimal mix of the quantities of all qualities was represented by each point on the indifference curve:

> We shall pay no attention to the problem how utility might be influenced by those changes in the quantities bought of the individual qualities which leave both x and p unchanged. We shall assume that for each pair (x, p) the quantities of the qualities are chosen such that utility is maximised subject to the condition implied by this pair. (Theil 1951–52, $n.3$, p. 130)

5. Theil's View of Income and Quality

After he explained the utility maximization process in (x, p) space, and the conditions required for an internal point of optimization, Theil subsequently relaxed the assump-

tion that income was fixed and analyzed the income-quality relationship. His conclusion regarding that relationship was that it is impossible to establish a priori that quality will increase (decrease) with an increase (decrease) in income. It is interesting, in light of the Duesenberry hypothesis regarding quality and income (Duesenberry 1949, pp. 20–29), that Theil cannot disprove the existence of a positive income-quality relationship. Here is Theil's explanation:

> [W]hat will happen if income increases or decreases? One might think that an increase of income always causes the consumer to buy more expensive qualities. However, this proposition is incorrect, at least it cannot be deduced from the stability condition. A case in which an increase of income causes the average price paid to be reduced is given in Diagram 2 [see Figure 3.2]. In this case the average price paid is reduced from $P_0 Q_0$ to $P_1 Q_1$ in spite of an increase of income from y_0 to y_1. (Theil 1951–52, p. 131)

Theil went on to point out that instead of simply a reduction in quality, it is also possible, under certain circumstances, that an increase in income could reduce both quantity and quality.

> Of course, in the case of one commodity it is impossible that quantity would be reduced as well, because then the product px would decrease contrary to the assumption that $y (=px)$ increases. However, if there are two or more commodities, such an effect may take place. (Theil 1951–52, p. 131)

We might add, in view of Brems's and Duesenberry's assumptions regarding a relationship between quality and saving, that a reduction in quantity is not impossible, even in the one-commodity case, if $y > px$ is allowed (i.e., if saving is allowed).

Finally, it is interesting that the entire discussion of a positive, negative, zero, or variable relationship of income to quality turns on the configuration of the preference map. Note that a homogeneous utility function would produce a positive income-quality relationship in Theil's (x, p) space.

6. The Grouping of "Qualities" to a Commodity, and Theil's Use of Quality Characteristics

Discussion of a negative income-quality relationship underscores the importance of how "qualities" group to form a commodity. Theil pointed out the arbitrary results that could be obtained by selectively grouping different sets of "qualities":

> Take, e.g., margarine; one may spread it on his bread or use it for cooking, etc. Let us assume that a consumer buys a more expensive quality [of margarine] for his bread. Now suppose that this income increases. Then it is possible that he will use butter (which is considered as a different commodity) for his bread and a slightly better quality of margarine for cooking such as to reduce both the average price paid and the quantity bought of [the original] margarine. . . . Of course, such a result is highly dependent on the way in which qualities are grouped to commodities. If we had considered butter and margarine as one commodity instead of two, the average price paid would have increased. But precisely the same is true for quantities: one can always, except perhaps in pathological cases, define commodities in such a way that an increase of income causes the quantity bought of none of the commodities to be reduced. (Theil 1951–52, p. 131)

From discussion of a one-commodity model, Theil expanded to the more general

n-commodity case. In this model, individual quality prices were allowed to change, and the quantity of the commodity was represented by x_i ($i = 1, \ldots, n$), where n is the number of commodities. Whereas previously the average price paid, p, was the only indicator of quality, in the n-commodity model Theil introduced the vector e_i to provide additional information on the quality of the ith commodity.

> Let us suppose that the qualitative nature of a quantity of x_i of a commodity i ($i = 1, \ldots, n$) can be completely described by means of a vector $e_i(e_{i1}, \ldots, e_{im})$. The elements of e_i may be quantitative things like specific gravity, etc., or may be qualitative such as colour, etc. (Theil 1951–52, pp. 131–132)

We should note that e_i is not an index of quality in the usual sense; instead, it more closely approximates the characteristics approach of Kelvin Lancaster and others. As we see below, Theil continued to employ price as the principal measure of quality; however, the e_i were permitted to influence p_i:

> It will be clear that the average price paid for a unit of commodity i, p_i, depends on the vector e_i. Hence we have the following side relation:
>
> $$\sum_{i=1}^n x_i p_i(e_i) - y = 0$$
>
> (Theil 1951–52, p. 132)

Although Theil was not explicit regarding the nature of the relationship of e_i to p_i, it seems reasonable to conclude that he generally assumed it was positive (Theil 1951–52, p. 132).

Against this new constraint Theil introduced the utility function $u(x_1, \ldots, x_n, e_1, \ldots, e_n)$, which, given a positive relationship between e_i and p_i, was a slight modification of the earlier $u(x, p)$. For this maximand and constraint he provided the following marginal conditions:

$$(\partial u / \partial x_i) - \lambda p_i = 0$$

$$(\partial u/\partial e_{ih}) - \lambda x_i(\partial p_i/\partial e_{ih}) = 0$$

$$(i = 1, \ldots, n; h = 1, \ldots, m)$$

where h represents a single quality element of the set of quality elements e_i that constitute the ith commodity, m is the total number of such elements in the ith set, λ is a proportionality constant (the Langrangian multiplier), and all other symbols are as previously defined. Note that in the one-commodity model the vector e_i would represent the quality elements contained within the individual goods (qualities) one through k of the single commodity. Theoretically, any change in a single e_{ih} would change at least one of the "qualities." Theil explained the above marginal conditions as follows:

> [T]he marginal utility of a quantity x_i is proportional to its price p_i; the marginal utility of an element e_{ih} of the vector e_i is proportional to the corresponding quantity x_i and the partial derivative of the price p_i with the respect to e_{ih}; . . . The first of these marginal conditions is identical with Gossen's Law. The second, too, is quite simple; roughly speaking, it tells us that, if (in equilibrium) an increment of e_{ih} has a large influence upon p_i (i.e. if this qualitative improvement is expensive) and if the quantity bought x_i is large, the marginal utility of e_{ih} must (in equilibrium) also be large. (Theil 1951–52, p. 132)

Note that in Theil's statement regarding the second marginal condition he implied $(\partial p_i/\partial e_{ih}) > 0$, namely, "if this qualitative improvement" (i.e., increase in e_{ih}) "is expensive" (i.e., increase in p_i). It appears he retained this assumption throughout the article.

There are some points we should make regarding Theil's use of e_{ih}. Recall that in the one-commodity model he defined the average price paid as either

$$p = (\sum_{i=1}^{k} q_i p_i)/x \text{ or } p = \sum_{i=1}^{k}(q_i p_i)/q_i,$$

where p was the average price paid for the single commodity, q_i was the quantity purchased of the ith quality, p_i was the price of the ith quality, k was the total number of

"qualities" in the single commodity, and x was the quantity of the commodity. Although we did not do so, we could have given the following formulation for the quantity x. Recall that Theil assumed the quantity of a single commodity could be represented as the summation of the quantities of the individual qualities of the commodity, or $x = \sum_{i=1}^{k} q_i$. As we change to the n-commodity model, the average price paid, p, becomes p_i, where i stands for the commodity and n is the total number of commodities ($i = 1, \ldots, n$). Similarly, x becomes x_i and i represents the commodity.

If we assume, as Theil did in many cases, that the quality elements e_{ih} are quantifiable and continuously differentiable, then we could assume that at least one relationship of p_i to e_i is as follows:

$$p_i = \sum_{j=1}^{k}(q_{ij}\{p_{ij}[e_{ih}]\})/q_{ij} \ (h = 1, \ldots, m) \quad (1)$$

where p_{ij} is assumed to have a functional relationship with e_{ih} such that $(\partial p_{ij}/\partial e_{ih}) \geq 0$. In equation (1), p_{ij} represents the price of the jth "quality," and e_{ih} is a set of quality elements.

Note that if only one element of quality were allowed to vary—for example, the hth element represents the quantity of fluid ounces of juice in an orange—then the change in e_{ih} would represent a change in the quantity of that single quality element. In such a situation, given that all other elements of quality are held constant, that is, the values of all other h-elements (other than fluid ounces of juice) are held constant, the different values of e_{ih} (the different number of fluid ounces of juice per orange) are the different "qualities" of the commodity. In this case, p_{ij}, the price per orange (the number of oranges being the quantity unit of measure), varies as the juice content of the orange varies.

In addition, note that Theil did assume the existence of the p_{ij}. In the section on the n-commodity model, under the subtitle "Commodities and Their Prices," Theil discussed two types of prices: the commodity price and the prices of individual qualities of the commodity:

> In this approach commodity prices have a dual nature. On the one hand the average prices [the p_i] can be chosen by the consumer, at least to a certain extent. On the other hand the prices of the individual qualities [our p_{ij}] (the average commodity prices [p_i] being simple functions of subsets of these prices [p_{ij}]) are data for him: they [the p_{ij}] are fixed by other subjects such as retailers, houseowners, the Government, etc. Now it is interesting to see what happens if these quality prices change [i.e., change in the p_{ij}]. The general approach of section (2.2) [where the n-commodity model is introduced] gives— in principle, at least—the opportunity to analyze such changes, because variations in quality prices [the p_{ij}] alter the way in which an element e_{ih} of the vector e_i influences the price p_i. Hence, by assuming some definite relation between each quality price [p_{ij}] and the way in which the corresponding p_i is influenced by the e_{ih} ($h = 1, \ldots, m$) one could analyze the influence of varying quality prices [p_{ij}] on the equilibrium values of x_i, e_i ($i = 1, \ldots, n$). (Theil 1951–52, p. 132)

Note that the expression in parentheses "(the average commodity prices being simple functions of subsets of these prices)" permits any one of a number of functional relationships, and equation (1) above is consistent with Theil's definition of average price in the one-commodity model.

7. The Concept of Quantity

The word "price" implies price "per unit" of something. The "unit" concept is particularly interesting in the case of the price, p_{ij}. The central difficulty in defining "unit" is the selfsame problem we have alluded to earlier— that is, the need to identify and separate the concepts of quantity and quality. Unless we assume that the "unit of measure" represents every aspect or characteristic that is variable within the good, we will need to separate that priced unit of measure from all other measures of the good. Note that we are not saying that price cannot capture all aspects of the good, but that the *unit of measure* to which the price is linked cannot measure all variable aspects of the good. One set of terms frequently used to identify and separate the "unit of measure," which is tied to price (i.e., the "unit" in the statement "price per *unit* of . . .") from all other units of measure of the good has been the terms "quantity" for the priced unit and "quality" for all other measures of the good. Note that it is an arbitrary decision as to which unit of measure of the good or service is given the title "quantity."[3] Some dimension of the good, however, must be so identified. We consider now the concept of "quantity" as it relates to the e_{ih} and p_{ij}.

In our interpretation of the Theil model, we assume p_{ij} is the price "per unit of quantity" of the jth "quality," and that the unit of measure for q_{ij} is identical to the unit referred to by p_{ij}. We also assume that changes in any e_{ih} contained in the jth "quality"— either changes in the quantity of an element or elements, or changes in the nature of an element or elements—will not, in and of themselves, cause a change in q_{ij} (i.e., the e_{ih} are orthogonal to q_{ij}). We do assume, however, that change in e_{ih} may bring about change in p_{ij} and possibly in p_i.

Note that in some instances change in the quantity of a quality element may also change the nature of the element. It is also possible that change in the quantity of one element may bring about change in one or more of the other elements.

Finally, we assume that change in the quantity q_{ij} of the jth "quality" may change the quality of the ith commodity, as measured by the average price, p_i. And, we assume change in the quality elements of the jth "quality" may change the "quality" to a different "quality." A change in j may also change the quality of the commodity.

To clarify the relationship of quality elements to the "qualities," and the "qualities" to the commodity, note that change in either the quantity of a "quality" (a change in q_{ij}) and/or change in the quality level of a "quality" (change in j) can produce a change in the quality of the commodity and a change in p_i. A change in the quantity of a "quality" (the change in q) will also produce a change in x_i, the quantity of the commodity. In the case of quality elements, conversely, a change in the quantity of a quality element and/or a change in the nature of a quality element may produce change in p_{ij} and possibly p_i. Unless specifically stipulated otherwise, the quantity of the jth "quality," or q_{ij}, will not be affected by any change in any element of the vector e_i. The reason for this distinction is that q_{ij} and x_i must be specified to have the same unit of measure, otherwise Theil could not sum the quantity of "qualities" to obtain the quantity of the commodity. However, there is no need to define the quantity unit of measure of a quality element to be identical with the quantity unit of measure of the "quality." In fact, to make such an assumption would limit the usefulness of the vector e_i.

With these assumptions we can establish equation (1). In addition, given our explanation of p_{ij}, q_{ij}, and e_{ih}, we now have

$$x_i = \sum_{j=1}^{k} q_{ij}. \tag{2}$$

As explained above, equation (2) assumes that the quantity unit of measure for each "quality" in the commodity is the same as the quantity unit of measure for x_i. Furthermore, q_{ij} and x_{ij} are assumed to be invariant to changes in quality.

With equations (1) and (2), Theil's constraint in the n-commodity model becomes:

$$\sum_{i=1}^{n} (\sum_{j=1}^{k} q_{ij}) \left[\sum_{j=1}^{k} (q_{ij} \{ p_{ij} [e_{ih}]\}) / q_{ij} \right] - y = 0, \tag{3}$$

and where in the case of $n = 1$, we have $q_{ij} p_{ij} - y = 0$.

Now, if we return to the first marginal condition quoted above, or $(\partial u / \partial x_i) - \lambda p_i = 0$, we observe that Gossen's Law is not as simple or obvious as suggested. Unless we stipulate that x_i is a quality-invariant measure of the quantity of the ith commodity, it is possible to permit x_i to increase via an increase in the quantity of progressively higher "qualities" (higher in terms of higher values for the e_{ih}) such that the traditional concept of diminishing marginal utility is rendered meaningless. This result arises from the fact that as quality changes, the good changes, and the arguments for satiation are weakened.

For example, if the quantity of the commodity x_i is parametrically held constant, say at one unit of the commodity, while the quality elements, the e_{ih}, are increased, would the consumer experience diminishing marginal utility for increases in e_{ih}? The answer is far from obvious, but it is doubtful that one can apply the usual interpretations of optimization equations in traditional consumer models to obtain the answer. The same question regarding diminishing marginal utility arises if quality varies along the x_i axis—that is, if x_i is not a quality-invariant measure of quantity. These points are similar to those raised by Wicksell (see chapter 2, section 2).

8. Theil's Treatment of the Grouping Problem: Additional Comments

With these comments we conclude our review of the e_{ih} and return to our discussion of the role of price in Theil's model. To explain how "qualities" group together to form commodities, Theil focused on price patterns of the p_{ij}. He explained his procedure as follows:

> We think that it has great advantages if the definition of a commodity depends on the behavior of quality prices [the p_{ij}]. So we shall define a set of qualities to be a commodity only if the prices of these qualities have a certain functional relationship to each other during the period considered. Such a relation-

ship might be that these prices move proportionally; it might be that the increments and decrements of these prices are identical; it might be that these prices obey a cubic with the same parameters, which are fixed by retailers, etc. (Theil 1951–52, p. 133)

Theil did not provide a theoretical explanation of how commodity boundaries are established; he used instead an empirical approach. There are weaknesses, however, with this approach. In what follows observe that Theil used intuition to preselect the data for his empirical work. This situation arises because he provided only a sufficient condition for a commodity group. In the following example, Theil illustrates how "outside" qualities could get mixed with the wrong commodity:

We may add that, if a set of qualities happens to be such a commodity and it appears that there is another quality the price of which has the same functional relationship to the prices of the first-mentioned qualities as these prices have among each other, it is not necessary to include the latter quality into this commodity. E.g., if a set of tea brands is such a commodity and if a quality of peanuts obeys the above-mentioned conditions, there may be sufficient reasons not to add this peanut quality to the set of tea brands. It will be clear that the above is in accordance with the words "only if" in the last paragraph. (Theil 1951–52, p. 133)

Theil's recourse to intuition in the separation of peanuts and tea was unfortunate, particularly in light of his views regarding what he called the "linguistic" approach to the definition of a commodity:

This grouping problem is usually solved in a linguistic manner. If the language one uses contains a substantive covering a set of qualities this fact alone is often responsible for the definition of such a set as a "commodity." It is clear that such a way of defining has no necessary advantages for economic analysis. Nevertheless, the qualities coming under a common substantive have often (but not al-

ways) a closely related significance for the satisfaction of the consumer's wants, so that in many cases at least the heterogeneity of such a commodity will not have so large a disturbing influence as to render further analysis useless. In spite of this a situation characterized by concepts that are based on linguistic considerations only cannot be called a highly satisfactory one. (Theil 1951–52, p. 133)

Theil utilized patterns within price data to identify "qualities" that had grouped (ex post) to form a commodity. (An interesting approach in light of contemporary time-series analyses, particularly co-integration, etc.) He did not suggest "how" nor "why" the "qualities" cluster together to form a group known as a commodity. The grouping of quality elements (e_{ih}) to form "qualities" likewise was not considered.

In the remaining portion of Theil's section on theory, he assumed changes in p_{ij} were proportional. With this assumption he introduced the proportionality constant, π_i, which is equivalent to $\partial p_i / \partial e_{ih}$ (Theil 1951–52, p. 134). The average price paid for a commodity is now "written as the product $\pi_i p_i$" (Theil 1951–52, p. 134), where p_i is defined as the same quality indicator as in the one-commodity model. The proportionality constant, π_i, was called a "price coefficient" (Theil 1951–52, p. 134) and was assumed to be datum to the consumer. The utility function became $u = u(x_1, \ldots, x_n; p_1, \ldots, p_n)$ and the constraint became

$$\sum_{i=1}^{n} \pi_i p_i x_i - y = 0.$$

Note that the constraint requires $\pi_i > 0$, which is consistent with $(\partial p_i / \partial e_{ih}) \geq 0$, as indicated earlier.

Given the utility function and budget constraint, Theil reiterated it was impossible to prove an increase in income would bring about an increase in the quality of items purchased. This result, of course, follows in part from the symmetrical relationship of x_i and p_i in the maximand and constraint. All of our points raised earlier on this matter are applicable here. Furthermore, as the following quotations indicate, Theil's empirical work did not eliminate $(\partial p_i / \partial y) > 0$, that is, a positive relationship between income and quality.

> The larger a family is, the more it is inclined to buy cheaper qualities of a commodity, because it needs larger quantities of, e.g., clothes and food. (Theil 1951–52, p. 140) [Note that, given a fixed income, the larger the family, the smaller the average income per family member.]

> Let us first compare the corresponding average values x [average quantity] and p [average quality] for the clerical [the high income group] and the manual workers [the low income group]. It appears that only a part of the differences can be explained by income differences (the average family size S is for both groups virtually the same); some differences must be due to sociological causes as to the habits of spending. It is found, e.g. that the quantities bought of tea, coffee and meat-products are larger for worker's families than for clerical families, in spite of the fact that the average income of the former group is less than one-half of the average income of the latter group.

> On the other hand, the average values of the p's [quality] show a much more regular pattern: they are all higher for clerical than for workers' families. (Ibid., p. 142)

> The results contained in this table [Table III] suggest that clerical families are more saturated with respect to the quantities and quality indicators considered than the other families with their much smaller incomes. (Ibid., p. 143)

> All income and family size elasticities of the average prices paid, for both sets of families, have the sign that can ordinarily be expected, viz. positive and negative respectively. (Ibid., p. 143)

Although we have identified a number of difficulties with the Theil model, it is not our intention to detract from the overall significance of his contribution. When we consider the disproportionately high degree of interest previously shown in the theory of the firm, Theil's research in consumer theory was a pioneering and long overdue piece of work. His model, along with that of Hendrik Houthakker, represents the first mathematical model of variable quality in consumption space. Finally, Theil was one of the first economists to suggest that the budget constraint in quantity-quality space was not linear.

Chapter 4

Theory of the Consumer and Variable Quality

The Contribution of Hendrik Houthakker

1. Introduction

Our discussion of Hendrik Houthakker's model of variable quality will retain the mathematical style utilized in the original work. Occasional reference will be made to contemporary mathematics, but only in footnotes. Ever since Houthakker's 1951 article appeared, theoretical and empirical models of variable quality have evolved considerably; nevertheless, the approach he developed and the issues he addressed remain relevant. Furthermore, the model he constructed is frequently cited as the foundation for many subsequent models of variable quality, as well as for empirical techniques utilized in the field.

This chapter lays the foundation for chapter 7 and subsequent chapters of part 2. In chapter 4 we present the original Houthakker model. Our discussion is based on his article, "Compensated Changes in Quantities and Qualities Consumed" (Houthakker 1951–52). Because diverse interpretations of the model persist to this day, it will be reviewed in considerable detail. In this chapter and in chapter 7 several questions are raised concerning the original model. In the process of responding to those questions, a modified version of the model is developed. This "Variation on a Theme by Houthakker" is presented in part 2. The principal focus of our review, in chapters 4 and 7, is the nature of Houthakker's constraint in quality-quan-

tity space. The modified model begins in chapter 7 and is further developed in subsequent chapters. The new model is significantly different from its parent, and has implications for both the theory of variable quality and for consumer theory in general.

2. The Houthakker Model of Variable Quality in Consumption Space

In the same volume of the *Review of Economic Studies* that contained Theil's article on quality is found the article by Hendrik Houthakker. The work opens with a description of the state of economic theory dealing with the subject of variable quality. Houthakker's introductory statements, wherein he defined his variables and constructed his model, are somewhat vague and have led to confusion.

In what follows, we present Houthakker's description of the model, and subsequently analyze each of his statements. This slow but, it is hoped, not too tedious process permits identification of his contributions, and they are significant. Throughout our discussion we compare the work of Houthakker with that of Theil.

Houthakker introduced his model with the following statement:

> We propose to study the quality problem by introducing qualities as separate variables, to be determined by the consumer in addition to quantities. This will be done in two stages:

first we assume that the quality of a commodity can be specified by one variable only; afterwards we shall briefly discuss multiple quality variables. (Houthakker 1951–52, p. 156)*

Note, first of all, that Houthakker assumed quality could be separated from quantity, at least to the extent that the consumer could make decisions between the two. Houthakker did not define quantity. Quality, however, he defined as a variety of the commodity, and it (quality) was assumed measurable by a unique price system. Although Houthakker introduced two models—a model where quality is measured by a single variable and a multiple variable model—the bulk of the article addressed only the single variable model.

The author's next paragraph was one of his most innovative and difficult. We will discuss it at length.

> In the simpler version of the theory the consumption of the i-th commodity will be described by two variables: physical quantity x_i and quality v_i. The latter number, which indicates the variety bought, is defined as the price per unit of that variety under some basic price system; the cost of x_i units of quality v_i will then be $x_i v_i$. We restrict our theory to price changes which cause the cost of this consumption $(x_i v_i)$ to become $x_i(a_i + b_i v_i)$ where a_i and b_i are constants ($b_i > 0$; $a_i + b_i v_i > 0$ for all v_i), to be called the *quantity price* and the *quality price* respectively. The former is identical with the price of a good in customary theory; the latter shows the price differential between various qualities. Under the basic price system, which may evidently be chosen anywhere, $a_i = 0$ and $b_i = 1$. The only permitted movements in the price scale of a commodity are therefore those which either increase the unit price of all varieties by a constant amount, or multiply all quality differentials by a positive factor, or do both.[2] If a variety is more expensive than another under one price system it will remain so after all permitted changes. (Houthakker 1951–52, p. 156)

His footnote reads as follows: "[2]This restriction to 'linear' price changes enables us to deal with the essentials of the problem without going into the theory of functionals and their derivatives" (Houthakker 1951–52, p. 156).

One of the most innovative ideas regarding variable quality was presented by Houthakker in the above paragraph. It was the notion that the price of a commodity could be divided into measurable subcomponents: a component that relates to the quantity of the commodity, and another that relates to the level of quality (variety) within the commodity. Houthakker's approach was similar to Theil's use of an average price of a commodity, where the average price was derived from the prices of individual qualities. Theil, however, was less explicit regarding the relationship of the commodity price and individual quality prices—except in his one-commodity model, where

$$p = (\sum_{i=1}^{k} q_i p_i) / x .$$

In the Houthakker model, the price of the commodity, p, may be defined as $p_i = (a_i + b_i v_i)$. The quantity of the ith commodity was measured by x_i, which was defined as the "physical quantity." His definition of v_i was that it is a "variety bought" (of the commodity) and could be measured "as the price per unit of that variety." The unit in "price per unit" was equivalent to the unit of measure in x_i. This relationship was established by Houthakker:

> [T]he different varieties of a commodity must be homogeneous to the extent that their quantities can be expressed in the same unit, else x_i would have no meaning. (Houthakker 1951–52, p. 156)

Note that Houthakker did not provide an expression for the quantity of an individual

---

variety; he only provided a price for each individual variety. Houthakker's use of the term "a variety" was identical to Theil's use of the term "a quality." Both terms stand for a single good, which represents a single level of quality, within a single commodity.

With the "quantity" unit-of-measure that is used for the variety price, v_i, equal to the "quantity" unit-of-measure for the ith commodity, x_i, and with the assumption that there is only one variety purchased of any given commodity, Houthakker states that "the cost of x_i units of quality v_i will then be $x_i v_i$." Note that he assumed only one variety is purchased per commodity, namely, that "only one variety of each good [commodity] must be bought, since the maximizing process to be considered does not allow for multiple equilibria" (Houthakker 1951–52, p. 156).

Note that v_i, which was defined to be the price per unit of the variety, cannot indicate the quantity of the variety purchased; this measurement task rests with x_i. Consequently, the result, $x_i v_i$, can be obtained—either in the case of a single quality variable per variety per commodity, or in the case of multiple quality variables—only if the quantity unit-of-measure for all varieties, regardless of the number of quality variables per variety, is identical for all varieties and equals the quantity unit-of-measure for the commodity, x_i.

Also note that Houthakker assumed, in his one-quality-variable model, that there is only one dimension of quality that is allowed to vary in each variety, that it is the same dimension for all varieties, and that it is the only aspect of quality that varies across all varieties (Houthakker 1951–52, pp. 156, 163). The reader should be careful not to confuse "quality variable" with a "variety." It is the change in a single quality variable that brings about a change in the variety, such that the variety becomes a different variety. In the case of multiple quality variables per variety, there is the additional requirement of

weighting the variables so as to obtain a ranking of the varieties.

The subject of interest at this juncture is the following: In the case of one variety purchased per commodity, the expression $v_i x_i$ represents a cost, and is identical with the more customary expression $p_i x_i$. Total expenditure, or the cost of the commodity, however, is not Houthakker's measure of quality. His method for measuring the quality of a commodity is to employ the indicator of which variety is purchased, and in the model where only one variety is purchased, the price of the variety serves as the indicator. In other words, it was the price of the variety, and no other measure, that served to indicate the level of quality. If Houthakker's v_i measured the same features of a variety as Theil's e_{ih} (an assumption that has been made by many authors), then $v_i x_i$ could not remain as originally defined by Houthakker. We conclude, therefore, that v_i is a price that also serves as an index. However, the index nature of v_i notwithstanding, we should keep in mind that v_i is the money measure of the value of a single unit of an individual variety of the ith commodity.

To continue the discussion of v_i, we introduce Houthakker's utility maximization process. In his words:

The theory has to relate the quantities x_i and the qualities v_i to the quantity prices a_i the quality prices b_i and money income M ($i = 1, 2, \ldots, n$, where n is the number of commodities). Introducing the (ordinal) utility function $u(x_1, \ldots, x_n, v_1, \ldots, v_n)$ to summarize a consumer's preferences we get the constrained maximum problem:

$$u(x_1, \ldots x_n, v_1, \ldots v_n)\text{max} \qquad (1)$$

subject to:

$$\sum_{i=1}^{n} x_i(a_i + b_i v_i) = M \qquad (2)$$

In addition, we should take into account the boundary conditions:

$$x_i \geq 0 \qquad (3)$$

and:

$$v_i^- \le v_i \le v_i^+ \tag{4}$$

where v_i^- and v_i^+ are the upper and lower limits of the permitted range of variation of v_i. (Houthakker 1951–52, pp. 156–157)

Although a great deal has been written regarding Houthakker's use of an indirect utility function, much less attention has been paid to the nature of his constraint. In this chapter, our task will be to gain a better understanding of that constraint. Our discussion begins with an examination of the expression $(a_i + b_i v_i)$.

According to Houthakker, the term a_i represents a "quantity price" and "is identical with the price of a good in customary theory." The use of the term "good" is equivalent to the term "commodity," as is shown by a careful reading of subsequent portions of his article. The term v_i, as discussed previously, "is defined as the price per unit of [a] variety under some basic price system." Houthakker's v_i performs the same function as Theil's p_{ij}. Note that in Theil's one-commodity model (with $k = 1$), and under equilibrium in Houthakker's model (i.e., where only one variety is purchased), we have Theil's $p = v_i$ of Houthakker.

Houthakker's term b_i was labeled a "quality price" and defined as "the price differential between various qualities." The relationship of the three terms is given by $(a_i + b_i v_i)$, with the boundary conditions ($b_i > 0$; $a_i + b_i v_i > 0$ for all v_i) and $v_i^- \le v_i \le v_i^+$. The values v_i^+ and v_i^- are, as explained before, "the upper and lower limits of the permitted range of variation of v_i." (Houthakker 1951–52, p. 157). Regarding the v_i, Houthakker adds the following:

> It will furthermore be assumed that the quality variable v_i is continuous within a certain range for each commodity, i.e. that for every unit price within a certain range some qual-

ity can be bought. Considering the large number of varieties in which most goods are sold, this hypothesis seems reasonable as a first approach. In addition all functions are assumed to be differentiable where necessary in the region considered. (Houthakker 1951–52, p. 156)

We digress for a moment and note that Houthakker has addressed the quality-grouping problem (i.e., the grouping of qualities to form a commodity) in a much more explicit fashion than Theil, or any other author we have previously considered. Houthakker, however, did not explain why varieties form into groups called commodities, nor did he explain how v_i^- and v_i^+ are determined.

We return now to our discussion of a_i, b_i, and v_i. To avoid the possibility that price changes of a single variety could rearrange the ranking of varieties between v_i^- to v_i^+, Houthakker limited price changes to the linear relationship $p_i = (a_i + b_i v_i)$. In his words,

> The only permitted movements in this price scale of a commodity [i.e., the change in p_i] are therefore those which either increase the unit price [v_i] of all varieties by a constant amount [i.e., a change in a_i], or multiply all quality differentials [the set of v_i, $v_i^- \le v_i \le v_i^+$] by a positive factor [b_i], or do both. (Houthakker 1951–52, p. 156)

Note that $p_i = a_i + b_i v_i$, along with the author's boundary conditions, can be interpreted to establish a $v_i p_i$ space, as illustrated in Figure 4.1. In this diagram the "quantity price," a_i, is the value of the intercept and b_i, the "quality price," is the slope, or $b_i = (dp_i/dv_i)$. Under the basic price system referred to by Houthakker, we have $a_i = 0$ and $b_i = 1$, or a 45° line through the origin. With the basic price system, $v_i = p_i$ for any value of $v_i > 0$, which gives $v_i x_i = p_i x_i$, as suggested earlier. Reference to the boundary conditions will show $v_i = 0$ is permitted, but in that case, $p_i = a_i$.

Although Houthakker defined b_i as "the price differential between various qualities,"

Figure 4.1 **Houthakker's Price Space**

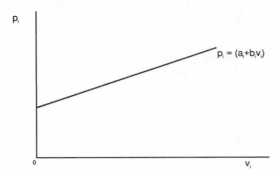

$p_i = (a_i + b_i v_i)$

Figure 4.2 **Equilibrium Condition in Price Space**

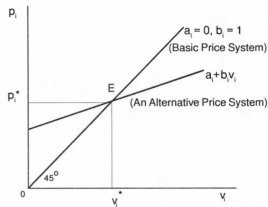

$a_i = 0, b_i = 1$
(Basic Price System)

$a_i + b_i v_i$

E

(An Alternative Price System)

45^0

it does not appear that he intended $b_i = dv_i$, but rather, $b_i = (dp_i / dv_i)$, where dp_i is the price differential for the commodity and dv_i corresponds to the change in price from one variety to another variety (i.e., a change in quality). This conclusion must be inferred as Houthakker did not make explicit reference to p_i. Definition of $v_i x_i$ as "the cost of x_i units of quality v_i," and the use of $(a_i + b_i v_i)$ as the price restriction on $(a_i + b_i v_i) x_i$ strongly suggest, however, that Houthakker intended $p_i x_i$ to become $(a_i + b_i v_i) x_i$ or $p_i = a_i + b_i v_i$. In the basic price system $p_i x_i = v_i x_i$, since $a_i = 0$ and $b_i = 1$, gives $(0 + 1 v_i) x_i = v_i x_i$. The existence of $p_i = a_i + b_i v_i$ suggests a price space as illustrated in Figures 4.1 and 4.2, where the prices of individual varieties of the commodity are mapped onto the price of the commodity.

The possibility that $v_i = 0$ was one of several features of Houthakker's model that distinguished it from Theil's and the work of all preceding authors. In Theil's two models, either the model for a single commodity or n-commodities, his measure of quality (i.e., p or p_i) could not go to zero unless the consumer's income went to zero. This limitation does not apply to Houthakker. With $v_i = 0$, he has $a_i x_i = M$ and his constraint still exists. Of particular interest, however, is the meaning of $v_i = 0$ and $p_i = a_i$, and, additionally, there is a need to further clarify the meaning of x_i.

3. A Definition of Quantity

With the commodity price ($p_i = a_i + b_i v_i$), and the boundary conditions discussed earlier, Houthakker provided a useful technique to identify the "quantity" unit-of-measure for a commodity. First note that $-(a_i / b_i) < v_i \leq v_i^+$, $-\infty < a_i < +\infty$, and $0 < b_i \leq +\infty$ are permissible ranges of variation for v_i, a_i, and b_i, respectively. Also, note that $-(a_i / b_i)$ is Houthakker's lower limit for v_i, or $v_i^- = -(a_i / b_i)$. We begin by assuming $a_i > 0$, such that $v_i = 0$ is possible.

To establish a "quantity" unit-of-measure for the ith commodity, we may select any variety from the set of varieties that we believe constitute the ith commodity, and designate that variety to have the value $v_i = 0$. After we have made our selection, we may temporarily ignore all other varieties. The price of the variety at $v_i = 0$ is not zero, but a_i. The price a_i is a price per some unit of measure of the variety (e.g., pounds, gallons, square feet, hours, or the simple number count of the "thing," and so forth). Whatever the unit of measure to which a_i refers, we will call it the "quantity" unit-of-measure of the variety at $v_i = 0$, and we will give it the symbol x_i.[1] This unit of measure for quantity has become, in effect, our numeraire or our invariant aggregator on the ith commodity.

Once we have identified the unit of measure for x_i, by Houthakker's assumption that "different varieties . . . [are] homogeneous to the extent that their quantities can be expressed in the same unit" (Houthakker 1951–52, p. 156), we can utilize the quantity unit-of-measure for the variety $v_i = 0$ to standardize the quantity unit-of-measure for all other varieties. Once this standardized quantity unit-of-measure has been adopted, the price per x_i per variety becomes the price of each variety (i.e., v_i), and the varieties can be ranked according to their prices.

Note that price does not determine the boundaries of the ith commodity set; that is an exercise that requires additional criteria (e.g., those provided by Abbott or Duesenberry). However, given existence of the set, Houthakker has a method to identify the quantity unit-of-measure for the commodity, and, as a result, he can rank the varieties within the set. This result is important, for it implies that without a quantity unit-of-measure, it is impossible to rank quality. We are reminded again of the necessity to define both quantity and quality.[2]

4. The Role of a_i and the Range of Variable Quality

Once the standardized unit-of-measure of quantity has been established across all varieties, it will not matter if subsequently $a_i \leq 0$. The unit of measure for x_i need not change. Note that for a constant value of money income, $M = \overline{M}$, and a fixed quantity of the commodity $\overline{x}_i$, we have $\overline{M} = a_i \overline{x}_i = p_i \overline{x}_i$ at $v_i = 0$, and $\overline{M} = b_i v_i \overline{x}_i = p_i \overline{x}_i$ for $a_i = 0$. In other words, for fixed values of M and x_i, p_i becomes fixed and the value of a_i, at $v_i = 0$ is equal to the value of $b_i v_i$ for $a_i = 0$. Or, $b_i v_i$ at $a_i = 0$ has become an "intercept." Quotation marks are used because by $p_i = (a_i + b_i v_i) > 0$ there can be no closed intercept on the v_i axis. The limit

value of $b_i v_i$, as p_i approaches zero, is an infinitely close approximation to any given value of such an "intercept," and for our purposes we assume, for $a_i < 0$, the "intercept" on the v_i axis is the lower limit to v_i or v_i^-. For $a_i = 0$, $v_i^- = 0$; and for $a_i > 0$, $v_i^- = -(a_i / b_i)$. In all cases, given Houthakker's linear quality-augmenting function, the lower limit of quality for the ith commodity, or v_i^-, is a function of a_i—the price of our numeraire variety.

Note that for negative values of a_i, some $v_i > 0$ disappear. In other words, for increasingly high negative values of a_i, less "low" quality varieties of the ith commodity are available to the consumer. Moreover, if v_i^+, the upper limit, is held constant, there will exist a sufficiently negative value for a_i such that $v_i^- = v_i^+$, and we have only one variety for the ith commodity. We might add further that, as the variety originally selected for $v_i = 0$ was assumed to have a price $a_i > 0$, the reduction of a_i to non-positive values suggests the non-desirability of the original variety $v_i = 0$, which could be the result of technological change for v_i^+, at the other end of the quality spectrum. If such were the case, then the likelihood of $v_i^- = v_i^+$ is small.[3]

On the subject of a lower boundary for v_i, if the grouping of varieties to form commodities were based on Abbott's or Duesenberry's assumptions of fulfilling "basic" human wants or needs, the Houthakker model appears capable of adjusting to changes in such wants or needs. The arbitrary manner in which $v_i = 0$ and a_i were selected is consistent with any "relativity" that might exist between the variability of quality and the subjectivity of human wants or needs. For the Houthakker model, there exists no similar procedure to identify the relative value of v_i^+, the upper limit.

Careful view of Houthakker's boundary conditions reveals $v_i < 0$ is permissible. The condition $(a_i + b_i v_i) > 0$, however, poses the limitation $p_i > 0$, which establishes the lower limit on v_i^- at $v_i > -(a_i / b_i)$. No significance whatsoever should be attached to the negative values for v_i, as the selection of $v_i = 0$ was entirely arbitrary.

We should also note that the value of b_i, $0 < b_i \leq \infty$, will influence the value of $[(dp_i/p_i) / (dv_i/v_i)]$, a form of quality elasticity, or what we could call the responsiveness of commodity price to a change in quality. For all price systems, other than the basic system, the "quality elasticity" of the ith commodity will vary for different values of v_i. We will have more to say on this topic later. (See also Dorfman and Steiner on quality elasticity in chapter 2, section 7.)

Finally, another complication should be considered. It is possible that as the price v_i varies within its relevant range, the quantity purchased of each variety could also change. Such changes in quantity would be reflected by changes in x_i.

If we held v_i constant at, say, $v_i = 0$, the quality of the commodity could not change; however, the quantity of the commodity x_i could vary as a result of variation of the quantity of the single variety. The same condition holds for any fixed value of v_i—that is, its quantity can vary but not its quality. Were quality to vary, then v_i, by definition, is not held constant.

If we return to Figure 4.1, we may note some additional similarities between the work of Henri Theil and the Houthakker model. Also, we may point out similarities to the hedonic technique.

As explained earlier, a major contribution by Houthakker was introduction of the price a_i. If we assume $a_i = 0$, a number of similarities between Houthakker and Theil become apparent. At $a_i = 0$ and $0 < b_i \leq \infty$ we have, in effect, Theil's n-commodity case under the assumption of proportional price changes. In such a case, Figure 4.1, with minor modifications, could apply equally to Theil as to Houthakker. The changes required are the substitution of P_{ij} for v_i on the horizontal axis. And, given our earlier discussion of $(\partial p_i / \partial e_{ih}) > 0$ (see chapter 3, sections 6 and 8), substitute p_{ij} for e_{ih} in Theil's π_i. The line $p_i = a_i + b_i v_i$, given $a_i = 0$, becomes $p_i = b_i v_i$, and is now equivalent to $p_i = \pi_i p_{ij}$, where $\pi_i = (\partial p_i / \partial p_{ij}) > 0$ as explained earlier. If $v_i = p_{ij}$, and Theil's average price paid for the ith commodity p_i equaled Houthakker's commodity price p_i (which would be the case for Theil's $k = 1$), then $b_i \equiv \pi_i$. The quantities x_i in both cases are identical.

The use of an indirect utility function and the primal-dual concept of optimization are still unique to Houthakker. However, the similarity of the Theil and Houthakker models, given $a_i = 0$, is clear.

5. Relationship to the Hedonic Technique: Introductory Remarks

Use of a_i and b_i in Houthakker's commodity price, $p_i = a_i + b_i v_i$, is sometimes cited as the foundation for the hedonic technique of adjusting price indices for variation in quality. The empirical method of the hedonic technique assumes commodity prices, p_{it}, where i represents the type of commodity and t the time period, are a function of a set of quality characteristics X, and some random disturbance factors u_{it}, or $p_{it} = f_t(X_{1it}, X_{2it}, \ldots, X_{kit}, u_{it})$ (Griliches 1971, pp. 57–58). To determine the influence of the set of quality characteristics X on p_{it}, the X_j ($j = 1, \ldots, K$) are regressed on the p_{it}. Where necessary, owing to quantitative limitations, dummy variables are sometimes utilized for the X_{jit}. Different functional relationships are possible; however, the semi-logarithmic form,

$$\log p_{it} = a_0 + a_1 X_{1it} + a_2 X_{2it} + \ldots + a_k X_{kit} + u_{it},$$

which relates the logarithm of price to the absolute values of the X_j, has been frequently employed (Griliches 1971, pp. 57–58, 988).

The similarity of the technique to Houthakker's commodity price is obvious. A simple comparison, wherein we assume each v_i represents a different quality variable (instead of the ith "variety" of the commodity), would permit $p_i = a_i + b_{ij}v_{ij}$, where Houthakker's $b_{ij} = (\partial p_i / \partial v_{ij})$ corresponds to the $a_1, \ldots, a_k$ coefficients above, and k represents the total number of quality variables. The v_{ij}, where j represents a specific quality variable, correspond to the set of quality factors X_j. For Houthakker, the index of such factors (in his case "varieties") is their individual prices. The introduction of v_{ij}, given $i \neq j$, expands the model to the case of a commodity that consists of two or more varieties. Previously only one variety was purchased. The a_o of hedonic regression do not correspond to the author's a_i, although they both represent intercept terms. There are other aspects of the Houthakker model and the hedonic technique that we will address later.

6. Introduction of Theil's e_{ih} into the Houthakker Model

On a different subject, although related to Theil's work and the hedonic technique, note that were we to introduce Theil's e_i vector, $e_i = (e_{i1}, \ldots e_{im})$, and assume Houthakker's v_i had some functional relationship to Theil's e_i (for example, assume $(\partial v_i / \partial e_{ih}) > 0$ for all h [$h = 1, \ldots, m$]), we could define each e_{ih} as one of Houthakker's quality variables. In the case of Houthakker's single-quality-variable model, assume that all change in a "variety," v_i, is derived from change in a single-quality variable (i.e., derived from change in a single e_{ih}).

One interpretation of the change in a single-quality variable is to assume that the "quantity" of that quality variable has changed. As we discussed earlier in our review of Theil, it is not necessary that the "quantity" unit-of-measure for the e_{ih} be the same as the quantity unit-of-measure for the v_i. It must be recalled, however, that the quantity unit-of-measure for the v_i (the variety) and the quantity unit-of-measure for x_i (the commodity) are identical.

In the case of m quality variables, a change in v_i (the variety) may now be produced via change in two or more of the e_{ih}. As before, one route via which change in e_{ih} might produce change in a single v_i is through change in the quantity of each of the individual quality variables—that is, a change in the quantity of each e_{ih}. Change in v_i, produced by a change in more than one e_{ih}, could arise, however, through other means.

Given $1 < h \leq m$, another form of change in e_{ih} that could affect the value of a single v_i is not a change in the "quantity" of each individual e_{ih} of a given subset of e_{ih} ($1 < h \leq m$), but rather the selection of a new subset of quality variables (e_{ih}) to "change." ("Change" in this context refers to change in the *quantity* of an individual quality variable—that is, a change in the *quantity* of a single e_{ih}.)

Given that not all quality variables (the e_{ih}) are subject to a change in quantity, and given that all quality variables are not equally weighted in their effect on v_i (the single variety), then if new e_{ih} from the set (m) are selected, it is possible that the new subset may have a greater or lesser impact on v_i than did the previous subset. Such a result could be obtained even if the number of e_{ih} in the first subset equals the number in the second.

To illustrate this point, assume that each subset contains only one quality variable, but that it is a different e_{ih} in each subset (e.g., subset A contains e_{i1} and subset B contains e_{i2}). If these two quality variables are not equally weighted in terms of their impact on v_i—for example, assume the weight of e_{i1} is greater than that of e_{i2}—then obviously a change in the quantity of e_{i1} will have a greater impact on v_i than will a similar change in the quantity of e_{i2}. In other words, given the selection of a new subset of quality variables, a change in the quantity of each e_{ih} in the new subset may have a greater or lesser impact on v_i than a corresponding change in the quantity of the previous subset of e_{ih}.

The above comments are intended to illustrate the possibility that, even with a fixed income, the consumer may still be able to select among alternative subsets of quality variables as long as the subset selected remains within the constraint, $M = \sum_{i=1}^{n} x_i(a_i + b_i v_i)$. Therefore, if the subsets of quality variables (e_{ih}) selected are not all equally weighted, the consumer may, for example, increase the quantity of a high-weighted quality variable, instead of increasing the quantity of a low-weighted variable. The effect of this type of decision would be to produce a relative increase in the quality of the variety (v_i) consumed. Again, it is assumed that the consumer remains within the budget constraint.

For example, the price per variety (v_i) of an orange could rise as a result of an increase in the juice content per orange (i.e., an increase in the quantity of a single-quality variable, e_{ih}, which measures juice content per orange); or, it (v_i) could rise as a result of an increase in the sweetness of the juice (where sweetness is another quality variable, possibly measured by the quantity of fructose per orange). Assume the quality variable for juice content is e_{i2} and the quality variable for sweetness is e_{i1}. Assume further that sweetness is weighted higher than juice content in determining the overall quality, v_i, for oranges. Our previous discussion would require that an increase in the quantity of e_{i1} result in a greater increase in v_i than an equal increase in the quantity of e_{i2}.

In summary, if we were to introduce Theil's e_{ih} into Houthakker's model, it would be necessary to have a mechanism that assures that change in e_{ih} (the quality variables) produce change in their corresponding v_i (Houthakker's price of the variety). As discussed earlier, change in the quantity of an individual e_{ih}, or change in the quantities of two or more e_{ih}, should be reflected by change in the corresponding v_i. The possibility that the e_{ih} may not all be equally weighted could also be in-

cluded in the model. In addition, there exists the possibility of trade-off and/or complementary relationships among the e_{ih}, and the v_i should also be capable of reflecting such phenomena. Finally, the relationship of v_i to Houthakker's p_i must be examined.[4]

7. The Relationship of v_i to p_i

We return now to Figure 4.1 and examine further the Houthakker constraint. Recall that in the simple version of his model only one variety is purchased at any given point in time (Houthakker 1951–52, p. 156). This restriction applies in either the case of a single-quality variable or in the case of two or more quality variables. We consider now the relationship of p_i (the commodity price) to v_i (the variety price), while bearing in mind the restriction that only one variety can be purchased at a time.

Recall that Houthakker defined v_i as the price per unit of the variety purchased. The commodity price, p_i, is defined as $p_i = (a_i + b_i v_i)$. If, at any point in time, only one variety is purchased of a given commodity, must $v_i = p_i$? For the moment, we will assume $v_i = p_i$ is required. We make this assumption based on the following: (1) Houthakker's definition of v_i—that is, it is a price; (2) the limitation of the consumer to purchase only one variety per commodity; and (3) the author's use of the basic price system, where $a_i = 0$ and $b_i = 1$.

Under the requirement that $v_i = p_i$, a form of "equilibrium" is introduced into the model. Because $v_i = p_i$ when $a_i = 0$ and $b_i = 1$, the intersection of $p_i = (a_i + b_i v_i)$ with the basic price system establishes "equilibrium" at E in Figure 4.2. We symbolize the equilibrium values by p_i^* and v_i^*. From here on we will call $p_i = (a_i + b_i v_i)$, with $a_i \neq 0$, the *alternative price system*.

One may question whether p_i^* must always equal v_i^* in the Houthakker model. Recall, however, the author's requirements—

that is, $M = v_i x_i$ and $M = p_i x_i$ (under the basic price system). It would seem, therefore, that p_i could never be greater than or less than v_i, as $p_i x_i$ greater or less than $v_i x_i$ is not allowed.

The implication of these requirements (i.e., that $v_i = p_i$ and that only a single variety is purchased) constrains the Houthakker model to solutions found under the basic price system. As demonstrated earlier, under such conditions, the results of the Houthakker model are essentially the same as those obtained by Theil. In other words, the locus of varieties purchased is not along the line $a_i + b_i v_i$ (the alternative price system), but along the 45° line from the origin, where $(dp_i / dv_i) = 1$. It should be noted that the hedonic technique presumes price behavior similar to the alternative price system, not the basic price system.

Under appropriate restrictions on a_i and b_i, the "equilibrium" condition could hold over a range of values of a_i and/or b_i for the alternative price system. Note that v_i must equal p_i under the equilibrium condition. Further, note that change in the equilibrium values of v_i^* and p_i^* could not occur unless the prices a_i and/or b_i change in such a manner as to establish a new "equilibrium" (i.e., a new intersection of the alternative price system with the basic price system).

Under the equilibrium condition, however, change(s) in a_i and/or b_i are constrained by a number of requirements. Note, for example, that for $a_i > 0$, we must have $0 < b_i < 1$ so as to retain an equilibrium value, $v_i^* = p_i^*$. Under such conditions, we have $(\partial v_i / \partial b_i) > 0$. See the upper diagram in Figure 4.3. For $a_i = 0$, we must have $b_i = 1$ to have $v_i^* = p_i^*$, and $(\partial v_i / \partial b_i)$ does not exist. See the upper diagram in Figure 4.4. However, for $a_i < 0$, we must have $b_i > 1$, to establish an equilibrium value, $v_i^* = p_i^*$, and we have $(\partial v_i / \partial b_i) < 0$. See the upper diagram in Figure 4.5. Because we have no restriction on a_i other than $p_i = (a_i + b_i v_i) > 0$, the result $(\partial v_i / \partial b_i) < 0$ is allowed.

Additionally, in all three cases described

above, $0 < b_i$ is required. Consequently, given $a_i > 0$, for any change in b_i, the direction of change in the equilibrium commodity price, p_i^*, is the same as the direction of change for the equilibrium price of the variety, v_i^*, and both p_i^* and v_i^* increase (or decrease) as b_i increases (or decreases). See Figure 4.3. Conversely, for $a_i < 0$, which requires $(dv_i / db_i) < 0$, as b_i increases, the equilibrium values of v_i^* and p_i^* decline, until they approach the limit $p_i > 0$. See Figure 4.5.

In addition to the requirements discussed above, other limitations are imposed by the $v_i^* = p_i^*$ condition. The additional limitations arise when a_i and b_i are analyzed under the restrictions of $v_i p_i$ space and $v_i x_i$ space. The quality-quantity space, $v_i x_i$ space, can be illustrated as shown in Figure 4.6. To specify the constraint in Figure 4.6, consumer income, M, and values for a_i and b_i must be selected.

Note that for the constraint illustrated in Figure 4.6, an intercept exists along the quantity axis at $x_i = (M/a_i)$. As discussed earlier, the intercept corresponds to the value $v_i = 0$ along the quality axis. A unique feature of the Houthakker model is the introduction of $a_i > 0$. Without a_i, the Houthakker and Theil models are essentially the same. Their relationship may be shown again here, where in $v_i x_i$ space with $a_i = 0$ (one of the requirements for Houthakker's basic price system), Houthakker's constraint becomes Theil's hyperbola and is asymptotic to both axes. As we shall see, only under special conditions does Houthakker's a_i produce a constraint in $v_i x_i$ space with intercept on the x_i axis. (See Muellbauer 1974, for an example of the $v_i x_i$ constraint with intercept.)

8. Further Restrictions on a_i and b_i

Of interest at this juncture is the set of additional restrictions on a_i and b_i that must be met when equilibrium and optimality conditions apply in $v_i p_i$ space and $v_i x_i$ space. We have already discussed the restrictions that apply in $v_i p_i$ space. We focus now on

Figure 4.3 **Price and Quality-Quantity Spaces: $a_i > 0$**

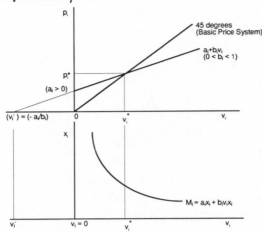

Figure 4.4 **Price and Quality-Quantity Spaces: $a_i = 0$**

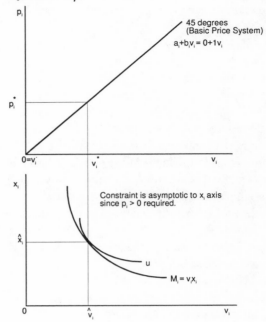

$v_i x_i$ space, and the requirements that arise when the two spaces are combined.

The constraint in $v_i x_i$ space is $M = (a_i + b_i v_i)x_i$. For specified M, a_i and b_i, there exists a constraint that represents a set of ordered pairs $< v_i, x_i >$, or alternative combinations of v_i (quality) and x_i (quantity) in $v_i x_i$ space. Note that each point, or ordered pair, on the constraint represents a different variety, and different quantity, of the commodity. Given the above, for specified M, v_i, and x_i, there exist additional restrictions on the range of values of a_i and b_i. And, as before, change in a_i is not independent of change in b_i.

We begin by examining the simple case of the constraint under the basic price system. Here $a_i = 0$, $b_i = 1$, and we have a constraint in $v_i x_i$ space that is identical to Theil's, that is, $M = v_i x_i$, which corresponds to Theil's $y = px$. The quality-quantity and price spaces are illustrated in Figure 4.4. Under this set of conditions, and assuming the constraint and utility function are well-behaved, utility maximization in $v_i x_i$ space produces an optimum identified as $\hat{v}_i$ and $\hat{x}_i$. Once the optimization process is complete, it seems reasonable to assume the v_i specified in $v_i x_i$ space will be identical to v_i^* found under the basic price system in $v_i p_i$ space, that is, $v_i^* = \hat{v}_i$. In other words, we assume the $\hat{v}_i$ established by constrained util-

ity maximization in $v_i x_i$ space is the same v_i^* established under the equilibrium condition, $v_i^* = p_i^*$, in $v_i p_i$ space. Compare the upper and lower diagrams in Figure 4.4.

Before discussing v_i^* in $v_i p_i$ space and $\hat{v}_i$ in $v_i x_i$ space, it will be useful to consider in further detail the Houthakker constraint. Houthakker and Theil were among the first economists to introduce a constraint in quality-quantity consumption space. Furthermore, the constraint they introduced was unusual; it was convex to the origin. Traditional micro-economic theory has the consumer face a linear constraint. Subsequent to Theil and Houthakker, other investigators have assumed the constraint in quality-quantity space is non-linear, but in some cases the constraint was assumed to be concave to the origin (see, for example, Newhouse 1970, p. 68).

Concave-to-the-origin constraints resemble production possibility contours. Of particular interest in this regard are the assumptions behind such contours—that is, that outputs are produced either under conditions of dimin-

Figure 4.5 **Price and Quality-Quantity Spaces:** $a_i < 0$

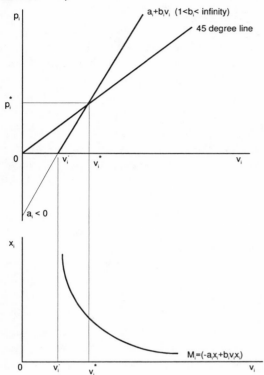

ishing returns, specialized input usage, or differing factor intensities. In the Houthakker and Theil models, convex-to-the-origin constraints exist in consumption space, instead of in output space. The curvature of the constraints, however, is analogous to increasing-returns-to-scale in consumption. The options available in quality-quantity space appear quite different from standard consumer theory. The existence of such a constraint was also suggested by Jack Hirshleifer (see chapter 5).

We return now to the limitations imposed on a_i and b_i as a result of the requirements encountered in $v_i p_i$ and $v_i x_i$ spaces. Consider the case of $a_i > 0$, $0 < b_i < 1$. See Figure 4.3. The consumer's budget constraint in $v_i x_i$ space is, as before, $M = (a_i + b_i v_i) x_i$. The price line in $v_i p_i$ space is $p_i = a_i + b_i v_i$. Given the price equilibrium condition, $v_i^* = p_i^*$, for $a_i > 0$

Figure 4.6 **Houthakker Constraint with Intercept**

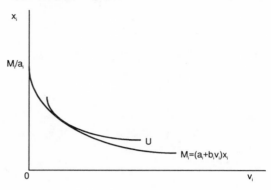

and $0 < b_i < 1$, we have $p_i = a_i + b_i v_i$, or $a_i = p_i - b_i v_i$, which, with $v_i^* = p_i^*$ (the equilibrium condition), becomes $a_i = v_i - b_i v_i$, or $a_i = (1 - b_i) v_i$ (at equilibrium). From the above, it follows that $b_i = (v_i - a_i)/v_i$.

The relationship of a_i to b_i establishes a range of values for a_i and b_i, along the budget constraint in $v_i x_i$ space, where the equilibrium condition imposed in $v_i p_i$ space is maintained. Under the equilibrium condition, changes in a_i and/or b_i are not independent. Additionally, these restrictions reveal that for any M in $v_i x_i$ space, and $a_i > 0$, $0 < b_i < 1$, in $v_i p_i$ space, the constraint in $v_i x_i$ space no longer has an intercept on the x_i axis. This result implies that in $v_i p_i$ space, although $v_i^- = (-a_i/b_i) < (v_i = 0)$, the value v_i^- can never be attained under the condition of $a_i > 0$, $0 < b_i < 1$. However, $(-a_i/b_i) < (v_i = 0)$ exists only under these conditions. See Figures 4.3 and 4.4. Further, the value $v_i = 0$, the standardized unit or numeraire, cannot be attained.

Recall that the equilibrium condition in $v_i p_i$ space corresponds to $b_i = (v_i - a_i)/v_i$ and $a_i = (1 - b_i) v_i$ along the constraint in $v_i x_i$ space. These results place boundary conditions on a_i and b_i. Specifically, b_i now imposes an upper bound on a_i, that is, $v_i^* > a_i$, if $b_i > 0$ holds; and $a_i = (1 - b_i) v_i$ requires $b_i < 1$, if $a_i > 0$ is to be maintained. Given $v_i^* > a_i$ (if $b_i > 0$ holds), and given $a_i > 0$, we have $v_i^* > a_i > 0$, and v_i^* cannot become $v_i^* = v_i = 0$. If v_i^* can only approach, but never attain, $v_i = 0$, then M/a_i is not possible, and the constraint has no intercept on the x_i axis. See Figure 4.6.

9. Problems Between the Equilibrium Condition and the Constraint

Review of Figure 4.3 shows that $v_i^* = p_i^*$, the equilibrium condition shown in the top portion of the diagram, corresponds to a specified value of x_i along the constraint in $v_i x_i$ space. The value of x_i will be labeled $\hat{x}_i$. Recall that $\hat{x}_i$ represents the quantity of the commodity. As illustrated in Figure 4.3, to move along the constraint in $v_i x_i$ space, the value of v_i^* must change in price space. Change in v_i^*, in turn, requires a change in the price equilibrium. (It should be noted that this requirement also applies to the case of $a_i = 0$, $b_i = 1$, the basic price system, under the equilibrium condition.) In the case of $a_i > 0$, $0 < b_i < 1$, however, any change in equilibrium must be accompanied by change in a_i and/or b_i. In other words, for each point on the constraint there is some combination of a_i and b_i that is consistent with the equilibrium value of v_i, both in price space and in $v_i x_i$ space.

If we assume b_i constant, then all new equilibrium values of $p_i^* = v_i^*$, produced along the 45° line, are the result of changes in a_i, or parallel shifts of the price line $(p_i = a_i + b_i v_i)$ in price space. Changes in price equilibrium could also result from changes in b_i, for a fixed value of a_i. Of course, change in both a_i and b_i could also produce change in the equilibrium. However, from the perspective of the constraint in quality-quantity space, to obtain consistency of v_i values between price space and quality-quantity space (i.e., in order to obtain $v_i^* = \hat{v}_i$) optimality in $v_i x_i$ space must be accompanied by appropriate adjustments of a_i and/or b_i in $v_i p_i$ space. These are extremely unusual restrictions on consumer theory.

From the perspective of traditional con-

sumer theory, it would appear that consistency of $v_i x_i$ and $v_i p_i$ spaces requires a two-step operation. In the first step, for example, utility maximization in quality-quantity $(v_i x_i)$ space could be employed to determine $\hat{v}_i$ and $\hat{x}_i$ for the consumer. Once this has been accomplished, appropriate values of a_i and b_i could be established in order to meet the requirements of equilibrium in $v_i p_i$ space.

Unfortunately, for the constraint to exist in $v_i x_i$ space, such that the process of constrained utility maximization could occur, it is first necessary to determine values for a_i and b_i. In other words, how can the process of constrained optimization identify if $\hat{v}_i$, $\hat{x}_i$ the constraint does not exist? And, how can a specific constraint, $M = (a_i + b_i v_i) x_i$, exist unless a_i and b_i are specified? The system, under the price equilibrium condition $v_i^* = p_i^*$, is indeterminate!

Conversely, if a_i and b_i are specified (other than $a_i = 0$ and $b_i = 1$), an equilibrium value in $v_i p_i$ space will be established by the intersection of the alternative price system with the basic price system. At the intersection of the two systems, $p_i^* = v_i^*$, for any combination of $a_i > 0$, $0 < b_i < 1$. If a_i and b_i are specified in $v_i p_i$ space, it would appear that the equilibrium value, v_i^*, established in $v_i p_i$ space, should be consistent with $\hat{v}_i$ selected in $v_i x_i$ space. Such consistency would place an additional restriction on consumer choice of v_i in $v_i x_i$ space. In fact, consumer choice becomes redundant. However, if values of a_i and b_i are not specified in $v_i p_i$ space, the constraint does not exist in $v_i x_i$ space, and we are back to the problem of indeterminacy.

It would appear that the two-step operation requires the first step be specification of a_i and b_i, instead of constrained utility maximization in $v_i x_i$ space. This arrangement, however, introduces the question of how a_i and b_i are determined. One approach might be to assume a_i and b_i are determined by producers. Another approach would be to assume a_i and b_i are determined by the market. We postpone consideration of both approaches to subsequent chapters.

10. Determination of b_i: Introductory Remarks

Here and in chapter 7, we will begin by addressing determination of b_i from the perspective of the consumer. Later, we will address separately the determination of a_i. A particularly interesting feature of the Houthakker model, similar to the Theil model, is the incorporation of consumer decision making into quality-quantity consumption space.

From our earlier discussion, recall $p_i = (a_i + b_i v_i)$. According to our interpretation of Houthakker, the price, p_i, is the price of the commodity, and v_i is the price of a single variety. In the case of the basic price system, $p_i = v_i$. Under the alternative price system, other results are possible. For example, the quantity price, a_i, may become the commodity price (i.e., $a_i = p_i$) if $v_i = 0$. (We now know that under current restrictions this result is impossible.) As discussed earlier, we have assumed $b_i = (dp_i/dv_i)$, that is, b_i is essentially a weight that indicates the magnitude of influence any given variety, v_i, has on the commodity price, p_i.

From the perspective of consumer theory, an additional hypothesis regarding the determination of a_i and b_i might be that individual consumers determine these values. Under this hypothesis, after the consumer selects values for a_i and b_i, the subsequent step consists of determination of $\hat{v}_i$ and $\hat{x}_i$ through constrained utility maximization. We should note, however, that under this hypothesis the consumer has acquired the ability to influence the constraint. As we shall see in chapter 6, ability to influence the constraint also arises in Lancaster's version of consumer theory, where consumer "perception" of product attributes modify the efficiency frontier in attribute space.

If the consumer is assumed capable of in-fluencing the constraint, it could be argued that b_i, Houthakker's "quality price," is the variable of primary interest. Recall that a_i is the "quantity price." Earlier we indicated that b_i could be interpreted as a weight that registers the impact of quality variation, dv_i, on the price of the commodity, dp_i. Another way to describe b_i might be that it is a weight that reflects consumer willingness-to-pay for different levels of quality.

A similar weight could be argued to exist for the producer's perceptions of quality (e.g., along the lines of the cost of v_i and/or reflecting producer perception of consumer preferences for v_i). The value of b_i could also include producer and/or consumer assessments of the impact of technological change and the introduction of new varieties. On producer versus consumer perceptions, see Hofsten 1952 and Triplett 1983. Finally, it could be argued that the consumer's determination of b_i, or what might be called b_i^c, is itself influenced by factors such as consumer income, level of education, age, sex, and other socioeconomic and demographic variables. This approach is consistent with current marketing research. Inclusion of these factors would influence the construction of consumer sampling frames to be utilized in the estimation of quality-adjusted consumer price indices. See Muellbauer 1974, Deaton and Muellbauer 1980, and Deaton 1992.

Unfortunately, Houthakker did not explain the process for determination of a_i or b_i. In his article, utility maximization was initiated under the basic price system, analogous to an initial feasible basis in linear programming. Once an optimal solution was found, he proceeded under an indirect utility function to perform a sensitivity analysis of the effects of compensated variation in consumer income M, and variation in quantity and quality prices, a_i and b_i. A major purpose of his article appears to have been the empirical investigation of variable quality based on market data. In other words, alternative price systems ($a_i \neq 0$,

$b_i \neq 1$) would be revealed through statistical analyses. Our approach here, which is continued in part 2, focuses on variable quality from the perspective of consumer theory. The determination of a_i and b_i plays a major role in subsequent chapters.

In this chapter we have introduced, in brief fashion, Houthakker's model of variable quality. In part 2 we continue our study of this important contribution. In the remaining chapters of part 1 we address the issue of quality-quantity trade-offs and the attributes approach to consumer theory, as well as other contributions. As we shall see, several authors have attempted to link the attributes approach of consumer theory to the study of variable quality. We discuss some of these matters in chapters 5 and 6.

Chapter 5
Quantity-Quality Trade-Offs
The Contribution of Jack Hirshleifer

The contribution of Jack Hirshleifer is not restricted to consumer theory, but rather addresses the issue of the *quantity-quality* trade-off as it relates to both the firm and the consumer. Inasmuch as his work is based on concepts originally developed by Theil and Houthakker, it seems appropriate to introduce his contribution at this juncture.

Prior to Houthakker and Theil, most authors who dealt with the subject of quality were concerned with the influence of quality on quantity demanded, or with the effect of quality on the costs of production. Little consideration was given directly to the quantity-quality relationship. Because the concepts of "quantity" and "quality" were rarely defined in any clear fashion, the looseness of definitions permitted, or more likely, were the cause of, a generally vague understanding of the quantity-quality relationship. A careful reading of most authors of the time shows that, for the most part, they assumed the quantity-quality relationship was inverse. Prior to Houthakker and Theil, however, the relationship was not treated explicitly.

In the Houthakker-Theil models of consumption space, the quantity-quality relationship was also hypothesized be to inverse. In addition, however, both researchers created models in which the quantity-quality contour was convex to the origin. Such a relationship was contrary to traditional linear budget constraints, isocost contours, and concave product transformation functions. The main purpose of the Hirshleifer article was to analyze the implications of a convex quantity-quality relationship, as well as to consider the frequency with which such contours are encountered.

Although the Hirshleifer analysis is introduced as "The Exchange Between Quantity and Quality" (Hirshleifer 1955), he does not provide a thorough definition of terms. Quantity, for example, is defined to be the "number" of the commodity at any level of quality (Hirshleifer 1955, p. 596). The unit of measure for "number" is left to intuition. The author appears to believe that once a commodity is identified, the nature of the commodity will suggest a "common sense" measure for quantity. Such may be the case for automobiles or airplanes, to use two of Hirshleifer's examples. In the case of service commodities (e.g., hospital services, legal services, or education) the quantity unit of measure is far from obvious, even though the commodity may be identified.

Hirshleifer defines quality to be a vector of characteristics that serve some purpose or human need (Hirshleifer 1955, pp. 598–599). His definition of quality is more satisfactory than that of quantity, but he fails to see that the unit of measure for quantity can be arbitrarily selected from among any of the variables in the quality vector. Consequently, although he attempts to clarify the relationship or exchange between quantity and quality, he has not clearly separated the two concepts. As a result, his contribution is limited more narrowly to the stability and optimization problems associated with convex constraints.

Hirshleifer's approach to the grouping problem, or the definition of a commodity, is handled in a manner similar to that of Lawrence Abbott or James Duesenberry. In the definition that follows note that he permits variation in only one quality characteristic—an identical procedure to that utilized by Houthakker in his single-quality-variable model:

> What seems to lie behind the intuitive concept is the idea that commodities may be grouped into families according to the purposes which these commodities ordinarily serve: some commodities provide transportation, others heat, others food, and so forth. Within a large category like transportation, we have subfamilies of commodities providing air transport, land transport, sea transport, and so forth. When the subfamily is sufficiently narrowly defined, it frequently becomes possible to find some objective technical characteristic which is, at least in the *ceteris paribus* sense, positively associated with performance—i.e., achievement of the purpose ordinarily served by the class of commodities in question. For the subfamily of commodities "transport aircraft," for example, reasonable though partial quality characteristics are cargo capacity, air speed, durability, etc. In almost all practical problems, quality would have to be represented as a vector of such characteristics, though it frequently happens that the conditions of the problem preclude variation in more than one or only a few of the conceivably variable characteristics. In this paper, we shall assume that only one quality characteristic can be varied, so that it alone serves as a sufficient measure of quality for our problem. (Hirshleifer 1955, pp. 598–599)*

Also on the same subject he notes:

> To avoid awkward circumlocution we shall use the term "commodity" throughout to refer to a group of similar products, rather than a unique good. A Cadillac and a Chevrolet are then different qualities of the commodity "automobile." (Hirshleifer 1955, p. 596)

To introduce indifference curves into quantity-quality space, Hirshleifer assumes that at any given point of optimization (1) a single model or variety of the commodity is purchased, or (2) the point represents an average quality of a mixture of purchases (Hirshleifer 1955, p. 598). After presentation of this background material, Hirshleifer proceeds to consider first the frequency with which the convex constraint is encountered in quantity-quality analyses, and the implications of the constraint for economic optimization processes.

He concludes that convex constraints may be encountered quite frequently and that such constraints may even exist, on occasion, in the exchange between two commodities (Hirshleifer 1955, pp. 599–601). This conclusion suggests that in any work dealing with quantity and quality one should not automatically assume the existence of concave or linear quantity-quality contours. As we shall see later, it is not even reasonable to assume that the quantity-quality relationship is always negative.

The mathematical implications of convex constraints in quantity-quality space have already been presented, in part, in our discussion of Henri Theil. Besides the stability requirements for an internal point of optimization, Hirshleifer considers the possibility of corner solutions and the economic implications of convex constraints. On the second topic, he states:

> Let us note here what a convex cost isoquant implies. It means essentially that movement at a given cost toward either extreme—very high quality with small numbers, or vice versa—can be made on more and more advantageous terms as you approach the extreme. In ordinary economic situations, as in the production of two commodities, we generally assume that the marginal rate of sub-

stitution increases (shifts unfavorably) as you push toward extreme combinations. More specifically, a convex cost isoquant means that instead of it becoming harder and harder to get additional quality (in terms of what you must sacrifice in quantity in order to keep cost constant) as you move from combinations already involving high quality and small numbers (and vice versa for the opposite case), it becomes easier and easier—until in the limit one can buy an indefinitely large increment of quality with an infinitesimal sacrifice of quantity. (Hirshleifer 1955, p. 599)

We should also note that a convex constraint also implies that quality deteriorates rapidly for slight increases in quantity, when quantity is extremely low.

In consumption space, Hirshleifer introduces the assumption that, for some commodities at any given time, there exists a maximum level of quality, q_0 (Hirshleifer 1955, pp. 602–604; see his Figures II and III). In some cases the maximum q_0 may be only approached; in other cases the maximum is attainable. In the former case, per unit cost (unit of quantity) becomes infinite as q_0 is approached. In the latter case, per unit cost may be high when q_0 is attained, but the cost will be finite:

> The crucial point turns out to be the behavior of the cost function as q [quality] approaches its limit q_0. To clarify this point it will be convenient to cite examples. If the ultimate level of quality can be approached but not actually attained, unit cost would be expected to go to infinity at $q = q_0$. This might be the case if our measure of quality were speed of a material object— either proceeding under its own power or accelerated by a gun or a cyclotron—since, at least under current physical theories, the limiting velocity of light can only be approached. . . . In the other case, the ultimate level of quality may be quite attainable, possibly at high but not at infinite cost. This might occur in practical problems if the quality characteristic in which we were interested was the absence of living bacteria in, say, a sample of milk or water—since, for reasonably sized samples, techniques are available which will kill literally all bacteria in the sample. (Hirshleifer 1955, pp. 602–603)

Once a maximum value of q exists, the author is prepared to discuss the possibility of corner solutions. Hirshleifer does not limit his analysis, as do Houthakker and Theil, to internal points of optimum. Instead, he acknowledges and utilizes corner solutions, as well as points of tangency, for a more general analysis of optimization processes in quantity-quality space:

> As has already been noted, the point of tangency of the cost and utility isoquants will be a nonoptimal solution if the former isoquant is more convex than the latter. From an a priori point of view, there seems to be no reason to believe that any particular convex curvature is more likely than any other, and so the practical possibility of failure of the tangency solution cannot be rejected. This situation may lead to a boundary solution, but in a wide class of cases we shall see that such a relation between the isoquants cannot hold throughout the graph and so a stable tangency solution exists. (Hirshleifer 1955, p. 602)

In addition to corner solutions at q_0, Hirshleifer discusses corner solutions involving either axis. In the process he introduces the possibility that, under certain isocost conditions, the point of optimum may jump from one corner to another. To explain this phenomenon, Hirshleifer employs a diagram similar to Figure 5.1 (Hirshleifer 1955, Figure III, p. 603). In Figure 5.1, C_1 and C_2 are isocost constraints, $C_1 < C_2$, and U_1 and U_2 are indifference curves, with $U_1 < U_2$ as usual. Quality is represented by q and quantity by n. Hirshleifer's explanation is as follows:

> The cost isoquants of Figure III have also been purposely drawn to illustrate another possibility, one which has actually occurred in a practical problem. In this case the cost isoquants are convex in the high-q low-n region but change to the "normal" concave shape in the high-n low-q region. For the curves as drawn, the line connecting optimal solutions runs along $q = q_0$. A small change in one or more of the parameters, however, will suffice to make solutions along the line FF' dominate these. In practical language, a

Figure 5.1 **Hirshleifer's Quantity-Quality Space**

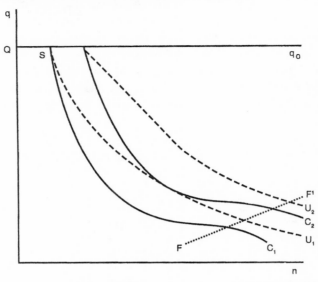

comparatively small change making quality more expensive than before relative to quantity may produce not a marginal change in the solution, but a radical shift from a choice involving a small number of very high-quality units to one using a large number of comparatively inferior units. (Hirshleifer 1955, p. 604)

Hirshleifer does not provide any additional information on this example, regarding the precise nature of shifts in the isocost constraint, or why *FF'* becomes the new locus of optimal solutions. The possibility of non-marginal changes in quantity and quality, conceivably from one corner solution to another, had not been considered by authors prior to Hirshleifer. (See Thom 1975 on butterfly and other cusps, etc.)

Hirshleifer closes with a few comments regarding his assumptions for the utility function in quantity-quality space. They are as follows:

> (1) all combinations involving zero quantity will be on the zero utility isoquant, and (2) all nonzero utility isoquants have a negative slope, with higher isoquants lying to the right and above lower ones. . . . (3) [U]tility isoquants are convex to the origin, at least in the large. . . .(4) For any combinations A, B, C such that A is preferred to B and B is preferred to C,

there is some "average" of A and C which is indifferent to B. (Hirshleifer 1955, pp. 604–605)

In a footnote to this material, Hirshleifer adds, "We shall avoid having to give a definition to the concept of zero quality by limiting our attention to the behavior of the cost and utility functions away from the lower limit on quality, if any" (Hirshleifer 1955, p. 604). Houthakker had a superior method for handling the concept of zero quality.

Hirshleifer began his article thus: "The question of quantity versus quality, though slighted by traditional theory, is in fact one of the most universal problems in the practical application of economic theory" (Hirshleifer 1955, p. 597). He closes with the statement,

> The practical significance of the considerations raised here is that, in the exchange between quality and quantity from the point of view of the consumer or of the firm, various possibilities arise which should make the economist careful in using his intuition trained in the exchange between quantities of different commodities. We have emphasized most the possibilities of decreasing marginal rate of substitution (convexity) in the cost isoquant, which may arise under quite plausible conditions. An important possible consequence is a certain tendency for extreme

solutions to occur, as in the case examined where small changes in one of the underlying parameters could lead not to a marginal modification of the solution but to a widely different outcome. (Hirshleifer 1955, p. 606)

Finally, although the subject of variable quality has continued to receive attention, the relationship of quality and quantity has generally gone ignored. Authors continue to speak of quantity at the intuitive level, and concave quantity-quality contours are assumed to exist. Examination of the contours, as to whether they are linear, concave or convex, has not changed a great deal since publication of Hirshleifer's article. His findings and admonitions have not received the attention they deserve.

Chapter 6

Wants, Characteristics, Price Indices, and Variable Quality

Ironmonger, Lancaster, Fisher and Shell, Muellbauer, and Others

After Theil, Houthakker, and Hirshleifer, the next major contribution to variable quality in economic theory came from characteristics-attributes models. Several researchers are identified with this approach. In the United States, the works of Kelvin Lancaster (Lancaster 1966a, 1966b, 1971), Richard Muth (Muth 1966), and Gary Becker (Becker 1964, 1965) are well known. In the United Kingdom and Australia there is, in addition, the contribution of Duncan Ironmonger (Ironmonger 1972).

The characteristics approach to consumer theory is sometimes assumed to have a theoretical link to the hedonic technique (see Muellbauer 1974). Intuitively, there appears to be a connection. Serious theoretical problems exist, however, between the two schools of thought. We will postpone consideration of these issues to a later section of this chapter. For now, we turn our attention to the work of Duncan Ironmonger.

1. The Ironmonger Model

Duncan Ironmonger's consumer theory is contemporary to that of Kelvin Lancaster and is similar in many respects, though there are significant differences. Ironmonger states that his ideas "were formulated at Cambridge during the period 1957 to 1960 and incorporated in a doctoral dissertation submitted in 1961" (Ironmonger 1972, p. xvii).* Neither author makes reference to the other in the main body of their work, although Ironmonger acknowledges Lancaster in his Introduction (Ironmonger 1972, p. 3). Of all the authors involved in development of the characteristics approach to consumer theory, none focused more on quality than Duncan Ironmonger.

The opening section of his book contains a critique of traditional consumer theory, particularly as developed by J.R. Hicks (Hicks 1946) and H. Wold (Wold and Jureen 1953). Ironmonger claims that prior to general acceptance of the mathematical requirements of calculus, several early economists held the view that commodities produce happiness indirectly through the satisfaction of human wants, and that such wants are many and varied. Included among such authors were Hermann, Bentham, Banfield, Jevons, Senior, Hearn, Carl Menger, von Thunen, and Alfred Marshall (Ironmonger 1972, p. 11).

According to Ironmonger, the concept of numerous wants was subsequently modified to a single dominant want—that is, satisfaction, happiness, or utility (Ironmonger 1972, p. 11). Whereas previously the concept of marginal utility was related to the priority ranking of wants (which were satisfied either by a single good or several goods), the simplified (more contemporary) version came to view marginal utility as the change in utility (the dominant want) derived from the consumption of a single good (Ironmonger 1972, p. 12). Ironmonger suggests that the reason economists adopted the dominant-want concept (utility), over the original and more theoretically rich concept of numerous wants, was that it fit more conveniently the requirements of calculus:

> The idea that commodities may only indirectly produce utility through first satisfying some particular separate wants has been dropped from the theory of consumer behavior. In the development of the theory, the idea of separate wants—an intermediate stage between the dominant want, happiness, and the commodities consumed—has been lost. . . . With the mathematical development of the theory of consumer behaviour stemming from the work of Pareto and Fisher in the 1890s and in the 1930s associated with the work of Hicks and Allen and the rediscovery of the work of Slutsky (1915), the distinction was dropped completely and commodities were invariably regarded as satisfying a single want. . . . The idea that some, if not most, commodities have several uses (i.e. are capable of satisfying several wants) was not made an integral part of the theory and is still dismissed as relatively unimportant. . . . As originally developed, the law of diminishing marginal utility seems to have been a law of priority among wants. . . . which states that the most important wants are satisfied before the least important. The present form of the law of diminishing marginal utility has neglected the discontinuous nature of the process of satisfying wants and has assumed that marginal utility decreases continuously. This assumption is to be found particularly in the mathematical treatment of the theory, where discontinuity would not lend itself to treatment by the infinitesimal calculus. (Ironmonger 1972, pp. 11–12)

Ironmonger developed his theory on the assumption that consumers desire commodities because commodities satisfy human wants. Although, in some ultimate sense, consumers may have only one want, happiness, this want (happiness) is assumed to comprise many other wants. And, he suggests, observation of how consumers satisfy their numerous wants will provide a better understanding of consumer behavior than attempting to analyze behavior based on a single dominant want.

For Ironmonger, a commodity may satisfy one or more wants, and several commodities may be used to satisfy a single want. Note that Ironmonger's "commodity" is analogous to Houthakker's "variety" or Theil's single "quality" (i.e., Ironmonger's commodity is comparable to a single "good").

Ironmonger provides the following definition of the term "want":

> [H]appiness is seen to be composed of many parts. It is these parts that will be referred to as wants. Warmth, shelter, entertainment, companionship, variety, distinction, knowledge, occupation, and freedom from thirst, hunger and pain are perhaps the main wants which comprise happiness. (Ironmonger 1972, p. 15)

The consumer is assumed to have a consumption technology that transforms units of a commodity into units of personal satisfaction of a want or wants. The transformation of commodities into want satisfaction is Ironmonger's definition and measure of quality (Ironmonger 1972, p. 17). His use of "want satisfaction" is similar to the approach taken by Abbott and Duesenberry, and it underscores the subjective nature of quality.

Ironmonger first presents the model of the individual consumer and then the model of group behavior. The specifications of his models were heavily influenced by the requirements of econometrics and the desire for statistical testability of his hypotheses. The requirements for hypothesis testing are particularly evident from his treatment of consumer ranking of wants.

For his model of the individual consumer, Ironmonger has the following variables:

x_j = number of units of commodity j used per unit of time.

z_i = number of units of satisfaction of want i obtained per unit of time.

w_{ij} = the number of units of satisfaction of want i obtained from consuming one unit of commodity j.

p_j = the price per unit of commodity j.

y = money income available to the consumer per unit of time.

The values of x_j, z_i, and w_{ij} are non-negative, and $p_j > 0$, $y > 0$. "Also the quantities x_j, p_j, and y are measurable or objective whereas z_i and w_{ij} are immeasurable or subjective" (Ironmonger 1972, p. 17). He assumes: "The consumer is regarded as having full knowledge of the amount of his income, the prices of all available commodities, his technology, and his wants" (Ironmonger, 1972, p. 16). Note that Ironmonger employs the concept of "quantity" without defining it. His concept of quality, as stated earlier, is represented by w_{ij}:

> The value w_{ij} is partly determined by the objective characteristics of the commodity and partly by the consumer's subjective valuation of these characteristics. It may be called the "i-th quality of the j-th commodity." (Ironmonger 1972, p. 17)

Throughout most of his book, Ironmonger assumes the w_{ij} are constant. He does allow, however, some instances where the w_{ij} are variable.

Review of the material previously discussed in chapter 2 of this text reveals a similarity between Ironmonger and the quality input-output model of Hans Brems. Ironmonger is closer to Brems than most advocates of characteristic-type models, as his use of w_{ij} as a measure of quality to consumers is analogous to Brems's treatment of the a_{ij} as a measure of quality in a production model.

Ironmonger opens his model of the single consumer by assuming the existence of a single want and a single commodity. In this case, we have $U = U(z_1)$ maximized, subject to $z_1 = w_{11}x_1$ and $y = p_1 x_1$. Utility is maximized where $x_1 = (y/p_1)$ and $z_1 = [(w_{11}y)/p_1]$, since $z_1 = w_{11}x_1$. As presented, the single-want single-commodity model does not allow consumer choice—provided saving is not permitted. Note, however, that if quality were variable, change in w_{ij} would introduce choice. Subsequently, he expands the analysis to two or more commodities (Ironmonger 1972, pp. 17–19).

He considers next the case of two wants: first, satisfied by a single commodity, and then by two commodities. The possibility of choice between wants, in addition to choice between commodities, introduces a number of new issues. As we shall see later, the manner in which these issues are addressed highlights some of the differences and similarities between Ironmonger and Lancaster.

In the case of a single commodity that is capable of satisfying two wants, Ironmonger assumes there are two possibilities: that of "joint satisfaction" and that of "common satisfaction." Joint satisfaction means that a unit x, of the single commodity j, may simultaneously, in some fixed proportion, satisfy two wants. He gives the example of "thirst and hunger being jointly served by the commodity milk" (Ironmonger 1972, p. 19). The consumer is assumed to have "no choice of the ratio in which he satisfies the wants. The only choice open to him is to choose the scale of satisfaction" (Ironmonger 1972, p. 19). We have, in effect, $U = U(z_1, z_2)$ maximized, subject to $z_1 = w_{11}x_1$, $z_2 = w_{21}x_1$, and $y = p_1 x_1$. As in the case of a single want and a single commodity, optimality occurs where $x_1 = (y/p_1)$. Because there is no choice in the allocation of x_1 between the two wants z_1 and z_2, because of the proportionality constant assumed in jointness, utility is maximized when all income is spent on x_1. As before, given constant w_{ij}, there is no choice in the model.

In the case of common satisfaction, the consumer can allocate units of the single commodity between two wants. "An example of common satisfaction is the case of thirst and washing being served by water" (Ironmonger 1972, p. 20). As before, $U = U(z_1, z_2)$ maximized, now subject to $z_1 = w_{11}x_{11}$, $z_2 = w_{21}x_{12}$, and $y = p_1x_1$, where $x_{11} = x_{11} + x_{12}$. With the introduction of choice, the optimal allocation cannot be determined without further knowledge of the utility function, or, given the author's definition of z_i, the preference between wants.

Before discussing preference, Ironmonger also introduced the case of two wants and two commodities. There are four possibilities. First, both commodities provide joint satisfaction of the two wants. Second, both commodities provide common satisfaction of both wants. Third, one commodity could provide joint satisfaction and the other provide common satisfaction. Last, and here the author introduced a totally new concept of the want-satisfying power of commodities: Each commodity could be tied specifically and exclusively to the satisfaction of a single want. The last case is defined as a "want-specific" commodity. "The simplest case to consider is where commodity 1 is specific to want 1 and commodity 2 is specific to want 2, for example, water serving thirst and bread serving hunger" (Ironmonger 1972, p. 20). With the want-specific case, we have $z_1 = w_{11}x_1$ and $z_2 = w_{22}x_2$, similar to our introductory example of one want and one commodity. Now, $U = U(z_1, z_2)$ maximized, subject to any one or combination of the z_i constraints discussed above, and $y = p_1x_1 + p_2x_2$.

In every case of two wants and one or two commodities, except for jointness in the one-commodity example, choice is involved in the satisfaction of wants, and sometimes in the allocation of commodities. In these cases, it is no longer possible to maximize both wants simultaneously. An increase in the satisfaction of one want—given fixed income, prices, and w_{ij}—will diminish satisfaction of the other.

Most importantly, we should note the central role of quality in Ironmonger's model. It is the individual consumer's consumption technology, the w_{ij} or transformation of commodities into units of satisfaction, that determines whether commodities provide joint, common, or want-specific satisfaction. A change in quality in Ironmonger's model not only can increase or decrease the efficiency of the want-satisfying power of a commodity but it can also direct that power to different wants and specify the type of transformation.

Given this definition of quality, several questions arise. For example, if the w_{ij} of commodity A for want 8 is lower than the w_{ij} of commodity B for the same want, yet the w_{ij} of commodity A for want 7 is higher than the w_{ij} of commodity B for want 7, what is the quality ranking of A to B? To continue, suppose commodity C excels all other commodities for satisfaction of want 6, but can satisfy no other want. Whereas commodity D, which has a much lower want-satisfying capacity for want 6 in comparison to commodity C, can be employed to satisfy many wants. What is the quality ranking of D to C? In the context of Ironmonger's model, preferences of the consumer would establish the ranking. Unfortunately, owing to the subjective nature of the w_{ij}, comparisons across individuals would be difficult, to say the least. The questions posed above also underscore the importance of commodity groupings according to a want criterion, as well as the importance of ranking wants. We consider now Ironmonger's views on consumer preferences and wants.

2. Preferences and Wants

Ironmonger opens his discussion of preference with the following comment:

> When the consumer is regarded as having many separate wants, the hypothesis about the form of the consumer's preferences requires stating as an hypothesis about the

form of his preferences between wants, rather than between commodities. (Ironmonger 1972, p. 21)

He follows this with some restrictive assumptions regarding consumer preferences in want space:

> This has some advantage in that economists may be prepared to make some rather different assumptions about the form of the function in the want space than they would be prepared to make about the form of the function in the commodity space. . . . It is probable that, as wants are not commodities, the preference function among wants is very different. In that circumstance, economists may have much to gain by making assumptions about the form of the function in the want space which will have sharper implications than those they are usually prepared to make about the form of the function in the commodity space. Provided the implications of an hypothesis are not refuted by evidence, their sharpness is a virtue, not a vice. (Ironmonger 1972, p. 21)

Ironmonger rejects, as unnecessary to want space, the usual assumption in commodity space that indifference curves are convex to the origin (Ironmonger 1972, p. 22). Based on his assumptions regarding the budget constraint, he argues that preferences need not be convex:

> [W]hen the budget restrictions . . . are translated to the want space, an "efficient budget" is obtained which is downward sloping and concave to the origin. Clearly when the budget restriction is concave to the origin it is no longer necessary to have the indifference curves between wants convex to the origin. All that is required is that the indifference curves shall be less concave than the budget restriction. (Ironmonger 1972, p. 22)

Based on the importance of rejectable hypotheses, Ironmonger argues that his theory would be precise enough to clash with the evidence. He suggests that what is needed is a theory of the consumer that stipulates a very precise pattern of behavior in want space. This precise pattern is constructed upon a concept of ranking satiable wants. (Ironmonger 1972, pp. 22–23)

He assumes that wants are satiable with finite income and non-zero prices, and that

as income is increased the consumer first satisfies his or her highest priority wants and then moves to lower wants. Although the ranking of wants is not a new assumption in economics, the preference assumptions introduced by Ironmonger are more restrictive than those usually encountered. In what follows, note the heavy emphasis on satiation and the ordering of wants to be satisfied:

> The system of priorities that the consumer is regarded as having is extremely simplified. These priorities are assumed to be so ordered that at a given income and prices the consumer will satiate as many wants as possible, going down the order of priority from the most important to the least. And if at these prices his income is increased by a marginal amount, this increase will be devoted to reaching satiation on his marginal want. The wants that have been completely satisfied can be called "supra-marginal" wants and unsatisfied wants "sub-marginal" wants.
>
> Notice that it is assumed that the consumer's wants are well-ordered, so that in any particular circumstance he has only one marginal want. The consumer aims at satiating one want at a time. This does not preclude the possibility of other wants being satiated incidentally to the satiation of the marginal want. This is always likely in cases where commodities provide joint satisfaction. . . .[1]
>
> The assumption of well ordered priorities among wants, together with the necessary satiation levels, what can be called the hierarchy principal, gives to the points in the want space an ordering with a very definite structure. All the indifference curves between wants are straight lines! This may appear to be a very simple assumption—one which is logically less probable. However, comparing two assumptions, the one which is logically less probable is also the one which is more falsifiable, and therefore more useful. (Ironmonger 1972, pp. 23–24)

Ironmonger was aware that these assumptions are restrictive. He believed, however, that they are better suited for empirical work, a matter of great importance to him.

> The assumption of well ordered wants is fairly restrictive, as it does not allow for the consumer to be indifferent between wants nor for

the wants to be joint. It may well be that wants at some places in the list of priorities are jointly desired. . . . It is indeed probable that wants are in some degree joint or competing. However, the ensuing analysis sticks to the simpler assumption that they are not. (Ironmonger 1972, p. 25)

The assumptions introduced by Ironmonger raise a number of questions regarding the processes of want-satisfaction. We will mention only a few here. First, note that Ironmonger's approach to "wants" is similar to James Duesenberry's, although there are differences. Ironmonger assumes that wants are ranked from highest to lowest, and that as income is increased the highest priority wants are the first satisfied. Duesenberry, in contrast, followed a procedure wherein, instead of step-by-step satisfaction of wants from higher to lower priority, assumed all consumers satisfy essentially the same wants, except that as income is increased, higher-quality goods are utilized to satisfy the same wants. With Duesenberry, low-income consumers satisfy essentially the same wants as do high-income consumers. At low income, however, wants are satisfied with low-quality goods and services, and at high income, higher quality goods and services are utilized (see chapter 3, section 2). With Ironmonger, higher income permits the satisfaction of lower priority wants, or the satisfaction of a greater number of wants. The rich and poor may have the same list of wants, according to Ironmonger, but the poor cannot satisfy as many of them as the well-to-do.

In addition to the problem of joint wants, referred to earlier by Ironmonger, there is the problem that consumers may not wait until one want is completely satisfied, or satiated, before moving down the list of wants to commence satisfaction of the next want. In fact, consumers probably allocate resources to the satisfaction of many wants simultaneously. Ironmonger is aware of such behavior, but he restricts his model to the marginal want.

With the assumption of ranked wants and

linear indifference curves, Ironmonger no longer utilizes, for example, $U = U(z_1, z_2)$, but has instead, where z_i^* represents the satiation level,

$U = U_1(z_1)$ where $0 \leq z_1 < z_1^*$ and
$z_2 \geq 0$, $(\partial U_1 / \partial z_1) > 0[.]$
$U = U_2(z_2)$ where $z_1 \geq z_1^*$ and
$z_2 \geq 0$, $(\partial U_2 / \partial z_2) > 0$
and where $U_2 \geq U_1$ [.] (Ironmonger 1972, p. 25)

This is the author's method of stating that, "whatever the level of z_2 while z_1 is in the range from zero to less than z_1^* (a certain constant), happiness is an increasing function of z_1 alone; and when z_1 is at least z_1^*, happiness is an increasing function of the level of z_2 alone" (Ironmonger 1972, pp. 25–26). Graphically, he illustrates this concept of ranked wants and satiation as shown in Figure 6.1 (Ironmonger 1972, p. 31, Figure 2.5).

In this diagram, the vertical lines from the origin to near the point z_1^* are indifference curves for the first want, z_1. At and beyond z_1^*, z_1^* being the satiation point for the first want, the horizontal lines represent the indifference curves for the second want, z_2. The arrows indicate the direction of utility maximization. Ironmonger is now prepared to discuss the determination of optimal resource allocation between two wants, and so forth.

When the consumer has two wants, three possibilities exist: the cases of common, specific, and joint satisfaction. In the case of two wants and common satisfaction from one commodity, we have:

If $(y/p_1) \leq (z_1^*/w_{11})$ then the solution is
$x_{11} = (y/p_1)$ and $x_{12} = 0[.]$
If $(y/p_1) > (z_1^*/w_{11})$ then the solution is
$x_{11} = (z_1^*/w_{11})$ and
$x_{12} = (y/p_1) - (z_1^*/w_{11})$ [.] (Ironmonger 1972, p. 26)

Note that x_{12} stands for the units of the first commodity utilized for the second want,

Figure 6.1 **Ironmonger's Ordering**

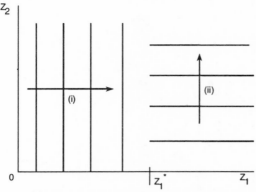

Source: Ironmonger, 1972, p. 31, figure 2.5. Reprinted with the permission of Cambridge University Press.

or x_{ji}. In this case, and most of those that follow, utility is maximized by first allocating all or sufficient income to satiate the first want, and then proceeding to the second want. In this case, $z_1 = w_{11}x_{11}$, $z_2 = w_{21}x_{12}$, $y = p_1x_1$, and $x_1 = x_{11} + x_{12}$. If income and price are such that the first want cannot be satiated, then all of the single commodity is devoted to the first want, or $x_{11} = (y / p_1)$. If $(y/p_1) > z_1^* / w_{11}$, then $x_{12} = (z_2/w_{21}) \neq 0$.

In the case of two commodities, both with specific satisfaction, $z_1 = w_{11}x_1$ and $z_2 = w_{22}x_2$, or $w_{12} = w_{21} = 0$, and we have:

If $(y/p_1) \leq (z_1^*/w_{11})$, then the solution is

$x_1 = (y/p_1)$ and $x_2 = 0$.

If $(y/p_1) > (z_1^*/w_{11})$, then the solution is

$x_1 = (z_1^*/w_{11})$ and

$x_2 = (y/p_2) - [(p_1 z_1^*)/(p_2 w_{11})]$.
(Ironmonger 1972, p. 26)

Ironmonger follows this with a discussion of the case where there are two wants, two commodities, and both commodities are capable of common satisfaction. He considers cases where one commodity is more (or equally as) efficient at satisfying both wants than is the other commodity. He also pre-

sents the case where one commodity is relatively more efficient for the satisfaction of one want (although not want-specific satisfaction), and the other commodity is relatively more efficient at the second want. He explains the situation of joint satisfaction of two wants by two commodities. Here he again considers cases where one commodity is greater, or equally efficient, at satisfying both wants.

Finally, there is the case where one commodity (although joint to both wants) is more efficient for one of the two wants than is the other commodity, and vice versa. In this last case, as well as in the others above, commodity choice is determined by which commodity best satisfies the satiable want, and by the level of consumer income and prices (Ironmonger 1972, pp. 26–27).

3. Budget Constraints

Next, Ironmonger introduces budget restrictions in want space. To accomplish this he utilizes two wants and three commodities, namely,

$$\begin{bmatrix} z_1 \\ z_2 \end{bmatrix} = \begin{bmatrix} w_{11} w_{12} w_{13} \\ w_{21} w_{22} w_{23} \end{bmatrix} \begin{bmatrix} x_1 \\ x_2 \\ x_3 \end{bmatrix}$$

with the budget restriction

$$y = (p_1 p_2 p_3) \begin{bmatrix} x_1 \\ x_2 \\ x_3 \end{bmatrix}.$$

(Ironmonger 1972, pp. 28–29)

In want space the coordinates for each commodity j, given a specified level of income, are $z_i = (w_{ij}y)/p_j$. By assuming that the consumer may spend his or her income on a single commodity, or on any pair of commodities, Ironmonger constructs a budget restriction in want space, as illustrated in Figure 6.2, where the R are coordinates for each commodity and designate their want-satisfying capacity. Note that were a commodity want-specific, its coordinate would lie on one of the axes. The consumer may satisfy wants

z_1 and z_2 by selecting any point in the subspace $R_1R_2R_3$, or on any boundary of the subspace. Points in the subspace, not on a boundary, represent the purchase of all three commodities. Efficient want satisfaction is found on the boundary between R_1–R_2 inclusive, or R_2–R_3 inclusive. The exact point of optimum choice is determined by the intersection of the efficient boundary to the map of straight-line indifference curves. Note that the coordinates for R_1, R_2, and R_3 are influenced by the value of the w_{ij}, the efficiency of transformation of commodities into want satisfaction, or Ironmonger's measure of quality.

The model can be expanded to m wants and n commodities; however, the well-ordered pattern of wants, and their sequence of satisfaction, continues throughout the set of all possible wants. Only the "last" want, z_m, remains insatiable (Ironmonger 1972, p. 32). Under the author's strict ranking of wants, utility maximization reduces to maximization of the marginal want, or:

Find x such that

$z_i = w_i x =$ max. (w_i is the ith row of **W**)

subject to the restraints

$w_{i-1}x \geq z_{i-1}^*$

$-p'x \geq -y$

$x \geq 0$. (Ironmonger 1972, pp. 33–34)

Note that utility is not maximized directly, but rather is subsumed in the ranking of wants and in the subjectivity of the w_{ij}.[2]

Ironmonger also presents a dual version of his model, namely,

Find s such that $z_i = [-z_{i-1}^* \vdots y]\, s =$ min. subject to the restraints

$[-w_{i-1}' \vdots p]s \geq w_i$

$s \geq 0$. (Ironmonger 1972, p. 34)

where, "s_1 to s_{i-1} are the imputed prices of satisfying the supra-marginal wants 1 to i–1; and s_i is the number of units of satisfaction of the

Figure 6.2 **Ironmonger's Constraint**

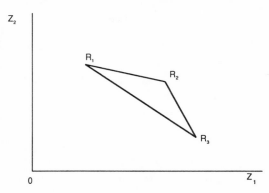

marginal want obtained from an extra unit of income" (Ironmonger 1972, p. 34).

He compares his model to the classic diet problem and provides a numerical example utilizing the calorie and vitamin figures given by Dorfman, Samuelson, and Solow (1958). In this example, Ironmonger utilizes as saturation values for z_i the minimum nutritional standards employed by Dorfman and coworkers (1958). Minimum standards, however, are hardly synonymous with satiation. This and other examples underscore some of the difficulties in application of the satiation concept.

Ironmonger also applied his theory to consumer durables. In many respects his approach is more useful than that developed by Lancaster (Lancaster 1971, pp. 104–107). By assuming, however, that want satisfaction comes exclusively from use and not from possession, the durables version of the Ironmonger model is only a slight extension of the basic model (Ironmonger 1972, pp. 35–39).

Under his basic model, Ironmonger discusses such topics as tastes, quality, prices, income, as well as the introduction of new commodities. We will focus on tastes, quality, and new commodities, and discuss price and income changes, only as they relate to quality.

4. Ironmonger on Taste, Quality, and New Commodities

According to Ironmonger, a change in taste is "limited to changes in the priority ordering among wants and in the saturation levels of these wants" (Ironmonger 1972, p. 48). It follows, therefore, from his efficient budget boundary in want space, that only if the marginal want is affected by such a re-ordering of wants will a change occur in the optimal allocation of commodities and in the wants satisfied.

In the case of quality change, instead of a re-ordering of priority among wants, there is "a change in one or more of the elements w_{ij} of the matrix $\mathbf{W}$." (Ironmonger 1972, p. 50). Ironmonger presents cases of single- and multiple-quality change. By a single-quality change is meant a change in one element of $\mathbf{W}$. Multiple-quality change is the change in two or more w_{ij} of $\mathbf{W}$. If quality change is limited to a single commodity, then the element(s) w_{ij} change only in the jth column of $\mathbf{W}$. A change in a single, or group of elements w_{ij}, will change the value of the vector for commodity j in want space. If the change in quality should be an improvement in quality, from an increase in either single or multiple element(s), then "for any given level of consumption of commodity j the quantity of satisfaction of the ith want is increased" (Ironmonger 1972, p. 50). Note that the commodity itself need not change, as a change in the consumer's evaluation of the commodity (i.e., the subjective aspects of w_{ij}) is sufficient.

As with taste change, a change in quality will only affect the optimum budget allocation if the quality change alters the efficient budget boundary in the region of the marginal want. Changes in quality that affect supramarginal and submarginal wants may alter the shape of the budget boundary, but unless it alters a vertex or line segment intersected by the maximum possible indifference curve (i.e., the point of the marginal want), there will be no change in the optimal satisfaction of wants nor in the consumption pattern of commodities (Ironmonger 1972, pp. 50–53).

The importance of this contribution by Ironmonger lies in the ability of his model to no longer require substitutability among varieties of a single commodity and to introduce, instead, substitutability among commodities (commodities in the sense of Houthakker-Theil). Furthermore, variation in quality may now result in no change in previous consumption patterns. According to Ironmonger, if a consumer's income is too low—for example, to permit satisfaction of the ith want, a change in the quality of the jth commodity, which commodity is frequently used to satisfy the ith want, will hold no significance for the low-income consumer. For the low-income consumer, with his or her present consumption pattern, the quality change, along with its attendant savings per unit of satisfaction, is considered unreachable, and therefore, ignored. This phenomenon also suggests that adjustment of price indices for quality change should apply only to those income cohorts capable of taking advantage of the change in quality.

Although not addressed by Ironmonger, there is in addition the possibility that, if the consumer is aware of the quality change but cannot take advantage of it (due to low income), this may lead to frustration, or envy, or a form of demonstration-effect à la James Duesenberry. This point raises the issue of interdependent utility functions, which in Ironmonger's model would also affect the ranking of wants and the w_{ij}.

Note that Ironmonger can also handle situations where, within a single commodity, say the jth, some quality elements increase, while others decrease. Consumption patterns will be affected only by those quality changes that impact the commodity consumed for satisfaction of the marginal want. If the jth commodity is that commodity, then the net effect of simultaneous increases and decreases in the quality elements, w_{ij}, may alter the coordinates of the commodity in want space. Consequently, the net quality change in the product may increase or decrease the want-satisfying power of the commodity, and therefore the consumption of the commodity, particularly if the previous coordinates for the commodity were near the satiation level of a want.

The introduction of a new commodity is empirically and theoretically difficult to discern from a change in quality. Usually the decision is subjective in nature and is related to our earlier discussion of the boundaries of quality variation for a commodity. New "qualities" of a commodity set are sometimes so different from previous qualities that it is difficult to decide whether the change represents improved quality of the original set, or the introduction of a totally new commodity—that is, creation of a new set.

For Ironmonger, the introduction of a new commodity, however discerned, "is represented by the insertion of an additional column in $\mathbf{W}$" (Ironmonger 1972, p. 54). The elements of the column are ordered according to the priority of consumer wants, and if the new commodity does not provide any satisfaction of a particular want, then the element of that row has a value of zero. Ironmonger assumes the consumer knows the want-satisfying power of all commodities, including the new one. He also assumes, quite unrealistically, "that none of the other elements of $\mathbf{W}$ changes because of the insertion of the new column" (Ironmonger 1972, p. 54). As in the case of quality change, the introduction of a new commodity does not assure a change in the budget boundary, nor in consumption patterns. The new commodity must be sufficiently efficient in its want-satisfying power to compete with or excel other commodities on the boundary. Only if the new commodity is efficient within the region of the marginal want will the new commodity be consumed.

5. Substitution and Complementarity

Finally, regarding the effect of price and income changes, Ironmonger defines substi-tute and complementary commodities on the basis of the relationship of their want-satisfying powers. For example, "If two commodities are perfect substitutes, then they provide satisfaction of wants in the same proportions, even though say physically different. In the want space the vectors for these two commodities will have the same slopes" (Ironmonger 1972, p. 61). Note that with a given income, if commodity prices are equal, their w_{ij} must also be equal. Thus, according to Ironmonger, quality, in addition to all of the other functions it performs, also should be included in evaluating the substitution and complementarity of commodities. (Recall our earlier discussion of Waugh, Chamberlin, and Abbott on this same topic.)

In conclusion, through Ironmonger's interpretation of the w_{ij} as measures of quality, our discussion of quality has come full circle from the firm or production-oriented approach of Hans Brems and others. The producer's criteria for quality, or the quality indices of a governmental regulatory body, are only significant to Ironmonger's consumer to the extent that they are absorbed into consumer technology and influence the value of individual w_{ij}. There is ample room for divergence between producer quality indices and the consumer's w_{ij}. It is also possible that the group of goods listed within producer quality indices may be utilized by the consumer to satisfy more or less (or different) wants than anticipated by the producer. Consequently, it is possible to have different grouping criteria between producers and consumers, in addition to different rankings within the groups. The decision as to which evaluation of quality—producer or consumer—is "correct" depends on the purpose of the index. (See Triplett 1983 for more on this topic.)

As we move on to the Lancaster model, we note that Lancaster's consumption technology is not defined in terms of quality, although he alludes to that possibility. The decision by Ironmonger to define the w_{ij} as measures of quality is unique in characteristics models. The notion that the want-satisfying power of goods and services serves as a definition and measure of quality can be traced back to Knut Wicksell and others. As always, the difficulty with such a concept lies in its measurement.[3]

Ironmonger does not place much emphasis on the grouping of commodities, or, in the language of other authors, the grouping of varieties to form commodities. Like Lawrence Abbott, he assumed that commodities are grouped around the wants they serve, and the higher the want-satisfying power of a particular commodity for a specific want, the higher the quality of that commodity, within the group of commodities that serve that want. As we stated earlier, Ironmonger's use of the term "commodities" is analogous to Houthakker's "varieties."

Ironmonger does not discuss the relationship of quality to quantity. An increase in the quantity of a good, through an increase in income or reduction of its price, will increase the units of satisfaction z_i for the ith want—up to the point of satiation. The increase in x_j (quantity) will increase z_i by the constant proportion w_{ij}. Thus, the quantity of the commodity can increase satisfaction of the ith want, without a change in quality, or change in w_{ij}. The *quantity-quality* relationship, in terms of the ith want, may be illustrated as in Figure 6.3. Clearly, x_j must be an isoquality measure of quantity. Comparison of Figure 6.3 with the quantity-quality trade-off constraints of Hirshleifer, Houthakker, or Theil is inappropriate, as Ironmonger's x_j does not represent a "commodity" in the sense of the previous three authors. Instead, x_j represents a "variety" or one constant-quality good within the set of goods constituting the commodity set (in the Houthakker context). Variation of the quality of x_j (i.e., a variable w_{ij}) would lead us back to the problem of subdivision of characteristics, and the issue of infinite downward nesting.

Figure 6.3 **Ironmonger: Iso-quality with Variable Quantity**

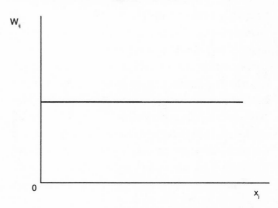

Ironmonger's constant w_{ij} (constant for changes in x_j) is consistent with our earlier discussion of "characteristics" of constant quality.

Note that with w_{ij} constant, we have $w_{ij} = (z_i/x_j)$. Recall that in the Houthakker model $b_i = (dp_i/dv_i)$, where v_i represents the level of quality. In the Houthakker model, quality may be viewed "outward" as it affects price. For Ironmonger, quality is viewed "inward" as it affects satisfaction of the consumer. In either case, as we hope to show in subsequent chapters, it is the consumer's reaction to, or evaluation of, "quality" that determines w_{ij} and b_i.

With these remarks, we conclude our discussion of the Ironmonger model. We consider next the work of Kelvin Lancaster.

6. The Lancaster Model

The main components of the Lancaster model can be found in the following works: Lancaster 1966a, 1966b, 1971. The most thorough development of his work is found in *Consumer Demand: A New Approach* (Lancaster 1971). Like Ironmonger, Lancaster begins his book with a critique of traditional consumer theory.

Both authors assume the existence of a consumption technology, but both the purpose of that technology and its composition are different. Goods, according to

Ironmonger, are desired by consumers because they satisfy wants. The transformation of goods to units of want-satisfaction is accomplished through his consumption matrix **W**. Goods, according to Lancaster, contain "characteristics," and consumers desire goods precisely because they contain characteristics. Characteristics are defined as the physical or otherwise quantifiable properties of goods. Only those properties relevant to consumers are defined as "relevant" characteristics:

> Any good possesses an enormous number of physical properties; size, shape, color, smell, chemical composition, ability to perform any one of a variety of functions, and so on. Because not all properties will be relevant to choice, we shall henceforth use the term *characteristics* for those objective properties of things that are relevant to choice by people. (Lancaster 1971, p. 6)*

The manner in which Lancaster utilizes "characteristics" is, initially at least, quite different from Ironmonger's treatment of "wants." According to Lancaster, "All goods possess objective characteristics relevant to the choices which people make among different collections of goods" (Lancaster 1971, p. 7). For Ironmonger, consumers desire goods for their want-satisfying power; for Lancaster, consumers desire goods for their characteristics.

We come now to one of the major differences between the two authors. For Lancaster,

> The relationship between a given quantity of a good (or a collection of goods) and the characteristics which it possesses is essentially a technical relationship. . . . Individuals differ in their reaction to different characteristics, rather than in their assessment of the characteristics content of various goods collections. (Lancaster 1971, p. 7)

Moreover,

> [e]very person in the economy is assumed to "see" the same consumption technology just as, in basic production theory, every producer sees the same production technology. (Lancaster 1971, p. 18)

Recall that for Ironmonger, the value of the individual elements, w_{ij}, of the consumption technology matrix **W** were "determined by the objective characteristics of the commodity and partly by the consumer's subjective valuation of those characteristics" (Ironmonger 1972, p. 17). In other words, for Ironmonger each consumer has his or her own consumption technology, which reflects individual assessment of the want-satisfying power of the good, that is, each consumer determines the value of his or her w_{ij}.

Lancaster, conversely, assumes all consumers have the same (identical) consumption technology matrix, as all consumers are assumed to "see" the same technical relationship of characteristics to goods. Individual consumers may react differently to the characteristics, but the nature of the characteristics, their specific dimensions, and their relationship to goods are "technical" and are the same for all consumers. Lancaster, consequently, places heavy emphasis on the measurability of characteristics, and, looking into the future, he foresees greater capacity for measurement, even of aesthetic characteristics:

> It is essential that the characteristic be an objective, universal property of the good. . . . Since aesthetic reactions are usually reactions to an extremely complex mix of a very large number of characteristics, we shall not pretend that our model will be operationally useful when aesthetic considerations are dominant in choice. The day may come when a computer can analyze the differences between an acclaimed work of literature and a piece

---

*From *Consumer Demand: A New Approach,* by Kelvin Lancaster. Copyright © 1971 Columbia University Press. Reprinted with the permission of the publisher.

of doggerel in terms of the objective arrangement of words, but it has not yet arrived. (Lancaster 1971, p. 114)

Before we proceed further with our comparison of these authors, it will be useful to review the variables in Lancaster's model. According to Lancaster, the consumer maximizes utility through the consumption of characteristics. The consumption technology is assumed to transform commodity space to characteristics space, where characteristics enter the utility function as arguments to be maximized, subject to the consumer's preference for them, and subject to budget restrictions. We have, then, $U = U(z)$ maximized, subject to $z = Bx$, $px \leq k$, and $x, z \geq 0$, where

> U is the utility function
> z is a vector of characteristics
> x is a vector of goods
> B is the consumption technology matrix
> p is a vector of prices for the goods in x
> k is income
> (Lancaster 1966a, pp. 135–136; Lancaster 1971, pp. 15–24)

Initially, the utility function is given the usual specifications—that is, transitivity and completeness of preferences, continuity, strict convexity, non-satiation—and all characteristics are positively desired. Later, the last two assumptions are relaxed (Lancaster 1971, pp. 20–21). The vector $z = [z_i]$ is the set of r characteristics, where the unit in which each characteristic is measured is the same for all goods possessing the characteristic (Lancaster 1971, pp. 15–16). (The reader is asked to recall our earlier discussion of a similar conclusion regarding the use of the e_{ij} in Theil and in Houthakker.) The quantity of each good j is represented by the vector $x = [x_j]$ ($j = 1, \ldots$, n). Lancaster provides no statement regarding specification of the quantity unit of measure. B is an r-by-n matrix of elements b_{ij}, where "b_{ij} is the quantity of the ith characteristic possessed by a unit amount of the jth good" (Lancaster 1971, p. 15). The rela-

tionship of x_j to z_i is established by the b_{ij}, which relationship is assumed to have the properties of linearity and additivity (Lancaster 1971, p. 15).

With the exception that B is the consumption technology of all consumers, instead of the individual W for each consumer, and z_i are "characteristics" instead of "wants," the models of Lancaster and Ironmonger are quite similar. As we shall see shortly, however, when the full Lancaster model has been presented, even these differences fade.

In the Lancaster model presented above (the one-stage model), given fixed income, prices, and b_{ij}, the "universal" consumption technology B transforms the budget constraint in goods space to a feasible set of characteristics in characteristics space (Lancaster 1971, pp. 25–35). The outer boundary of the feasible set is concave to the origin and is titled the "efficiency frontier" (Lancaster 1971, pp. 35–36). The feasible set is analogous to Ironmonger's budget-restricted set, and the efficiency frontier is equivalent to Ironmonger's efficient budget boundary. The only difference, again, is the fact that, for Lancaster, only one efficiency set and frontier exists for all consumers, given B and fixed prices. Consumers with different incomes "are related by homogeneous scalar expansions or contractions" (Lancaster 1971, pp. 53–54). For Ironmonger, each consumer determines his or her own consumption technology matrix; therefore, each faces a different feasible set and efficiency frontier.

In addition to the model presented above, Lancaster has an enlarged version, or what he terms the two-stage model. In this version, the consumption process is broken into two-stages (hence the name). Whereas previously the transformation of goods into characteristics was handled by $z = Bx$, we now have an intermediate step called a "consumption activity." With this version of the model, goods are converted to characteristics by passing through one or more consumption activities, or in other words, goods are inputs to consumption activities, which activities produce characteristics (Lancaster 1971, p. 47). As before, the characteristics, not goods, enter the utility function. With the introduction of consumption activities, the model becomes $U = U(z)$ maximized, subject to $z = By, x = Ay, px \leq k,$ and $x, y, z \geq 0$ (Lancaster 1971, pp. 47–48; Lancaster 1966a, pp. 135–36).

The activity matrix A is n-by-m, where each activity a_{kj} "is assumed to be linear and to require goods in fixed proportions" (Lancaster 1971, p. 47). The B matrix, which no longer represents the entire consumption process and thus may not be titled "the" consumption technology, is a matrix of order r-by-m. The elements b_{ij} indicate "the amount of the ith characteristic derived from unit level of the jth activity" (Lancaster 1971, p. 47). If each consumption activity requires only one good, x_j, and each x_j is used in only one activity, then A is a diagonal matrix and we have only a linear transformation interposed between goods and activities, or we have $z = Bx$, where the b_{ij} account for the linear activity transformation (Lancaster 1971, pp. 47–49). Throughout most of his presentation, Lancaster utilizes $z = Bx$, instead of the two-stage model. We will continue our discussion based on his use of the one-stage model.

With the feasible set established in characteristics space, utility is maximized where the highest indifference curve is tangent to the efficiency frontier or intersects a vertex on that frontier. Were our discussion to stop here, we would conclude that there are four major differences between Lancaster and Ironmonger: (1) B is universal for all consumers (instead of W for each consumer); (2) indifference curves are convex (instead of linear and corresponding to ranked wants); (3) consumers desire characteristics (instead of want-satisfaction); and (4) consumption technology is broken up into two stages (instead of a single stage). However, as we proceed with the Lancaster model we discover

there is only one difference, that between the B and W matrices. Subsequently, we show that even this difference is not significant when each model is subjected to empirical work.

7. Similarities and Differences Between Lancaster and Ironmonger

The Lancaster model approximates that of Ironmonger when Lancaster attempts to explain whether or not a characteristic is "relevant." He must establish this criterion because "It is clear that if we count as a characteristic every property of a good that is objectively observable, the number of such 'characteristics' approaches the infinite" (Lancaster 1971, p. 140). In fact, if Lancaster cannot reduce the number of characteristics to something less than the number of goods analyzed, the practical application of his theory "has no great superiority over the traditional model" (Lancaster 1971, p. 140). Consequently, Lancaster introduced the following criterion for relevancy of a characteristic:

> A characteristic is "relevant" to a situation (by which we mean the relationship of a consumer or consumers to a set of goods) if ignoring its existence would lead to different predictions about the choice or ordering of the goods by the consumers. (Lancaster 1971, p. 140)

In the final analysis, then, for Lancaster it is the consumer who determines the set z_i. And, as we shall discover, consumers identify (select) characteristics based on whether the characteristics are relevant to the satisfaction of human wants. Before we consider that topic, however, we need to review Lancaster's concept of grouping.

Given the universe of goods and characteristics, it is useful to reduce the total set to various subsets. At this juncture, Lancaster further refines the term "relevant." He does so by separating goods and characteristics on the basis of whether they are relevant to a given group:

The first requirement for any attempt at operational use of the model, therefore, is to find the circumstances (assuming they exist) under which we can analyze part of the total consumption universe in relative isolation from the remainder.

Once we have established the possibility of concentrating on a group of goods of manageable size, the chief operational problems are those of identifying the characteristics relevant to this particular group. (Lancaster 1971, p. 116)

Once Lancaster has separated goods, and their corresponding characteristics, into groups (relevancy being defined in terms of relevancy of a good or characteristic to the group), the next question becomes: What determines "relevancy" of the group?

At this juncture, Lancaster, rather reluctantly, introduces the concept of wants. He is uncomfortable with a "wants" approach to consumer theory, and he generally avoided use of the term. The essence of a loosely defined wants-approach, nevertheless, runs throughout his model. The following quotes provide examples of his "wants" approach, as well as his reluctance to use the term:[4]

> In the earlier marginalist goods were considered to be related to people because they satisfied "wants." This is no place for a discussion of what these writers really meant by "wants." It is sufficient that they were considered entirely human properties that were, in some way, matched with or "satisfied" by certain goods and that preferences depended on the relationship between wants and the properties of goods. (Lancaster 1971, p. 146)

> Characteristics, in our model, are observable properties of goods, but their relevance to people lies in their ability to generate some response (perhaps negative) in consumers. In this sense we could refer to a characteristic as "satisfying wants" in some fashion. Because of its conceptual redundance we shall generally avoid this way of stating the relationship, but there is an undoubted similarity to what the earlier writers had in mind. Since a characteristic is only a single property of a good, which may possess many, there is a closer matching of single characteristics with single psychological aims than there is of single goods. (Lancaster 1971, p. 146)[5]

> A characteristic is totally irrelevant if it does not appear in consumers' preference functions ("satisfies no wants"), either positively or negatively. (Lancaster 1971, p. 146)

> A prominent feature of the "wants" approach, which we wish to take up, is hierarchy. (Lancaster 1971, p. 147)

At this stage, Lancaster introduces the hierarchy-dominance concept, and the notion of satiation effects (Lancaster 1971, pp. 147–156). Lancaster's approach is more thorough than Ironmonger's, particularly his use of open and closed satiation (Lancaster 1971, p. 148), but the parallels with Ironmonger are numerous. Both authors utilize the diet problem in their examples, and one variation presented by Lancaster (where calories and flavor are the characteristics) provides a particularly useful comparison of each author's preference system.

To illustrate his hierarchy-dominance-satiation preference system in characteristics space, Lancaster produced a diagram similar to Figure 6.4 (see Figure 9.6 in Lancaster 1971, p. 155). The reader should also compare Figure 6.4 with Ironmonger's Figure 6.1. The indifference curves $IC_1 < IC_2 < IC_3$ are identical in meaning with Ironmonger's vertical indifference curves of his Figure 6.1. Similarly, Lancaster's vertical indifference curves $IC_5 < IC_6 < IC_7$ have the same interpretation as Ironmonger's horizontal indifference curves beyond z_1^*. Note that c^* in Figure 6.4 of this text would correspond to Ironmonger's z_1^*. Also, the IC_1 through IC_3 and vertical IC_5 through IC_7 of Figure 6.4 in this text show the hierarchical ordering and dominance of characteristics, or "wants" to use Ironmonger's terminology. The principal difference between the two systems is that Lancaster provided for closed satiation (i.e., disposal costs are not zero), and he permitted simultaneous choice between characteristics (i.e., negative and positive sloped indifference curves). In this regard, Lancaster's model is theoretically richer than Ironmonger's model.

Figure 6.4 **Lancaster's Ordering**

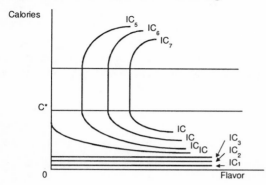

Source: From *Consumer Demand: A New Approach,* by Kelvin Lancaster. Copyright © 1971 Columbia University Press. Reprinted with the permission of the publisher.

Finally, although Ironmonger does not split his consumption technology into two stages, the introduction of "consumption activities" by Lancaster is theoretically harmonious with the Ironmonger model, and could be easily included. The difference between the "subjectivity" of **W** compared with the "objectivity" of **B** is more apparent than real.

First of all, note that in every numerical example provided by Ironmonger he employed objectively quantifiable characteristics, the same as did Lancaster. In fact, both authors employ data on easily quantifiable physical characteristics (e.g., vitamins for the diet problem), or they use aggregated data on consumer purchases and industry-aggregated evaluations of performance factors (e.g., driving time for the automotive industry). In Ironmonger's case, the use of aggregated data means that instead of **W** being interpreted as the consumption technology faced by an individual consumer, the consumption technology becomes the average **W** faced by all consumers, or the *representative consumer*. This result is similar to Lancaster's interpretation of the universal **B** matrix. We find, therefore, that in their use of data and interpretation of the results, the matrices of both models are essentially the same.

8. The Characteristics Approach and Variable Quality

In a characteristics model of consumer behavior the components of "quality" are usually viewed as quantifiable through the subdivision of goods and services into numerous characteristics. Such characteristics are typically viewed as arguments in the utility function. Lancaster placed heavy emphasis on the objective, quantifiable nature of characteristics. Whether quality is defined as the transformation of goods into units of satisfaction, as in the Ironmonger approach, or simply as the summation of characteristics, the characteristics approach permits quantification of something more than "quantity" of the product. (Although identification of the "quantity" unit-of-measure from among the numerous other characteristics of a good or service is not always a simple matter.)

The identification and the quantification of characteristics have led some researchers to conclude that the concept of quality could be absorbed within the characteristics approach. In other words, "quality" is viewed as a term that previously was useful to account for unexplained aberrations of consumer behavior (i.e., when quality entered the utility function). Under such circumstances, quality served as a sort of disturbance term. With development of the characteristics approach, however, other previously unaccounted-for factors (the characteristics) now enter the utility function, reducing the size of the unexplained disturbance, and hence the need for the term "quality."

The choice of terms is, of course, arbitrary. It should be noted, however, that the characteristics approach did not reduce the need to identify a quantity unit-of-measure for each good or service. The reason for this requirement rests with the nature of the **B** and **W** matrices discussed previously, or with any other matrix that transforms goods space to characteristics or wants space. The transformation of goods into characteristics, or into units of satisfaction (i.e., the b_{ij} or w_{ij}), is measured via the ratio of the *quantity* of the good (in goods space) to some other unit of measure of the characteristic (in characteristics space). With the linear assumptions behind the b_{ij}, whatever the unit-of-measure for quantity of the good, it (the quantity of the good) must be able to vary without causing any variation in the ratio of the quantity of characteristics to the quantity of the good.

Obviously, the characteristics approach has not eliminated the need for a measure of "quantity" (either for the good or for the characteristic), and, the introduction of characteristics space in consumer theory simply provides a clear dichotomy between quantity and quality: "Quantity" is the measure of the good in goods space; "quality" is the measure (either singularly or in some weighted aggregation) of characteristics in characteristics space. Under this interpretation, both the quantity of characteristics and the value of the transformation coefficients influence the "quality" of a good or service. Note that all of the above applies to consumer assessment of quality and not to producer assessment, although similar transformations could be made in production space (see Rosen 1974).

Also, note that in terms of the quantity-quality model of Jack Hirshleifer, the interpretation of characteristics as measures of quality alters Hirshleifer's two-space analysis. Whereas previously, Hirshleifer measured quality along a single axis, the characteristics approach of Lancaster and other researchers requires the measurement of quality in n-space, where n is the number of characteristics. Combined quantity-quality space thus becomes an $n + 1$ space. Instead of comparing the relationship of quantity along a single axis to quality along another, the relationship becomes that of comparing quantity along a single axis to an n-dimensional space,

which measures quality. To obtain the single-axis measure of quality, as in Hirshleifer's two-space analysis, quality characteristics must be weighted, aggregated and ranked to form a single, continuous index, and the quantity measure must be separable from the quality index.

The applicability of Lancaster's model to the analysis of variable quality can be extended further. The following quote is his only direct reference to quality and its bearing on our previous remarks is obvious:

> A related problem is that of quality changes. New models are introduced, prices change. Has the price of the good, per unit of "quality," changed or not? Again, the idea of quality is a broad generalization of the idea of characteristic content. "Quality improvement" means, if anything, increased quantities of some characteristics per unit of the good, and some kind of approach via the characteristics analysis seems mandatory. (Lancaster 1971, p. 122)

The unit in "characteristics per unit of the good" is, of course, the issue addressed by our previous statements regarding quantity. The essence of Lancaster's statement on "quality improvement" is, in the language of hedonic theorists, a repackaging approach to the measurement of quality.

Finally, Lancaster suggested that the characteristics approach to consumer theory provides a superior methodology for the development of indices:

> Does the modern urban dweller really obtain as much more of relevant characteristics, compared with the simple peasant. . . .
>
> We can attempt answers to these problems much better by looking at characteristics than at goods themselves. How much does it cost, in different periods or different countries, to obtain some fixed bundle of characteristics by the most efficient choice of goods for the purpose? (Lancaster 1971, p. 122)

As we shall see, this approach to indexing is similar to that employed in the hedonic technique and in World Bank instruments such as the Human Development Index. Both the effectiveness and the accuracy of Lancaster's index, which he titled a "constant-characteristics evaluation index" (Lancaster 1971, p. 123), rest with identification of "the most efficient choice of goods"—that is, consumer "ignorance" and learning are assumed (see Lancaster 1966b, pp. 19–20). Obviously, because information costs for knowledge of the goods-characteristic relationship are not zero, both in terms of time and money, consumer ignorance is a real possibility, and, as in other indices, could introduce "bias" into his index.

Also, Lancaster must assume, for all characteristics in a fixed bundle, that the "quality" of the characteristics does not change—that is, the "quality" of each characteristic, per quantity unit of the characteristic, is assumed constant. This gets us back into the endless subdivision or nesting problem we discussed earlier.

As regards the application of his model to the construction of indices, if the quantity of characteristics per good and/or the transformation of characteristics from goods are interpreted as the measures of quality, then Lancaster's concepts of substitution, income change, negative characteristics, grouping, hierarchy-dominance-satiation, technical and human irrelevance could be utilized to explain the reactions of consumers to changes in quality. There remains, however, the task of weighting the characteristics in terms of an overall assessment of the quality of a good or service. For an individual consumer, the weighting could be handled via his or her preference system, but for aggregate ranking of the quality of goods and services across consumers, problems remain. It is also here, with preference systems and the weighting and ranking of quality, that some problems arise in establishing linkage between Lancaster and the hedonic approach. We turn now to the hedonic technique.

9. Variable Quality and the Hedonic Technique

The empirical techniques of the "hedonic" price index can be traced to Andrew Court (1939) and Richard Stone (1956). Theoretical support for the technique is occasionally attributed to Houthakker (see Adelman and Griliches 1961; Rosen 1974), and to the characteristics approach (see Griliches 1967; Rosen 1974; Triplett 1971). The author usually credited with revival of interest in hedonic price indexes is Zvi Griliches (Griliches 1964, 1967, 1971). In this and subsequent chapters, we highlight some of the theoretical issues, rather than offer a history of applications. Our focus is on the technique and its relationship to the characteristics approach to consumer theory.

From our earlier discussion of the hedonic method, recall that it attempts to discover the relationship between change in the price of a commodity and change in the characteristics or quality elements of the commodity. A change in price attributable to variable quality may be employed to adjust price indices. The technique involves regressing prices, or the logs of prices, of different varieties of the commodity, on such characteristics as size, performance measures, durability, and so forth.

The concept of quality utilized in hedonic work, either from the side of the consumer or the producer, typically involves the use of attributes or characteristics. In actual practice, the technique is utilized more from the resource-cost or user-value perspective of producers (see Triplett 1983, 1986, 1990).[6] In what follows, several contributions to the hedonic literature are presented. In line with our focus on consumer theory, the material on producer measures of inflation, or the characteristic approach as applied to producers, is neglected. Of particular interest are the authors' concepts of quality, especially as these apply to the consumer. Four works are cited: Adelman and Griliches, Triplett, Fisher and Shell, and John Muellbauer.

9.1 The Adelman and Griliches Definition of Quality

Irma Adelman and Zvi Griliches defined quality as follows:

> We propose that the quality of a commodity be regarded as a composite of a number of different characteristics. Each trait will represent a particular quality dimension of the item in question. The entire list of these characteristics, plus one indicator of each, constitutes the quality specification of the product considered. . . . With this definition of quality, to any given commodity i there will correspond n_i different quality dimensions α_{ij}. Naturally, n_i, the number of quality specifications will be different for each commodity, and the value assumed by each α_{ij} will vary with time as well as with the grade of the good. (Adelman and Griliches 1961, p. 539)

In conjunction with this definition, Adelman and Griliches introduced a regression model similar to Houthakker's equation, and estimated the change in price associated with change in the α_{ij} (Adelman and Griliches 1961, pp. 539–542).

9.2 Triplett on the Definition of Quality

A more extensive consideration of quality was provided by Jack Triplett. In his early work he identified three concepts of quality. They were as follows:

> 1. "[Q]uality" is synonymous with "property", "attribute" and "characteristic"; it is an element "which belongs to something and makes or helps to make it what it is". Thus, one might say that pine and oak have different "qualities", which mean that the attributes and characteristics of the two woods differ (perhaps making them best suited to different purposes). (Triplett 1971, p. 5)

> 2. "[Q]uality" refers to the character, basic nature, or essence of a thing—that which distinguishes one thing from another. Thus, a chair differs qualitatively from a refrigerator, and an armchair can be distinguished from a rocking chair by its quality, or essential nature. The first concept of quality identified it with a particular attribute; the second focuses on the whole set of attributes or characteristics of a thing, taken together. (Triplett 1971, pp. 5–6)

> 3. "Quality" is associated with a ranking of products (or services) according to grade, desirability, usefulness, or degree of excellence. With this concept, quality differences are exclusively differences in the level of quality. Where the second concept (noted above) really referred to a listing of the set of attributes or characteristics possessed by a product, the third is concerned with the amounts of quantities of the various characteristics. (Triplett 1971, p. 6)

Triplett concluded that the third concept was the most appropriate one for use in the hedonic technique, and probably for economic analysis in general (Triplett 1971, pp. 6–8). He notes

> that elements from the second concept of quality have occasionally crept into the economic literature on quality and quality measurement. But to view quality as synonymous with variety, or identical to nonhomogeneity in products, results in confusion. Some variation in products may be related to quality, but other differences may be unrelated. (Triplett 1971, pp. 6–7)

The suggestion to utilize only the third concept of quality conveniently avoids two issues discussed earlier in this work—that is, the need to determine boundaries of quality variation for a given commodity (the grouping criteria), and the need to distinguish between quality variation and introduction of a new commodity. In subsequent work, Triplett addressed some of these issues, but primarily from the point of view of producers (see especially Triplett 1983).

Regarding the three categories presented above, note that the first concept of quality could be viewed as equivalent to *defining* the group of characteristics of a specific good, within a set of goods constituting a commodity. The second concept could be interpreted as the *listing* of goods (by their individual characteristics) within the set of goods constituting a commodity. Finally, the last concept could be viewed as the *ranking* of the goods within the set constituting the commodity. To suggest that the ranking of goods is the only appropriate definition and function of quality may be appropriate for some circumstances, but is too restrictive an approach for our analysis.

Triplett criticized Lawrence Abbott for incorporating (and supposedly confusing) elements of the second and third concepts of quality (Triplett 1971, p. 7, see note 9). Triplett's uneasiness with Abbott's use of the term "variety" was justified. Such terms can lead to confusion, as can almost any lexicon regarding quality, which is the reason for our lengthy discussion of terms in our reviews of Abbott, Brems, Houthakker, Theil, Ironmonger, Lancaster, and others. Note that Triplett's criticism of Abbott (i.e., his use of the terms "variety" and "quality," etc.) applies equally to Brems, Theil, and Houthakker, among others.

From his three concepts of quality, Triplett proceeds to discuss service flows and characteristics. He suggests that goods may be grouped according to the degree of similarity of their characteristics (in this respect he is similar to Lancaster), and that quality can be defined in terms of characteristics (Triplett 1971, p. 12; Triplett 1983, pp. 277–287, 293–298, 300–303). He assumes that a quantity unit-of-measure for each characteristic can be identified, and that the "quality" of each characteristic can be held constant during changes in the quantity of the characteristic (Triplett 1971, pp. 13–14, 21, note 21). The importance of how quantity and quality are defined is also underscored in the following example, in which he states that

fuel economy, in a durable good, would—under *ceteris paribus* conditions—normally be regarded as a quality attribute. Yet, if the unit of pricing is shifted from, say, a truck to a unit of transportation service, then fuel economy, as a quality attribute, disappears: For a ton-mile of drayage, fuel is simply a cost element. (Triplett 1971, p. 38)

As we have discussed previously, selection of the appropriate unit-of-measure for quantity is important in theoretical work on variable quality, and, as suggested by Triplett, it is also important in applications of the hedonic technique and efforts to adjust price indices for change in quality.

10. Fisher and Shell on Price Indices and Quality

One of the most rigorous treatments of variable quality, price indices, and the hedonic technique was that provided by Franklin Fisher and Karl Shell (Fisher and Shell 1971). Their work addressed issues of taste and quality change, the introduction of new goods, and the construction of cost-of-living indices.

On the subject of cost-of-living indices, Fisher and Shell point out that the traditional approach is formulated in a non-quantifiable manner; thus,

a frequently encountered view of the true cost-of-living index is that it is designed to answer the question: "What income would be required to make a consumer faced with today's prices just as well off as he was yesterday when he faced yesterday's income and yesterday's prices?" (Fisher and Shell 1971, p. 18)*

The difficulty with this formulation lies in the statement "just as well off as he was yesterday." Fisher and Shell point out that even with constant tastes, price indices cannot answer the question as stated:

---

*From *Price Indexes and Quality Change* by Franklin Fisher and Karl Shell, ed. Z. Griliches. Copyright © 1971 by the President and Fellows of Harvard College. Reprinted by permission of Harvard University Press.

Yet reflection on this shows that the same difficulty appears even if tastes do not change. While it is apparently natural to say that a man whose tastes have remained constant is just as well off today as he was yesterday if he is on the same indifference curve in both periods, the appeal of that proposition is no more than apparent. In both periods, the man's utility function is determined only up to a monotonic transformation; how can we possibly know whether the level of true utility (whatever that may mean) corresponding to a given indifference curve is the same in both periods? The man's efficiency as a pleasure-machine may have changed without changing his tastes. (Fisher and Shell 1971, p. 18)

On the same subject, they add, "One never steps into the same river twice, and the comparison between a man's utility now and his utility yesterday stands on precisely the same lack of footing as the comparison of the utilities of two different men" (Fisher and Shell 1971, p. 18).

To provide a better methodology to account for taste and quality change, and to provide a quantifiably meaningful index, Fisher and Shell suggest that equivalent opportunities for choice—not equivalent levels of utility—become the basis for intertemporal comparisons (Fisher and Shell 1971, pp. 19–20). Given this approach to cost-of-living indices, the authors proceed to address not only the issues of taste and quality change but also the introduction of new commodities. As we have seen previously, all three forms of change are related, but Fisher and Shell present some useful procedures to identify each.

Of particular importance are the two authors' comments regarding similarities and differences between a change in taste, on the one hand, and a change in quality, on the other. The following example illustrates the problem:

> [J]ust what [do] we mean by a taste change as opposed to a quality change[?] To take a slightly different idealized case, suppose that consumers suddenly learn to use a certain fuel

more efficiently, getting a certain number of BTU's out of a smaller quantity of fuel. If the relevant axis on the indifference map is the amount of fuel purchased, then there has been a taste change; if it is the number of BTU's gained from such fuel, there has not been a taste change but a quality change—a change in the opportunities available to consumers. The change can be consistently treated in either way, but the two treatments will differ. When the phenomenon is treated as a quality change, the true cost-of-living index will decline; when it is analyzed as a taste change, this will not be the case. The decision turns on whether the cost of living should be said to decrease just because consumers are better at consuming. If we are concerned with the delivery to the consumer of certain "basic satisfactions," a quality change is involved; this is an extension of the position taken in the construction of hedonic price indexes. If, on the other hand, we are concerned with the valuation of opportunities as available in the market, then treatment of the change as being one of tastes is more appropriate. (Fisher and Shell 1971, p. 24)

The reader is again asked to note the central role played by the unit-of-measure selected to serve as "quantity." If quantity is defined as the amount of fuel, or as the BTU's (service flow from the fuel), this will determine whether there exists a change in taste or a change in quality, respectively.

Further, notice that the idea that "consumers are better at consuming" is handled in the Lancaster and Ironmonger models through change in the elements of the consumption technology matrices B or W. The "basic satisfactions" or wants approach of Ironmonger would classify the change as a quality change. The Lancaster model, which would emphasize the characteristic, "BTU's gained from such fuel," instead of "fuel purchased" (a goods space analysis), would also classify the change to be (by Fisher and Shell's criterion) a change in quality. The dichotomy between taste and quality changes presented by Fisher and Shell suggests another difference between traditional consumer theory (goods space) and the characteristics approach to consumer theory. The former would define the fuel example to be a change in taste; the latter could define it as either a change in quality, or a change in taste.

According to Fisher and Shell, adjustment of cost-of-living indices to account for variation of quality may also involve, among other things, determination of whether the quality change affects only the good experiencing the change, or whether the quality change of a single good impacts the consumption of other goods. The simplest form of quality change, one that may be limited to the immediate good involved (a good-augmenting type of quality change), or may affect other goods, is the case of repackaging. Quality change along the lines of repackaging can be described as a change in the flow of services from the good, without a change in the quantity unit-of-measure of the good:

> If widgets are sold by the box and twenty widgets now are packed into the same size box as previously held ten, it is clear that this is equivalent to a halving of the price of widgets. Somewhat more generally, if one new widget delivers the same services as two old ones, this may also be considered to be simply a repackaging of widgets and thus equivalent to a price reduction. (Fisher and Shell 1971, p. 42)

Note that repackaging may be viewed, in the Ironmonger model, as equivalent to a change in w_{ij}, where the quantity unit-of-measure for j remains constant.

Fisher and Shell show that only in the case of repackaging of the good-augmenting type is it appropriate to adjust the cost-of-living index by exclusively adjusting the price of the affected good (Fisher and Shell 1971, pp. 47–49). In all other cases, the prices of other goods will also need adjustment. To illustrate the type of quality change, where the effects of the change extend beyond the immediate commodity involved, the authors provide the following example:

> [S]uppose that there is a quality change in refrigerators. If this change simply makes one new refrigerator deliver the services of some larger number of old ones, then the simplest price adjustment in the cost-of-living index is indeed an adjustment in the price of refrigerators. On the other hand, if that quality change also increases the enjoyment obtained from a quart of ice cream, then an adjustment in refrigerator price will not suffice; an adjustment in the price of ice cream is also called for. Indeed, if the only effect of a refrigerator quality change is to augment the enjoyment obtained from ice cream, then the simplest adjustment is one made only in the price of ice cream, even though the quality change takes place in refrigerators. In this case, an adjustment in the price of refrigerators can be made to suffice; the magnitude of that adjustment, however, will depend on the quantities demanded of all goods. An adjustment in the price of ice cream will also suffice; the magnitude of that adjustment, however, will only depend on the quantity of ice cream and the quantity of refrigerators. (Fisher and Shell 1971, p. 43)

In general, Fisher and Shell (1971) recommend "that the simplest adjustment of the cost-of-living index may be an adjustment in the price of one or more goods other than the one whose quality has changed" (pp. 43, 51–54).

Finally, the authors indicate that the hedonic technique is appropriate only in the case of repackaging:

> It should come as no surprise that the extension of the results of hedonic price index investigations outside the sample period in which the market observations are made is strictly appropriate only in the repackaging case. The theory of hedonic price indices treats a new quality of a given good as a repackaging of a bundle of underlying attributes. Only if the attributes enter the utility function through the "package," rather than directly, will hedonic price index adjustments be more than locally appropriate. (Fisher and Shell, p. 43, n.21)

This limitation regarding repackaging and the hedonic technique underscores our earlier comments regarding the importance of varieties in the Houthakker model. In other words, how the e_{ih} are bundled to form varieties may be quite important to consumers. In many applications of the hedonic technique, however, the varieties are bypassed and the analysis goes directly from the e_{ih} (the characteristics) to the commodity price p_i. Under Fisher and Shell one must ask whether the package is the commodity or an individual variety within the commodity. Because the "package" actually purchased by the consumer typically is a variety (under Houthakker's terminology), it seems reasonable to define the variety as the package. Consequently, if the variety is ignored, it would appear the hedonic technique is not meeting the Fisher and Shell repackaging criterion.

11. John Muellbauer on Characteristics and the Hedonic Technique

Considerable attention has been given to the possibility of a connection between the characteristics approach of consumer theory and the hedonic technique. As suggested by Fisher and Shell, the bridge between the two schools of thought may be quite narrow. The narrowness of the connection was further demonstrated by John Muellbauer. In his article "Household Production Theory, Quality, and the 'Hedonic Technique,'" Muellbauer outlined, among other things, the requirements necessary to link the hedonic technique to the Lancaster model (Muellbauer 1974). In addition, he identified three classes of theories that provide support for empirical work on variable quality. For each class, moreover, Muellbauer identified restrictive conditions that must be met to preserve consistency between theory and empirical results.

11.1 The First Class of Theories

The first class of theories addresses the relationship between a constant utility price

index and the utility maximization process of a household production model. The constant utility price index is the "true" price index, and it is defined "as the relative expenditure under two price regimes required to reach a given level of utility" (Muellbauer 1974, p. 978).*

If we define y_t^* as the minimum expenditure necessary to attain the level of utility in the base period (i.e., U_0), then the true price index (with U_0 constant) is given by (y_t^*/y_0). To this point, Muellbauer assumes tastes and quality are constant, and he concludes:

> If tastes are constant and there is no quality change, the form of the functional relationship between expenditure on the one hand and prices and utility on the other is constant. In this case the traditional Laspeyres and Paasche approximations to a true index are valid and well known. (Muellbauer 1974, p. 978)[7]

If quality change is introduced, however, Muellbauer demonstrates that the Laspeyres index no longer serves as an upper bound on the true price index (Muellbauer 1974, pp. 978–983).[8] This result weakens the argument that the hedonic technique (the estimated shadow prices π of the characteristics z) can approximate the true index. Muellbauer, however, further indicates that if the π are independent of z (which requires constant returns for the cost function as well as nonjointness in the inputs x), or if the household production function has constant returns and the utility function is homothetic, then the Laspeyres index continues as an upper bound on the true index, and the approximation of the hedonic technique still holds. Unfortunately, a considerable price is paid for these restrictions.

Note that the requirement of nonjointness in the first solution "is unrealistic for many examples of household production and poses serious problems in practical identification of z" (Muellbauer 1974, p. 979). The first limitation was also imposed by Reuven Hendler (Hendler 1975).[9] The nonjointness requirement also applies to the Ironmonger model and implies that all goods are want-specific or provide common satisfaction (Ironmonger 1972, pp. 156–157). (Unfortunately, through most of his model Ironmonger assumed goods provide joint satisfaction.)

The problems associated with identification of z (the characteristics) introduce additional difficulties for the hedonic technique:

> It is implausible to regard Z as being embodied in the goods. Nonjointness implies that the level of each input can essentially be split into separate parts, each of which is used in only one branch of production. Thus if $x_i = x_{i1} + x_{i2}$, the production of z_1 depends on x_{i1} and that of z_2 on x_{i2}. Many types of consumption are not, however, of this type. (Muellbauer 1974, p. 985)

The assumption of nonjointness does assist with the problem of aggregation across consumers. The implications of nonjointness for the consumption technology matrix—namely, that each consumer faces the same technology and shadow costs "irrespective of tastes" (Muellbauer 1974, p. 985)—are less restrictive for Lancaster than for Ironmonger. Recall that for Lancaster the technology matrix **B** was identical for all consumers, whereas for Ironmonger the **W** matrix was unique for each consumer.

The requirement of homotheticity of the utility function also imposes some unrealistic limitations on household production models. First, note that constant returns in production combined with homothetic preferences results in consumption along a ray in characteristics space, and our earlier comments on linear combinations and the Hendler contribution are recalled (see also Roth 1987, chapter 3). Homotheticity also implies unitary income elasticities of demand for all characteristics, a requirement inconsistent with Ironmonger's and Lancaster's assumptions of hierarchy, dominance, and satiation of wants or characteristics. And, as Muellbauer points out, the requirement is "usually refuted by empirical work" (Muellbauer 1974, p. 986). These restrictions also create difficulties in the use of semi-log price-characteristic regressions, in application of the hedonic technique to the Lancaster model (Muellbauer 1974, pp. 979, 986–988).

11.2 The Second Class of Theories

The second class of theories relating consumer behavior to the hedonic technique are theories associated with repackaging of quality and homothetic separability in the utility function. According to Muellbauer:

> Under this hypothesis, it is assumed that each market good has a quality index which is a function of a set of physical characteristics. This relationship is the same for all market goods of a general type ... and being a question of tastes, is independent of market variables. Under this assumption ... market goods of a given type can be aggregated; the aggregate is simply the sum of the quality indices weighted by the number of units of each good purchased. (Muellbauer 1974, p. 988)

The utility function is given by

$$U = U[X_0(\sum a_i x_i), X_1, \ldots, X_n]$$

where $X_0(\ )$ is the category utility function for the group of goods $(x_1, \ldots, x_m)$—recall our earlier discussion surrounding the importance of grouping goods to form commodities—and X_1 through X_n are all other market goods. The indifference curves for $x_1, \ldots, x_m$ are linear (like Ironmonger). Note that X_1 through X_n can likewise be presented as groups within this category utility function. The a_i are quality indices for the corresponding goods; they are functions of the characteristics, and they are assumed to be independent of market variables. For example, in the case of two characteristics, $a_i = g(b_{1i}, b_{2i})$, where the b are characteristics (Muellbauer 1974, pp. 988–989). As discussed above, there may be empirical problems and limitations associated with the selection of some forms of $g( )$ (Muellbauer 1974, pp. 988–989).

Given similar tastes across consumers, the $g( )$ provide a linkage with the hedonic technique:

> If everyone has similar tastes, then it is assumed that competition will force relative prices to be approximately equal to relative quality indices at each point in time, i.e., p_i will be approximately proportional to $g(b_{1i}, b_{2i})$. Over time, the general level of prices changes and the constant of proportionality can be interpreted as a price index. Thus $p_{it} = \bar{p}_t g(b_{1it}, b_{2it})$. This becomes a linear regression model after a log transformation. It is estimated on pooled times-series/cross-section data and corresponds to the second variant of the hedonic technique mentioned in the introduction [(Muellbauer 1974, p. 977)]. Thus, $\log p_{it} = \log \bar{p}_t + \log g(b_{1it}, b_{2it})$. (Muellbauer 1974, p. 989)

As indicated by Muellbauer, it is quite probable that consumer tastes differ. An even greater problem is introduced, however, if a_i or $g( )$ are nonhomothetic; that is, instead of a_i being a function strictly of the set of physical characteristics, a_i, or equivalently $g( )$, are dependent on utility U or the category utility X_0. Should this occur,

> it implies that for different income levels consumers will have different marginal rates of substitution. It therefore calls into question the assumption that competition will force relative prices into equality with relative quality indices. If quality means different things at different levels of income, we have a serious problem of how to interpret the above regression model based on aggregated market data. (Muellbauer 1974, p. 989)

Muellbauer had no easy solution to this problem. He suggested that hedonic analysts endeavor to subdivide markets into segments based on commodity groupings, thus increasing the probability that consumers have similar marginal rates of substitution (Muellbauer 1974, p. 980). This approach, unfortunately, is not without its own empirical limitations. For example, cross-sectional variation and intertemporal desegregation become much more limited. The commodity-grouping approach, however, imposes fewer restrictions on the repackaging model of variable quality than on the Lancaster model. Muellbauer recommended, therefore, repackaging as the superior method to address the effects of variable quality on consumer behavior (Muellbauer 1974, pp. 980, 990).

There are, nevertheless, various conditions identified by Muellbauer that, if met, would permit the results of the two models to coincide: The utility function in both the Lancaster and repackaging models must be separable, and the category function $X_0( )$ must be linear and additive both for goods and for characteristics. Thus, $\sum a_i x_i \equiv \gamma_1 z_1 + \gamma_2 z_2$, and $a_i = \gamma_1 b_{1i} + \gamma_2 b_{2i}$. Given these limitations, in addition to those associated with maintaining an upper bound for the Laspeyres index, "the gain in generality of the Lancaster model relative to simple repackaging is not great" (Muellbauer 1974, p. 990).

11.3 The Third Class of Theories

Muellbauer's third approach utilized the Houthakker model (Houthakker 1951–52). In his brief review of the model, Muellbauer suggested that the pricing system of the constraint $M = x_i(a_i + b_i v_i)$ is comparable to a two-part tariff. (Care should be taken not to confuse Muellbauer's use of b with Houthakker's b_i.)[10] To avoid the limitation that only one variety is purchased, Muellbauer adopted a category utility function. Under his alterations (i.e., $v_i x_i = z$ and b_i as the price of $v_i x_i$) the utility function in Houthakker's model becomes a category function that will handle one-variety purchases (corner solutions), as well as Houthakker's two-stage utility maximization process. The new function can be generalized by making the quality index parameters, a_i (Muellbauer's a_i), functions of the level of utility U or of the category utility (Muellbauer 1974, p. 992). However, as explained above for the repackaging approach, nonhomotheticity of the a_i permits marginal rates of substitution (MRS) to vary for different levels of income (Muellbauer 1974, pp. 989–990, 992). Thus, the Houthakker and repackaging approaches suffer the same trade-off: Generality to many goods results in dissimilar MRS across income, versus constant MRS and corner solutions.

Variable MRS across income levels, either in the Houthakker or repackaging models, combined with consumer shadow prices that do not directly reflect a_i (Muellbauer 1974, pp. 991–992), can produce bias in cost-of-living indices. Divergence of shadow prices from a_i results from the requirement that the a_i be independent of market variables (Muellbauer 1974, p. 988), whereas the shadow prices are generated from market data. According to Muellbauer, the problem is twofold: (1) We do not know "whether shadow prices are internal or external to household decision making" (Muellbauer 1974, pp. 991–992), an issue not easily resolved with market data[11]; and (2) even if shadow prices are known internally to consumers, such prices may not adequately reflect the quality index a_i.

Construction of Muellbauer's a_i quality index is no easy matter. He described the a_i as

> a quality index which is a function of a set of physical characteristics. This relationship is the same for all market goods of a general type (say refrigerators or some grouping of refrigerators) and being a question of tastes, is independent of market variables. (Muellbauer 1974, p. 988)

The difficulties arising here have to do with the role of tastes, and with the procedure for "grouping" products and services. Muellbauer's emphasis on physical charac-

teristics as the basis for the index is similar to Lancaster's universal **B** matrix. However, introduction of tastes supports the existence of as many indices as there are, for example, consumers, or representative consumers, and introduces problems of aggregation.

Independence of Muellbauer's a_i from market variables, conversely, suggests that the impact of advertising on tastes, for example, is minimal; something marketing experts would reject out of hand. Furthermore, how reasonable is it to assume that consumer decision making regarding the quality of something sold in markets operates independently of the market? As regards problems associated with grouping, Muellbauer addressed these matters in an earlier portion of his article, and, within the context of his a_i quality index, they continue to present problems here. Although Muellbauer highlighted the importance of the grouping problem, he did not resolve it. It is, essentially, an issue for sampling—that is, the accuracy of stratified-clustered samples of cohorts of consumers—each sample representing a different cohort, a different representative consumer.

Given the limitations Muellbauer identified via his three classes of theories (i.e., restrictions on shadow prices and the a_i, as well as variability of the MRS) we conclude that under the Muellbauer criteria, the bridge spanning a characteristics version of consumer theory, variable quality, and the hedonic technique is even more narrow than appeared earlier under the Fisher and Shell criteria. Given these limitations in linking theory and empirical investigation, Muellbauer concludes that measures of inflation may be distorted, that is, cost-of-living indices may be biased across social groups and income levels in modern societies. For example, he found "that in the United Kingdom at least, the cost of living indices of different income groups have increased at different rates (most for the poorest in recent years)" (Muellbauer 1974, p. 980).

12. Conclusions

It seems reasonable to conclude that considerable theoretical work remains before we can link variable quality, consumer theory, and cost-of-living indices. Empirical work in this field stands in need to a unified theoretical foundation. At present, only the repackaging approach combined with separable homothetic utility functions can consistently relate empirical work to the behavior of consumers. The limitation of consumption to linear expansion paths in characteristics space, however, is hardly an adequate explanation of consumer behavior in the world of variable quality. The introduction of variable MRS is probably required, as "quality" more than likely has different meaning to different income (and education) levels, and so forth. Such a result places higher demands on data definition, measurement, and collection. The day appears to have arrived when consumer theory in microeconomics should be subdivided into subsets corresponding to different socioeconomic–demographic characteristics of the consuming population. The days of a universal "Theory of the Consumer" appear to be gone.

The problems discussed above are multiplied many times over when decision making on the part of the firm is introduced. Divergence of consumer and producer criteria for quality, introduced by Waugh and Brems, is an unresolved issue to this day.

In an effort to resolve this difficulty, Sherwin Rosen introduced a model based on producers' and consumers' indifference curves that "kiss" along a market hedonic or implicit price function (Rosen 1974, pp. 38–48). His model attempts to surmount the potential disequilibrium problems encountered in markets with variable quality. However, the model does not explain the process of equilibrium, but rather, given the existence of equilibrium, it attempts to analyze empirically the corresponding supply and demand functions (Rosen 1974, pp. 48–51). As we shall see, it is possible that the problems of equilibrium, as well as those associated with generation of quality indices for adjustment of cost-of-living indexes, may be unresolvable.

As mentioned earlier, many authors interested in variable quality and the hedonic technique make reference to the theoretical contribution of Houthakker. In addition to the limitations explained by Muellbauer, in chapter 4 we found what may be considered a problem internal to the Houthakker model itself. We return now to that issue and seek a solution.

Part 2

A New Economic Theory
of the Consumer
Variations on a Theme by Houthakker

Chapter 7

Interpretations of the Houthakker Constraint

As we have seen with Muellbauer, Fisher and Shell, and others, any attempt to include variable quality in a model of consumer theory, and to relate such models consistently to price indices, is no easy matter. The Houthakker model frequently plays a role in these endeavors. As indicated in chapter 4, however, some theoretical difficulties exist in the Houthakker model itself. In part 2 we address these difficulties and propose a solution. The "solution" becomes a variation on the original Houthakker model. The new model has implications for the hedonic technique, but is not intended to resolve any difficulties in the linkage between Houthakker and the hedonic approach. Likewise, the new model is not intended to resolve linkage problems with Lancaster-type models.

1. Attempts to Resolve Indeterminacy

As explained in chapter 4, unless values are specified for a_i and b_i, the Houthakker constraint does not exist in $v_i x_i$ space. There is one exception. The constraint exists under the basic price system, that is, when $a_i = 0$ and $b_i = 1$. See Figure 4.4. Recall that under these conditions the constraint does not have an intercept on the x_i axis.[1] Under the *basic price system*, and under the equilibrium condition in price space, a special form of constraint, what could be called the *basic constraint,* exists in $v_i x_i$ space. The basic constraint is analogous to the basic price system in price space. The basic constraint is the constraint illustrated in Figure 4.4, where $M = (a_i + b_i v_i) x_i$, but as $a_i = 0$ and $b_i = 1$, all we really have is $M = v_i x_i$.

At all points along the basic constraint, the equilibrium condition in price space is satisfied. Under this set of conditions, if an optimum point is first specified on the basic constraint (e.g., by utility maximization), it is possible to subsequently vary a_i and/or b_i in such a manner as to pass through the point initially specified on the basic constraint. Houthakker's sensitivity analysis essentially follows this procedure.

Under this procedure, however, for each value of a_i and/or b_i, we have created another constraint. We call such constraints *alternative constraints*. All of the alternative constraints must intersect the basic constraint at the previously specified optimum point (i.e., the point initially determined through utility maximization). In this sense, we recognize that each point on the basic constraint represents an infinity of possible alternative constraints through that point. Correspondingly, on each alternative constraint there exists a point where $p_i = v_i$ in price space (i.e., the point of intersection of the alternative constraint with the basic constraint).

Under this procedure, utility maximization establishes $\hat{v}_i$ and $\hat{x}_i$; however, variation of a_i and/or b_i admits an infinite set of alternative constraints through the point $(\hat{v}_i, \hat{x}_i)$ on the basic constraint. Each alternative constraint represents a different pair $<a_i, b_i>$. In other words, even with v_i and x_i specified, the problem remains of how to determine a_i and b_i when they are freed from the basic price system. This "solution," then, is essentially not a solution to the problem of indeterminacy, although it is the starting point for

Houthakker's sensitivity analysis under indirect utility.

As stated earlier, our analysis is not concerned with application of indirect utility, but rather with the constraint and the characteristics of $v_i x_i$ and $v_i p_i$ spaces, and the relationship of these two spaces. As seen from Figure 4.4, under the basic price system the constraint exists in $v_i x_i$ space, and utility maximization is possible.

In what follows, we discuss the circumstances that arise when quantity and quality prices, a_i and b_i, are restricted to values other than those of the basic price system. Such combinations of prices, a_i and b_i, will create price systems different from the basic price system. As indicated earlier, we call such price systems *alternative price systems*.

Our procedure involves two steps. First, we consider the model where the price equilibrium condition, $p_i = v_i$, is retained. In the second step, we drop the price equilibrium requirement.

As illustrated in Figures 4.3 and 4.5, the price equilibrium condition requires the price line, $p_i = a_i + b_i v_i$, to intersect the basic price system (i.e., intersect the 45° line). Once we drop the assumption that $a_i = 0$ and $b_i = 1$, that is, once we allow the existence of alternative price systems (and alternative constraints), we are confronted with the question of how a_i and b_i are determined.

Assume that money income, M, is constant. Under the basic price system, once M is specified, a basic constraint, corresponding to basic prices and income, is specified in quality-quantity space. In our discussion of the basic constraint, we introduced the possibility of numerous alternative constraints, where for each combination of a_i and b_i (with M fixed), there existed a unique alternative constraint. Under the price equilibrium condition, alternative constraints intersect the basic constraint at a single point, the point where $\hat{v}_i$ in quality-quantity space equals the equilibrium value of v_i in price

space. In price space, v_i^*, the equilibrium value of v_i is determined by the condition $p_i^* = v_i^*$. On the basic constraint, $\hat{v}_i$ is determined through utility maximization.

In addition to questions surrounding determination of a_i and b_i, under the price equilibrium condition there is the question of how equality is established between v_i^* in price space and $\hat{v}_i$ in quality-quantity space. In a later section we address this matter. Here, we continue the discussion of a_i and b_i.

As mentioned earlier, any point on the basic constraint may have an infinity of combinations of a_i and b_i, or an infinity of alternative constraints, through that point. Consequently, utility maximization against the basic constraint does not specify the alternative values of a_i nor b_i. If utility maximization is to occur against an alternative constraint, the alternative values of a_i and b_i must be specified in advance (i.e., before the process of utility maximization occurs). Furthermore, it should be noted that it is possible to determine values for , $\hat{x}_i$, $\hat{v}_i$, v_i^*, and p_i^*, and still place no limitation on the alternative values of a_i and b_i, either for an alternative constraint in $v_i x_i$ space, or for the alternative price line, $p_i = a_i + b_i v_i$ in $v_i p_i$ space.

2. Preferences and the Constraint

One approach to this problem might be to assume configuration of the preference map in quality-quantity space, along with curvature of the basic constraint, could be used to place limits on the range of variation in a_i and b_i. This arrangement is analogous to Houthakker's use of indirect utility, where compensated variation in a_i, b_i, and M is allowed against a fixed indirect utility surface.[2]

Following this procedure, with direct utility fixed in $v_i x_i$ space, an internal solution on the basic constraint separates the infinite set of alternative constraints through that point into two subsets, each of which is also infinite: a set that is attainable at the optimal point and a complement set that is not. Note that for fixed M, the slope of each alternative constraint is influenced by the curvature of the indifference surface tangent at the optimal point.

The intersection of an infinite number of alternative constraints, corresponding to the infinite number of combinations of a_i and b_i, is illustrated in Figure 7.1. In this diagram the point m on the basic constraint indicates a solution to the utility maximization process. Through this point an infinite number of alternative constraints may pass (all with M equal to $\overline{M}$ of the basic constraint). However, the infinite set of alternative constraints through m are constrained to also pass through the shaded regions to the northwest and southeast of m. These are the attainable sets, given the usual assumptions regarding well-behaved preferences. As illustrated in Figure 7.1, each alternative constraint pivots through the point m and is constrained to the shaded areas.

Introduction of the utility surface, tangent to the basic constraint at the point m, reduces the size of the shaded areas. In other words, the width of the arc through m is reduced. To the extent that quantity, x_i, and quality, v_i, change from complements to substitutes in the direct utility function, the preference map will reduce the range of arc, or degree of pivot, of the alternative constraints through the point m. This is equivalent to reducing the range of variation of a_i and/or b_i. In other words, the range of variation in a_i and b_i is inversely related to the degree of substitutability of quantity, x_i, and quality, v_i, in the utility function. The higher the degree of substitutability, the smaller the range of variation in a_i and/or b_i. The higher the degree of complementarity in the preference map, the greater the range of variation in a_i and/or b_i.[3]

It is important to note that under this approach consumer preferences are influencing the range of price variation in a_i and/or

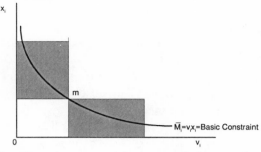

Figure 7.1 **Preferences and the Constraint**

b_i. The prices, a_i and b_i, in turn, influence the alternative constraint. In other words, consumer preferences influence the nature of alternative constraints in quality-quantity space.

How this process operates, unfortunately, is not very precise. The approach hypothesizes that there is a range of variation in a_i and/or b_i, and that configuration of the preference map can establish boundaries on the range. Under this approach, alternative constraints pivot through the point m, and, correspondingly, alternative price lines in price space pivot through the equilibrium point, p_i^* = v_i^*. The degree of variation is influenced by the nature of the preference map, but there is no global measure of the surface. (Sensitivity analysis might produce local measures about the point m.) Following the line of argument on the degree of substitution between quantity and quality, it appears that (for a given M) as a_i approaches the value zero and b_i approaches the value 1, the degree of pivot through m is reduced, and in the limit approaches zero. In other words, in the limit, the alternative constraint approaches the basic constraint. Correspondingly, in price space, in the limit the alternative price system becomes the basic price system. This solution is not very satisfying.

3. Repackaging and the Constraint

Another approach to determine a_i and b_i would be to adopt a repackaging approach. Given issues of separability, as well as efforts to link the Houthakker and hedonic models to the Lancaster model, repackaging has been argued to be the only acceptable method of handling variable quality. (See Fisher and Shell, and Muellbauer.) As we shall see, a repackaging model possesses some useful features for addressing some of the problems associated with variable quality. It does not, however, resolve the problem of indeterminacy of a_i and b_i away from the basic price system.

Under repackaging, if we assume the measure x_i is invariant to quality change (i.e., x_i is an isoquality measure of quantity), then we may assume x_i is the "basic package" or numeraire to which quality variation is applied.[4] With a repackaging model, where x_i is the basic package, a_i may be defined to be the price of the basic package, or Houthakker's price of "quantity." In a sense, this approach is analogous to the use of product lines in price theory. The product line may consist of three categories: good, better, and best. Under a repackaging approach, the "good" category may be defined as the basic package. Price differentials above the price of the "good" category indicate higher categories of quality—that is, the "better" over the "good," and the "best" over the "better." Houthakker's quality price, b_i, which reflects the price differential between Houthakker's "varieties," may be argued to measure such price adjustments above the basic package.

Under a repackaging approach it is common to assume that producers determine the price differentials on all grades or quality levels of the product line. Obviously, producer interaction with consumers in markets will bring about adjustments to prices initially established by producers. However, the prices that enter the market are p_i and/or v_i, not a_i and b_i. At this juncture, one option is to assume that producers determine a_i and b_i. This assumption is not the only option, however.

4. Producer Determination of a_i and b_i

In what follows, it is assumed that producers establish values for a_i and b_i. It is further as-

sumed that such values are different from the basic price system. It is also assumed that the values selected for a_i and b_i fall within, and are consistent with, all previously identified boundaries and other conditions for a_i and b_i.

Given that M is constant, once producers specify values for a_i and b_i, a specific alternative constraint is established in $v_i x_i$ space. But note, once the constraint is established, the model becomes overdetermined. Intersection of the alternative constraint (constructed with a_i and b_i values chosen by producers) with the basic constraint establishes, as one example, the point m. (See, e.g., Figure 7.1). Utility maximization is no longer required. In fact, utility must be maximized at the point m, unless we allow two solutions on the constraint. Further, note that the problem of overdetermination also exists if the consumer selects b_i in the repackaging model. (Assuming the basic package price, a_i, is already set, either by producers or by consumers, or via some other arrangement. We will have more to say on this topic later.)

For now, the problem of overdetermination of the solution in $v_i x_i$ space can be resolved if we are willing to drop the equilibrium condition in price space. So, for now, we make that change and no longer require $p_i = v_i$. As we shall see, however, this step eliminates some problems, but introduces others.

First of all, the problem of overdetermination at the point m is eliminated, since by deletion of the equilibrium requirement we also eliminate the basic constraint in $v_i x_i$ space. Our utility maximization process now proceeds against the single alternative constraint, which corresponds to the producer-selected values of a_i and b_i. This internal solution (we continue to assume the preference map and constraint are well-behaved and produce internal solutions) will identify $\hat{x}_i$ and $\hat{v}_i$. The determination of a_i and b_i will also create a price line in price space. We assume the line intersects the 45° line from above (as in Figure 4.3). Because we have dropped the equilibrium requirement, p_i^* is no longer established by the intersection of the price line

$(p_i = a_i + b_i v_i)$ with the 45° line. We need to know, however, how p_i^* is determined.

From $v_i x_i$ space, we assume utility maximization determines $\hat{v}_i$. One approach to determination of p_i^* would be to assume $p_i^* = a_i + b_i \hat{v}_i$ (for $a_i \neq 0$, $b_i \neq 1$); in other words, find the solution off the alternative price line, instead of from the 45° line. Under this approach, $p_i \neq v_i$ is possible. However, if $p_i \neq v_i$, which price does the consumer pay? (Remember we are examining Houthakker's single-variety case.)

There exists still another question. Because p_i is determined by the selection of $\hat{v}_i$, consumer preferences in $v_i x_i$ space establish the value of p_i, and the position of the constraint on the x_i axis in $x_i x_j$ space ($i \neq j$). We could eliminate this difficulty by introducing the assumptions of separability of x_i in the utility function and decentralization of the ith commodity in the consumer's budget. The assumptions of separability and decentralization would restrain the influence of consumer preferences (for quality and quantity of the ith commodity) to the ith commodity. We will discuss this option later. At this juncture, however, we turn to another approach.

We could assume p_i is not determined endogenously, but is given from $x_i x_j$ space and, consequently, is taken as fixed in $v_i p_i$ space. If p_i is fixed from $x_i x_j$ space (let $\bar{p}_i$ designate the fixed value of p_i), what is the relationship of $\hat{v}_i$ to $\bar{p}_i$? If we have $\bar{p}_i$ (from $x_i x_j$ space) and $\hat{v}_i$ (from $v_i x_i$ space), and we use the repackaging model where producers determine a_i and b_i, then again we have an overdetermined system. Remember that we must have a_i and b_i specified in order to generate the constraint in $v_i x_i$ space. Utility maximization in that space will give $\hat{v}_i$ and $\hat{x}_i$. However, with p_i specified in $x_i x_j$ space, does $\hat{x}_i$ in $v_i x_i$ space equal the $\bar{x}_i$ selected in $x_i x_j$ space? Assume for now that it is the same x_i for both spaces (i.e., $\hat{x}_i = \bar{x}_i$), then utility maximization in $v_i x_i$ space is not required, as a_i, b_i, and $\bar{x}_i$ (from $x_i x_j$ space) will

Figure 7.2 **Alternative Constraint and Price Space**

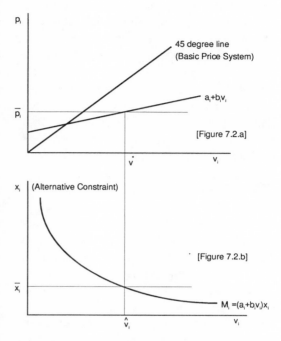

establish $\hat{v}_i$. The problem before us is how to use $\bar{p}_i$ and $\bar{x}_i$, from $x_i x_j$ space, and not have an indeterminate nor overdetermined system in $v_i x_i$ and/or $v_i p_i$ spaces.

Examination of Figure 7.2 will illustrate the problem. Here we have $\bar{p}_i$ and $\bar{x}_i$ given from $x_i x_j$ space. Note that the equilibrium condition in price space ($v_i = p_i$) has been dropped. Also, note the use of M_i. Here we are decentralizing M_i in $v_i x_i$ space from M in the remaining dimensions of consumption space, (i.e., $M_i = M - p_j x_j$) or the income not spent on the other commodity(s), x_j. In other words, we have introduced the assumption that the consumer can decentralize his or her budget for a specific commodity. (On the concepts of decentralization and separability, see Blackorby et al. 1978.) The existence of a utility-maximized optimal value in $x_i x_j$ space is assumed in the (solution) values for $\bar{x}_i$ and $\bar{x}_j$. We also assume the utility function is separable in x_i. The x_j may be viewed as a composite commodity (all other commodities), or the x_j axis may be spanned to n dimensions for the n other commodities.

M_i is income spent on commodity i, the quantity and quality aspects of which are measured by x_i and v_i, respectively. Note that from $M_i = M - p_j x_j$, the size of M_i is influenced by M, p_j, and consumer preferences for x_j (as reflected in the optimal value, $\bar{x}_j$).[5]

Given that $\bar{p}_i$ and $\bar{x}_i$ are established in $x_i x_j$ space, our problem becomes determination of a_i, b_i, and v_i in price and quality-quantity spaces for commodity i. If we assume a_i and b_i are set by producers, then from price space we have $\bar{p}_i = a_i + b_i v_i$, and from $v_i x_i$ space we have $M_i = (a_i + b_i v_i)\bar{x}_i$. From $x_i x_j$ space we have $M = p_i x_i + p_j x_j$ and $M_i = M - p_j x_j = p_i x_i$, therefore $(a_i + b_i v_i)\bar{x}_i = M_i = p_i \bar{x}_i$ or $(a_i + b_i v_i)\bar{x}_i = \bar{p}_i \bar{x}_i$ where $\bar{p}_i$ is given from $x_i x_j$ space. From before, this reduces to $\bar{p}_i = a_i + b_i v_i$, and the value of $\hat{v}_i$, determined once a_i and b_i are chosen, must be consistent for both price space and quality-quantity space. Note that this equality of $\hat{v}_i$ for both spaces must hold without the requirement $v_i = p_i$. Further note that in the process just explained, $\hat{v}_i$ was determined after $\bar{p}_i$ and $\bar{x}_i$ were determined. In other words, in this version of a two-stage decision-making process, quantity (x_i) is specified first, and then the level of quality (v_i).

This is unlike some other interpretations of a two-stage decision process in quality-quantity models. The usual approach to two-stage, or two-part tariff decision models, where the quality of the commodity is variable, is to assume the consumer first selects the level of quality of the commodity (i.e., selects v_i), and then selects the quantity of the commodity (x_i). (See, for example, Muellbauer 1974.) Further, note that under our two-step arrangement, utility maximization in $v_i x_i$ space is no longer required to obtain a solution.

Earlier we indicated that if p_i were determined endogenously through utility maximization in $v_i x_i$ space, combined with producer-determined prices (a_i and b_i) in price space, then the consumer influenced the constraint in $x_i x_j$ space. In the approach we have just discussed, the reverse is true, namely optimization in $x_i x_j$ space establishes price (p_i) and quantity (x_i) in $v_i p_i$ and $v_i x_i$ spaces. We may now elaborate further on this development.

We begin by expanding upon Figure 7.2. In Figure 7.3 we have reconstructed Figure 7.2, but with the addition of subdiagram 7.3c. The diagram illustrates an expanded version of $x_i x_j$ space; specifically, we now have $x_i x_j x_h$ space. In subdiagram 7.3.c we assume x_i is separable in the utility function from x_j and x_h. Whatever the level of consumption selected for x_i, it in no way influences preferences for x_j and x_h. Solutions for x_j and x_h are illustrated by $\hat{x}_j$ and $\hat{x}_h$, respectively.

As described previously, utility maximization in 7.3.b, given producer-selected values of a_i and b_i, can produce a solution for quantity ($\hat{x}_i$) and quality ($\hat{v}_i$). The x_i so chosen must correspond to the x_i solution in subdiagram 7.3.c. (Note that $\hat{x}_i$ in 7.3.c is orthogonal to the solution value for x_j and x_h in 7.3.c.) The solution $\hat{v}_i$ provides the value for v_i in $p_i = a_i + b_i v_i$, the price line in 7.3.a. Recall that the equilibrium condition, $p_i = v_i$, is no longer required. The solution for price space is p_i^*, as illustrated.

Under "normal" circumstances (i.e., without decentralization), the value of p_i^* from price space would influence the slope of the constraint in $x_i x_j$ space and the slope of the constraint plane in $x_i x_j x_h$ space. The solution in $x_i x_j x_h$ space is the point of tangency between preference map and constraint, where $x_i = \hat{x}_i, x_j = \hat{x}_j$, and $x_h = \hat{x}_h$. Note that without decentralization, a change in p_i will affect the solutions for x_j, x_h, and x_i. (A change in p_i brought about by a new solution value in $v_i x_i$ space will change $\hat{x}_i, \hat{x}_j, \hat{x}_h$ in $x_i x_j x_h$ space.) In other words, the price solution in $v_i p_i$ space must conform to the $\hat{x}_i$ solution in $v_i x_i$ space; but without decentralization, p_i will influence the corresponding x_i solution in $x_i x_j x_h$ space.

Figure 7.3 **The Introduction of $x_i x_j x_h$ Consumption Space**

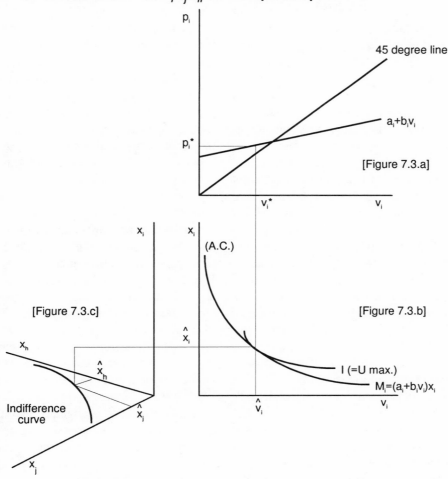

This will be the case, as $M = p_i x_i + p_j x_j + p_h x_h$, where $p_i = a_i + b_i v_i$, or $p_i x_i = (a_i + b_i v_i) x_i$. Note, however, that v_i is selected by the consumer to get $\hat{v}_i$; therefore, the consumer's preferences are in $\hat{v}_i$, which in turn influences p_i^*, and hence the constraint in $x_i x_j x_h$ space. This can be further illustrated as follows:

$$M = p_i x_i + p_j x_j + p_h x_h$$

$$x_i = (M/p_i) - (p_j/p_i) x_j - (p_h/p_i) x_h.$$

Substitution of $(a_i + b_i v_i) = p_i$ gives

$$x_i = [M/(a_i + b_i v_i)] - [p_j/(a_i + b_i v_i)] x_j - [(p_h/(a_i + b_i v_i)] x_h.$$

The slope of the constraint in $x_i x_j$ space is

$$(\partial x_i / \partial x_j) = -[p_j/(a_i + b_i v_i)].$$

Similar results follow for $x_i x_h$ space. Again, v_i, which would become $\hat{v}_i$ through optimization, is a variable influenced by the consumer, and it is in the constraint.

As suggested earlier, one approach to restrict consumer influence on the constraint in $x_i x_j x_h$ space is to assume separability of the ith commodity in the utility function and decentralization of the ith commodity in the consumer's budget. Separability can produce a preference map similar to the one illustrated in Figure 7.3.c. Separability of the objective function is not sufficient, however; budget decentralization of the ith commodity in the constraint, in $x_i x_j x_h$ space, is also required. For our model, decentralization of the ith commodity requires an accurate projection of expenditures on i, a projection further compounded by the need to simultaneously know the solution values of x_i, p_i, and v_i. To be able to acquire the information necessary to make such decisions requires strong assumptions regarding consumer knowledge and information-processing capabilities.

Another approach—to avoid the prospect of the consumer influencing the constraint (either in $v_i x_i$ or higher spaces)—would be to assume that the consumer selects the variety $\hat{v}_i$. Once the variety is selected, the producer's pricing algorithm, $p_i = a_i + b_i \hat{v}_i$, then identifies the price that corresponds to the selected variety. In this sense, the consumer is not influencing the constraint, rather only choosing from a set of prices (predetermined by the producer) the price that corresponds to the selected variety. No consumer-induced shifting of a constraint occurs under this interpretation.

Several difficulties, however, exist with this interpretation. First, to eliminate the possibility that the consumer influences the constraint in, for example, $x_i x_j x_h$ space, this interpretation allows the consumer to open and/or close variety spaces from v_i^- to v_i^+, across all varieties of the ith commodity. For the consumer, only that variety space is spanned, in $x_i x_j x_h$ space, which corresponds to his or her selection of $\hat{v}_i$.

A second difficulty relates to the nature of consumer behavior required under this interpretation. Traditional consumer behavior assumes the consumer knows his or her income and the prices of products to be purchased. The consumer then maximizes utility against a budget constraint, which is specified by income and prices. The utility-maximizing process determines the optimal quantity of products to be purchased. Under the present alternative interpretation, the consumer first selects the quality (variety) of a commodity. Subsequently, through the price algorithm, $p_i = a_i + b_i v_i$, the solution of $\hat{v}_i$ in quality-quantity space identifies the price, p_i, the consumer will pay. The choice of x_i is not influenced by the price p_i, but rather by a_i and b_i (which we have assumed are set by producers), as well as by M_i and consumer preferences for v_i and x_i in $v_i x_i$ space. Note that the solution for x_i in $v_i x_i$ space must be the same solution for x_i in $x_i x_j x_h$ space. In other words, p_i is unnecessary information for consumer decision making. This result is highly unusual.

Finally, in this model (without decentralization) where producers determine a_i and b_i, note that consumer preferences for quality (i.e., choice of v_i) influence p_i in an unusual way. Specifically, if the consumer preference map in $v_i x_i$ space establishes a tangency at a "low" level of v_i, a correspondingly "low" price p_i is determined in $v_i p_i$ space, and (if we dropped decentralization) the constraint in $x_i x_j x_h$ space moves out the x_i axis. The "low" v_i in $v_i x_i$ space occurs at a "high" x_i or quantity of the commodity. The opposite result would follow if the tangency in $v_i x_i$ space occurs at a "high" v_i. Note that the constraint in $x_i x_j x_h$ space moves out the x_i axis for a reduction in p_i, and given the indifference curves required under our separability condition, this may result in a higher level of utility. In opposite fashion, as the v_i selected in $v_i x_i$ space tends toward higher v_i, price (p_i) rises and the constraint in $x_i x_j x_h$ space moves down the x_i axis, resulting in lower levels of utility. In other words, "high" quality in $v_i x_i$ space results in "low" utility in $x_i x_j x_h$ space, and "low" v_i in $v_i x_i$ space results in "high" utility in $x_i x_j x_h$ space.

To this point, we have discussed a number of approaches to resolve the problems of indeterminacy or overdetermination of the model. In the process, we have introduced a number of questions regarding the relationships of $\hat{p}_i$, $\hat{x}_i$, $\hat{v}_i$, a_i, and b_i. As yet, we have not resolved these matters. Regarding the "prices" a_i and b_i, we have assumed, to this point, that they were determined by the producer. We consider next the alternative where the consumer determines a_i and b_i.

5. Consumer Determination of a_i and b_i

Instead of assuming a_i and b_i are set by the producer, we now assume these values are determined by the consumer. In the process, we encounter another set of interesting yet difficult questions.

Recall that in price space, $b_i = (dp_i/dv_i)$. As discussed earlier, under certain conditions the e_{ih} from Henri Theil may be linked to the v_i of Houthakker, that is, the conditions require that the e_{ih} cluster as bundles, in some fashion, to each variety v_i, and that they meet certain invariance conditions regarding an iso-quality aggregator. The use of e_{ih} as characteristics of the ith commodity introduces a possible linkage to the hedonic technique. In the hedonic case, however, b_i becomes $b_i = (\partial p_i/\partial e_{ih})$ and is typically interpreted as a coefficient that measures the impact on commodity price (p_i) of change in the quality characteristics, e_{ih}.

Previously, to avoid an indeterminacy in the Houthakker model—which can arise whenever the model operates outside the basic price system—we encountered the need to specify alternative (non-basic price) values for a_i and b_i. Further, recall that unless the Houthakker model can expand beyond the basic price system, it is essentially the same model as that developed by Henri Theil.

As we shall discover throughout the remainder of this and subsequent chapters, several unusual problems arise under the assumption that the consumer determines a_i and/or b_i. For example, under consumer determination of b_i we will discover there may arise circumstances wherein there is no way for the consumer to know, a priori, his or her constrained optimum in quality-quantity consumption space. As one example of how this problem might arise, the consumer may not have preferences established for all levels of quality, that is, for all levels of v_i from v_i^- to v_i^+.

In some respects these difficulties are comparable to those encountered in earlier debates regarding "revealed preference," but they are also related to issues of consumer decision making in the world of risk and uncertainty, decision making involving expected utility, as well as issues of search costs, signaling, and so forth. In addition, contributions from cognitive psychology, the notion of perception frames and context effects, the Competence-Difficulty or C-D gap and reliability condition may come into play regarding consumer decision making in quality-quantity space, and particularly, in our case, in the consumer's determination of a_i and b_i.

6. Quality and Consumption Experience

One of the principal difficulties alluded to above can be stated as follows: Even though the consumer may have information regarding the quality of a product or service, "information" may not be sufficient for accurate decision making regarding the value of, for example, b_i. The consumer may also need his or her own personal assessment of the product or service, and that personal assessment or evaluation is obtained only through the act of firsthand consumption of the product or service. In other words, information may not be equivalent to firsthand "experience," a special form of information. More specifically, the act of consumption may be required to acquire the "experience" necessary to determine a_i and/or b_i. The state of having information may not be equivalent to the state of having personal experience, and it could be argued that "experience" is necessary to determine a_i and b_i. If this is the case, then the consumer cannot know, ex ante, the value of a_i and/or b_i. The best the consumer can do is guess.

If we assume the consumer determines a_i

and/or b_i, then, as stated earlier, the consumer determines both the constraint and the preference map in $v_i x_i$ space. This is an entirely new process for consumer decision making and it could lead to indeterminacy. In other words, the problem initially encountered in chapter 4 persists. As we hope to show in part 2, however, there may be a way out of this problem. We devote the remaining chapters of part 2 to this new decision-making process.

Returning to our earlier discussion of limitations on consumer decision making, if the consumer determines (e.g., b_i) for a product or service for which he or she has no previous consumption experience, then, in the initial period of consumption, an "accurate" constraint in $v_i x_i$ space does not exist. The consumer, nevertheless, may find a "solution." As we shall see shortly, the method for reaching such solutions may be quite unlike anything previously considered in consumer theory.

In one sense, what we may have encountered in quality-quantity consumption space is a situation where the consumer (the "observer" and perceiver of quality) is no longer independent of the "observed" (the constraint), which is the boundary of feasible options within that space. Note that this inseparability of consumer from constraint, observer from observed, is not the Hawthorne effect or testing effect associated with experimental and quasi-experimental designs.

In other words, the phenomenon we describe here is not the same as that of an economist (an outside observer) disturbing consumer decision making in quality-quantity consumption space, simply through the act of observing that decision making. This latter case presumes a situation where the economist-observer distorts the "true" solution by the act of observation or testing. Our problem arises from the inseparability of consumer (the observer) from the observed (the constraint), that is, the inseparability of consumer in the preference map from consumer in the constraint. Outside observation and/or

testing by the economist, therefore, does not create this problem, although it may introduce other problems. We will argue (later) that inseparability of consumer preferences in the objective function from consumer perceptions of the constraint characterizes consumer decision making in $v_i x_i$ space, if the consumer determines a_i and/or b_i.

Note that all of the previous economic works cited on variable quality hold to the assumption that the consumer is apart from, and unable to influence, the constraint.[6] According to these other models, the consumer may be ignorant of the constraint (e.g., lack information regarding prices), or the consumer may be less than perfectly informed about the product, and so forth. Probabilistic methods, inclusive of Bayesian heuristics regarding search costs and price signals, are sometimes recommended as methods to assist consumers in reaching decisions under these conditions—in other words, to help the consumer estimate, or locate, the "true" constraint. The prospect, however, that the consumer influences the constraint, the inseparability issue, has not arisen in these models.[7] We believe that the consumer decision-making problem we have encountered in quality-quantity space is different from the problems addressed by these other models. We further believe that the problem we have stumbled upon is serious and holds extensive implications for microeconomics.

At this juncture, a few comments are in order regarding determinism and stochasticism in our model. What we believe occurs in $v_i x_i$ consumption space is stochastic decision making. In other words, the model is stochastic, but not simply in the sense of empirical estimation of deterministic parameters. Our model is stochastic in its very essence; that is, it is not a deterministically constrained optimization model of consumer theory. As in mixed-strategy game theory, we believe consumer decision making in quality-quantity consumption space is stochastic in nature—in other words, that deterministic consumer models are inadequate to the task.

7. First-Time Assessment of Quality: The Case of No Previous Consumption Experience

In what follows, we focus first on consumer determination of b_i. Subsequently, we will discuss in separate fashion, consumer determination of a_i. As previously discussed, in the case of a variety for which the consumer has no consumption experience, if the consumer determines b_i, then he or she has no basis upon which to judge the quality of that variety, and, therefore, no basis to determine b_i. The consumer may guess at the value of b_i, but has no assurance, a priori, of the accuracy of the guess. This situation is analogous to determining one's demand reservation price for an item offered in a Dutch auction, where the item is totally new to the consumer—that is, it is something with which the consumer has no previous firsthand consumption experience. The more complicated the product or service, and the less informed and/or educated the consumer, the greater will be the difficulty in assessing quality. Within the context of Ronald Heiner's model, the greater the C-D gap, the greater the likelihood of "inaccurate" quality valuation (see Heiner 1983, 1985a, 1985b, 1985c, 1986). Such "inaccuracy" could also be reflected in the magnitude of a distance function indicating the difference between the consumer's initial value for b_i and its "final" value.

The word "final" is placed in quotation marks because consumer decision making in the world of variable quality may be in a constant state of flux, reflecting changes in the consumer's consumption technology, among other things. Change in consumption technology could arise, for example, as a result of changes in age, education, related consumption experiences, changes in tastes (which could include *acquired tastes*), and so forth. To the extent habit is important to a consumer—that is, a repetitious consumption pattern for v_i fixed at some constant level—the more likely b_i will become accurate and final for that consumer. The greater the extent to which a consumer is willing to risk having new consumption experiences, at previously unknown levels of quality, the less likely b_i will stabilize. All of these factors contribute to a variable consumption technology.

To continue the topic of consumer determination of b_i, note that the "reality" of a given (constant) level of quality is influenced by the consumer's perception of that "reality," that is, by consumer perception of some specified level of quality.[8] Quality, like beauty, is in the eye of the beholder. This, in turn, must lead economists to consider issues such as perception and cognition, and it introduces into microeconomics the prospect of subjective "reality," and individual "realities." More succinctly, it opens the possibility that the reality (or nature) of the constraint in $v_i x_i$ consumption space is not established for the consumer until the consumer perceives and creates it, and the consumer creates the constraint through the act of consumption, and the subsequent learning that arises from that consumption. This is a loopy process. For first-time consumption, the consumer has to guess at some value of b_i so as to initiate the process, similar to a Bayesian heuristic process. For a variety never previously consumed, the initial value chosen for b_i may be based on intuition, other consumers' experience, knowledge passed on by parents and culture, advertising, other sources of information, and so forth. If, however, the variety has never been previously consumed by the consumer,[9] the value of b_i is not based on consumption experience. The value of b_i must be a guess.

8. The Value of a_i and a Basic Package

At this juncture it is useful to recall our discussion of repackaging. Earlier, we assumed a_i was the price per unit (where x_i was the quantity unit-of-measure) of the basic variety, or the variety at $v_i = 0$, and we assumed that a_i was fixed (see chapter 4). Recall that the basic variety was the standardized variety, or basic package, to which quality characteristics were then added (i.e., quality augmentation or variation could be viewed as a process of repackaging the basic package). Here, we assume that the consumer selects a value for a_i only once, possibly based on previous consumption at $v_i = 0$ (the basic package), and that afterwards a_i remains fixed. All subsequent change of price is accomplished through change in b_i, which accompanies change in quality characteristics beyond the basic package.

After the consumer selects (guesses) an initial value for b_i, the constraint in $v_i x_i$ space appears (assuming a_i already exists) and the utility maximization process previously described, with separability and decentralization, may occur. After the experience of consuming $\hat{v}_i$ (the new variety not previously consumed), the consumer may come to realize that he or she needs to reevaluate the initial b_i. That is, the initial b_i may not be accurate (i.e., the b_i that the consumer assigns after the initial consumption experience may differ from the initial b_i). In other words, if the consumer continues to consume variety $\hat{v}_i$, there may be a learning process that, in iterative fashion, adjusts b_i to better approximate the consumer's perception of $\hat{v}_i$, where this perception is now based on firsthand consumption experience. The iterative learning process may approach some final value of b_i, call it $\lim b_{it} = b_i^*$, where t stands for time and b_i^* is the "final" (accurate) value. It is assumed that b_{it} will follow the pattern of a learning curve. Note, however, that this explanation is based on the assumption that the consumer continues to consume $\hat{v}_i$. This is what we will call the *special case*.[10]

9. When the Consumer Holds Quality Constant

Under the *special case*, where $\hat{v}_i$ is fixed in $v_i x_i$ space, any subsequent change in b_i (by

the consumer) must also change x_i, the quantity purchased. If we assume the consumer thinks (first) in terms of purchasing a specific variety, $\hat{v}_i$, and then (second) selects a value for b_i, then the consumer is assessing quality at the level of an individual variety. Note that once b_i is selected, not only does the constraint emerge in $v_i x_i$ space, but the price line, $p_i = a_i + b_i v_i$, is positioned in price space. (We assume a_i is set initially by the consumer and thereafter remains constant.) With subsequent changes in b_i, both the constraint and price line change. Since in the special case $\hat{v}_i$ is assumed fixed, a change in b_i produces change in p_i and x_i. (For now we ignore the separability and decentralization conditions in $x_i x_j x_h$ space discussed earlier.) For a new b_i, a new x_i is specified.

Note that if, after consumption of $\hat{v}_i$, the consumer decides to lower b_i, this means that (from the consumer's perspective) the price, p_i, is too high and should be reduced for that variety. In this sense, it is as though the consumer's willingness-to-pay has declined, and the variety $\hat{v}_i$ is priced too high. (We will have more to say on willingness-to-pay in section 12 and in subsequent chapters.) A reduction in b_i will also mean (ironically) a higher quantity x_i in $v_i x_i$ space. Further, note that in the special case the learning process applies only to a specific level of quality, or $\hat{v}_i$. Subsequent different levels of quality would similarly have to be learned.

10. When the Consumer Changes the Level of Quality

In the more *general case*, we assume the consumer is allowed to change the level of quality, $\hat{v}_i$.[11] If the level of quality should change, the learning process—previously described for a single level of quality (variety $\hat{v}_i$)—may not occur. By this we mean that if the level of quality were to change frequently, the quality learning process could be disturbed. When learning curves exist, they may be truncated before reaching b_i^*.[12]

In the general case, after establishing an initial value for b_i and then consuming $\hat{v}_i$ for the first time, the consumer may change (raise or lower) the value of b_i. Once such a change in b_i occurs, the constraint in $v_i x_i$ space will change slope and convexity. Now, unlike the special case, we do not assume the consumer makes an effort to continue to consume the initial variety $\hat{v}_i$. Instead, in the general case, we allow the consumer to change varieties. New values for $\hat{v}_i$ and $\hat{x}_i$ may have little relationship to previous values. Obviously, frequent change in v_i may interfere with the learning process previously described.

Once the consumer selects a value for b_i, the initial constraint in $v_i x_i$ space is created. Given existence of the constraint, constrained utility maximization may proceed to find solution values $\hat{v}_i$ and $\hat{x}_i$. Consumption at the solution point permits the consumer to gain experience regarding the new $\hat{v}_i$ and to subsequently evaluate b_i in light of that experience.

11. The Value of b_i and Configuration of the Constraint

We examine now what happens to the constraint as the consumer reevaluates b_i. We begin by first examining the effects of b_i on the constraint.

For the constraint $M_i = (a_i + b_i v_i)x_i$ in $v_i x_i$ space, a change in b_i (or a_i) will shift the constraint and change its convexity. The slope of the constraint is given by

$$(dx_i/dv_i) = -[(b_i M_i)/(a_i + b_i v_i)^2] < 0; \quad (1)$$

convexity is given by

$$(d^2 x_i/dv_i^2) = [(2M_i b_i^2)/(a_i + b_i v_i)^3] > 0. \quad (2)$$

Review of either derivative indicates that b_i will influence the slope and convexity of the constraint. The effect of db_i on x_i and v_i is unclear from equation (1). If, however, we differentiate the constraint for dx_i/db_i and dv_i/db_i we obtain the following:[13]

$$(dx_i/db_i) = -[(v_i M_i)/(a_i + b_i v_i)^2] < 0 \quad (3)$$

$$(dv_i/db_i) = [(a_i x_i^2 - M_i x_i)/(b_i x_i)^2]. \quad (4)$$

The value of equation (4) will be negative if $M_i > a_i x_i$, which will occur if $M_i = a_i x_i + b_i v_i x_i$, for $b_i v_i x_i > 0$. Note that equation (4) has a value of zero if $M_i = a_i x_i$ or $(M_i/a_i) = x_i$, the intercept value where $v_i = 0$ (i.e., a corner solution). Consequently, for most circumstances we can assume $(dv_i/db_i) < 0$.

From the above, we assume that in most cases an increase (decrease) in b_i will decrease (increase) x_i, given v_i constant; and an increase (decrease) in b_i will decrease (increase) v_i, given x_i constant.

At this juncture, we point out some additional characteristics of the Houthakker constraint. The product $b_i v_i$ in the constraint converts the traditional linear constraint of microeconomic consumer theory into an hyperbola. In Houthakker's constraint, it is the ratio of the "prices" a_i to b_i that determines curvature of the constraint. Note that for "high" (a_i/b_i) values the constraint approaches the usual linear form. Further note that if $b_i = 0$, the constraint becomes $M_i = a_i x_i$, or a_i becomes equivalent to p_i, and we have the traditional constraint in consumer theory. For the basic price system, $a_i = 0$ and $b_i = 1$, the constraint becomes as illustrated in Figure 4.4. We should further add that the magnitude of consumer income does not influence the curvature of the constraint. See Appendix A for additional information on the constraint.

12. The Meaning of Change in b_i: Introductory Remarks

In a model where consumers determine b_i, there is a need to examine the meaning of change in b_i. It should be noted at the outset that previous remarks regarding change in b_i were not addressing the issue of consumer demand. Our topic was, and to this point still is, more limited. We are only discussing the effects of change in b_i on the boundary of the feasible consumption set in $v_i x_i$ space.

Earlier we presented a situation where the consumer initiated consumption in $v_i x_i$ space by selecting, or guessing, some initial value of b_i, or $b_{it=0}$, where $t = 0$ represents the initial time period. Once a decision had been reached regarding the value of $b_{it=0}$, the constraint appeared in $v_i x_i$ space (a_i having been previously selected). After consumption of the initial variety, $\hat{v}_i$, the consumer may subsequently reevaluate the magnitude of $b_{it=0}$.

Assume that after initial consumption, the consumer learns that the initial value he or she selected for $b_{it=0}$ was "inaccurate." As one possibility, assume that the consumer now perceives the quality of $\hat{v}_i$ to be higher than originally estimated. In our model this would mean that the initial value given $b_{it=0}$ was too low. Because b_i measures the change in p_i with respect to a change in v_i (where the change in v_i may include a change in the perception of v_i),[14] a higher value for $b_{it>0}$ would mean a higher p_i for the same v_i, or a steeper slope of the price line in $v_i p_i$ space. (Recall that we assume a_i is fixed, so the price line pivots at a_i.) This result can be interpreted as a higher willingness to pay for $\hat{v}_i$, once the perception of the quality of $\hat{v}_i$ is adjusted upward. It is assumed that the evaluation of $\hat{v}_i$ is a personal and subjective exercise.

If the consumer adjusts b_i upward, after initial consumption of $\hat{v}_i$, it means the variety $\hat{v}_i$ is perceived (by the consumer) to be of higher value than initially reflected in $b_{it=0}$. For now we assume that this action on the part of the consumer does not change the ordering of v_i within the range v_i^- to v_i^+. The upward adjustment of b_i means that the consumer's satisfaction derived from consumption of $\hat{v}_i$ has changed (upward in this case), which means that all other b_i for v_i above $\hat{v}_i$ are also raised (at least) by the same proportion. Lower v_i (i.e., lower than $\hat{v}_i$) may be unaffected. How these adjustments are accomplished can alter the nature of the quality-augmenting function (heretofore linear) and the role played by b_i in that function. We will discuss this matter shortly. To continue discussion of b_i and v_i, it will be useful to assume v_i is continuous for all varieties in the range v_i^- to v_i^+ inclusive (Houthakker's assumption).

Finally, as mentioned previously, by adjusting b_i upward we assume the consumer is revealing a greater willingness-to-pay for $\hat{v}_i$. This result introduces an interesting question: If, after initial consumption of $\hat{v}_i$, the consumer's willingness-to-pay is higher than what he or she had to pay at the initial price p_i, does this mean that in quality-quantity consumption space there exists a phenomenon analogous to consumer surplus? If so, how do we interpret consumer surplus in the context of variable quality?

Chapter 8
Consumer Surplus, Willingness-to-Pay, Perception, and b_i

1. Consumer Surplus and Variable Quality

As in traditional microeconomics, our model assumes there are psychological aspects to the concept of consumer surplus. Given the introduction of consumer perception of quality, we assume the only person qualified to determine what he or she would be willing to pay for a given level of quality is the particular individual consumer involved. There are other factors that might also influence the magnitude of consumer surplus—for example, "consumption experience."

Our model raises several questions regarding the role of "quality" in the process of consumption. A sample of such questions is given below. In what follows, the term "variety" is used according to Houthakker's definition.

Is "experience" in the consumption of a specific variety necessary in order to determine the size of consumer surplus for that variety?

Is consumer surplus variety-specific?

Is consumer surplus "learned" as a result of previous consumption experience?

Are there "expectational" aspects to consumer surplus?

Are expectations adjusted through learning and experience? In other words, could we have an analog to the expression: "Don't knock it till you've tried it," i.e., "You don't know how much you'd be willing to pay for something until you've tried it."

If producers charge according to what they perceive "the market will bear," does a private market, with variable quality of the product or service, possess phenomenon comparable to a free rider problem?

In our model, might it be rational for consumers to hide their "true" preferences, i.e., to hide their "true" willingness-to-pay for quality?

In the original Houthakker model, where the consumer may select v_i from the range v_i^- to v_i^+ of the commodity set, and in our model where the consumer may determine a_i and b_i (recall that a_i is currently assumed to be fixed), consumer surplus becomes three-dimensional. After selection of v_i, the surplus reduces dimension to the more common two-dimensional case.

To discuss the properties of a three-dimensional consumer surplus, we draw upon the work of Robert Willig (Willig 1976). We also employ a modified version of Willig's work utilizing an approach by Maurice, Phillips, and Ferguson (Maurice et al. 1982). We begin discussion with the traditional case of a two-dimensional surplus. Later we expand to three dimensions with variable quality, quantity, and price (p_i).

Figure 8.1 **Maurice et al. on Willig's Consumer Surplus**

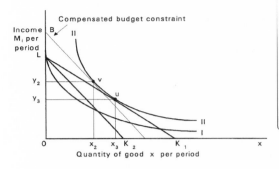

2. Variable Quality Under a Willig Assessment of Consumer Surplus

The statement "What a consumer would be willing to pay" was analyzed by Willig within the context of Hicksian compensated demand—specifically, where a price change is compensated by a change in income.[1] Recall that in Houthakker's use of indirect utility, in addition to income compensation, one price change (e.g., da_i) could be employed to compensate another price change (e.g., db_i). In Willig's analysis the good may be either income-normal or income-inferior. As presented in his paper, the good is generally assumed to be normal (i.e., an increase in price is compensated by an offsetting increase in income). For Willig the income compensation function (Willig 1976, p. 591) is structured in terms of dx (quantity) under an indirect utility function. In our model, over the range of quality variation v_i^- to v_i^+ (i.e., before the consumer selects $\hat{v}_i$), the income-compensation function will likewise be defined in terms of quantity (dx_i). It is interesting to note, however, that instead of dx_i over fixed quality $\hat{v}_i$, we could also investigate consumer surplus over variable quality, dv_i, for a fixed quantity, $\hat{x}_i$.

Concepts of income-normal and income-inferior, however, do not seem readily transferable from the quantity measure (e.g., $(\partial x_i/\partial M) > 0$) to the quality measure (e.g., $(\partial v_i/\partial M) > 0$). For example, if $\hat{x}_i$ is fixed, does $(\partial v_i/\partial M) > 0$ mean quality variation is normal with respect to income, or does it mean that preceding levels of "lower" quality, bypassed as income grew, are inferior? What precisely does $(\partial v_i/\partial M) > 0$ mean? Furthermore, how do we interpret $(\partial v_i/\partial M) < 0$? Are these v_i inferior varieties?

In our model these questions are addressed, in part, by studying the optimization process (path) between the preference map and our unusual constraint, as we allow change in consumer income (dM_i). Much, of course, depends on the nature of the preference map (e.g., is it homothetic?) and the "prices" a_i and b_i. Given change in convexity of the Houthakker constraint, interior solutions are by no means assured.

For now, we continue the discussion of consumer surplus according to Willig's income-compensation function defined over dx_i. Our review of Willig will utilize an interpretation provided by Maurice, Phillips, and Ferguson. For Maurice et al. (1982) the linkage between consumption space and Hicksian compensated demand is accomplished by redefining the vertical axis in a two-space consumption diagram. Instead of comparing two goods, the vertical axis is defined as income, say M_i, and the remaining good is assumed income-normal. An example is provided in Figures 8.1 and 8.2 (Maurice, Phillips, and Ferguson 1982, pp. 151–152). For Willig's analog in demand space, see his Figure 1 (Willig 1976, p. 592).

As shown in Figure 8.1, if the consumer is at point L on the vertical axis, no quantity of x is purchased—that is, the consumer does not spend (saves all) income. At the original point of tangency between the constraint LK_1 and the indifference curve II (i.e., the point U), the consumer purchases x_3 and has OY_3 income left (in

Figure 8.2 **Maurice-Willig: Compensated and Ordinary Demand**

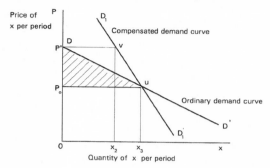

other words, LY_3 of income is spent on x). Assume a price increase that pivots the constraint at L such that the new constraint is LK_2. Here, Maurice et al. create a corner solution at L through use of an indifference curve with intercept at L. (We will ignore the theoretical difficulties associated with indifference curves that possess intercepts.) The Marshallian (ordinary) demand curve derived from these solutions in consumption space is the curve DD' in Figure 8.2. The compensated demand curve, which reflects only the substitution effect, is derived by an income-compensated shift of the constraint, the dashed line in Figure 8.1. The new compensated solution is at the point V. The movement from U to V, associated with the income-compensated price change, is the demand curve D_1D_1' in Figure 8.2. (The move from U to V in Figure 8.1 illustrates the Compensating Variation form of income-compensated price change.)

As illustrated in Figure 8.2, the customary notion of consumer surplus is the area under the ordinary demand curve DD' (the area $P_0P'u$). However, as demonstrated by Willig, the use of ordinary demand curves underestimates consumer surplus (or as in Willig's analysis, underestimates the amount of income the consumer would be willing to exchange in return for the right

to purchase x at the original price, P_o). Thus, the "true" measure of the loss associated with the price increase, or the "true" measure of consumer surplus, is the area under the compensated demand curve D_1D_1' (or $P_0P'vu$).

For our model, with both variation in quality as well as quantity, the constraint in Figure 8.1 must be modified and becomes Figure 8.3. The equation for this diagram begins with $M = p_ix_i + p_jx_j$, which rearranges to $x_j = (M/p_j) - (p_i/p_j)x_i$, as in the standard case. This will create the constraint in x_ix_j space, and, consistent with Maurice et al., we define the x_j axis as income, either spent or not spent on x_i. Note that in x_ix_j space both axes are closed boundaries. Now, to span v_ix_i space, we introduce Houthakker's $p_i = a_i + b_iv_i$ in the above equation, or $x_j = (M/p_j) - [(a_i + b_iv_i)/p_j]x_i$, which multiplied through becomes $x_j = (M/p_j) - (a_i/p_j)x_i - [(b_iv_i)/p_j]x_i.^2$ The constraint in x_ix_j space is now with intercept (M/p_j) on the x_j axis and has slope $-(a_i/p_j)$. In v_ix_i space the x_j intercept is likewise (M/p_j) and the slope, after rearranging, is $-[(b_ix_i)/p_j]$. Here, however, the v_i axis is open, since quality cannot exist without quantity. Quantity, it is recalled, also does not exist without quality, except possibly as the basic package. There are quality dimensions, however, even to the basic package. We clarified this issue in our discussion of the numeraire value of quality at $v_i = 0$, which lies between v_i^- and v_i^+. This explanation is also consistent with the repackaging model, where $v_i = 0$ is the basic package. (See chapter 4 and the discussion of Muellbauer in chapter 6.)

The constraint in v_ix_i space is, as before, $M = (a_i + b_iv_i)x_i$, with no intercept on the v_i axis, and only under special conditions is there an intercept on the x_i axis. These conditions are as follows: Houthakker's equilibrium condition, $p_i = v_i$, must be dropped, that is, no use of the basic price

Figure 8.3 **Relationship of Variable Quality to $x_i x_j$ Space**

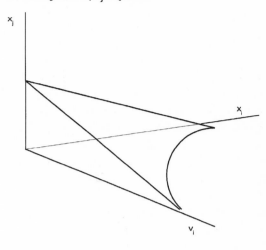

system as it does not allow $v_i = 0$ (because $p_i \neq 0$ by Houthakker's condition $(a_i + b_i v_i) > 0$); and, the equilibrium ranges imposed on a_i and b_i must be exceeded; see chapter 4.[3] As regards the constraint in $v_i x_i$ space, it is, as before, convex to the origin, and, as here presented, is also dependent on the level of x_j (i.e., we are not, at this juncture, assuming separability or decentralizability). Finally, as stated earlier, in conformity with Maurice et al. (1982) we assume the x_j axis represents income, or income spent (expenditure) on all other goods. With this background, we may proceed to analyze our constraint in the context of consumer surplus.

As indicated previously, we begin by focusing on consumer surplus in the context of variable quantity over a fixed quality, or dx_i given v_i constant. Insofar as Figure 8.3 is concerned, we commence from the perspective of a side view through the $x_i x_j$ plane onto the constraint in three-dimensional space. Here, once v_i is fixed (e.g., $\hat{v}_i$), the analysis of consumer surplus in $x_i x_j$ space proceeds as previously discussed.

If we assume an increase in the price of x_i (i.e., an increase in a_i), which is compensated by an offsetting increase in income, and if we assume utility maximization that always attains an internal solution,[4] then the income-compensated price change will give results similar to those previously described. Note, however, that the initial position of the constraint in $x_i x_j$ space is influenced by the selection of $\hat{v}_i$, and by the assumption that, notwithstanding price change in a_i, the consumer continues to consume $\hat{v}_i$ (our special case). Note further that as far as the constraint is concerned, the lower the value of $\hat{v}_i$, the higher the initial constraint in $x_i x_j$ space— which suggests that a change in quality also could be used to compensate for the change in a_i. Houthakker identified this trade-off through use of db_i to offset da_i.

The linkage to demand curves from consumption space, identified by Willig, also follows in our model, except that we assume the curves are isoquality demand (both the ordinary and compensated curves). The connection to Willig will be loosened somewhat once we introduce the assumptions of separability and decentralization and the requirements that follow, namely, conditional utility and conditional demand curves. For now, however, we ignore these complications and proceed with our discussion based on Figure 8.3.

Instead of examination of the constraint in Figure 8.3 through the $x_i x_j$ plane, we turn now to the perspective through the $v_i x_j$ plane. Here we find dv_i and $\hat{x}_i$, or the unusual case alluded to earlier wherein quality varies across a fixed quantity. As before, we change price, in this case b_i, and employ a change in income to compensate the price change. We assume $(\partial v_i / \partial M) > 0$ (i.e., a "normal goods" assumption), although as mentioned earlier, the meaning of this relationship is unclear. From this as-

Figure 8.4 **Iso-Quantity Curves in v_ib_i Space**

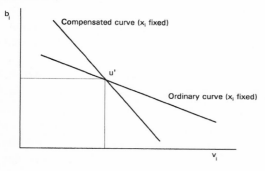

sumption it follows that an increase in b_i can be compensated by an increase in income, and, analogous to our previous remarks, it can also be compensated by a decrease in the level at which x_i is fixed.

We should note that under compensating variation (e.g., from a change in income) the consumer remains on the same indifference curve but at a different point on the curve. In v_ix_j space this means the consumer stays on the same indifference curve but at a different level of quality (i.e., v_i changes along the indifference curve). Under equivalent variation the consumer is on a lower indifference curve, but at the same relative position on the curve with respect to the v_i axis (that is, the consumer stays at the same level of quality, no change in v_i). Equivalent variation gives results analogous to the special case; that is, the case where the consumer seeks to remain at the same v_i in the utility maximization process in v_ix_i space. Compensating variation gives results analogous to the general case. Note that indifference curves in the Houthakker model imply the consumer can rank and compare trade-offs of bundles of different combinations of quantity, x_i, and quality, v_i. With this information, our results in v_ix_j consumption space (with x_i fixed) are comparable to those we obtained previously for dx_i with v_i fixed. Unusual problems arise,

however, when we try to link v_ix_j consumption space with demand curves (both ordinary and compensated), as was previously accomplished for x_ix_j space.

One of the problems encountered is the meaning of the curves in v_ib_i space. Previously, we spoke of ordinary and compensated "demand curves" in x_ia_i space, a type of quantity-price space, with quality fixed. Now we have a quality-price space with fixed quantity. As before, ordinary and compensated curves can be generated in v_ib_i space, just as in x_ia_i space; however, these downward-sloping curves are not demand curves, at least not under the usual definition of demand. An illustration of $v_i b_i$ space is provided in Figure 8.4.

As shown, these curves are not isoquality curves, but rather iso-quantity curves. Each point on either curve represents a different level of quality, or different variety, as indexed by v_i. The traditional concept of demand is constructed in terms of "quantity purchased," at various prices, other things being equal. Under such a definition it is possible to construct a concept of consumer surplus, which is also a price-quantity relationship. Here, however, quantity is held constant and quality (the varieties v_i) is allowed to vary. It follows, therefore, that these curves are not demand curves, nor are they capable of generating consumer surplus. Specifically, the area under either curve (ordinary or compensated), to the left of the point u', for example, is not consumer surplus. In fact, the product of b_i and v_i does not give total revenue (nor expenditure).

The curves in Figure 8.4 are a variation on the idea of price-quality consumption paths, one of which is compensated and the other is not. As illustrated, either one of these curves would show that, for a "low" v_i, the consumer would be willing to pay a higher price (b_i) than the price, say, at u'.

At higher v_i, the consumer pays a lower price. These results, of course, do not fit our intuition. If, however, time were introduced into the analysis, with early time periods corresponding to low values of v_i, then these price-quality consumption paths might be interpreted to show the effect of technological change across time—that is, the frequently encountered phenomenon of rising quality concurrent with falling prices.[5]

In summary, we conclude that in $v_i x_j x_i$ space, the phenomenon known as consumer surplus should be analyzed only from the perspective of $x_i x_j$ space, for specified values of v_i. Examination of $v_i x_j x_i$ space reveals that parametric variation of v_i will produce change in consumer surplus, but such change can only be measured in $x_i x_j$ space. Variation of v_i may also result in shifts in isoquality demand, both ordinary and compensated. We return now to the process of consumer selection of b_i and our earlier remarks regarding b_i as a parameter that reflects consumer willingness-to-pay.

In the next section we discuss separability in the preference map and decentralizability of the budget. One implication of these assumptions is the requirement that utility and demand functions become conditional—that is, conditional utility (for commodity i, given no change in preferences for other commodities) and conditional demand (conditional on the expenditure for commodity i at the isoquality level selected for v_i of commodity i). This means, of course, that consumer surplus must also become conditional; that is, conditional on preferences for other commodities (other than commodity i), and conditional on the decentralized budget expenditure projected for commodity i at variety level $\hat{v}_i$.[6] With these remarks, we return to the discussion of consumer determination of b_i.

3. Further Comments on the Meaning of Consumer-Induced Change in b_i

Earlier we assumed that if the consumer determines b_i, not only did such decision making influence the constraint in $v_i x_i$ space, it also reflected the consumer's willingness-to-pay based on his or her perception of quality (of a variety, $\hat{v}_i$). We have also assumed that when quality is introduced into demand theory, the concept of consumer surplus may include the consumer's perception of quality. As we shall see later, in our model the inclusion of quality also introduces an alternative to the demand reservation price. We now examine change in b_i, initiated by the consumer, and its effect on the constraint.

From our previous discussion of b_{it}, we begin with a situation where the consumer has gained experience (learned) from an initial consumption of $\hat{v}_i$, and where he or she subsequently perceives the quality of $\hat{v}_i$ to be higher than originally estimated with $b_{it=0}$. In other words, we begin where the consumer has changed b_i such that $b_{it=1} > b_{it=0}$. We examine the effects of this change on the constraint in $v_i x_i$ space. An illustration is provided in Figure 8.5.

Recall from our previous discussion of consumer determination of b_i—where the consumer learns from consumption experience and adjusts b_{it}—that if b_{it} approaches b_{it}^*, then learning may lead to a stable b_i. This phenomenon applied to the special case, the case where v_i remained constant.

Now, although we continue to assume learning occurs, our focus is on the constraint in $v_i x_i$ space, as the consumer adjusts b_{it}. As part of the b_i adjustment process, we assume learning is an integral part of consumption activity, and that consumer perception and learning, along with other factors, may shift the constraint and change its convexity.

Figure 8.5 **Houthakker's Constraint Under an Increase in b_i**

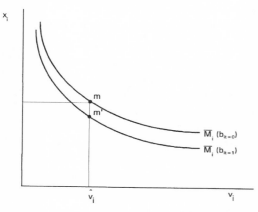

The discussion that follows does not assume change in b_{it} always results in a stable solution. A number of unique phenomena may arise. We begin with the situation depicted in Figure 8.5.

As shown in Figure 8.5, the consumer, after consumption of $\hat{v}_i$, reevaluates his or her initial $b_{it=0}$, and decides b_i was too low. As shown in the diagram, the subsequent $b_{it=1}$ is higher, and the constraint has shifted toward the origin.[7] What is the meaning of this change in b_i? If we assume the special case, where the consumer continues to consume $\hat{v}_i$, then the higher $b_{it=1}$ has several interpretations.

First, an upward adjustment in b_i indicates that the initial "guessed" value of $b_{it=0}$ was inaccurate—in this case, too low. Recall from $v_i p_i$ price space that $b_i = (dp_i / dv_i)$, and that v_i may vary from v_i^- to v_i^+. For the consumer we assume b_i reflects willingness-to-pay for v_i.

We have sufficient background information now to be more specific about b_i. In particular, we now address how b_i is a derivative (dp_i / dv_i), in Houthakker's model, while in our model b_i measures willingness-to-pay for individual v_i (i.e., b_i at $\hat{v}_i$). For Houthakker, $p_i = a_i + b_i v_i$, and as illustrated in price space (see Figure 4.3), b_i is interpreted as the constant slope of the price line. Note that b_i is also the slope in the basic price system, with $a_i = 0$ and $b_i = 1$. In our model b_i may be interpreted as a weight that reflects consumer perception and evaluation of (willingness-to-pay for) an individual variety, and is capable of change from variety to variety. In effect, for our model the equation for the price line is rearranged such that $b_i = (p_i - a_i)/v_i$, where a_i may be held constant. In other words, b_i is interpreted as the difference, over and above a_i (the price of the basic package in a repackaging model), that the consumer attributes to a specific variety, $\hat{v}_i$, for the quality characteristics perceived to be in that variety, over and above the characteristics in the basic package. Because we have assumed a_i constant, then for any variety, the b_i corresponding to that variety is equal to the reciprocal of that variety times the price difference (markup) between the quantity (or basic package) price (a_i) and the overall price p_i, where p_i is variable. (Recall that we are still using Houthakker's single-variety model.)

This interpretation applies to b_i for any given v_i, and it allows b_i to vary across v_i. To be sure, b_i may still be a derivative, but now the consumer is assumed able to influence the derivative and hence the price line. There is no conceptual problem with using a derivative as a weight. In our analysis, however, the derivative is adjustable, and it is influenced by consumer perception of quality.

In the Houthakker model, if b_i is interpreted as a weight, it would have to be interpreted as a constant weight across all varieties. The magnitude of the weight for any single variety is simply the same constant b_i found in the equation for the price line $(p_i = a_i + b_i v_i)$, and, obviously, if b_i is, for example, increased for any v_i, this will lead to an increase in p_i for all v_i. In Houthakker's model, the consumer cannot weigh quality separately for any individual variety. A change in b_i for one variety changes the weight for all varieties in the commodity set. It is as though b_i were an average weight (or average price adjuster) across all varieties in the commodity set. This phenomenon results from Houthakker's linear price aggregator, a variation of J.R. Hicks's concept of a composite commodity. In our model, we question the assumption that the relationship of price across v_i is, in fact, linear. One consequence of this change in assumptions is the need to reexamine the process of aggregation of varieties to form a commodity set. We look into that matter in more detail later. The notion of a commodity set is an important topic and it appears directly and indirectly at several junctures throughout this and subsequent chapters. We now return to our discussion of consumer behavior and the process of adjusting b_i.

The price the consumer pays, in the single variety model, is p_i. Note the price paid for variety v_i is p_i, a price per quantity unit of v_i. Expenditure on variety v_i is $p_i x_i$, or $(a_i + b_i v_i)x_i$ for a specified v_i. The impact of the variety v_i on the price the consumer pays is determined by the weight, b_i, given a repackaging model with a_i constant. In other words, the importance to the consumer of the variety, v_i, as measured by the magnitude of p_i, is influenced by the size of b_i, and b_i is determined by the consumer's perception of v_i. Later, we argue that the consumer's perception of v_i is influenced by the number, type, and configuration of e_{ih} (characteristics) within each variety. In other words, the e_{ih} influence b_i via the consumer's perception of the e_{ih} in each variety. (Note that this is similar to, but not identical with, Ironmonger.) The consumer's perception and evaluation of varieties, in turn, permit the consumer to rank-order varieties. We assume the ranking is based on each variety's ability to satisfy individual consumer wants, similar to the Abbott and Ironmonger models. Such wants are assumed to be subjective, and to vary across time within each consumer and across consumers. Wants are also assumed to vary across such sociodemographic factors as age, sex, culture, race, education, income, and so forth. With these comments, however, we have advanced considerably ahead of the material for this chapter. We return now to our discussion of the phenomena occurring in Figure 8.5.

In Figure 8.5, the consumer has "guessed" at the initial value of $b_{it=0}$ because, as we have assumed, he or she had no previous experience from consumption of that variety. After selection of an initial guessed value of b_i, the constraint emerges in $v_i x_i$ space, and utility maximization results in a solution at m. (Recall our previous assumptions regarding well-behaved constraint and objective function that produce internal solutions.) The consumer consumes variety $\hat{v}_i$.

4. Targeting, Guessing, Neighborhoods, and Budgets

There are two important issues regarding this optimization phenomenon. First, the process implies the consumer knows in advance which variety will be selected by utility maximization, that is, b_i corresponds to a specific v_i, $\hat{v}_i$. It is possible, however, that the consumer does not know in advance. In such circumstances, we assume, alternatively, that the consumer has a general idea of what he or she wants in advance of purchase,[8] and that "shopping" involves not only collecting information, but also evaluating varieties within a "neighborhood." We assume shopping is a process involving perception and evaluation, typically against some current want.[9]

The process of "guessing," for first-time consumption of a new variety, also involves guessing about a decentralized budget for the new variety. In other words, the process of decentralized budgets is not focused at the level of the commodity, but is nested downward to the level of an individual variety, or neighborhood around a variety. A neighborhood may be defined as a range along the v_i axis proximate to the targeted v_i, $\hat{v}_i$. A similar range would constitute a neighborhood along the constraint in $v_i x_i$ space.

We assume that the projected decentralized budget for a variety is based on two estimates. First, there is the consumer's perception of v_i, which is reflected in b_i. (Parenthetically, we note that perception of a single variety may be influenced by other proximate varieties in the neighborhood.) Second, there is the consumer's estimate of the budgeted expenditure to set aside for that variety.[10] Both of these processes involve perception and expectation; that is, they are subjective and dynamic.[11]

Another issue in the optimization process is the prospect that the entire constraint in $v_i x_i$ space is created by an estimate of b_i for a single variety, the targeted variety, $\hat{v}_i$. How is this phenomenon consistent with our previous remarks regarding variable weights? There are a couple of ways to resolve this apparent inconsistency; both employ the concept of a neighborhood around $\hat{v}_i$.

First, we could assume b_i constant over the range of the neighborhood. For those segments of the constraint outside the neighborhood, we could assume b_i is fixed, variable, or unknown. In other words, for the consumer, the nature of the constraint might be known only within the neighborhood of $\hat{v}_i$.[12] Outside the neighborhood, any

of the following assumptions might apply: the constraint exists; the constraint does not exist; or the constraint is stochastic. We assume that when the consumer focuses attention on varieties outside the original neighborhood, and initiates the consumption and evaluation process, a constraint is created in the new neighborhood. The old constraint may cease to exist, or may continue to exist (in the previous neighborhood). Finally, it is important to note that all remarks concerning neighborhoods and the constraint in $v_i x_i$ space also apply to the price line in price space.

The second method for resolving the apparent inconsistency of b_i constant and b_i variable is to assume that b_i is constant over the entire length of the constraint. The value of b_i is defined as its value at $\hat{v}_i$. Under this approach, we assume the act of consumption occurs only within the $\hat{v}_i$ neighborhood. Consequently, the nature of b_i and the nature of the constraint, outside the neighborhood, are essentially of no importance. This approach will work for the single-variety model, but it will lead to problems in the case of multiple varieties.

The reader is again reminded that the discussion up to now is strictly from the point of view of the consumer. Nothing has been stated regarding the interaction of consumer and producer, of demand and supply, nor of market phenomena.

We return now to Figure 8.5. After initial consumption of $\hat{v}_i$, and based on that consumption experience, the consumer discovers that $\hat{v}_i$ is of greater value than the price, p_i. (See also Figure 7.2.) Based on that consumption experience, the consumer adjusts b_i upward to reflect a higher value of $\hat{v}_i$, or a higher willingness-to-pay for $\hat{v}_i$. The change in b_i results in a shift of the constraint. Figure 8.5 provides an example of such a shift.[13] Although not shown in Figure 8.5, the rise in b_i will also cause the price line in $v_i p_i$ space to swing up-ward, pivoting at the fixed intercept of a_i on the p_i axis. This change in price space will result in a higher price, p_i, for the variety $\hat{v}_i$.

5. Expectation and Experience

The process of adjusting b_i is iterative and does not end until the b_i selected by the consumer becomes stationary—at least for some reasonable time period.[14] We define b_i as stationary when $(b_{it=k+1}) = (b_{it=k})$. Attainment of this stationary state corresponds to attainment of b_i^* in the learning process. At the stationary value of b_i^*, what the consumer expects from $\hat{v}_i$, and is willing to pay for $\hat{v}_i$, is, in fact, the price, p_i, which the consumer pays for $\hat{v}_i$. Furthermore, when b_i is stationary, the consumer's *expectation* of satisfaction from variety $\hat{v}_i$, and the consumer's *experience* of satisfaction received from consumption of that variety, are the same.

Until such time as the stationary value of b_i^* is attained, we assume the iterative adjustment of b_i continues—as long as the consumer continues to be interested in consuming variety $\hat{v}_i$. The process of searching for a stable b_i for $\hat{v}_i$ might go on indefinitely.[15] During the process of adjusting b_i, change in the consumer may truncate or otherwise interfere with the learning process, such that an asymptotic approach to b_i^* is delayed. For example, there could be change in consumer expectations of $\hat{v}_i$ and/or change in the consumer's interpretation of the experience gained from the consumption of $\hat{v}_i$. Either of these phenomena could change b_i^*, and thus contribute to over- or underestimation of b_i relative to a new b_i^*. Under such circumstances, it is possible that b_i becomes unstable (i.e., is unable to attain b_i^*). The non-stationary condition of b_i may continue as long as the consumption technology and preferences of

the consumer continue in a state of flux. It is possible that some forms of change in the consumer have little or no effect on b_i, and that other types of change have to be sufficiently large (i.e., have crossed some threshold value) before they affect b_i. The dynamic nature of the consumer, however, and the potential effects of these changes on the estimation of b_i, must not be ignored. In addition to the above, the potential for human error, for example, the C-D gap of Ronald Heiner could be included in the model (Heiner 1983).[16]

All of the factors that produce either stationary or non-stationary patterns for b_i also force the constraint in $v_i x_i$ space to become either stationary or non-stationary. In other words, the iterative and either asymptotic, periodic, or unstable evaluation of b_i by the consumer renders the constraint in quality-quantity space similarly asymptotic, periodic, or unstable. In any case, under consumer determination of b_i the constraint becomes dynamic.

Another complication of consumer decision making in quality-quantity space is the counterintuitive shift pattern of the constraint. Note that as the consumer adjusts b_i upward (to continue with our previous example), the constraint shifts inward toward the origin (see Figure 8.5). For internal (non-corner) solutions to constrained utility maximization (either of the special or general case), the inward shift of the constraint forces the consumer to a lower indifference curve. It is as though consumer adjustment of b_i in the constraint is working at cross purposes with utility maximization. How do we explain this phenomena?

6. Utility Maximization and Perception of the Constraint

Although it appears that b_i adjustment by the consumer is working at cross purposes with maximization of utility, such is really not the case. The counterintuitive aspect of b_i adjustment is, in fact, related to another phenomenon that has a long history in microeconomic theory. Specifically, the issue addressed here—consumer adjustment of b_i—is compatible with, and may give further insight into, the concept of a "demand reservation price." It is possible that our new model of consumer decision making in quality–quantity space may provide an improved understanding of how consumers establish reservation prices. In addition, we hope to show that the model is compatible with recent developments in cognitive psychology and other research on human decision making processes.

Finally, as regards the appearance that consumer adjustment of b_i is working at cross purposes with utility maximization, in the new model we must first justify a new assumption. In our model we assume that consumer decision making in quality–quantity space involves the consumer in both the preference map and the constraint. This assumption presumes that consumer perception of options in quality–quantity space (i.e., consumer perception of the constraint) is as important to consumer decision making in $v_i x_i$ space as "intentional behavior," or what the consumer strives to do, the maximization of utility reflected in the objective function.[17] Another way of stating this dual role of the consumer is as follows: "What you want to do" (intentional thoughts or aspirations reflected in the objective function), and "what you perceive you can do" (your perception of options or possibilities as reflected in the constraint), are related to each other and influence one another. These two thought processes are assumed to be interactive (i.e., there is feedback between them; each influences the other). They are part of a loopy system. "What you want to do" influences "what you perceive you can do," and "what

you perceive you can to (accomplish)" influences "what you desire to do." Perception is important to both activities. We will have more to say on this topic in chapter 9 and in subsequent chapters.

In what follows, it is important to remember that our discussion continues to be restricted to consumer phenomena, particularly to consumer influence over the constraint through adjustment of b_i. Producer influence of the constraint, and identification of options that the consumer can attain, will be addressed later. At that time, we will reconcile what the consumer is willing-to-pay with what the consumer actually must pay.

To return to Figure 8.5, recall that we have assumed the consumer begins consumption at the point m, with $b_{it=0}$, the initial guessed value of b_i for $\hat{v}_i$. After initial consumption, the consumer adjusts b_i upward, $(b_{it=1}) > (b_{it=0})$, reflecting a higher willingness-to-pay for $\hat{v}_i$. We have assumed the consumer targeted $\hat{v}_i$ as the desired level of quality of the ith commodity (i.e., the special case). With upward adjustment of b_i the constraint shifts as illustrated, and the consumer (through an honest revelation of willingness-to-pay)[18] consumes $\hat{v}_i$ at the new point m'. The new point on the lower constraint corresponds to a lower quantity, x_i, of the commodity.

For the moment, let us assume $b_{it=1}$, which produced the lower constraint, is the stable value for b_i, or $(b_{it=1}) = b_i^*$. In other words, $b_{it=1}$ is "accurate" in measuring the consumer's willingness-to-pay for $\hat{v}_i$. Note that the new (higher) willingness-to-pay, brought about by the rise in b_i, can be measured in two ways: first, through the increase in p_i in price space, brought about by the increase in b_i (for $v_i = \hat{v}_i$); or, second, through a reduction in x_i, which reflects the effect of increased b_i on the constraint in $v_i x_i$ space (again for $v_i = \hat{v}_i$). If we assume the consumer does not have to

Figure 8.6 **The Constraint Under Increase or Decrease in b_i**

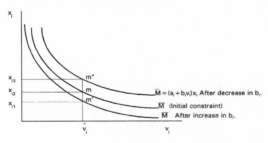

pay the amount indicated as willing-to-pay, then the vertical distance (at $v_i = \hat{v}_i$) between the two constraints, between m and m' in Figure 8.5, may be interpreted as a measure of "potential" consumer surplus. The exact magnitude of the surplus cannot be determined until we consider the role of the producer in $v_i x_i$ space.

In Figure 8.6, we consider the consumer's option to either increase or decrease b_i. Before discussing Figure 8.6, however, a few additional remarks are necessary regarding movement from m to m' in Figure 8.5. As stated earlier, the downward shift of the constraint induced by an increase in b_i, or the move from m to m', represents an increase in willingness-to-pay for $\hat{v}_i$. In addition to our previous remarks on consumer surplus and willingness-to-pay, we need to elaborate on three categories of willingness-to-pay.

7. Additional Concepts of Willingness-to-Pay

The first type of willingness-to-pay we have already introduced; it is the category known as "Willingness-to-Pay-to-Keep," or WTP(TK). This category can be defined as either the higher price, p_i, or reduced quantity, x_i, that the consumer would be willing to pay to continue to consume $\hat{v}_i$. In other words, it is the WTP to keep $\hat{v}_i$. In Figure 8.5, the movement from m to m' illustrates the quantity of the ith commod-

ity, at variety level $\hat{v}_i$, which the consumer would be willing to give up (pay) so as to be able to continue consuming $\hat{v}_i$. In Figure 8.6 this movement is shown as the reduction in x_i from x_{i2} to x_{i1}. The corresponding "potential" consumer surplus is the distance between x_{i2} and x_{i1}. The surplus is not the area of the rectangle with corners at x_{i1}, x_{i2}, m, m'. In other words, the increase in b_i indicates a higher WTP(TK) at quality level $\hat{v}_i$, and a "potential" consumer surplus of $x_{i2}-x_{i1}$. The "potential" is realized provided the consumer pays the price, p_i, associated with x_{i2} at the point m. The actual price the consumer pays depends on the interaction between producer and consumer. Interaction between consumer and producer is discussed in chapters 11 through 15.

Another manifestation of WTP(TK) occurs when the consumer remains at $\hat{v}_i$, but has learned, from consumption experience, that the initial guessed value of $b_{it=0}$ was too high. We assume that under such circumstances the consumer subsequently reduces b_i. The reduction in b_i (for $v_i = \hat{v}_i$) reveals that the initial value of b_i was inaccurate, and it implies that the consumer may have been "disappointed" (experienced a negative surprise)[19] from the initial consumption experience of $\hat{v}_i$. Subsequently, the consumer adjusts b_i downward to "more accurately" reflect his or her current estimate of willingness-to-pay. Under this set of circumstances, the change in WTP(TK) is not positive, relative to point m, as was the case in the previous example. In the new situation we assume that the consumer must be compensated, in some fashion, so as to be willing to continue to consume (keep) $\hat{v}_i$. The reduced WTP(TK) is revealed through the higher quantity, x_i, required for the consumer to remain at $\hat{v}_i$. The lower b_i shifts the constraint outward, and the solution moves from m to m''. Such movement implies the reverse of consumer surplus, a phenomenon we will call consumer disappointment, or simply "disappointment." In $v_i x_i$ space, the magnitude of disappointment is measured by the distance between x_{i3} and x_{i2}. Similar to our previous remarks, disappointment is not the area of the rectangle with corners at x_{i2}, x_{i3}, m'', m.

Note that for WTP(TK), both for an increase in b_i (the consumer surplus case) and for a decrease in b_i (the disappointment case), the consumer continues to consume $\hat{v}_i$.[20] In both cases, stable values of b_i are assumed to exist, either at m'

and m''. In the remaining two categories of willingness-to-pay, we encounter decision making wherein the consumer moves away from $\hat{v}_i$. These categories of willingness-to-pay will be called: "Willingness-to-Pay-to-Acquire" WTP(TA), and "Willingness-to-Accept-Payment-to-Relinquish" WTAP(TR).[21] We examine these new categories of willingness-to-pay in chapter 10. In the next chapter, we continue with WTP(TK), but turn our attention to the stability conditions for b_i.

Chapter 9

Stability of b_i, Attractors, and Self-Perception

A Feigenbaum Model of Consumer Decision Making

1. Stability of Consumer-Determined b_i

Recall that earlier we defined stable b_i to be $(b_{it=k+1}) = (b_{it=k})$. In this section we expand upon the conditions for stability. In Figure 9.1, the axes are $b_{it=k}$ on the horizontal and $b_{it=k+1}$ on the vertical. For both axes the b_i values range from 0 to 1, inclusive. The diagram is a phase space on the unit square with 45° bisecting line. On the 45° line, we have $(b_{it\,=\,k+1}) = (b_{it\,=\,k})$; however, this may not be sufficient to establish a stable solution. Note that $0 \leq b_{it} \leq 1$ for Figure 9.1, which is similar, but not identical, to the condition required in Figure 4.3. In Figure 4.3, $0 < b_i < 1$ is required. Here, on the other hand, we allow closure on the boundaries 0 and 1, because we have relaxed the price-space equilibrium condition, $p_i = v_i$.

Previously, we had $(b_{it=k+1}) = (b_{it=k})$ as the stable value for b_{it}. At this juncture, it will be useful to consider not only the existence of stable values for b_i, but whether consumer-generated b_i converge to such values. To examine these properties, it is both interesting and useful to apply the analysis of attractors found in nonlinear dynamics. Specifically, in this section we examine whether points on the 45° line are stable, as well as the conditions under

Figure 9.1 **Expectation-Experience Phase Space**

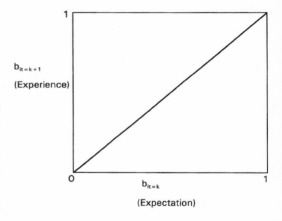

which consumer evaluation of quality (the process of consumer determination of b_i) converges to the 45° line, or evolves into patterns of oscillation, or degenerates into chaotic patterns. Note that our earlier definition of stability is comparable to a point of equilibrium over some time period. In our model, the equilibrium may be defined as agreement between consumer "expectation" and consumer consumption "experience." Throughout the discussion that follows, we limit our remarks to the special case.

Before discussing stability, we consider the matter of existence. We utilize Brou-

Figure 9.2 **Folded Function in Expectation-Experience Space**

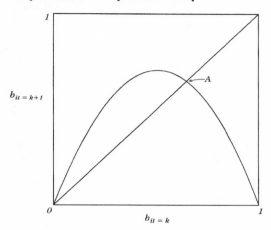

Figure 9.3 **Period-One Attractor**

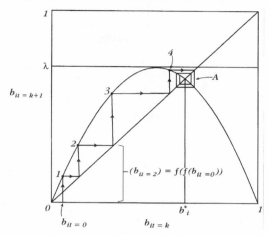

wer's fixed-point theorem and apply it to the b_{it} variables of Figure 9.1. We commence by assuming "experience" to be a function of "expectation," and define "experience" to be $b_{it=k+1}$ and "expectation" to be $b_{it=k}$.[1] We further assume the mapping of $b_{it=k}$ onto $b_{it=k+1}$ is continuous, and that the set of all b_{it} is closed, bounded and convex. By Brouwer's fixed-point theorem, given such a mapping, there exists at least one fixed point such that $(b_{it=k+1}) = (b_{it=k})$.

To specify the model further, we assume the mapping to be an inverted parabola (see Figure 9.2), where:

$$(b_{it=k+1}) = [(4\lambda b_{it=k})(1-b_{it=k})] \quad (1)$$
$$0 < \lambda \leq 1.$$

This mapping is simply intended as an example. Any quadratic extremum will suffice.

In Figure 9.2 a fixed point occurs where the function intersects the 45° line (i.e., at the point A). A second fixed point occurs at the origin. Of particular importance is the stability of the solution at A. To examine stability at A, we employ methods drawn from nonlinear dynamical systems.

One of the simplest explanations of such systems is provided in an early work by Douglas Hofstadter.[2]

We begin by examining a stable solution. Consider Figure 9.3, which is identical to Figure 9.2, based on the same inverted parabola, but where a convergent path toward b_{it}^* is presented. The path originates at the initial "guessed" value of b_i, or $b_{it=0}$. The initial value is called the "seed." The path toward a solution is indicated by the arrows. The path is derived from Mitchell Feigenbaum's analysis of attractors and is based on phenomena that exhibit patterns of feedback or loops, in other words, a loopy system (see Feigenbaum 1981).

The model we are developing is an example of a dynamic system, where the output of a previous time period is fed back into the system as a subsequent input. In our model of consumer behavior, the feedback, or loop, links consumer "expectation" of quality in time period k to consumer consumption "experience" of quality in time period $k+1$. The consumption "experience" then loops around, or feeds back, and influences "expectation" in the next time period.[3] In the words of Douglas Hofstadter:

From the simplest of such loops, it seemed, both stable patterns and chaotic patterns . . . could emerge. The difference was merely in the value of a single parameter. Very small changes in the value of this parameter could make all the difference in the world as to the orderliness of the behavior of the loopy system. This image of order melting smoothly into chaos, of pattern dissolving gradually into randomness, was exciting to me. (Hofstadter 1981/1985, p. 22)*

As Hofstadter and others point out, the analysis of attractors is based on the process of iteration of some real-valued function that exhibits the behavior of a sequence of values such as x, $f(x)$, $f(f(x))$, $f(f(f(x)))$, and so forth. Generally, these functions are required to exhibit cyclical or near-cyclical behavior. Specifically, the function should "switch back," or be a nonmonotonic function whose graph is folded. Our inverted parabola is a good example, and is, in fact, used by Hofstadter. Instead of x, we use b_i. In Figure 9.3, for any value of $b_{it=k}$ in the interval 0 to 1 inclusive, the resultant output, or $b_{it=k+1}$, will always have a value between 0 and λ. This arrangement assures that the output (consumption experience) always feeds back into the function as an input (the next period's expectation), which, in turn, influences the next period's consumption experience. It is the fold in the function that guarantees iteration. And, as we shall see, it is the value of λ that determines whether there is convergence, oscillations around a single fixed-point attractor, or patterns that may ultimately dissolve into chaos. Dependence on the value of λ holds, regardless of where we place the seed, the initial value of b_i.[4]

In the case of convergence to a stable fixed point, assume we begin at $b_{it=0}$, the "seed," as illustrated in Figure 9.3. From the initial value $b_{it=0}$ on the horizontal axis, we proceed vertically until we hit the parabolic curve. This point indicates the value of $b_{it=k+1}$ on the vertical axis, or $(b_{it=1}) = f(b_{it=0})$. This corresponds to Hofstadter's $y_o = f(x_o)$. To iterate the function further, we draw a new vertical line located at the new $b_{it=k}$ value (now $k=1$), which value will equal the previous $b_{it=k+1}$ value, that is, $b_{it=0+1}$. This will occur where the first horizontal arrow meets the 45° line. We now repeat the operation by drawing a second vertical arrow, which proceeds from the 45° line (at the new value of $b_{it=1}$) to the curve. This second vertical arrow will hit the curve at a height, $(b_{it=2=1+1}) = f(b_{it=1}) = f(b_{it=0+1}) = f(f(b_{it=0}))$. Note that the height is identified by $(b_{it=2}) = f(f(b_{it=0}))$ in brackets in Figure 9.3. From here on we just repeat the iterations until convergence at the point A.

As described by Hofstadter, the solution at A "is a special kind of fixed point, because it attracts iterated values of $f(x)$" (Hofstadter 1981, p. 28). In our case, the fixed point at A attracts iterated values of $b_{it=k}$, or iterated values of expectation. The attractor at A attracts every non-zero value of the seed, the initial guessed value of b_i. For this reason, it is called an "attractive fixed point." The other fixed point at the origin, by contrast, is a repellent or an unstable fixed point. In describing stable attractors, Hofstadter observes:

Note that sometimes the iterates of f will overshoot x^* [the solution point], sometimes they will fall short—but they inexorably draw closer to x^*, zeroing in on it like swallows returning to Capistrano [and, we might add, like consumers seeking an accurate assessment of the quality of products and services they buy]. (Hofstadter 1981, p. 28)

Regarding the stability of the fixed point at A, and the contrasting instability of the origin, it is the slope of the curve at the fixed point that determines stability versus instability. The rule for stability is that the slope of the curve at any fixed point be less than -1.

In the example provided, which is identical to Hofstadter's (except for relabeling of axes), the value of λ is 0.7. This value produces a stable solution at A. As indicated earlier, several investigators maintain that the value of λ is the only significant variable in the determination of whether solutions are stable (either to a fixed point or to patterns of oscillation), or whether the iterations lead to chaos. Chaos, or chaotic patterns, arise when λ exceeds the value 0.892486418. . . . For values of λ "close" to 0.89, patterns of oscillation around one or more fixed points can arise. Generally, the lower the value of λ the simpler the orbit pattern, and of interest to us, the greater the likelihood of convergence to a single fixed point (Hofstadter 1981, p. 31).

Suppose, in our example, we increase the value of λ. This will change the location of the fixed point, A, and change the slope of the curve as it passes through the point. When $\lambda = 0.75$ the curve intersects the 45° line (falling) at a 45° angle. Let us examine the effect of this change on the stability of the (new) solution. As illustrated in Figure 9.4, where we have used the same seed for b_i, the path now orbits around the fixed point. It will do so indefinitely. This is a 2-cycle pattern of oscillation. This pattern has identified two values of b_i, (b_i^1 and b_i^2), which, combined as a pair, become an attractor of period two.[5] The 2-cycle pattern is stable, it attracts b_i values to the orbit, instead of to a fixed

Figure 9.4 **Period-Two Attractor**

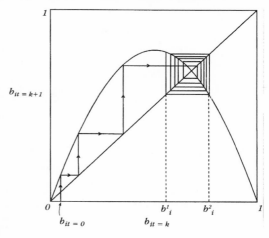

point. From our point of view, the consumer now oscillates between two values of b_i, one below and the other above a single-valued, or "accurate" solution. Recall $b_{it} = b_{it}^*$ defines accuracy (i.e., expectation equals experience).

This process continues for higher values of λ. For example, when λ reaches a value of 0.86237 . . . , we encounter a 4-cycle pattern, or a pair of 2-cycle attractors. The 4-cycle pattern explodes to an 8-cycle pattern for $\lambda = 0.87$ (approximately). This process continues doubling (bifurcating) for smaller and smaller increases in λ, where λ is approaching a critical value (λ_c) of size 0.892486418 . . . (Hofstadter 1981, pp. 28, 31).[6] As we increase λ, the attractor values for b_{it} exhibit the pattern shown in Figure 9.5.

For λ beyond λ_c we move into the chaotic regime. Here, further iteration of the function can yield, for some seeds or initial values of $b_{it=0}$, orbits that are aperiodic—that is, orbits that do not converge, or "converge to no finite attractor," (Hofstadter 1981, p. 31). Under such circumstances, for most b_i seeds the orbit will remain periodic, but the periodicity may be difficult to detect; the period may be ex-

Figure 9.5 **Fragmentation of b_i for Higher Values of λ**

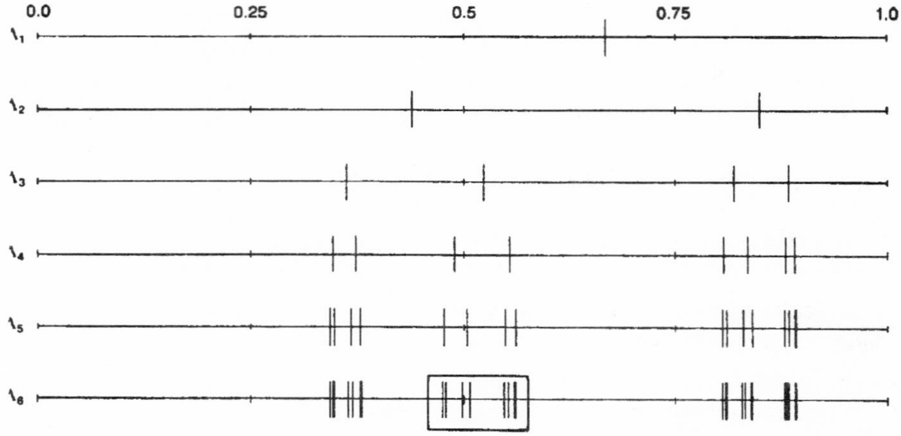

Source: Figure 16.5 (p. 374) from *Metamagical Themes: Questing for Essence of Mind* by Douglas R. Hofstadter (Viking, 1985) copyright © 1985 by Basic Books, Inc. Reprinted by permission of Basic Books, a member of Perseus Books, L.L.C.

tremely high, or simply too complex to detect patterns. Under these circumstances,

> [a] typical periodic orbit, instead of quickly converging to a geometrically simple attractor, will meander all over the interval [0,1], and its behavior will appear indistinguishable from total chaos. Such behavior is termed ergodic. Furthermore, neighboring seeds may, within a very small number of iterations, give rise to utterly different orbits. In short, a statistical view of the phenomena becomes considerably more reasonable beyond λ_c. (Hofstadter 1981, p. 31)

An illustration of what happens beyond λ_c is provided below in Figure 9.6. It is the now famous picture of cascading bifurcations. (See, for example, Kadanoff 1983, p. 51.)

As a closing comment on this material, please note that for high seed values (that is, $b_{it=0}$ to the right of a non-zero fixed point, that is, to the right of the point *A*) the process is essentially the same as presented for low seed values. The only difference is in the first iteration.[7] See Figure 9.7. We return now to consumer determination of b_i and consider an application of attractors to our study of variable quality.

2. Attractors and WTP(To Keep)

Earlier, we defined $b_{it=k}$ to be "expectation" and $b_{it=k+1}$ to be "experience." We have limited our discussion so far to WTP(To Keep), that is, the special case. From the theory of attractors, we have learned that in unit phase space it is the slope of a folded curve through the 45° line that determines stability of a solution, and that λ influences the slope of the curve.

Of interest to us at this juncture is the process of determining the nature of the folded function. In this regard, Hofstadter and others have emphasized the magnitude of λ. We formulate the matter in a slightly different manner.

In our model, which involves consumer perception of quality, we assume the consumer (consciously or unconsciously) generates the curve. We assume the curve to be a mathematical representation of mental

Figure 9.6 **Cascading Bifurcations**

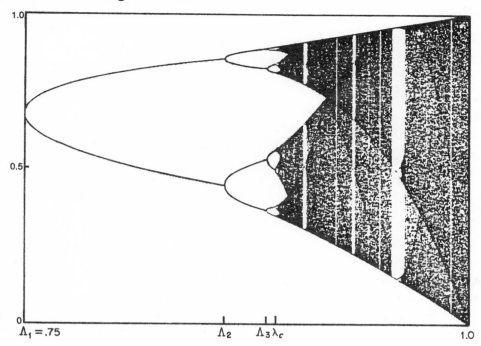

Source: Reprinted with permission from Leo P. Kadanoff, "Roads to Chaos," *Physics Today,* December 1983. Copyright © 1983, American Institute of Physics

phenomena that occur within the consumer, specifically the interaction of consumer expectation and consumption experience.

To begin, note that if the consumer is extremely accurate, he or she will place the seed, the guessed value of $b_{it=0}$, at the fixed point (i.e., at the intersection of the curve with the 45° line). Such a degree of accuracy, however, raises the subject of whether there would exist a curve at all of such a consumer. In other words, for the highly accurate consumer, only points on the 45° line would be chosen; in effect, the curve has become the 45° line.[8]

For most consumers, however, it is likely that there would be inaccuracy and a learning process. In fact, we assume that the curve is generated by the degree of inaccuracy, or discrepancy, between expectation and experience. We also assume that the learning capacity and learning speed of each consumer are able, over time, to reduce the magnitude of discrepancy between expectation and experience. (See Heiner 1983 on the C-D gap for a similar concept.) In the world of perception and variable quality, we assume consumer mental processes create and adjust the curve through learning associated with consumption.

All statements regarding inaccurate expectations are to be interpreted in terms of the relationship of expectation to consumption experience. This is not equivalent to saying expectations are high or low relative to some absolute "reality," for we are dealing with individual consumer perception. Our model assumes that each individ-

Figure 9.7 **Period-One Attractor for High-Valued Seed**

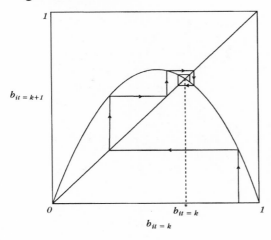

$b_{it = k}$

ual has a concept of "reality," and that the concept involves learning loops associated with individual self-perception and perception of the surrounding world.[9]

To return to our analysis of variable quality, the greater the disparity between expectation, $b_{it=k}$, and consumption experience, $b_{it=k+1}$, the greater the likelihood the consumer will become confused in his or her personal assessment of the quality of the variety, $\hat{v}_i$. Confusion, or possibly chaotic thinking, may be revealed through erratic and/or unending changes in b_{it}. To return to $v_i x_i$ space, such confusion means that b_i^* (the stable value of b_i) is not found. This means, in turn, that the constraint in $v_i x_i$ space is in constant motion, changing with each act of purchase-consumption.[10] In the WTP(TK) case, the consumer remains at $\hat{v}_i$, although willing to pay different amounts in order to continue consuming $\hat{v}_i$. The quantity, x_i, purchased of that variety changes with each change in the constraint, that is, with each change in b_i.

This pattern of behavior in $v_i x_i$ space suggests that inaccurate expectations of quality on the part of consumers may result in unstable buying patterns, and, depending on consumer behavior in the aggregate,

could also result in unstable markets. As mentioned earlier, in the WTP(TK) case such instability is reflected in change in the quantity, x_i, of a fixed variety, $\hat{v}_i$, and in change in p_i. The dimension of these phenomena is enlarged when we introduce the cases of WTP(TA) and WTAP(TR), where variation in quality (i.e., change in v_i) is also permitted. Variation in v_i introduces the general case. Before we consider these other categories of willingness-to-pay, however, a few additional comments are necessary regarding the perception of quality and WTP(TK).

3. Quality and the Self

As stated in the introductory chapter to this work, our analysis of variable quality is restricted to the quality of products and services at the level of retail transactions between consumers and firms. In part 2 our approach has been restricted, thus far, to the consumer and the role of variable quality in consumer theory. In this section we introduce assumptions regarding the role of self-image in the perception of variable quality and in the interpretation of consumption experience.

In what follows, we argue that both consumer "expectation" of quality (corresponding to a single variety, $\hat{v}_i$) and consumer interpretation of consumption "experience" (derived from consumption of $\hat{v}_i$) are influenced by the consumer's concept and perception of self. Under this scenario, what may be perceived and interpreted as high quality by one consumer, contrarily may be perceived and interpreted as low quality by another. Via this understanding, variation in quality rankings across consumers arises, in part, because the "quality" of products and/or services depends on how effectively such products and/or services serve to enhance and/or protect each consumer's self-image, or concept of Self.

Under this approach to consumer theory, the concept of quality is defined, and ordered, *first* in terms of the *security/survival* of the self—conceivably within a niche in some psychological space, where the quality of products and services is perceived in terms of establishing and/or protecting the self. The approach involves issues of turf in a psychological space (initially within a family and later within schools, the work environment, and other communities), and it incorporates aspects of rent-seeking behavior, where the rent is the long-term effectiveness of the niche in terms of establishing, protecting, and enhancing the self.[11] The *second* priority in the definition and ordering of quality is the perception of quality in terms of the ability of products and services to *enlarge, enhance,* and/or allow *growth* of the self.[12]

Under these assumptions, consumer perceptions of quality and preference-orderings based on those perceptions are assumed to originate from, and be strongly influenced by, individual consumer self-image. In other words, perception of the quality of products and services is influenced by perception of Self. The quality of products and services is perceived through the eyes of the self. Any change in self-image might result in change in the consumer's perception of quality, and, therefore, change in the consumer's corresponding preference-orderings for goods and services. Change in self-image could produce change in the b_i corresponding to goods and services.

The self, in this model, is seen as surrounding "itself" with support images, or in carrying out activities of self-reinforcement and/or self-enhancement. Such activities are assumed to involve loopy learning processes. The support images sought by and maintained around the Self include products and services purchased, as well as the images provided by family, friends, work environment, religion, culture, and so forth. Such images may be viewed within the context of an object-relations concept of a real self.[13] In our model of consumer behavior under conditions of variable quality, we assume the evaluation of quality, and the market decision-making processes associated therewith involve these, and other, sociopsychological activities.

It is important to note that within our model what may be viewed by the self as a high-quality product or service at one point in time, may not be esteemed very highly by the self at a subsequent time. Such change in the perception and evaluation of quality could arise from personal experience, maturation, as well as from other forms of change within the self.

With these remarks, we conclude our discussion of perception and the WTP(TK) process. We proceed next to expand the model to include WTP(To Acquire) and WTAP(To Relinquish). With the introduction of these two additional concepts of willingness-to-pay, the model is no longer restricted to the special case. The foundation is laid for the General Case.

Chapter 10

Willingness-to-Pay, Targeting, Learning, and Demand Prices

1. The General Case: Additional Concepts of WTP

In Figures 8.5 and 8.6 the consumer was assumed to be at the point m, based on an initial "guessed" value of b_i. Under WTP (to Keep), the consumer remained at the targeted variety, $\hat{v}_i$. In quality–quantity space, any variation in willingness-to-pay was restricted to change in the quantity, x_i. In addition, in price space, variation in willingness-to-pay was reflected in change in p_i. In this chapter we relax the assumption that the consumer remains at $\hat{v}_i$.

As before, we assume the consumer is at the point m, as shown in Figure 8.6. We also assume, as before, that after initial consumption of $\hat{v}_i$, the consumer reevaluates $b_{it=0}$, and based on that consumption experience may either adjust b_i upward or downward. If we assume, as in Figure 8.5, that the consumer adjusts b_i upward, the constraint shifts inward toward the origin. With this shift in the constraint, and deletion of the requirement that the consumer remain at $\hat{v}_i$, we encounter consumption options as illustrated in Figure 10.1. (Note that in Figure 10.1 we have identified the initial quantity by $\hat{x}_i$.) As shown by the arrows, there are numerous options open to the consumer on the new constraint. The arrows serve only as examples of an infinite number of new solutions.

We assume the new b_i ($b_{it=1}$) is stable and that it applies to the entire range of the constraint. This may be a questionable assumption, but it facilitates introduction of the *general case*. To identify new solutions for v_i and x_i, we assume that the consumer pursues a process of constrained utility maximization, but one that is not necessarily targeted to $\hat{v}_i$. In fact, the consumer's preference map may select any combination of v_i and x_i allowed by the new constraint. Note, however, that with regard to the initial point m, the consumer may choose bundles with either lower v_i and lower x_i, or trade-off bundles involving higher v_i and lower x_i, or vice versa. Let us assume that the consumer's new optimal solution, obtained via utility maximization against the new constraint, is one in which v_i is higher (relative to the initial $\hat{v}_i$), and in which there is a corresponding reduction in x_i. In Figure 10.1 this path is indicated by the arrow (1). This is a case involving willingness-to-pay-to-acquire.

2. Willingness-to-Pay-to-Acquire

As mentioned earlier, willingness-to-pay-to-acquire, or WTP(TA), involves a change in the variety, v_i. WTP(TA) may also involve a change in quantity, x_i. The type of change in v_i assumed here is an increase of

Figure 10.1 **Multiple Consumption Paths Under Increased b_i**

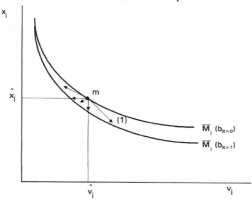

Figure 10.2 **Multiple Consumption Paths to Higher Quality**

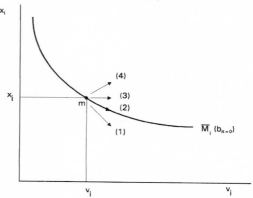

v_i to a value higher than the previous $\hat{v}_i$. In other words, the consumer is "acquiring" a higher level of quality. The process of moving from lower to higher v_i can unfold in several ways. Before discussing these alternative paths, it is important to remember that we are still confined to consumer behavior and to consumer determination of b_i. Although we occasionally make reference to utility maximization, our primary focus remains the constraint in $v_i x_i$ space.

Of the several paths to acquire higher quality, four are illustrated in Figure 10.2. As indicated earlier, we begin by considering the first path. This path is the same as that illustrated by the arrow (1) in Figure 10.1.

To create path (1), we assume the consumer determines, after consumption of $\hat{v}_i$ at the point m, that b_i at m is inaccurate.[1] In the case of path (1), the consumer adjusts b_i upward and subsequently targets on the new constraint at a point where v_i is higher than the initial $\hat{v}_i$ and x_i is lower than the previous $\hat{x}_i$. As illustrated in Figure 10.1, the increase in b_i shifts the constraint downward and increases its convexity. The downward shift of the constraint permits a path such as path (1). Note that the reduction in x_i along path (1) is greater than would be required had the consumer targeted the same new variety, but remained on the original constraint. In other words, the reduction of x_i along path (1) is greater than it would be along path (2) in Figure 10.2. Also, note that the same point in $v_i x_i$ space, attained at the terminus of path (1), could be attained under the original constraint if we allowed saving on the part of the consumer.

Finally, note that the upward adjustment of b_i, and corresponding downward shift of the constraint, can be constructed in terms of a targeted neighborhood of $\hat{v}_i$, or region along the constraint. In this sense, we have a case that is intermediate between the special case and the general case. For the intermediate case, there is a region along the constraint that is the target or focus of the consumer. To the extent the region is enlarged and extends along the constraint, it approaches the entire length of the constraint (i.e., it approaches the general case). To the extent the region is reduced in size, it approaches a point on the constraint and becomes the special case (that is, targeted on a single variety).

To return to our discussion of path (1), we assume the next step, after the downward shift of the constraint, is movement from m to m' (see Figure 10.3). This is equivalent to our previous case, WTP(to

Figure 10.3 **Stepwise Path Under WTP(TA)**

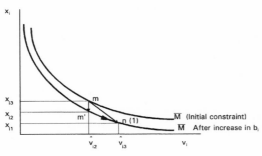

Keep). Assume for now that the point at *m'*, and the corresponding b_i at *m'*, are stable—that is, the new constraint does not shift further. In other words, the first step is essentially the path followed under the special case.

In step two, however, we assume a different form of consumer behavior. Here the consumer is assumed to "move" along the constraint from *m'* to the point *n*, with a corresponding change in v_i from $\hat{v}_{i2}$ to $\hat{v}_{i3}$. The consumer "moves" to a higher level of quality because it is assumed he or she desired and targeted a higher v_i, the v_i at *n*, or $\hat{v}_{i3}$. The previous v_i, $\hat{v}_{i2}$, ceases to be the target.

3. Utility Maximization and Targeting

A subtle question, related to the movement along the constraint from *m'* to *n*, is the difference between the process of utility maximization and the process of targeting. In our current example, it is a question of whether the new v_i, $\hat{v}_{i3}$, is targeted, or the result of utility maximization. We assume that "simple" utility maximization occurs when the consumer does not focus on or target a specific variety, nor is there targeting on a neighborhood along the v_i axis. Under a non-targeted process for selection of v_i, the consumer accepts the variety obtained from the process of utility maximi-

zation. In a sense, it is as though the consumer does not know specifically which variety he or she wants in advance. By way of further refinement of this process, we identify two categories of "simple" utility maximization. If utility maximization occurs along the entire length of the constraint, we define the process as Full Constraint Simple Utility Maximization, or FCSUM. Alternatively, if a neighborhood has been identified, and utility maximization is used to select a single v_i from within the neighborhood, we define the process as Neighborhood Simple Utility Maximization, or NSUM.

If targeting occurs, then the consumer preselects a variety, or a neighborhood, and then restricts the process of utility optimization to that variety or neighborhood. The NSUM approach introduced above is an intermediate case that involves both utility maximization and a limited form of targeting. The targeting approach is similar to the behavior of preference maps in characteristics or attributes space, where preference can identify the desired combination or cluster of attributes—which in our model would correspond to the desired configuration of attributes (or elements e_{ih}) in a variety (i.e., the targeted variety). In the case of targeting a single variety, utility maximization applies only to the "quantity" of the preselected variety—that is, it applies to x_i for the targeted $\hat{v}_i$.[2] The isoquality, or homogeneous, model of consumer utility maximization is an example of this case.

In the NSUM case, another factor to consider, regarding movement along the constraint, is the breadth of the neighborhood. Specifically, in the case of the initial variety, $\hat{v}_{i2}$, is the size of the neighborhood around $\hat{v}_{i2}$ sufficiently large to extend from $\hat{v}_{i2}$ to $\hat{v}_{i3}$? Recall that in Figure 10.3 the value of b_i was determined by the consumer on the basis of his or her assessment of $\hat{v}_{i2}$, or possibly on the basis of other varieties within a neighborhood of $\hat{v}_{i2}$. What is important here is whether the b_i employed for the new constraint, that is, the b_i based on an assessment of $\hat{v}_{i2}$, is sufficiently accurate for the range of quality variation from $\hat{v}_{i2}$ to $\hat{v}_{i3}$. It seems reasonable to assume that the accuracy of b_i at m' fades as the consumer moves outward along the constraint toward the point n. A consequence of this potential inaccuracy is that the "solution" at point n may not be stable—that is, the b_i at m' does not extend to n, and hence there is the need to evaluate $\hat{v}_{i3}$ at the new "solution." A new WTP(to Keep) evaluation of $\hat{v}_{i3}$ may be necessary. For now, however, we assume that the solution at n is stable (i.e., that the b_i at m' "reached" to n). Obviously, the shorter the "distance" between m' and n, the more reasonable is this assumption.

Note that this two-step process can be broken up into infinitely smaller segments (smaller segments of m to m' and m' to n) such that the sequence of two-step operations approximates the path known as path (1). The reason for this two-step approach is the potential for consumer ignorance, or lack of consumption experience, across v_i, and, therefore, the corresponding difficulty for the consumer of accurately assessing b_i at the higher v_i, $\hat{v}_{i3}$. This suggests that higher v_i, or higher v_i neighborhoods, may be targeted, which is to say, the consumer has some general idea of the level of quality, or neighborhood thereof, which he or she desires prior to the act of purchase and consumption. The process of "shopping" may be assumed to include gathering information on either individual v_i or v_i neighborhoods.[3] In fact, we assume that under most circumstances the consumer does not follow the process of FCSUM, but rather focuses or targets his or her utility maximization on a specific variety or neighborhood around a variety.

4. Jumping, Guessing, and Stability of the Constraint

Along this line of thought, it is conceivable that the consumer does not move along a path (m to n) in Figure 10.3. Instead, the consumer simply jumps from point m to point n, without any intermediate consumption along a path toward n, either from m to n or m' to n. In other words, there are consumption points, and these points can jump about without being approached via a consumption path. In order for the jumping phenomenon to occur, however, we assume that the WTP(TK) process is used to evaluate each new point (e.g., the point n). We also assume that the "jumping" process for new v_i will involve the previously described "guessing" process of $b_{it=0}$ (the seed) for initial consumption of some variety not previously consumed. The guessing process applies when the "reach" of a former b_i^* (stable b_i) is not adequate for a distant variety (i.e., b_i^* is inaccurate outside its neighborhood along a given constraint). Here again, the consumer will have to undertake the guessing process for $b_{it=0}$, and follow the WTP(TK) process to obtain an accurate b_i for the new variety.

In other words, as we move along a fixed constraint, away from a targeted variety (e.g., $\hat{v}_{i2}$), or away from a targeted v_i neighborhood, the previously accurate b_i (e.g., the b_i at m' in Figure 10.3) may become inaccurate. When this happens, b_i may become unstable—that is, when the original b_i is applied to v_i beyond the limit of the original neighborhood, it may become unstable.[4] This means that as we move away from the point m' on a fixed constraint we may lose the single fixed-point attractor that previously applied to $\hat{v}_{i2}$. Thus, as the consumer moves away from m' in Figure 10.3, but continues to use the value of b_i corresponding to m', it

Figure 10.4 **Constraint Fragmentation Outside the Neighborhood**

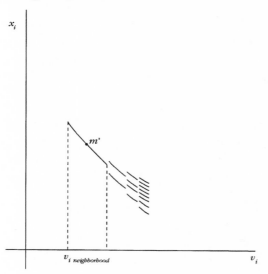

is conceivable that the expectation-experience equilibrium for the original $\hat{v}_{i2}$ does not produce equilibrium of expectation and experience at the new, higher $\hat{v}_{i3}$. Such phenomena may indicate that the curve in expectation-experience phase space has changed. To employ the same set of expectations and interpretations of consumption experience for one $\hat{v}_i$ (e.g., $\hat{v}_{i2}$) to an alternative $\hat{v}_i$ (e.g., $\hat{v}_{i3}$) may produce disequilibria of expectations and experience. Furthermore, it is conceivable that as the consumer moves further away from the original $\hat{v}_{i2}$, the magnitude of discrepancy between expectations and experience grows. Our previous discussion of accuracy and stability of b_i (chapter 9) may now be used in reverse; not only does accuracy of expectation with consumption experience establish stability of b_i, but instability of b_i implies, and provides evidence of, inaccuracy of expectations and interpretation of experience.

By retaining the b_i at m', the constraint exists. Outside the $\hat{v}_{i2}$ neighborhood, however, we assume that the original b_i be-

comes increasingly inaccurate. The further the distance from the original neighborhood, the greater the degree of inaccuracy and instability of b_i. Another way to view such phenomenon would be to conceive the original constraint as gradually breaking up as the consumer moves outside the original neighborhood. The process of breaking up the constraint would proceed according to the pattern of 2-cycle, 4-cycle, and higher period attractors. The process of going from one to increasingly numerous constraints, as the consumer moves further outside the $\hat{v}_{i2}$ neighborhood, is analogous to increasing the number of b_i as λ increases in value. (See Figure 9.5.) There is a separate constraint for each b_{it} obtained via this process. There is, correspondingly, a different constraint for each time period. The constraint has become dynamic. See Figure 10.4 for an example of the constraint breaking up as a result of inaccuracy of b_i for regions beyond the original v_i neighborhood. The greater the distance from the neighborhood, the greater the fragmentation of the constraint, reflecting higher period attractors for b_i.

To return to our previous discussion, we assume that as the consumer moves outside the neighborhood associated with the point m', the value of λ begins to rise. This implies that along the constraint in $v_i x_i$ space the value of λ is not necessarily constant. We assume that within the neighborhood of a targeted v_i, if b_i is stable (i.e., $b_i = b_i^*$), λ is constant and sufficiently below λ_c such that a period-one attractor is established. This assumption does not, of course, imply the reverse: that a constant λ means b_i is stable. A neighborhood is created when the consumer focuses attention on a region along the v_i axis.

As described earlier, the stability of b_i is established by the expectation-experience learning process that the consumer goes through as he or she consumes a specific variety—that is, the WTP(TK) process discussed under the special case. Recall that the value of λ determined whether b_i corresponded to a first-period attractor or higher-period attractors. As explained earlier, we assume that as the consumer moves out of the previous v_i neighborhood along the constraint, inaccuracy commences between expectation and experience. The inaccuracy is assumed to arise because the consumer is purchasing a variety that is unfamiliar to him or her. The initial guessing and learning process must begin anew. It is further assumed that the further the new variety is from the consumer's previous consumption experience, the greater the potential for, and/or the greater the magnitude of, inaccuracy. And, it is assumed that the magnitude of inaccuracy can be represented by the distance between λ and $λ_c$. We assume that learning processes of the consumer are capable of influencing the fold of the expectation-experience function in b_{it} phase space. In other words, learning ultimately influences λ.

5. Learning Patterns and Creating Patterns

We assume that learning reduces confusion for the consumer, that is, reduces the gap between expectation and consumption experience, and that the first step to learning involves pattern recognition. In the present context, learning involves recognition of the pattern between the value of $b_{it=k}$, the expectation associated with a targeted v_i (e.g., $\hat{v}_{i3}$), and the value of $b_{it=k+1}$, the consumption experience derived from that variety. In cases where expectation exceeds experience, disappointment may occur. There is strong evidence of learning from disappointment or negative surprise. In cases where consumption experience exceeds expectation, pleasant-surprise or acquired-taste phenomena may arise.[5]

We also recognize, however, that learning involves not only the recognition of patterns but also the creation of patterns. Learning from consumption experience can lead to change in what is expected, which in turn opens the possibility to a new relationship (or pattern) between expectation and experience.

In addition, recall that we have assumed consumption experience is interpreted by the consumer in terms of self-image. Interaction between the self and its surrounding world is an example of pattern creation. Perception and the creation of categories (of, e.g., varieties and/or commodities), and how these categories serve consumer wants and maintain and/or enhance self-image, are all mental activities involving pattern recognition and pattern creation—and these activities arise (self-organize) within the consumer. These patterns derive through the processes of perception, interpretation, and meaning produced within the consumer, as the consumer goes through the experience of consumption and evaluation of v_i against previous expectations.

In other words, we assume a link exists between pattern recognition and pattern creation, which is a loopy dynamic process that occurs within the consumer. The ability to carry out these learning processes is assumed to be reflected in the magnitude of λ, and the speed with which the consumer can reduce λ to obtain a single fixed-point attractor (accuracy) in expectation-experience phase space.

6. The Relationship of WTP(TA) to WTP(TK)

We return now to the topic of willingness-to-pay-to-acquire, WTP(TA). From our previous remarks regarding movement along the constraint, we now adopt the assumption that, in most cases, the process of "targeting" is required for the consumer to obtain a stable b_i for a new variety outside the previous neighborhood. We assume that only the WTP(TK) process, associated with a targeted variety or targeted neighborhood, is capable of producing a stable constraint, for example, at and around $\hat{v}_{i3}$ in Figure 10.3. In effect, the WTP(TA) process is a more general form of b_i evaluation that subsumes the WTP(TK) process. In other words, when the consumer decides to increase quality (move to a higher variety), he or she initiates the WTP(TA) process by first selecting, or targeting, which variety, or neighborhood, will become the new targeted variety or neighborhood. After the new target is selected, the WTP(TK) evaluation process begins with an initial guessed value for b_i in expectation-experience phase space. The initial guess is the seed. In this context, the relationship of WTP(TA) and WTP(TK) could be described as one where WTP(TK) is nested within WTP(TA). As we shall see later, WTP(TK) is also nested within willingness-to-accept-payment-to-relinquish, WTAP(TR). These relationships can be viewed as nested, hierarchical, and recursive decision making. They are clearly adaptive decision making.

As pointed out earlier, it is conceivable that the consumer jumps from one targeted $\hat{v}_i$ to another (e.g., from $\hat{v}_{i2}$ at m to $\hat{v}_{i3}$ at n in Figure 10.3). The jumping process involves targeting a new $\hat{v}_i$, and then guessing an initial b_i value for that variety—unless that variety was previously consumed, in which case guessing might not be required. Several interesting issues are associated with jumping.

7. Effects of Targeting on the Constraint and Preference Map

We consider first the implications of targeting for the constraint in $v_i x_i$ space. For each point of consumption on the v_i axis (established by the consumer in the process of targeting on a variety), there exists a point on the constraint. If the consumer targets on a neighborhood, instead of on a single variety, then there exists a segment of the constraint. The segment corresponds to the range of the neighborhood along the v_i axis. Following from this, we assume that the constraint does not exist in $v_i x_i$ space in those regions where there have been no targeting and consumption processes undertaken by the consumer. As a result of the jumping process, and the attendant b_i learning and evaluation process, it is now possible that the constraint in $v_i x_i$ space is truncated. In other words, for an individual consumer, we can no longer assume that the constraint exists throughout $v_i x_i$ space. Full constraint simple utility maximization (FCSUM) is no longer possible, unless the "full constraint" is defined as that range of $v_i x_i$ known to the consumer (i.e., the constraint becomes conditional on consumer knowledge and experience). The quality–quantity constraint becomes unique to each individual consumer.

A second implication arises for the preference map. Given the truncated constraint in $v_i x_i$ space, it follows that there would exist corresponding limitations on the objective function. We assume such is the case and that the process of utility maximization in $v_i x_i$ space is correspondingly restricted to the v_i neighborhood; or if variety-specific targeting occurs, utility maximization is restricted to the specific variety. Utility maximization is no longer full-constraint simple, but rather is neighborhood simple, or restricted to the quantity of a specifically targeted variety. The map of consumer preferences, in other words, does not exist throughout $v_i x_i$ space. It exists only within the region(s) where the consumer has consumption experience or is in the process of targeting and learning from consumption experience.

Figure 10.5 **Preference Map Under Single-Variety Targeting**

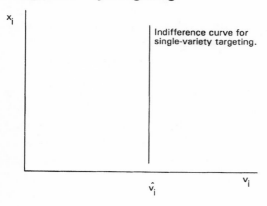

Furthermore, if the consumer has targeted a single variety (e.g., targeted $\hat{v}_{i3}$), then correspondingly it is conceivable that the preference map consists of a single straight line vertical to the targeted variety (i.e., perpendicular to the v_i axis at $\hat{v}_{i3}$). An example is provided in Figure 10.5. Straight line preference maps were also employed by Leontief and Ironmonger. We will have more to say on utility maximization in chapters 11 through 15.

8. WTP, x_i, and p_i

To return to our discussion of willingness-to-pay, note that insofar as the path from m to n is concerned (see Figure 10.3), willingness-to-pay may be measured either by the change in x_i in v_ix_i space and/or by the change in p_i in v_ip_i price space. In the case of WTP(TA), the payment can be broken into two parts. As shown in Figure 10.3, the path from m to n may be seen as a movement from m to m' and then from m' to n. The movement from m to m' involves a reduction of x_i from x_{i3} to x_{i2}. This payment is equivalent to that which would be obtained exclusively by the WTP(TK) process (see Figure 8.6). The movement from m' to n involves a reduction of x_i from x_{i2} to x_{i1}. This payment, as we explained earlier, may involve an iterative adjustment

of b_i to reach the point n—that is, a WTP(TK) process that is focused at $\hat{v}_{i3}$ and results in the point n.

The reduction in x_i represents the payment made by the consumer to acquire $\hat{v}_{i3}$. The increased willingness-to-pay, revealed by the increase in b_i, is paid in x_i. The change in $\hat{v}_i$, b_i, and x_i may affect expenditure or budgeted funds for the ith commodity, as well as the expenditure on other commodities. These conditions require additional comment.

9. Targeting, Separability, and Decentralization

Presently, we assume that targeting on v_i, and the iterative evaluation of b_i (with attendant changes in x_i), are consistent with the requirements of separability within the utility function and decentralization of the budget. Separability within the utility function may be assumed necessary for consumer decision making to focus, or target, on a single variety or neighborhood, and ignore all other varieties or neighborhoods.[6] Note that depending upon the type of separability, there may be no substitution of v_i (among v_i) taking place when the consumer goes through the WTP(TK) process on a targeted v_i. Under some circumstances, substitution of v_i within a neighborhood may be permitted.[7]

Targeting on $\hat{v}_i$ in the preference map must be accompanied by targeting of budgeted expenditures for $\hat{v}_i$ in the constraint. Budgeted expenditures (p_ix_i) for the targeted variety, $\hat{v}_i$, are required in order to span v_ix_i space; however, the spanning of that space must not disturb budgeted expenditures for commodities other than commodity i. In other words, all other commodities j ($j \neq i$) must be invariant to change in v_ix_i space. The invariance is established through separability in the utility function and decentralization in the constraint. Decentralization of the constraint in

$v_i x_i$ space assures that the impact of change in b_i (for a targeted v_i or targeted v_i neighborhood) is isolated to the expenditure on $\hat{v}_i$, or on the targeted neighborhood.

To have decentralization of the targeted v_i from all other v_i, the expenditure on $\hat{v}_i$ must be "budgeted",[8] or set aside so as to not allow variation in expenditure on $\hat{v}_i$ to affect other v_i.[9] For example, a change in b_i, when a_i is held constant (which we have assumed under repackaging), will change the p_i and x_i that correspond to $\hat{v}_i$; therefore, the budgeted expenditure for $\hat{v}_i$ might be affected. If expenditure on $\hat{v}_i$ is affected, not only may other v_i be affected[10], but the budgeted expenditure for commodity i may be affected and, therefore, the decentralizability of x_i within $x_i x_j x_h$ space. To eliminate any effects on other v_i, as well as on other commodities, we assume the budget constraint in $v_i x_i$ space can be decentralized on $\hat{v}_i$ or its neighborhood.

Decentralization of the constraint on the targeted v_i is another example of nesting. In this case, nesting a subspace for $\hat{v}_i$ within $v_i x_i$ space, which, in turn, is nested within $x_i x_j x_h$ space. In effect, we have a hierarchy. Separability of $\hat{v}_i$ within the utility function, and the decentralization of budgeted expenditure on $\hat{v}_i$ within the constraint, are both necessary so as to allow the process of targeting and to employ the attractor model. As regards targeting and the consumer learning process under WTP(TK), the expectation-experience phase space is nested within a point—the targeted $\hat{v}_i$ or $\hat{v}_i$ neighborhood—along the constraint in $v_i x_i$ space, and $v_i x_i$ space is nested within the constraint in $x_i x_j x_h$ space.

10. Other Paths to Higher Quality

If we return now to Figure 10.2, we can proceed, in rather straightforward fashion, to examine the remaining paths, namely, paths (2), (3), and (4). Path (2) is ostensibly the same as the movement from m' to n in Figure 10.3, and the explanation of that movement is, for the most part, adequate for path (2). The only additional explanation required is that path (2) assumes no change in b_i. In other words, path (2) is analogous to the movement from m' to n in Figure 10.3, where the "reach" of b_i at m' (in Figure 10.3) is adequate for a path that extends from the point m' to the point n. The neighborhood reaches or extends to the end of the path. The constraint does not shift or change convexity, because b_i does not change. If b_i does not reach to the end of the path, then the WTP(TK) process must be initiated for the new targeted v_i at the end of the path. Furthermore, if b_i does not reach, then the constraint may start breaking-up as the consumer moves out along path (2). If this occurs, however, we do not have path (2).

11. The Special Case of Fixed Quantity and Variable Quality

Path (3) of Figure 10.2 presents an alternative version of the special case. In the case of path (3), the constraint shifts outward and upward, reflecting a downward adjustment in b_i. The adjustment occurs through the WTP(TA) process. In this case, however, instead of an offsetting increase in x_i to compensate for the reduction in b_i, the consumer now chooses to increase v_i, while remaining at the former $\hat{x}_i$. This represents an important case; especially common is the case where $\hat{x}_i = 1$. Path (3) allows us to examine the process of upgrading the quality of a single item: for example, the purchase of a home, an automobile, a category of household appliance, other consumer durables, and so forth.

This type of targeting (e.g., $\hat{x}_i = 1$) is analogous to the special case for $\hat{v}_i$, only here the target is "quantity." Invariance now exists with respect to "quantity," instead of "quality." However, unlike the case of variable x_i with fixed $\hat{v}_i$, in the case of fixed x_i and variable v_i, our quantity measure is no longer isoquality. In this alternative version of the special case we have an iso-quantity (or constant) "quantity." Under these circumstances, a repackaging approach to variable quality proves once again to be a useful concept. The repackaging approach is necessary for the consumer to make comparisons of different varieties, which is to say, to compare different levels of quality across a fixed quantity.

12. Further Comments on the Basic Package

To utilize a repackaging approach, it is necessary to identify a "basic package." In the present context, the question is which combination of $v_i x_i$ represents the basic package? For most circumstances we will assume $\hat{x}_i = 1$, although cases may arise where this assumption could be relaxed. To continue, against which "package" or "bundle" of $v_i x_i$ does the consumer make comparisons, as though in a process of adding and/or subtracting various combinations of quality characteristics (the e_{ih}), in order to compare the merits of alternative packages? Consistent with our earlier discussion of "quantity" (see chapter 4), we assume the basic package is that v_i for which $v_i = 0$ and $a_i = \phi$, where ϕ is some constant. For most empirical work we assume ϕ is non-negative. This assumption precludes cases where $(v_i = 0) < v_i^-$. (See Figure 4.5.)

From the point of view of an individual consumer, a second yet related question concerns whether there could exist more than one basic package. Our model would suggest that, under some circumstances, multiple basic packages could arise. For each value of $\phi > 0$, given $v_i = 0$, there exists a basic package. If however, at some future time, the consumer should choose a different $v_i = 0$ (possibly due to technological change and/or the elimination of the previous basic package), then there would arise a new basic package. Note, however, that at any point in time, we assume the existence of only one basic package. As discussed earlier, the basic package is a relative concept, but one that is necessary for the consumer to be able to compare and rank varieties.

Another question, related to the second one, concerns whether the basic package is stable for "reasonable" time periods. If consumers change the basic package "frequently," what factors contribute to such change? Some possible sources for change could be changes in the consumer, the introduction of new alternative varieties (especially new substitutable varieties brought about by technological change), elimination of the previous basic package, and so forth. The basic package is, in many respects, similar to the base period in a price index, and the criteria for change of base periods in price indices might apply equally well to changes in a basic package.

With the numeraire of the basic package, it is possible for an individual consumer to make comparisons, such as upgrading the quality of one's home, under the $x_i = 1$ case. In our model, however, it may be possible for the consumer to make comparisons without knowledge of the basic package. For example, consumers might simply compare packages, none of which are the numeraire or basic package. Or, they may change the basic package so often as to render it meaningless. Either way, such behavior on the part of consumers could lead them to cycling patterns of quality assessment.[11]

As suggested earlier, trade-offs and complementarities may exist among the quality characteristics, e_{ih}, between two or more varieties. For our purposes, it is assumed that the consumer is capable of weighing the e_{ih} within each bundle (variety), that the consumer can also evaluate and compare bundles, and that the consumer can evaluate trade-offs between bundles, such that all varieties (at least within a neighborhood) can be accounted for and rank-ordered.[12] The ranking of varieties is the ordering that exists along the v_i axis. We assume the v_i axis serves as an index of rank ordered bundles of e_{ih}, where each bundle represents a variety. It should be noted, however, that these assumptions introduce the possibility, indeed the likelihood, that the v_i axis is different for each consumer! This condition further complicates empirical work on variable quality. We will have more to say on this topic in chapters 13 through 15.

It is assumed that for each consumer there exists a basic package of characteristics, a ''basic'' bundle of e_{ih}, which serves as the origin ($v_i = 0$) or basis for the ordering. The basic package is equivalent to a numeraire in a repackaging model. The existence of the basic package also facilitates elimination of the cycling problem, which could otherwise arise along the v_i axis. As stated earlier, however, cycling remains possible for individual consumers.

Finally, in line with our earlier discussion of v_i neighborhoods, a corollary assumption is that any ordering along v_i axes exists only within neighborhoods where consumers have consumption experience.

For each individual consumer, the basic package is assumed to be invariant over varieties within a single commodity, or at least within a neighborhood of that commodity. As explained previously, the basic package can be viewed as a numeraire within an aggregator function. In this sense, the higher v_i are aggregated on the basic package and the process of aggrega-

tion reflects the ordering, or index, which is the v_i axis. Finally, by way of summary, we have assumed that the entire process of v_i aggregation over an invariant basic package is an activity nested within a commodity, the ith commodity, and we have assumed that commodity to be invariant to changes in all other commodities, and that the other commodities are correspondingly invariant to changes in the ith commodity (i.e., strict separability). As discussed earlier, separability assumptions place restrictions on the substitutability of commodities. These restrictions can be relaxed later.

To return to our discussion of consumer behavior along path (3) of Figure 10.2, we assume that the consumer must either (a) have identified a basic package and constructed an ordering of v_i on that package[13] or (b) that cycling among v_i, for a fixed x_i, is permitted. Acceptance of cycling of v_i should not appear too unreasonable, especially in light of the roles of perception and learning in our model, and the otherwise strong assumptions required of human memory under a non-cycling hypothesis. Given current rates of technological innovation and the not uncommon shortsightedness of consumer decision making, it is conceivable that some consumers are unaware of their cycling patterns. The reader is again reminded of the similarity between Arrow's voting paradox, cycling of v_i, and a period-two attractor.[14] Note that many comments regarding path (3) also apply to the other paths. The requirements of the basic package, however, arise most directly to the case of fixed x_i and variable v_i.

Finally, we assume that movement along path (3), from the point m in Figure 10.2, may involve the WTP(TK) process. We make this assumption to assure there is a new, stable solution at the end of the path. In other words, the b_i adjustment process must establish $b_i = b_i^*$ for the new $\hat{v}_i$ at the end of the path. Only if the new b_i stabilizes at a value such that $x_i = \hat{x}_i$ (the original fixed value of $\hat{x}_i$) do we have path (3). The requirement to use the WTP(TK) process for movement along path (3) applies only to cases where the path extends beyond the original $\hat{v}_i$ neighborhood around m. Under such circumstances, the original b_i may be inaccurate and, therefore, necessitate the reevaluation and adjustment of b_i for the new $\hat{v}_i$.

It should be noted that there is no process comparable to WTP(TK) for $\hat{x}_i$ (as there is in the special case for $\hat{v}_i$) because $b_i = (\partial p_i / \partial v_i)$, that is, there is no x_i in b_i, $b_i \neq (\partial p_i / \partial x_i)$. Recall that Houthakker has a_i serve as the price of quantity, or the price of x_i. Change in a_i could serve as an indicator of consumer willingness-to-pay for x_i, or what we might call change in the consumer's willingness-to-pay for the basic package. To this point in development of the model, we have assumed a_i fixed, and the only dimension of willingness-to-pay that we investigate applies to the quality of varieties above the basic package, or b_i for $v_i > v_i = 0$. We will consider variation in a_i later.

13. Payments Under WTP and Higher Quality

In our previous discussion of WTP(TA) as applied to paths (1) and (2) (Figure 10.2) the payment component of willingness-to-pay was measured in terms of reduction in x_i, either for the case where the consumer remained at $\hat{v}_i$ (the special case), or the case where the consumer shifted to a higher v_i. Note that in terms of the x_i payment (reduction in x_i), the payment is smaller for path (2) than for path (1), for any higher value of v_i. This result reflects the relatively higher b_i, or WTP(TA), behind path (1) than is associated with path (2). For path (3) of Figure 10.2, the payment, in terms of x_i, is zero. As noted earlier, for

paths higher than path (2), for example, paths (3) and (4), b_i is lower relative to the b_i of path (2). This phenomenon reflects a lower willingness-to-pay for v_i higher than the previous v_i at m in Figure 10.2. It is usually presumed, however, that consumers will prefer higher quality. Paths (3) and (4) do not support this presumption. The lower b_i of these paths might reflect either consumer disappointment with, or satiation toward, levels of quality (varieties) higher than the v_i at m in Figure 10.2.

Earlier, we stated that for path (3) the payment, in terms of x_i, was zero. For path (3) there is no reduction in x_i. Furthermore, via path (3), v_i has increased. How are these results understood in terms of willingness-to-pay? In other words, what is the payment?

Recall from our discussion of the special case, where a single v_i is targeted, that it is possible to have circumstances where the reverse of "payment" might arise. The reverse of payment, or a negative payment, can be viewed as a "bribe," or some form of compensation to induce the consumer to continue to consume some specified level of quality. (See chapter 8, section 7.) In the special case the consumer is compensated or bribed to remain at $\hat{v}_i$. In our present case, path (3), the payment may again be interpreted as a bribe, or incentive. In this case, however, it is an incentive, or negative payment, to remain at $\hat{x}_i$. In the x_i targeted case, any payment (positive or negative) is reflected by a change in p_i in $v_i p_i$ price space. In the present case (path 3) the reduction in b_i results in a lower p_i.

The direction of path (3) is consistent with the idea that, under some circumstances, the consumer may not want higher quality—at least not within the ith commodity. The lower value of b_i (as contrasted with, e.g., path 2) reflects a lower willingness-to-pay for quality higher than the v_i at m in Figure 10.2. This may arise because the consumer has decided to seek higher quality in some other commodity. As discussed earlier, such behavior must be supported in decentralized budgets. Decision making of this nature (between commodities i and j) requires, however, relaxation of our separability and decentralization requirements.

As regards path (4) of Figure 10.2, WTP(TA) is lower, as reflected in reduced b_i, than the b_i corresponding to path (3). In this case, however, the compensation or bribe is larger and is measured as an increase in x_i, as well as reduction in p_i. As with path (3), behavior of this sort might indicate that the consumer is not interested in levels of quality higher than the v_i at m, at least not within the ith commodity. For the consumer, the variety at the point m may be the highest acceptable level of quality. The consumer may prefer, instead, to target higher levels of quality in some other commodity or commodities. Such behavior would be consistent with, for example, Ironmonger's model of satiation and the rank-ordering of consumer wants (see chapter 6).

14. Demand Reservation Price and Demand Maintenance Price

Of particular interest, regarding paths (3) and (4), is the introduction of a new type of demand price. Previously, when discussing an increase in b_i, we noted that such decision making on the part of consumers was analogous to an increase in the consumer's "demand reservation price" (see chapter 8, section 6). In the case where b_i has decreased, however, the concept of "payment" is inappropriate.

A decrease in b_i is analogous to a decrease in the demand reservation price, a decrease in willingness-to-pay. Relative to the previous magnitude of willingness-to-pay, the new payment is smaller, and the

change in payment is negative. Such change in willingness-to-pay, or $db_i < 0$, may elicit compensation or a bribe. In other words, for the consumer to be willing to continue to purchase the same variety, after willingness-to-pay has decreased, he or she must be compensated or bribed—that is, given a greater quantity of the variety and/ or a reduced price, p_i. In similar fashion, on some occasions, for the consumer to become "interested" in some higher level of quality, for example, higher than the consumer's targeted v_i neighborhood, it may be necessary to compensate or otherwise make attractive, the higher variety.

In terms of demand theory, a decrease in b_i and receipt of compensation, or a "bribe," may be viewed as the counterpart to a demand reservation price, a price we shall call the "demand maintenance price." A demand maintenance price can be defined as the price required to assure that the consumer continues to purchase the same variety, even though he or she has experienced a reduction in willingness-to-pay for that variety. The demand maintenance price can also be defined as the price required to assure that the consumer "select" a higher level of quality. Compensation is necessary in cases where the consumer would not otherwise chose to "acquire" the higher quality—that is, not purchase a variety higher than those found in his or her v_i neighborhood.

In $v_i x_i$ space the compensation or bribe is an increase in x_i given to the consumer; it is, in effect, a type of volume discount. In $v_i p_i$ price space the compensation or bribe is a decrease in p_i, given a_i constant. The combined concepts of demand reservation price (DRP) and demand maintenance price (DMP) provide a more flexible and in-depth consideration of the processes necessary to determine a consumer's willingness-to-pay. The combined forces of DRP and DMP, through the "higgling and bargaining'' (Smith 1776/1952, p. 13) of prices by both producers and consumers, are assumed necessary to ''accurately'' determine the consumer's ''true'' willingness-to-pay. As will be discussed shortly, unlike most models of consumer behavior, our model introduces interaction between consumers and producers in $v_i x_i$ consumption space, in addition to $x_i p_i$ market space. The insights gained from a deeper, more downward nested level of interaction between consumers and producers are considerable.

Consistent with our earlier comments on consumption experience and v_i neighborhoods along the constraint, the price line in $v_i p_i$ space, likewise, may exist only where the consumer has consumption experience, and it may be truncated and/or contain kinks. We will have more to say on this topic later. We will also have more to say regarding demand maintenance prices and consumer demand.

To return to Figure 10.2, note that across paths (1) through (4) the WTP(TA) process indicates that for paths below the original constraint, the consumer has changed b_i such that $db_i > 0$, which reveals a new demand reservation price. For paths above the original constraint, the consumer has changed b_i such that $db_i < 0$, which reveals a demand maintenance price. For a path that remains on the original constraint, that is, path (2), there is neither a new demand reservation nor maintenance price. In this case, the original b_i remains accurate, no new evaluation of v_i or the v_i neighborhood is necessary. As presented in our model, the concepts of demand reservation price and demand maintenance price are relative to the price of some previously consumed $\hat{v}_i$.

Specifically, such ''prices'' are relative to previous b_i and v_i. As an aside, note that the introduction of a demand maintenance price raises an interesting question regarding consumer surplus: Does the existence of a demand maintenance price imply zero (or negative) consumer surplus?

To return to our discussion of Willingness-to-Pay-to-Acquire, note that across all of the paths illustrated in Figure 10.2, WTP(TA) declines as one proceeds from path (1) to path (4). Figure 10.6 provides another illustration. In Figure 10.6, $\hat{v}_{i2}$ represents the initial variety. The point m is analogous to m in Figure 10.2. The variety $\hat{v}_{i3}$ represents some higher level of quality, higher than $\hat{v}_{i2}$. In Figure 10.6 we assume the b_i evaluation process is stable for each path toward $\hat{v}_{i3}$—that is, the end point of each path represents a different but stable value for the b_i evaluation of $\hat{v}_{i3}$. There can exist, however, an infinite number of paths that lead from the point m to any point on the vertical line perpendicular to $\hat{v}_{i3}$. Each path would correspond to a b_i value between zero and 1. The four paths illustrate the possible options. For high values of b_i, the consumer pursues paths such as path (1). For successively lower (stabilized) values of b_i, the consumer pursues such paths as (3) or (4). In other words, the various paths for WTP(TA) reflect a b_i adjustment process on a targeted (higher) v_i similar to the adjustment process we explained earlier regarding WTP(TK) for a fixed v_i (i.e., the special case). When b_i stabilizes at some value $(0 \le b_i \le 1)$, then a specific path is established.

If b_i is not stable for varieties higher than v_{i2}, the constraint breaks up as discussed earlier. See Figure 10.4 for an illustration of a constraint breaking up.

15. Willingness-to-Accept-Payment-to-Relinquish

Willingness-to-Accept-Payment-to-Relinquish, WTAP(TR), presumes the consumer is already at a given level of quality of the

Figure 10.6 **Willingness-to-Pay for Higher Quality**

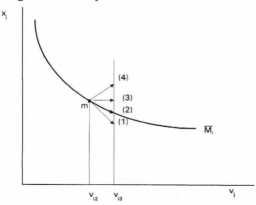

Figure 10.7 **Willingness-to-Pay for Lower Quality**

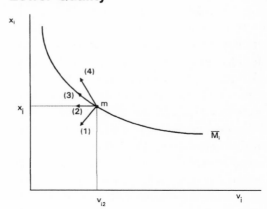

commodity, call it variety $\hat{v}_{i2}$. The WTAP(TR) seeks to determine the magnitude of payment required for the consumer to willingly relinquish $\hat{v}_{i2}$ and accept a lower level of quality in its place.[15] In terms of a figure comparable to Figure 10.2, WTAP(TR) investigates change in v_i such that the new v_i is lower than $\hat{v}_{i2}$. An illustration is provided in Figure 10.7.

Much of what was previously explained regarding WTP(TK) and WTP(TA) applies to the process of WTAP(TR). As before, the payment or compensation is manifest through change in b_i, which, in turn, is reflected in change in x_i and/or p_i.

Paths (1) through (4) in Figure 10.7 cover four general categories of WTAP (TR). As with WTP(TA), movement to v_i lower than $\hat{v}_{i2}$ presumes the consumer targets on a $v_i < \hat{v}_{i2}$. Once a lower v_i has been targeted, the consumer proceeds through the WTP(TK) process. As before, this process involves evaluating and adjusting b_i through learning, which arises from consumption experience. If the learning process is accurate, such that expectations equal experience, then b_i becomes stable for the new (lower) v_i.

If the b_i at m is accurate, and has a neighborhood that extends to the new

lower v_i, then the consumer may proceed along path (3) in Figure 10.7. The payment along paths (3) and (4) is an increase in x_i. In other words, as discussed earlier, the payment is a bribe or compensation, which is necessary for the consumer to relinquish $\hat{v}_{i2}$ and accept a lower v_i. Under these circumstances, the b_i corresponding to paths (3) and (4) reveal demand maintenance prices. Note that b_i is constant for path (3) and b_i is reduced for path (4)—that is, b_i is lower for path (4) than for path (3).

Path (2) of Figure 10.7 is analogous to path (3) in Figure 10.2 for WTP(TA), and the explanation of that path can be utilized here. Instead of a decrease in b_i for a higher v_i with x_i constant (path 3 of Figure 10.2), there is an increase in b_i for a lower v_i with x_i constant. The increase in b_i, given a_i constant, means p_i is higher for the lower v_i. The following explanation of path (1) applies as well to path (2).

Path (1) of Figure 10.7 is analogous to path (4) in Figure 10.2. Here, however, the consumer, after consumption of a lower v_i, decides to increase b_i—that is, the b_i at the original $\hat{v}_{i2}$ is lower than the b_i at the new (lower) v_i. Under WTP(TK), the increase in b_i (at the new lower v_i) has a payment that is revealed as a reduction in x_i and an increase in p_i. The increase in b_i, relative to the b_i at $\hat{v}_{i2}$, translates as a higher demand reservation price for the lower v_i! The explanation of such decision making on the part of the consumer is essentially the same as that which applied to path (4) of the WTP(TA) case. In the case of path (1) of WTAP(TR), the original variety, $\hat{v}_{i2}$, has become a level of quality higher than currently desired by the consumer. It is assumed that the consumer's assessment of quality has changed. In the present case, the consumer would prefer, and be willing to pay more to obtain, a v_i lower than the previous $\hat{v}_{i2}$. Such behavior might be unusual, but in our model it cannot be ruled out as an option to consumers. This is not the only explanation for this behavior. We will have more to say on this matter in chapters 13 through 15.

Similar to WTP(TA), paths (1) through (4) in Figure 10.7 assume that all new b_i values are stable. If they are not, breakup of the constraint may occur.

With these remarks, we conclude our discussion of willingness-to-pay associated with consumer determination of b_i.

Chapter 11
Consumer–Producer Interaction and the Market

1. Summary of Consumer Perception and the Constraint

In contrast to the constraint in the Houthakker model and in most of microeconomic theory, our model assumes consumer perception, learning, and other decision-making processes influence the position, convexity, and length of the constraint, as well as influence the preference map. Such phenomena occur in quality-quantity consumption space. The constraint employed in our model is the original Houthakker constraint: $M = (a_i + b_i v_i)x_i$. Consumer influence upon the constraint is accomplished primarily through consumer determination of the parameter, b_i. The consumer may also influence a_i. Our model introduces consumer perception of quality as the perception of each variety, and/or perception of a v_i neighborhood. The model introduces willingness-to-pay for quality through the parameter b_i, which may be defined as a weight that registers consumer willingness-to-pay for a single variety, or for varieties within a neighborhood. This redefinition of b_i is consistent with the interpretation of Houthakker's b_i as, $b_i = (dp_i/dv_i)$. The magnitude of payment, however, may be registered by changes in either x_i and/or p_i.

Earlier, we argued that b_i, for $b_i \neq 1$, is indeterminate in the Houthakker model. We noted that a_i also is indeterminate away from the basic price system. In an effort to resolve these matters, we investigated a number of options. One approach was to introduce consumer determination of b_i. Consumer determination of b_i, however, allows the consumer to influence the constraint. Consumer determination of b_i also opened the possibility that the constraint could become truncated and potentially unstable. More specifically, when the consumer determines b_i, through the expectation and consumption-experience process—focused on a targeted variety, or $\hat{v}_i$ neighborhood—we discover that it is possible for the constraint to exist only as a point or as a neighborhood around $\hat{v}_i$. An illustration of a truncated constraint is provided in Figure 11.1. Finally, in our model the constraint exists at a point in time, or over some time interval. The constraint is stable as long as b_i is stable—that is, as long as b_i has a period-one attractor.

Across time, b_i may change from one stable value to another. When time is introduced, the constraint becomes dynamic and may exhibit patterns of shifting segments of various lengths and convexity. The dynamic constraint reflects change in b_i and in v_i neighborhoods across time. The pattern of shifting constraints may reflect b_i adjustments under conditions of WTP(TK), WTP(TA), and/or WTAP(TR), depending upon whether or not the con-

Figure 11.1 **Truncated Constraint in Quality–Quantity Space**

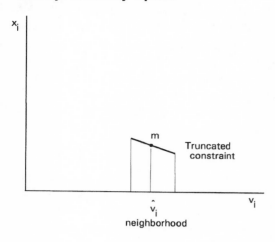

2. Producer Determination of b_i

For an individual producer to complete a transaction with a consumer, we assume another type of constraint exists in the v_i neighborhood of the consumer. We identify this other constraint as a constraint established through producer determination of b_i. We call this constraint the Producer-Determined Constraint, or PDC. Similarly, from now on we label the constraint, which is perceived by the consumer, the Consumer-Determined Constraint, or CDC.

In $v_i x_i$ space we assume that only on that portion of the producer's constraint (PDC), which lies on or above the consumer's constraint (CDC), can transactions occur between an individual consumer and producer. This phenomenon reintroduces the problem identified earlier by Frederick Waugh and Hans Brems: specifically, the potential for disagreement between producer and consumer over the perception, assessment, and evaluation of quality, and the possibility that exchange might not occur as a result of these differences. Here, the differences are manifest in the constraints generated by the parties to the transaction.[1] In subsequent chapters we discuss the interaction of consumer and producer constraints. For now, we focus on producer determination of b_i and producer influence on the constraint in $v_i x_i$ space.

In chapters 4 and 7 we discussed the problem of indeterminacy of b_i, an innovative parameter introduced by Houthakker in his constraint: $M = (a_i + b_i v_i)x_i$. To this point, we have focused on consumer determination of b_i. We now symbolize consumer determination of b_i as b_i^c. In this section, we discuss producer determination of b_i, which will be shown as b_i^p. (See chapter 7 for an earlier discussion of producer influence on b_i.)

In the case of b_i determination by producers, we assume b_i^p is a weight that pro-

sumer changes v_i. The nature of the b_i adjustment process—whether there are single-period or multiple-period attractors—influences the pattern of the constraints.

Although at a point in time only a single constraint exists, when the constraint becomes dynamic, the model is capable of producing, across time, numerous constraints in $v_i x_i$ consumption space. This phenomenon occurs for a single consumer. At any point in time, only a single constraint is operative. At subsequent times, other constraints may become operative.

For any individual constraint to exist, it is necessary that the consumer be able to purchase and consume the targeted variety, or varieties, from within a $\hat{v}_i$ neighborhood. In some instances, the purchase and consumption of some varieties may not be possible. We should note that the opportunity to purchase and consume a variety, at some point in time, does not necessarily guarantee repetition of that opportunity at a subsequent time. These results have implications for the attractor model previously discussed. Under such circumstances, v_i neighborhoods may become more useful than the restriction to individually targeted varieties, $\hat{v}_i$.

ducers assign to varieties v_i, $v_i^- \leq v_i \leq v_i^+$. Recall that we assume $b_i = (dp_i/dv_i)$, or that b_i adjusts price, p_i, for the quality level of each variety. Heretofore, this evaluation process has been from the point of view of the consumer, and interpreted as the consumer's willingness-to-pay for different varieties of the ith commodity. The consumer evaluation process was assumed based on consumer expectation and consumption experience with any given variety, or v_i neighborhood.

In the case of the producer, b_i^p is assumed to reflect producer estimates of consumer willingness-to-pay for a variety, or varieties within a v_i neighborhood, of the ith commodity. It is further assumed that producer estimates of consumer willingness-to-pay may be stratified by consumer income cohorts. At this juncture, for purposes of simplification we assume that the M_i estimates utilized by producers are accurate (i.e., producers accurately estimate consumer income). We also assume a_i is the same for both producers and consumers. (We will have more to say on both of these assumptions in subsequent chapters.) As a result of these assumptions, the only differences between the two constraints in $v_i x_i$ space arise from differences in b_i^p, b_i^c, and in the level of quality, v_i. Empirical estimation of these phenomena will require examination of the relationship of consumer income to v_i neighborhoods and to b_i^c, or the relationship of M_i to b_i^c, controlled for v_i neighborhoods. We examine some of these and other empirical issues in chapters 12 through 15 and in Appendix B.

It is assumed that each producer is prepared to sell numerous varieties of the ith commodity. Producer estimates of consumer willingness-to-pay may be based on market research, such as consumer surveys, case studies, focus groups, and so forth. If markets are segmented, these estimates may differ from one market to another.

It is possible that $b_i^p \neq b_i^c$ for any given variety, or neighborhood of a variety. This is the Waugh-Brems problem alluded to earlier. As we will discover, however, transactions between producers and consumers may occur if $b_i^p \neq b_i^c$, as long as $b_i^p \leq b_i^c$, for targeted $\hat{v}_i$ or $\hat{v}_i$ neighborhoods.

As in the case of the consumer, b_i^p determined by the producer may vary across time. It is also possible that an expectation-experience learning process, as previously explained for the consumer, applies as well to producers. Similarly, the attractor model, with some redefinition of variables, may also be applied to producers. In the case of the producer, however, we assume the expectation-experience process is based on producer expectations and experience regarding sales of targeted varieties, or of varieties in a targeted neighborhood.

The accuracy of producer sales "expectation" in relationship to sales "experience" depends on the accuracy of producers in estimating willingness-to-pay by consumers for a given variety or neighborhood of a variety—that is, how closely b_i^p approximates b_i^c for a targeted $\hat{v}_i$, or $\hat{v}_i$ neighborhood. This may be viewed as a loopy system in which producers learn, and as they learn, b_i^p approaches the target, b_i^c. Two versions of attractor analysis are applicable here: one for consumers and another for producers. The interaction of these two dynamic processes may, in turn, lead to complex or emergent behavior, conducted within markets for the ith commodity.

If the b_i^p based on producer estimation of consumer willingness-to-pay is inaccurate, the inaccuracy will be reflected in disparity between sales expectation (on the part of a producer) and sales experience. The greater the disparity between sales expectation and sales experience, the greater the likelihood of two-cycle or higher-cycle attractors. The possibility of chaos (con-

Figure 11.2 **Transactions in Quality-Quantity Space**

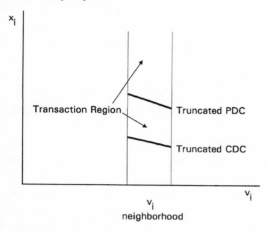

fused decision making on the part of producers) also exists, in which case the number of transactions between consumers and producers may fall. For the most part, however, we assume producers learn relatively quickly, such that b_i^p approaches b_i^c.

As in the case of the consumer, b_i^p may be viewed as a shift parameter for a single constraint over the entire range of v_i (v_i^- to v_i^+), or for a truncated constraint targeted on a single $\hat{v}_i$ or on a $\hat{v}_i$ neighborhood. If producer determination of b_i is seen as a single constraint across all v_i, in order for at least one transaction to occur between the producer and a consumer, the producer-determined constraint (PDC) must lie on or above at least one consumer-determined constraint (CDC). Where the PDC does not lie on or above at least one CDC, no transactions occur for that producer.

Finally, if we assume a producer's constraint exists over only a portion of the range v_i^- to v_i^+ (i.e., it exists in a v_i neighborhood), then for transactions to occur within the neighborhood of the truncated producer's constraint, the PDC must lie on or above at least one consumer constraint in the same v_i neighborhood. The nature of these constraint relationships has to do with the conditions necessary for transactions to occur between producers and consumers. Transactions occur only along PDC that lie within the v_i range of consumer constraints, and where the PDCs, or portions thereof, lie on or above CDCs. In other words, transactions may occur along the PDC where $b_i^p \leq b_i^c$, and where the b_i correspond to the same time period. An illustration of this condition is provided in Figure 11.2.

If, at a point in time, the PDC lies everywhere below the CDC, transactions will not occur between that producer and consumer. Note that in Figure 11.2, a transaction region has been identified. The region is the area on and above the CDC. For a transaction to occur, it is necessary that the PDC pass through the transaction region. Transactions occur only on the PDC, but the CDC identifies the portion of the producer's constraint, if any, where transactions might occur.

3. Refinements on Utility Maximization and the Selection of Quality

Utility maximization, either FCSUM or NSUM, may determine where on the producer's constraint a transaction will occur—unless targeting is applied to a specific $\hat{v}_i$. Neighborhood simple utility maximization (NSUM) may be employed to determine v_i within a neighborhood. If consumer targeting on a specific v_i is involved, neither form of utility maximization (in terms of determination of v_i) is applicable. Unless quantity, x_i, has also been targeted, a process we will call double-targeting, utility maximization would still apply to quantity of the targeted variety. In other words, utility maximization may apply to consumer decision making in $x_i x_j$ space, once quality has been determined. As before, in the case of a targeted variety, separability of the utility function to that variety identifies the variety to be transacted; however, a transaction will not occur unless $b_i^p \leq b_i^c$ for that variety.

Constrained utility maximization in quality-quantity space cannot occur unless a constraint exists. In our model, however, we have two versions of constraint: one as perceived by the consumer, and another as presented by the producer. Furthermore, even with the existence of a PDC and a CDC, transactions will not occur in $v_i x_i$ space unless the producer's constraint passes through the transaction region established by the consumer-determined constraint (i.e., unless $b_i^p \leq b_i^c$ within the transaction region).

The constraint against which consumers may maximize utility, or on which they may target, is the PDC, given that it is equal to or above the consumer-determined constraint. If a portion of the producer constraint lies below the CDC, transactions will not occur along that portion. The portion of the producer constraint where $b_i^p \leq b_i^c$ is the effective constraint. The preference map for targeting on a single variety may be a variation of the Leontief perfect-complements map or an Ironmonger map. Unless quantity is also targeted, for example, $\hat{x}_i$ as in path (3) under WTP(TA) or path (2) in WTAP(TR), utility maximization may be used to determine the optimal quantity of the variety. If both v_i and x_i are targeted (double-targeting), then no form of utility maximization is applicable, and the preference map becomes a point in $v_i x_i$ space (i.e., discrete choice). Furthermore, such a point can be attained only if $b_i^p \leq b_i^c$ at that point. It is also worth noting that in the case of double-targeting, no transaction regions exist—unless saving and/or resale options exist for the consumer. A transaction may occur at the point, depending on whether the point in $v_i x_i$ space is feasible (i.e., $b_i^p \leq b_i^c$).

In addition to the issues of utility maximization and targeting in $v_i x_i$ space, there are issues of utility maximization and targeting in characteristics space. As to the mapping of e_{ih} space to $v_i x_i$ space, recall from chapters 3 and 4 that our model assumes the e_{ih} are orthogonal to the v_i axis.

As regards the processes of utility maximization or targeting in $v_i x_i$ space, we assume the consumer has preferences regarding clusters of e_{ih}. Some e_{ih} may not register in the conscious decision making of the consumer, and other e_{ih} may have to exceed some threshold values before they become "significant" for decision making. As far as our model is concerned, we assume that some, but not necessarily all, characteristics enter the consumer preference map, and therefore might influence either the process of utility maximization or targeting. Further, we assume it is possible that variation could exist between e_{ih} within a specific variety, $\hat{v}_i$. In other words, not all e_{ih} are capable of changing v_i. This phenomenon may be true for both consumers and producers.

In our model it is assumed that consumers have preferences over varieties and that they are able to rank-order those preferences. (See, however, our earlier remarks on cycling of the basic package and v_i ordering.) The configuration of e_{ih} associated with individual v_i is not necessarily important to our model. What is important are the "clusters" of e_{ih}, which clusters are labeled "varieties" in our model, and consumer decision making regarding those varieties.

The configuration of e_{ih} in the basic package, under a repackaging model, is also unimportant to our model. The existence of a basic package is important, but, as discussed earlier, the basic package might change across time, across consumers, and even within a single consumer. Finally, in our model there may be differences of opinion between consumers and producers as regards the configuration of e_{ih} in the basic package.

4. Consumer and Producer Interaction

At first glance it may appear that, under these conditions, the frequency of transactions between producer and consumer would be quite low. This result might hold for transactions between any individual producer and a specific consumer. With an increase in the number of both producers and consumers, however, the likelihood of transactions increases.

For a producer-determined constraint to exist for an individual consumer, either many producers must provide the alternative varieties, v_i, that the consumer might purchase, or a few producers (conceivably one) provide many varieties. The existence of many varieties in the ith commodity market is essential for the consumer to perceive them, purchase them (a transaction), and then consume them. It is, after all, the consumption process that opens the possibility for the consumer to learn from consumption experience, and then, if necessary, adjust b_i^c. Without alternative varieties from which to choose, the constraint for an individual consumer, or conceivably all consumers, could be quite narrow.

In our model, an individual producer is not assumed to provide all varieties from v_i^- to v_i^+. Many producers may correspond to the range from v_i^- to v_i^+. In $v_i x_i$ space, at any given point in time, each consumer has his or her own constraint. We assume that it is possible for many consumer-determined constraints (one per consumer) to exist simultaneously in the markets of the ith commodity. From the perspective of producers, therefore, there would exist a market version of quality-quantity space, and a market version of an aggregated constraint in that space. The full constraint version of $v_i x_i$ space corresponds to this version. We assume it is the objective of producers to "satisfy" the maximum number of CDCs in $v_i x_i$ space, given each producer's cost requirements.

As in the case of the consumer who may purchase from many producers, a single producer may sell to many consumers. We assume that any individual producer might have more than one PDC in any given time period. Given cost considerations, a producer might have as many constraints (PDC) as deemed necessary to attract or capture the "optimum" number of consumers in quality-quantity space. Consumers, however, are assumed to have only one CDC at any point in time. (We are still operating under Houthakker's single-variety hypothesis.)

The existence of many consumers increases the likelihood that $b_i^p \le b_i^c$ among a subset of consumers, such that transactions occur between consumers and individual producers. The existence of many consumers increases the likelihood of transactions along the constraint (PDC), or constraints, of an individual producer. The extent to which producer constraints are truncated, as well as the extent of targeting on varieties by producers (on individual v_i or on v_i neighborhoods), will influence the breadth of v_i^{-P} to v_i^{+P}, which represent the lower and upper boundaries for the constraints (PDC) of an individual producer. The aggregation of individual producer constraints determines the boundaries of v_i^- and v_i^+ available to all consumers in the market of the ith commodity. As with consumer constraints, individual producer constraints are assumed to be dynamic—that is, across time, PDC may change position, convexity, neighborhoods, and so forth. Similarly, the rank-ordering of varieties to form the v_i axis may vary across producers, just as it may for consumers (see chapter 10, section 12). We assume, however, that producers seek to match up well with the

v_i neighborhoods of consumers. Producers may also seek to influence those neighborhoods, as well as the v_i orderings of consumers.

As stated earlier, a producer may complete a transaction with any given consumer, if the PDC lies on or above the corresponding CDC (i.e., the PDC lies within the transaction region of the consumer). Obviously, producers will seek to maximize the number of consumer transaction regions intersected by their constraints (i.e., by their PDC). It is assumed that for any b_i^p, for which transactions do not occur, or for which the number of transactions is below some "acceptable" frequency, the producer will adjust the b_i^p, and/or change v_i neighborhoods, so as to optimize the frequency and revenue value of transactions.

One way to accomplish this goal would be to lower b_i^p, the markup for quality over the basic package (see chapter 7, section 8, and chapter 8, section 3). The optimum strategy for producers would be to have the PDC on or slightly above the CDC. Unfortunately, the closer the producer's constraint is to any individual consumer-determined constraint, the greater the likelihood of passing below the consumer constraint, and thereby eliminating the transaction. In this case, for all affected consumers, transactions would cease. For a producer, we assume the goal is to establish b_i^p as high as possible, for any given (expected) quantity, x_i, of the variety offered for sale—that is, the markup (of b_i^p over and above the price of the basic package, a_i) would be as high as possible for a specified quantity of the variety sold.[2] Obviously, there will be guessing and learning by producers in their efforts to discover the optimum b_i^p. Especially is this likely to be

the case when we recall the dynamic nature of consumer constraints. We assume that producers will conduct periodic analyses of alternative values of b_i^p so as to maximize revenues for the varieties they offer in the market.[3] We assume it is the goal of producers to maximize revenues for all of the varieties they offer for sale.

Our model assumes there is a feedback-loop learning process for producers, wherein they adjust to consumer willingness-to-pay for specified varieties. The model further assumes that consumer and producer learning behaviors are both dynamic and interactive. In other words, in quality-quantity space there is learning on the part of both parties to transactions, there are hunter-prey phenomena, and, as we shall see shortly, there may well be gaming behaviors on the part of both consumers and producers. As regards the consumer, the learning process is nested within and reflected by the CDC in $v_i x_i$ space, as well as in the preference map. According to the model, all of the behaviors discussed, on the part of both consumers and producers, influence data that becomes manifest as transactions in ith commodity markets.

Our model includes perception of quality by the consumer, as well as the producer's need to assess and adjust to any changes in consumer perception. Producers may also strive to influence consumer perception. In the next chapter we consider, in more detail, the role of b_i^p and b_i^c in empirical work involving variable quality. As we shall discover, many of the issues raised by the new model may also be significant for the hedonic technique and for the adjustment of price indices under variable quality.

Chapter 12

Transaction Regions, Neighborhoods, and Targeting

1. Transaction Regions and $v_i p_i$ Price Space

Consumer decision making in $v_i x_i$ space is linked with decision making in $v_i p_i$ space. In chapter 4 we discussed Houthakker's use of v_i and p_i, and showed that a reasonable interpretation was $p_i = a_i + b_i v_i$. Figure 4.2 in chapter 4 provides an illustration of $v_i p_i$ space, along with the basic price system ($a_i = 0$, $b_i = 1$), and an example of an alternative price system. Recall that we have dropped the requirement $v_i = p_i$, since we are interested in solutions away from the basic price system. In addition, we have examined the relationship between $v_i x_i$ space and $v_i p_i$ space. (See chapter 4, Figures 4.3, 4.4, and 4.5 and corresponding discussion).

In chapters 10 and 11 we introduced the concept of a transaction region between consumers and producers, and the existence of two constraints in $v_i x_i$ space. One constraint is generated by an individual consumer (the CDC) and the other by an individual producer (the PDC). To this point, our discussion of transaction regions has been limited to the two constraints, their corresponding b_i, and to quality-quantity space, $v_i x_i$. Owing to the relationship, however, that exists in the Houthakker model between quality-quantity space and price space (see Figures 4.3 to 4.5), it

is reasonable to assume the existence of transaction regions in $v_i p_i$ space.

We begin this section by retaining the assumption that a_i is fixed. Later, we relax the assumption and introduce two versions of a_i: one for the consumer, a_i^c; and one for the producer, a_i^p. Initially, we have $a_i^c = a_i^p = \phi$, a constant, and we assume $\phi \geq 0$.

With M_i constant and the same value for both the Consumer-Determined Constraint (CDC) and the Producer-Determined Constraint (PDC), the only difference between the two constraints is b_i. Under full constraint simple utility maximization (FCSUM), corresponding to the two constraints in $v_i x_i$ space, there exist two price lines in $v_i p_i$ price space. We identify these price lines as the consumer-determined price line (CDPL) and the producer-determined price line (PDPL). The CDPL can be viewed as the range of prices acceptable to the consumer, the consumer price acceptance line, or as a boundary identifying maximum acceptable prices to the consumer. The PDPL can be viewed as a set of prices offered by the producer, or as the producer price offer line. A PDPL is illustrated in Figure 12.1. If we now introduce a CDPL with the same value for a_i, but where $b_i^p < b_i^c$, we have in $v_i p_i$ space price lines as shown in Figure 12.2.

From our previous condition for transactions in $v_i x_i$ space (i.e., $b_i^p \leq b_i^c$), and

Figure 12.1 **The Producer-Determined Price Line**

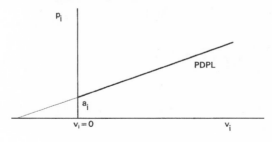

where transactions occur along the producer-determined constraint (PDC), we now have in $v_i p_i$ space a transactions surface that occurs along the producer-determined price line (PDPL). In Figure 12.2 transactions may occur anywhere along the PDPL.

Obviously, if the CDC and PDC are full constraint simple (i.e., without neighborhoods), the condition $b_i^p < b_i^c$ is sufficient to establish transactions throughout the region ($v_i = 0$) to v_i^+. If we had the reverse (i.e., $b_i^p > b_i^c$), then Figure 12.2 converts to Figure 12.3, and no transactions occur. Throughout these illustrations, recall $v_i = 0$ is the basic package, a_i is its corresponding price, and that a_i has been restricted to non-negative values.

2. Alternative Interpretations of a_i in Price Space

Earlier we discussed basic packages that correspond to individual consumers (see chapter 10, sections 11 and 12). We continue now with a_i, the price of the basic package, and consider consumer determination of a_i, or a_i^c. Here, as in the case of the b_i^c, we assume a_i^c is established by individual consumers and may be unique to each consumer. In other words, not only do the b_i^c reflect individual consumer perception and willingness-to-pay, based on individual consumption experience and

Figure 12.2 **Transactions in $v_i p_i$ Price Space**

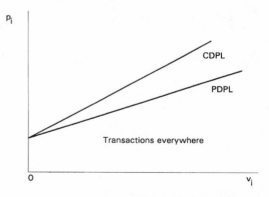

Figure 12.3 **No Transactions in Price Space**

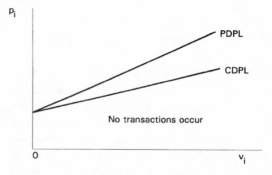

learning, but the a_i^c as well reflect individual consumer perception, willingness-to-pay, consumption experience, and so forth.

With a_i unique to each consumer, Figures 12.2 and 12.3 may have different intercept values for the CDPL and PDPL. Several different price line relationships could arise. In Figure 12.4 we have $b_i^p < b_i^c$, but $a_i^p > a_i^c$. Under these conditions, transactions may occur along the PDPL only where the PDPL lies on or below the CDPL. The segment of the PDPL where transactions may occur has been identified by a thick line (i.e., the line segment to the right of the intersection at E). We call such line segments a transaction surface. Note that corresponding to the transaction surface of the PDPL is a range along the v_i axis and along the p_i axis. The upper limit

Figure 12.4 **Limited Transaction Surface in Price Space: I**

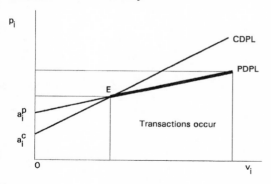

Figure 12.5 **Limited Transaction Surface in Price Space: II**

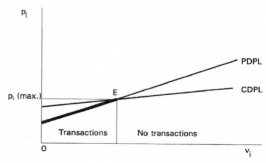

to each range depends on the length of the PDPL to the right of E (Figure 12.4).

Also, under the conditions illustrated in Figure 12.4, the lower bound of p_i is greater than a_i, and hence the range of transactions along the v_i axis excludes the basic package. This is true for either a_i^c or a_i^p. Also, to the right of E a type of consumer surplus is evident, since CDPL > PDPL. Recall, however, our earlier remarks regarding consumer surplus in the absence of any measure of quantity (see chapter 8, section 2).

In Figure 12.5 we have the reverse of Figure 12.4. Here $b_i^p > b_i^c$ and $a_i^c > a_i^p$. As shown, transactions occur along the PDPL to the left of E. Again, the transaction surface is along the PDPL on or below the CDPL. Under these conditions the basic package may be purchased, and a_i^p establishes the purchase price. Variation in p_i is constrained to the range $a_i^p \leq p_i \leq p_i$ (max.). The maximum price, p_i(max.), corresponds to the price at E. In other words, the lowest possible value for p_i identifies the value of a_i. Under these conditions the price value of the basic package could be estimated from market data. (There are empirical implications here for the hedonic technique.) Note that these conditions in price space also require the constraint in $v_i x_i$ space to have a positive intercept on the x_i

axis (see our earlier requirements for such an intercept in chapter 4, sections 7 and 8).

3. Transactions and v_i Neighborhoods

Finally, as regards transactions in $v_i p_i$ space, we consider circumstances that involve v_i neighborhoods and/or single-variety targeting in $v_i x_i$ space. Corresponding to the conditions for transactions in $v_i x_i$ space (i.e., that the PDC lies on or above the CDC), the reverse is true in price space (i.e., that the PDPL lies on or below the CDPL). An illustration involving a v_i neighborhood is provided in Figure 12.6. As shown, the full length of the PDPL lies beneath the CDPL.

As in the case of PDC, which crosses the CDC, similar intersections of CDPL by PDPL are possible. Although issues of convexity are not involved for line segments in price space, difference between a_i^c and a_i^p may produce intersecting line segments in $v_i p_i$ space. In the case of intersecting price lines, the transaction surface remains that portion of the PDPL on or beneath the CDPL.

The existence of v_i neighborhoods and their corresponding constraint segments, as well as the existence of transaction surfaces and their corresponding price line segments, do not diminish the importance of Houthakker's quantity price, a_i. More spe-

Figure 12.6 **Quality Neighborhoods and Transactions**

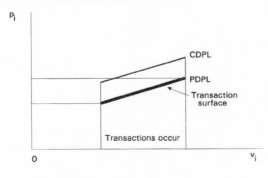

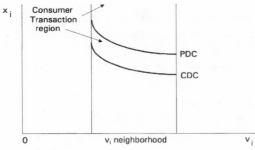

Figure 12.7 **Truncated Price Line and the Basic Package**

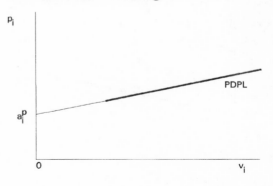

cifically, even though the price line may no longer extend to the p_i axis in price space (Figure 12.6), the importance of both the basic package, and its corresponding price remain. The existence of v_i neighborhoods and truncated transaction surfaces, however, raise questions as to how to define, identify, and measure a_i. (This is another topic with implications for the hedonic technique.)

Previously, a_i was the intercept of the price line $p_i = a_i + b_i v_i$ in $v_i p_i$ space. The price line was linear, not broken into segments, and extended throughout price space. Additionally, a_i corresponded to the value of $v_i = 0$, which is the variety assumed to represent the basic package. Difficulties arise, however, once line segments are introduced in price space. Which v_i becomes $v_i = 0$, the basic package? And, what is the value of a_i that corresponds to that v_i?

We resolve these difficulties by first as-

suming $v_i = 0$ remains at the origin in $v_i p_i$ space. As regards a_i, we may utilize a linear projection of the price line segment to the p_i axis. A projection is illustrated in Figure 12.7, utilizing only the PDPL. The dotted line represents the projection. We assume a_i remains the intercept on p_i, where the projected price line intercepts the p_i axis. A similar process of projection would apply to the CDPL. Under this interpretation, the basic package remains the variety at $v_i = 0$ and its corresponding price is a_i, the intercept on the p_i axis.

An alternative explanation for a_i, under the conditions of v_i neighborhoods and transaction surfaces, would be that for each v_i neighborhood a separate $v_i p_i$ space exists (i.e., to each v_i neighborhood there corresponds a $v_i p_i$ subspace). One way to define such a subspace would be that a_i corresponds to the lowest value of v_i in the range of v_i constituting the v_i neighborhood. In other words, a new origin for $v_i p_i$ space is established at the lowest value of v_i in the v_i neighborhood. The p_i axis remains as before. Under this interpretation, a_i remains an intercept, but is the value of the intercept on the line segment orthogonal to the lowest value of v_i in the neighborhood. An illustration is provided in Figure 12.8, where the p_i axis has been shifted rightward from the original origin at $(v_i = 0)_1$

Figure 12.8 **Quality Neighborhood and Price of Basic Package**

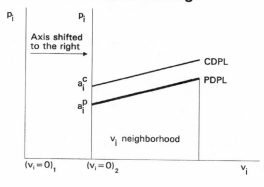

Furthermore, the problem of cycling across subspaces becomes possible, as it was earlier across basic packages. There arises, correspondingly, the need for a numeraire or invariance operator across the subspaces, if both rank-ordering and comparison of subspaces by consumers are to occur without cycling.

One possible numeraire or invariance operator under these circumstances would be the self-concept of the individual consumer. As discussed earlier, at the retail level (where we have remained throughout this study) the concept of quality is assumed to be strongly correlated with, and influenced by, each consumer's concept of self or self-image (see chapter 9, section 3). Given the role we have posited is played by self-image, one numeraire against which comparisons could be made, either of varieties or subspaces of varieties, is how effectively individual varieties or v_i neighborhoods serve the consumer's self-image.

If we employ self-image as the invariance operator, however, we should bear in mind that across the life cycle of human beings self-image changes. Nothing is constant. Nevertheless, over relatively short time periods self-image might serve as a numeraire. For empirical purposes, such an approach would require aggregated data on expenditure patterns by age, sex, and other life-style dimensions of consumer cohorts. Unfortunately, as stated earlier, consumers may not utilize long-term memory, but rather make comparisons based simply on their most recent purchases, which is to say, consumers may not be aware of any cycling within their expenditure patterns.

to a new origin at $(v_i = 0)_2$. Note that $(v_i = 0)_2$ corresponds to the lowest value of v_i in the v_i neighborhood.

This approach is consistent with our previous remarks regarding the subjective nature of b_i^c, the individual consumer rank-ordering of varieties along the v_i axis, the subjectivity of the basic package, and so forth. Under this approach, the subspace(s) of $v_i p_i$ space may be unique to each consumer. The only consistent dimension of the space has been, and remains, the p_i axis. Similar conditions of subjectivity apply to the v_i axis in $v_i x_i$ space. We have already examined how the constraint in $v_i x_i$ space is subjective for each consumer. As always, preference maps are assumed to be subjective.

In summary, when $x_i p_i$ space is opened to become $v_i x_i$ and $v_i p_i$ spaces, the subjectivity of quality—the processes of perception and interpretation of consumption experience—is introduced. Only the p_i and x_i axes remain objective in nature. If the a_i change from $v_i p_i$ subspace to $v_i p_i$ subspace, and/or the basic package changes from subspace to subspace, the comparison task for consumers is now raised to the level of comparing $v_i p_i$ subspaces associated with different v_i neighborhoods and transaction surfaces (i.e., not simply comparing varieties, as discussed earlier).

4. Targeting and $v_i p_i$ Space

Finally, we come to the process of targeting on a single variety, $\hat{v}_i$. This phenomenon must be addressed both from the point of view of $v_i x_i$ space and from price space.

Figure 12.9 **Variety Targeting in** $v_i x_i$ **and** $v_i p_i$ **Spaces**

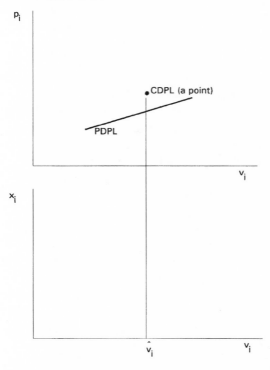

In Figure 12.9 we have expanded the targeting phenomenon to both $v_i p_i$ price space and $v_i x_i$ consumption space. As illustrated in price space, transactions occur because the p_i and v_i coordinates of the targeted variety $\hat{v}_i$ lie above the PDPL.

In addition to targeting by the consumer, it is possible that producers also target on single varieties (in addition to targeting on consumers' v_i neighborhoods). When this occurs, producers must not only match the consumer target—that is, the producer's $\hat{v}_i^p$ must match the consumer's $\hat{v}_i^c$—but producers must also continue to meet the requirement $b_i^p \leq b_i^c$. In addition, in the case of single-variety targeting, questions arise regarding a_i^p and a_i^c.

For example, earlier we raised the question of whether v_i neighborhoods create subspaces along the v_i axis. Corresponding to such subspaces, there arose the question of whether a_i remained as the intercept on the original p_i axis, or whether a_i corresponded to the lowest v_i in a v_i neighborhood. Assume for the moment the latter case. In this case it is as though the p_i axis had been repositioned such that a new origin is established at the lowest v_i, and the v_i neighborhood becomes a new $v_i p_i$ space (see, again, Figure 12.8). If repositioning of the origin ($v_i = 0$) is assumed to occur, what happens in the case of single-variety targeting (i.e., the v_i neighborhood has contracted to a point on the v_i axis)? Does a_i continue to exist? Has a_i replaced b_i?

In the case of consumer targeting on a single variety, $\hat{v}_i$, where no corresponding neighborhood exists, the lowest v_i equals $\hat{v}_i$. Obviously, the highest v_i also equals $\hat{v}_i$. Previously, we suggested a_i could correspond to the lowest v_i in the neighborhood. Can we still utilize that assumption when $(v_i = 0) = \hat{v}_i$? Furthermore, when v_i is a point on the v_i axis and a dot in $v_i p_i$ space, what is the meaning of $b_i = (dp_i/dv_i)$, the slope of a price line, which has collapsed to a dot in $v_i p_i$ space?

Recall that at $v_i = 0$, we have $p_i = a_i$, that is, from $p_i = a_i + b_i v_i$, with $v_i = 0$, $b_i v_i$ disappears. When $\hat{v}_i = (v_i = 0)$ under single-variety targeting, a_i is equivalent to p_i, the price of the targeted variety. Previously a_i^c was defined as the price the consumer was willing to pay for the basic package. Now, however, under single-variety targeting, has the target become the basic package? If so, does such a phenomenon lead to an increased likelihood of cycling?

Another perspective on a_i, again under conditions of single-variety targeting, would be to assume a_i remains along the p_i axis and $(v_i = 0) \neq \hat{v}_i$. Assume $(v_i = 0) < \hat{v}_i$. We could define such a_i as freestanding. By this we mean, a_i is not necessarily an intercept of a price line through $v_i p_i$ space, nor is a_i the price of the lowest v_i in a v_i neighborhood. In other words, a_i stands free of a v_i neighborhood and/or of its corresponding price line.

In the case of single-variety targeting with free-standing a_i in price space, we have, in effect, two varieties: one corresponding to the targeted variety, $\hat{v}_i$, and the other corresponding to the basic package at $v_i = 0$. If we compare the two varieties, would we expect the price (p_i), corresponding to $\hat{v}_i$, to be higher than the price (a_i), corresponding to the basic package? Under the case of free-standing a_i, would the difference in price, between the free-standing a_i and the price corresponding to $\hat{v}_i$, represent the markup of $\hat{v}_i$ over the price of the basic package? See Figure 12.10.

If the price a_i is the same as the price for $\hat{v}_i$, does this imply no markup? If so, does it mean $b_i = 0$? If the price of the free-standing a_i equals the price of the targeted variety $\hat{v}_i$, do we have two basic packages? Has $\hat{v}_i$ become equivalent to a basic package, or does a_i remain the basic package? What of the intervening v_i (i.e., the values of v_i between $v_i = 0$ and $\hat{v}_i$)? If p_i at $v_i = 0$ is the same as p_i at $\hat{v}_i$, is this analogous to our previous discussion of repositioning the p_i axis? What if the free-standing a_i at $v_i = 0$ is greater than p_i for $\hat{v}_i$? Is such a result possible? Should we restrict a_i to values less than or equal to the price of $\hat{v}_i$?

Earlier we spoke of the "reach" of b_i along a constraint in $v_i x_i$ space. Another question regarding a_i is whether the consumer considers a_i in his or her evaluation of any given v_i—that is, does the basic package enter consumer decision making in the evaluation of a variety? If the reach of b_i does not extend to $v_i = 0$ and therefore include a_i, could the consumer make such an evaluation and comparison? Is it possible that the concepts of a basic package and its corresponding price a_i are simply useful mental constructs for firms and social statisticians, but rarely, if ever, utilized by consumers? Worse still, is it possible that consumers are totally unaware of the concept of a "basic package," except

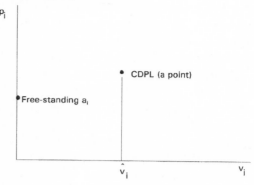

Figure 12.10 **Free-Standing a_i in Price Space**

possibly when they hear the advertising phrase "the stripped-down version," and so forth. The evolution of our model has opened the door to the possibility that consumers may be unaware of, uninformed regarding, and/or unconcerned about a basic package.

From the point of view of consumer perception, expectation, and consumption experience, how likely is it that consumers have consumption experience regarding the basic package? Maybe it is just the lower income groups that have such experience, and they may not be aware that the goods and/or services they purchase are "the basic package."

To return to our earlier discussion of numeraires and invariance operators, is it possible that the rank-ordering of varieties occurs through people of one income group comparing themselves to people of other income groups, and using these comparisons as proxies for rank orderings and a hypothetical basic package?

5. Targeting on Quantity: The Case of $\hat{x}_i = 1$

In addition to single-variety targeting in $v_i x_i$ space, there is the issue of targeting on a specific level of quantity, or targeting on $\hat{x}_i$ in $v_i x_i$ space. We begin by examining consumer decision making in probably the most common form of quantity-targeting, the case of $\hat{x}_i = 1$. We note, however, that just as in the case of v_i targeting, there may exist neighborhoods for x_i and targeting on x_i neighborhoods. We commence our discussion with the quantity-specific case of $\hat{x}_i = 1$.

Earlier we introduced the $\hat{x}_i = 1$ case when we discussed WTP(TA) and WTAP (TR) (see chapter 10). Note that in $v_i x_i$ space, if $\hat{x}_i = 1$, we must have either a change in consumer income, M_i (i.e., a change in the budgeted income devoted to the ith commodity), change in a_i, and/or change in b_i, in order for the constraint to shift and allow variation in v_i over fixed x_i. In other words, in $v_i x_i$ space, with $\hat{x}_i = 1$ there must be a locus of points corresponding to variation in v_i brought about by shifts in the constraint. In price space, for $\hat{x}_i = 1$ there is a pattern of price lines that either pivot or shift, either upward or downward, depending upon whether a_i is constant, with change in b_i; b_i is constant and change occurs in a_i; or both a_i and b_i change simultaneously. Change in M_i will not affect the CDPL.

We begin by assuming a_i^c fixed and that change occurs only in b_i^c. As our focus is on the consumer, the CDPL will pivot at the a_i^c intercept. As illustrated in Figure 12.11, a shift in the consumer-determined constraint brought about by a change in b_i^c, in this case a reduction in b_i^c, will swing the CDPL downward in price space.

In this example it is assumed M_i and a_i^c are constant. Recall $b_i = (dp_i/dv_i)$ gives the slope of the price line. (Note that $b_i^c = (dp_i/dv_i)$ gives the slope of the CDPL.) Also, recall that in our model b_i^c may change for different values of v_i—that is b_i^c may change for different points, or neighborhoods, on the v_i axis. If the change in v_i, as illustrated in Figure 12.11, pertains to a v_i neighborhood, then we would have a piecewise-linear consumer-determined price line within that neighborhood in price

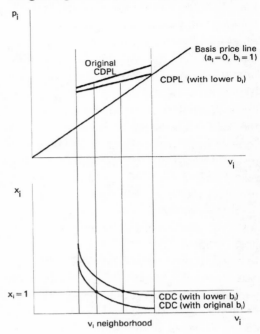

Figure 12.11 **Effects of Quantity-Targeting in $v_i x_i$ and $v_i p_i$ Spaces**

space. Conversely, if change in v_i corresponds to different v_i neighborhoods, then we could have separate price lines (CDPLs) in price space—each linear but (conceivably) with different slope for each neighborhood. Similar arguments hold for changes in b_i^p for producers and the PDC and PDPL when $x = 1$, or for other fixed values of x_i.

6. Double-Targeting

The next issue, regarding transactions in price space, is the issue of double-targeting. Recall that double-targeting involves targeting on a single variety, $\hat{v}_i$, and targeting on a specific quantity, $\hat{x}_i$. We begin with targeting conducted by the consumer.

Under double-targeting in $v_i x_i$ space, instead of a constraint line segment, there exists a constraint dot or point. Under these conditions there exist no opportunities for utility maximization, either FCSUM or NSUM (i.e., not even quantity can be maximized). Furthermore, under double-targeting the transaction region in $v_i x_i$ space reduces to a point, the point of the double target. Accordingly, for producers to realize transactions with consumers who have double-targeted, the PDC in $v_i x_i$ space must pass through or above the point-constraints of individual consumers. If the PDC is above the constraint point, it must nevertheless allow the consumer to meet both targets (i.e., meet $\hat{v}_i$ and $\hat{x}_i$). Note, furthermore, saving and/or resale of extra x_i must be allowed.

Recall that transactions occur on the PDC. The condition $b_i^p \leq b_i^c$, and hence the PDC above the consumer's double-targeted point, does not negate the requirement that transactions occur on the PDC. In the case where the PDC rests above the consumer's double-targeted point, the consumer may chose either not to purchase (no transaction occurs), or the consumer may purchase the excess x_i and then subsequently monetize the involuntary ''consumer surplus'' (generate monetized savings) by resale of the excess x_i. If negotiation time costs and storage costs are important to consumers, the likelihood of such transactions is small.

If a_i^p and b_i^p are such that the PDC in $v_i x_i$ space passes through or above the consumer's constraint point, then a transaction may occur between that producer and consumer. Corresponding to those a_i^p and b_i^p values, there will be a PDPL in $v_i p_i$ space. Given the existence of a transaction surface in price space (i.e., that $PDPL \leq CDPL$ over a range inclusive of the targeted v_i), then there exists a price, p_i, corresponding to the double-targeted bundle, $\hat{v}_i$, $\hat{x}_i$. From the consumer's perspective, given $\bar{M}_i = p_i \hat{x}_i = (a_i^c + b_i^c \hat{v}_i^c) \hat{x}_i^c$, where $\hat{v}_i^c$ and $\hat{x}_i^c$ represent the consumer targets and $\bar{M}_i$ is a fixed (constant) decentralized subbudget

for the ith commodity, there exists a targeted price for the consumer in price space that corresponds to the double-targeted v_i and x_i in quality-quantity space. This price we identify as $\hat{p}_i^c$. Thus, for transactions to occur along the transaction surface in price space, the PDPL must permit attainment of the consumer's targeted price, $\hat{p}_i^c$. This price can be defined as the consumer's maximum acceptable price (see section 1 of this chapter).

Clearly, strong implications abound here regarding elasticity of demand. If the price p_i^p required by the producer is higher than $\hat{p}_i^c$, no transactions will occur, unless the consumer is willing to change his or her decentralized budget for the ith commodity (i.e., is willing to increase M_i). (Recall that throughout our discussion we have restricted ourselves to Houthakker's single-variety case, the case where consumer purchases only one variety of the varieties constituting the ith commodity.) If $\hat{p}_i^p < p_i^c$, then saving (consumer surplus) may accrue to the consumer. Such saving may be transferred to another commodity or commodities—a result with implications for the separability and decentralization requirements discussed previously—or it may be retained as savings. We will continue our discussion of the various forms of targeting in chapters 13 through 15.

7. Clustering Patterns of e_{ih} to v_i

Earlier we discussed the characteristics approach to quality, which we presented in the form of Theil's elements e_{ih}, and we introduced the issue of how elements cluster to form a variety. The question of how the e_{ih} cluster to individual v_i is important, although it is often ignored. In the format of our model, the process of clustering or grouping of quality elements, e_{ih}, to individual varieties involves a mapping of an n-dimensional e_{ih} space to a v_i axis. We have touched upon some of the conditions associated with mapping characteristics to an invariant aggregator when we discussed the works of Theil, Ironmonger, Lancaster, Muellbauer, and others. (See also our discussion of isoquality measures of quantity, chapter 4, section 3.)

The clustering pattern of e_{ih} to v_i has implications for the hedonic technique. The typical application of the technique involves linear regression, frequently in log form, where the characteristics of a product or service are regressed on a dependent variable, the price of the item, or service. Under this method it is important to note that an implicit assumption has been made, namely that the manner by which the e_{ih} cluster to the v_i does not matter. In other words, the mapping of characteristics to varieties is presumed to be insignificant to an understanding of how quality characteristics influence the price of a product or service. The hedonic technique proceeds directly from the e_{ih} to p_i. Recall that we have interpreted Houthakker's b_i as $b_i = (\partial p_i / \partial v_i)$; however, the typical hedonic approach presumes $b_i = (\partial p_i / \partial e_{ih})$. Further, recall our earlier discussion of $[(\partial p_i / \partial v_i) (\partial v_i / \partial e_{ih})]$ (see chapter 4, sections 4 through 6).

In line with our earlier discussion of consumer perception of varieties, such perception processes may in fact be influenced by the bundling and configuration of the quality characteristics, e_{ih}, to individual varieties. Also, as discussed earlier, the ordering of v_i along each individual consumer's v_i axis likewise may be influenced by how the e_{ih} cluster to the v_i. The manner in which the e_{ih} are perceived by the consumer, both individually and in the clusters or bundles that become varieties, is an important issue and merits further research.

Chapter 13

Individual Consumer Demand from Quality–Quantity Space

1. Individual Consumer Demand Under Variable Quality: Introductory Remarks

Given all that has been discussed to this point, it is now possible to integrate our model of consumer behavior in *quality–quantity* consumption space with individual consumer demand, and with market concepts of demand. Chapters 13 through 15 are devoted to this goal.

Expansion of our model to this level involves concepts drawn from discriminating monopoly and non-Walrasian markets. In line with non-Walrasian markets, we assume transactions between producers and consumers may occur away from market equilibrium (i.e., on the short side of the market). A diagram illustrating such phenomena is provided in Figure 13.1, where the short sides are identified by bold lines (see Benassy 1986).

We begin our discussion under conditions where quality does not enter into consumer decision making (i.e., under conditions of isoquality or the homogeneous goods and services assumption). We commence with $b_i = 0$, $a_i > 0$. An illustration of $v_i x_i$ and $v_i p_i$ spaces, under these conditions, is given in Figure 13.2. Note that $p_i = a_i$, as previously discussed, and consumption space is limited to quantity, x_i. The consumer would, for example, com-

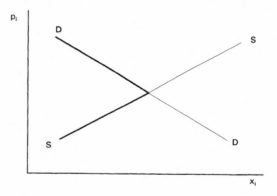

Figure 13.1 **Short Sides of the Market**

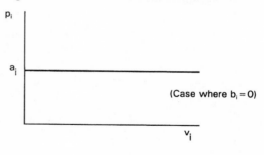

Figure 13.2 **The Traditional Case**

(Case where $b_i = 0$)

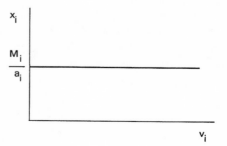

Figure 13.3 **Opening the Houthakker Model**

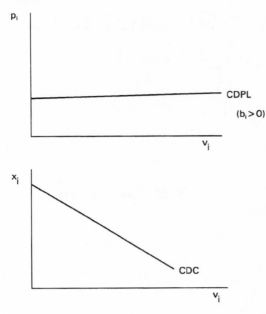

Figure 13.4 **Utility Optimization in v_ix_i Space**

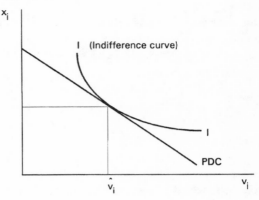

pare commodity i and commodity j, and would face the usual linear budget constraint in x_ix_j consumption space. Demand curves and all of the traditional topics of substitution and income effects, ordinary versus compensated demand, and so forth, would follow.

If we now introduce Houthakker's full constraint, with $b_i > 0$ and $a_i > 0$, we enter his quality-quantity consumption space and may proceed with the new model. We commence with an (a_i/b_i) ratio sufficiently high such that the constraints (CDC and PDC) are approximately linear in quality-quantity (v_ix_i) consumption space.[1] In v_ip_i price space, with "high" a_i and "low" b_i, the price lines (CDPL and PDPL) have slopes greater than zero (we assume $b_i > 0$). Consider Figure 13.3, where only the CDPL and CDC are illustrated, and where b_i is assumed to be slightly greater than zero.

Initially, we assume $a_i^p = a_i^c$ and $b_i^p \leq b_i^c$, such that transactions may occur between an individual producer and an in-

dividual consumer. With $a_i^p = a_i^c$ we assure that transactions may occur anywhere on the PDC and on the PDPL. Under these conditions, we further assume that utility maximization in v_ix_i space results in interior solutions on an approximately linear constraint (i.e., on the PDC; see Figure 13.4.[2]

To introduce isoquality demand for an individual consumer, we assume the consumer's preferences are such that v_i remains at $\hat{v}_i$ in quality-quantity consumption space (i.e., the *special case*). The price p_i, in price space, is taken from the producer's PDPL and indicates the transaction price the consumer must pay for quality level $\hat{v}_i$ and its corresponding quantity, x_i. We should note that, under conditions of CDPL > PDPL (or $b_i^c > b_i^p$), the demand reservation price and corresponding consumer surplus may be greater than revealed in market transactions. Only when CDPL = PDPL ($b_i^c = b_i^p$) does the transaction price, p_i, accurately reflect maximum willingness-to-pay on the part of an individual consumer for some quantity of a specified level of quality, $\hat{v}_i$.

In demand space, the p_i and x_i generated above, corresponding to $\hat{v}_i$, represent a point on the consumer's (ordinary) demand curve. To create an isoquality demand curve, we assume a_i remains fixed, but that the consumer changes b_i^c. We also assume M_i, the budgeted amount allocated for the ith commodity, is fixed. We now utilize the material discussed earlier regarding consumer willingness-to-pay under conditions of the special case.

Similar to the special case, we assume the consumer first increases and then decreases b_i^c, and through the consumption-learning process attains accurate values for b_i^c—that is, expectation equals experience. At this juncture, we also assume consumer decision making applies to the entire length of the v_i axis (i.e., no v_i neighborhoods exist).

Under conditions of the special case, recall that as the consumer raises b_i^c, the CDC is lowered in $v_i x_i$ space and the CDPL rises in $v_i p_i$ space. Through the process of raising b_i^c, the consumer indicates a willingness to reduce the quantity, x_i, of the variety $\hat{v}_i$, and a willingness to raise the price, p_i^c, which he or she will pay per unit for the variety $\hat{v}_i$. In other words, a higher b_i^c in quality-quantity consumption space is revealed as a higher price, p_i, and lower quantity, x_i, along an isoquality demand curve in demand space. It should be noted that along a traditional ordinary demand curve, which is also assumed to be isoquality (i.e., $\hat{v}_i$ targeted), willingness-to-pay is not constant—that is, b_i^c varies along the demand curve. Higher b_i^c are at the upper end of the demand curve and are reflected as higher prices and lower quantities. This result, of course, is consistent with the concept of diminishing marginal utility along demand curves in traditional consumer theory. Recall, however, our earlier discussion of Knut Wicksell on variable quality and diminishing marginal utility (see chapter 2).

See Figure 13.5 for an illustration of rising b_i^c and its effect on p_i and x_i. Just the reverse of these processes is true when the consumer decreases b_i^c, while remaining at $\hat{v}_i$.

2. Consumer and Producer Surpluses

To consider non-Walrasian markets, we now address decision making (regarding price, quantity, and quality) on the part of firms: in our present case, on the part of a single producer. In chapters 11 and 12 we discussed consumer-producer interaction, the producer's b_i^p, and so forth. In the case of non-Walrasian markets, we assume, in addition to the usual costs of production and return to owner's equity, the firm's supply strategy includes the firm's estimate of consumer willingness-to-pay for different levels of quality. In other words, the supply curve represents the lower bound on the price, p_i^p, the firm will accept in order to sell a specified quantity, x_i, at the quality level, $\hat{v}_i$. As we shall see, this subject involves producer's surplus.

Recall from chapter 11, section 2, b_i^p represents the firm's estimate of what an individual consumer, or cohort of "similar" consumers, would be willing to pay for some specified level of quality. If we return to Figure 13.1, we may elaborate further on the interaction of consumers and producers, within the context of supply and demand and a targeted level of quality.

In the traditional explanation of consumer and producer surpluses, equilibrium price established at the intersection of supply and demand partitions the surpluses. In a non-Walrasian market, where transactions may occur away from equilibrium, above-equilibrium prices result in transactions on the short side of demand. In these cases, consumer surplus is smaller than that established at a market equilibrium price. Consumer surplus exists only for consumption to the left of the transaction point—that is, to the left of the transacted quantity. Depending on elasticities of supply and de-

Figure 13.5 **Generation of Iso-Quality Demand: Simple Case**

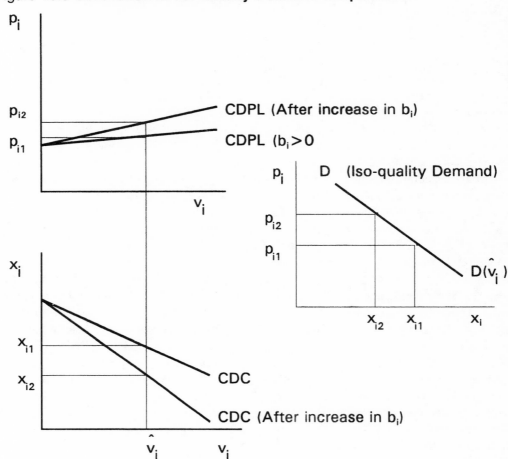

mand, producer surplus on the short side of demand may be larger than at the equilibrium price. An illustration of consumer surplus is provided in Figure 13.6. (In this figure only the short sides of demand and supply are shown.)

If we focus exclusively on the transacted quantity (as illustrated in Figure 13.6), the partitioning of consumer and producer surpluses may now be viewed in the context of the interaction of consumer willingness-to-pay and producer estimates of that willingness (i.e., between b_i^c and b_i^p). As before, we continue to assume a_i fixed and equal for both consumer and producer. For

now, we assume the consumer continues to demand the transacted quantity in Figure 13.6.

For that transacted quantity, we find the new model provides additional insight into the concept of a demand reservation price and how that price relates to consumer surplus. Note that as presently constructed, the demand reservation price for the transacted quantity, x_i, is conditional on remaining at the quality level, $\hat{v}_i$. Within the context of our previous discussion of double-targeting (chapter 12, section 6), we find that a demand reservation price (DRP), p_i^c, requires double-targeting—that is, holding both

Figure 13.6 **Consumer Surplus on the Short Side of Demand**

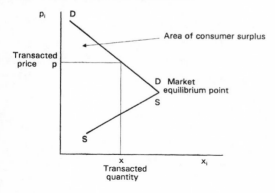

Figure 13.7 **Producer Surplus Away from Market Equilibrium**

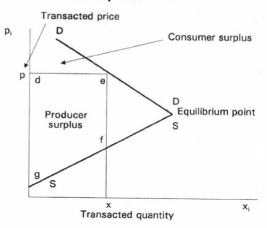

quantity and quality constant and then discovering consumer willingness-to-pay for $\hat{x}_i$ and $\hat{v}_i$.

Under conditions illustrated in Figure 13.6, if a producer accurately estimates a consumer's b_i^c, such that $b_i^p = b_i^c$ for some specified $\hat{v}_i$, then the PDPL will be equal to the CDPL for that specified level of quality. The same will hold true for the CDC and PDC (i.e., CDC = PDC for the specified $\hat{v}_i$). The corresponding price, p_i, and quantity, x_i, will likewise be the same for both producer and consumer. We identify these conditions as: $p_i^p = p_i^c$ and $x_i^p = x_i^c$.

Under these conditions there will be less surplus for the consumer than under an equilibrium price. The producer will capture the surplus between the transacted price on the demand curve and the area above the supply curve (i.e., the area "defg" in Figure 13.7). Note that consumer surplus exists to the left of the transacted quantity—that is, the area under the demand curve and above the transacted price. We assume that supply and demand, as well as the transacted price and quantity, are identical for Figures 13.6 and 13.7.

To the extent the producer underestimates consumer willingness-to-pay for $\hat{v}_i$,

and/or to the extent the consumer is able to hide his or her "true" b_i^c, consumer surplus may be larger. In what follows, we assume the consumer continues to target $\hat{v}_i$. Additionally, we assume the consumer who purchased the transacted quantity, x_i, in Figure 13.7 continues to desire that quantity (i.e., there is double-targeting by the consumer).

Different from our previous example, where we had $b_i^p = b_i^c$, we now assume that the producer has established b_i^p such that $b_i^p < b_i^c$. As a consequence, as PDPL < CDPL and PDC > CDC, the transacted price, $p_i = p_i^p$, and it's corresponding quantity, $x_i = x_i^p$, on the isoquality demand curve ($v_i = \hat{v}_i$), are a lower price and higher quantity than the previous transacted quantity targeted by this consumer. In other words, for this consumer the desired quantity, of variety $v_i = \hat{v}_i$, is $x_i = x_i^c$ (which is the previous transacted quantity), and this consumer is willing to pay a price $p_i = p_i^c$ for that quantity of $\hat{v}_i$. See Figure 13.8. Given that the transacted price is p_i^p, and given that this consumer purchases the quantity x_i^c, the consumer has added the area "deih" to his or her consumer surplus.

Figure 13.8 **Producer Underestimates Consumer WTP**

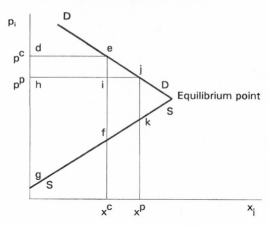

If we assume that this isoquality demand curve represents willingness-to-pay on the part of more than one consumer (we will have more to say on this shortly), there may exist a consumer who will purchase at the new price, p_i^p. For this consumer (whom we might call the "marginal consumer"), $p_i^p = p_i^c$, and correspondingly, for this consumer, $b_i^p = b_i^c$. Recall that we have assumed a_i constant and equal for both consumer and producer.

We now expand the assumption and assume a_i is constant and equal for all consumers and all producers. We further assume that all consumers represented by this isoquality demand curve have selected $\hat{v}_i$ as the level of quality. Clearly, for those consumers where $b_i^c > b_i^p$, the greater the magnitude of b_i^c over b_i^p, the greater the magnitude of individual consumer surplus. As we explained earlier, b_i^c is higher at the upper end of the demand curve, where prices, p_i, are higher. As the transacted price, p_i, falls, additional consumers commence consumption of variety, $\hat{v}_i$. Infra-marginal consumers receive additional consumer surplus.

From the point of view of producers of variety $\hat{v}_i$, whereas previously pro-

ducer surplus was the area "defg," with the new transacted price, p_i^p, and transacted quantity, x_i^p, the area of producer surplus becomes "hjkg" (see Figure 13.8). The overall addition to consumer surplus, inclusive of the infra-marginal and marginal consumers, is the area "dejh." Should the transacted price fall such that it is on the short side of supply, consumer surplus is further increased and producer surplus reduced. The gap between b_i^c and b_i^p, ($b_i^c > b_i^p$), becomes greater for transaction prices on the short side of supply than on the short side of demand.

As in the case of the consumer and the demand curve, we assume the firm's supply curve is isoquality, and we further assume that it is targeted at the same level of quality as that of the consumer (i.e., $\hat{v}_i^p = \hat{v}_i^c$). In this fashion, we have assumed away some aspects of the Waugh–Brems problem. In our model, the disequilibrium aspects of that problem may be stated in two ways: $\hat{v}_i^p \neq \hat{v}_i^c$ and $b_i^c \neq b_i^p$.

Finally, just as b_i^c varies along an isoquality demand curve, we assume producer estimates of consumer willingness-to-pay, b_i^p, may vary along an isoquality supply curve. We will have more to say on this later.

3. Effects of Increased Convexity of the Houthakker Constraint

We began this chapter by assuming the (a_i/b_i) ratio sufficiently high such that the constraints, CDC and PDC, were approximately linear. We return now to $v_i x_i$ space and examine what happens when the ratio (a_i/b_i) is reduced. Figure 13.9 illustrates the constraint under different values of (a_i/b_i). The value of M_i is held constant. Note that as (a_i/b_i) falls the constraint becomes more convex to the origin—that is, the focus point of the hyperbola shifts toward the origin. In terms of consumer decision making in quality-quantity space, the trade-off between v_i and x_i varies depending on the level of quality, $\hat{v}_i$, or on the location of the v_i neighborhood.

For "low" values of (a_i/b_i), the change in x_i corresponding to change in v_i, or dx_i/dv_i, will be higher for v_i values close to the origin than for v_i values far from the origin. Specifically, the quantity response to a change in the level of quality will be greater for v_i values to the left of the focus point (the focus point of the hyperbola) than for v_i values to the right of that point. The slope of the constraint, $-(dx_i/dv_i)$, is higher for v_i to the left of the focus point than for v_i values to the right of the point. Furthermore, the lower the (a_i/b_i) ratio, the greater the difference in $-(dx_i/dv_i)$ depending on the location of v_i with respect to the focus point. Note that the (a_i/b_i) ratio falls as the price of the basic package, a_i, falls in relationship to the quality markup, b_i. Also, note that the (a_i/b_i) ratio must be high (e.g., approximately in excess of 250) in order for the constraint to approach linearity (see note 1 and appendix A). Consumer income does not influence the range of linearity across the constraint, neither for the full constraint nor for neighborhoods along the v_i axis. Other things constant, for specified v_i neighborhoods, change in allocated (decentralized) income, M_i, does not change convexity of the constraint. The feasible region in $v_i x_i$ space, however, is larger for high M_i owing to outward movement of the constraint. Convexity of the constraint does not change for change in M_i.[3]

In the case of isoquality demand (i.e., $\hat{v}_i$ targeted), convexity of the constraint and location of $\hat{v}_i$ along the v_i axis are no less important than in the *general case*, where v_i is allowed to vary along the constraint.

In the case of targeted v_i, the change in quantity, x_i, corresponding to a change in b_i, depends on the magnitude of the shift in the constraint, the change in convexity, and the location of the v_i target. Recall from chapter 7, section 11, equation (3), that change in x_i derived from change in b$_i$ is given by: $(\partial x_i/\partial b_i) = -[(v_i M_i)/(a_i + b_i v_i)^2]$. See also note 13, chapter 7.

To reiterate, for a low value of (a_i/b_i) and constant M_i, the change in x_i will be greater for change in $\hat{v}_i$ to the left of the focus point than for change in $\hat{v}_i$ to the right of that point. An implication of this finding is that, for low (a_i/b_i) and constant M_i, the quantity response to a change in b_i will be greater for "low" levels of quality than for "high" levels. These results, in turn, may influence own-price elasticity of demand in $x_i p_i$ space. The conditions for such influence are $(\Delta p_i/\Delta b_i) > 0$, given a_i constant. In terms of transactions, the appropriate b$_i$ is b_i^p.

The new model projects that, for low (a_i/b_i) and constant M_i, own-price elasticity of demand, $(dx_i/x_i)/(dp_i/p_i)$, will be higher along isoquality demand curves with "low" $\hat{v}_i$, than along isoquality demand curves with "high" $\hat{v}_i$. Recall that $\hat{v}_i$ represents the targeted variety, or specified constant level of quality, for an isoquality demand curve. The model implies that, under the conditions described above, isoquality demand curves become more inelastic as the targeted level of quality is increased, and that this phenomenon occurs regardless of the level of budgeted consumer income, M_i. For a fixed (a_i/b_i) ratio, as M_i is increased (decreased) the constraint does not change convexity for a specified v_i or v_i neighborhood. We should note that these results regarding own-price elasticity say nothing as to the nature of shift patterns of isoquality demand (e.g., when the targeted level of quality has in-

Figure 13.9 **Houthakker Constraint Under Variable a_i/b_i Ratio**

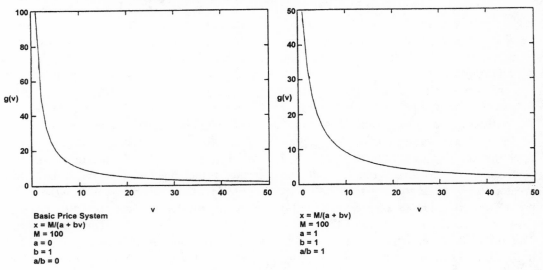

Basic Price System
$x = M/(a + bv)$
$M = 100$
$a = 0$
$b = 1$
$a/b = 0$

$x = M/(a + bv)$
$M = 100$
$a = 1$
$b = 1$
$a/b = 1$

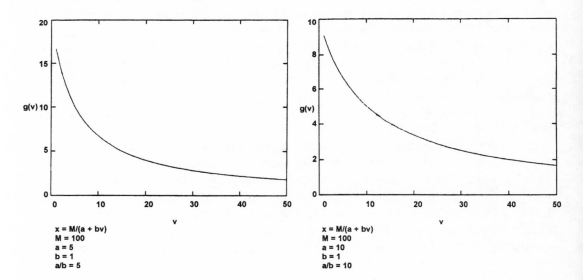

$x = M/(a + bv)$
$M = 100$
$a = 5$
$b = 1$
$a/b = 5$

$x = M/(a + bv)$
$M = 100$
$a = 10$
$b = 1$
$a/b = 10$

creased or decreased). We address this topic in the following section.

4. Shifts of Isoquality Demand Curves

Our discussion to this point has centered on isoquality demand, where the consumer targets on a specific level of quality, on $\hat{v}_i$.

We now address the topic of change in isoquality demand, or shifts of an isoquality demand curve.

It is important to be clear as to what is included in this phenomenon. For example, it is typically presumed that an increase in quality will induce an outward shift or increase in consumer demand. In our model,

Figure 13.9 (continued)

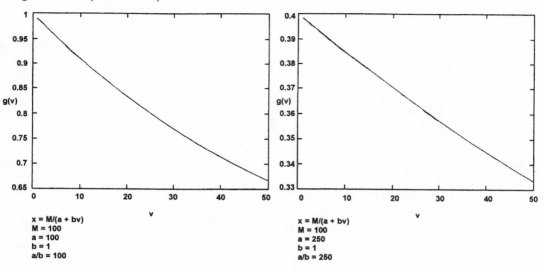

x = M/(a + bv)
M = 100
a = 100
b = 1
a/b = 100

x = M/(a + bv)
M = 100
a = 250
b = 1
a/b = 250

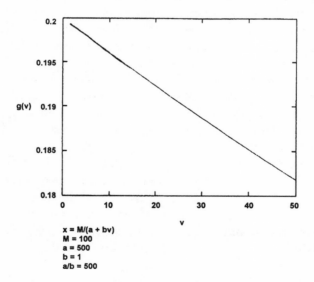

x = M/(a + bv)
M = 100
a = 500
b = 1
a/b = 500

however, the shift patterns of isoquality demand curves are less predictable. First, in the case of an isoquality demand curve fixed at $\hat{v}_i$, shifts could arise due to a change in quality (i.e., through $\Delta \hat{v}_i$), or shifts could arise for other reasons. In the second case, quality remains constant (i.e., remains at $\hat{v}_i$); however, a change in demand still occurs. For example, a change in demand could arise as a result of a change in consumer technology (à la Fisher and Shell or Ironmonger), where the change in consumer technology rearranges the ranking of v_i. A change in demand could also arise owing to a change in taste. (See, also, Ironmonger on change in priority of wants across commodities as a change in taste.) A change in demand could arise owing to a change in b_i^c. Finally, a change in demand could arise as a result of a change in budgeted income, M_i.

As before, unless there is a consistent definition of quantity, a change in that definition could result in a "change in taste" being interpreted as (or confused with) a "change in quality," or vice versa (see Fisher and Shell). We will have more to say on these matters later.

Additionally, confusion can arise from a variable-quality demand curve, that is, a demand curve where v_i varies along the curve. Studies of change in demand attributable to change in quality need to be conducted carefully so as not to confuse shifts in isoquality demand with movements along, or shifts of, a variable-quality demand curve. In empirical studies it is often difficult to control and isolate isoquality demand from variable-quality demand. We will also have more to say on this topic later.

For now, we focus on the theoretical aspects of shifts in isoquality demand. We begin with the case where quality has increased and examine the assumption (presumption) that higher quality induces an outward shift or increase in consumer demand.

5. Individual Consumer Demand Under an Increase in Quality

To facilitate discussion of shifts in isoquality demand, we open with the simplifying assumptions that consumer technology does not change and that the ordering of v_i on the v_i axis does not change. Later, we relax these conditions. The assumption that, for a constant price (p_i), an increase in quality (an increase in v_i) will result in an outward shift in individual consumer demand, is illustrated in Figure 13.10,

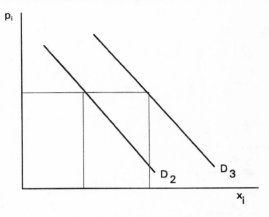

Figure 13.10 **Increase in v_i Results in Increase in Demand**

where $\hat{v}_{i2}$ corresponds to D_2 and $\hat{v}_{i3}$ to D_3, and $\hat{v}_{i3} > \hat{v}_{i2}$.

We should first note that the increase in quality could arise from at least two sources: the consumer and/or the producer. We begin by assuming the latter. We also assume that the consumer had previously targeted on a single variety, $\hat{v}_{i2}$, and that the producer had accurately matched that target (i.e., $\hat{v}_{i2}^p = \hat{v}_{i2}^c$). We further assume that the producer has accurately estimated b_{i2}^c, such that $b_{i2}^p = b_{i2}^c$. As previously, we assume $a_i^c = a_i^p$ and that the price of the basic package has remained unchanged over the relevant time period. In price space and $v_i x_i$ space, consequently, we have a set of conditions as portrayed in Figure 13.11. In these diagrams we have assumed there are no v_i neighborhoods. Also, the (a_i / b_i) ratio is assumed sufficiently low such that the constraint is non-linear.

We commence by assuming that the producer introduces a higher v_i to the consumer. Assume v_{i3}^p is higher than $\hat{v}_{i2}^p = \hat{v}_{i2}^c$. At this juncture we ignore the issue of whether v_{i3}^p is a "new" variety or a variety that previously existed. In $v_i x_i$ space we have the situation illustrated in Figure 13.12.

We now address the following two questions: Will the consumer become interested

Figure 13.11 **Initial Conditions in $v_i x_i$ and $v_i p_i$ Spaces**

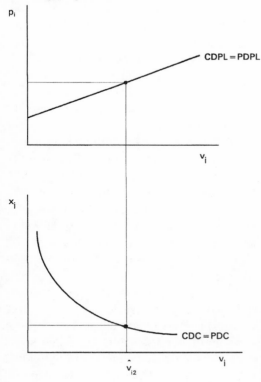

Figure 13.12 **An Increase in v_i in $v_i x_i$ Space**

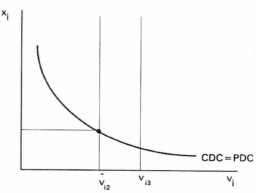

habit in consumer consumption patterns may inhibit purchase of higher v_i by some consumers.

For now, let us return to the question of whether higher quality can induce an increase in demand. Assume the consumer becomes interested in v_{i3}^p. Will individual consumer demand for the ith commodity increase—that is, produce an outward shift?

Recall that throughout our discussion of the Houthakker model we have held to the assumption that only a single variety of the commodity is purchased during the time period under examination (i.e., the single-variety case). Under these conditions, quantity of the single variety may change, but only a single variety (a single level of v_i) is purchased by any given consumer at some specified time period.

A surprising result of the new model is the conclusion that, ceteris paribus, an outward shift or increase of individual consumer demand is unlikely to accompany an increase in quality. An aggregated market demand curve, representing many consumers, may shift outward, reflecting the addition of new consumers to the market as a result of higher quality. For an individual consumer, however, if nothing else changes except the level of quality, there will be no increase in individual demand.

in v_{i3}^p and switch to the higher variety? And, if such a switch does occur, will this produce an outward shift of individual consumer demand?

According to our model, when producers offer higher quality products or services there is no guarantee individual consumers will accept the higher v_i. As explained earlier, if a higher v_i exceeds the upper bound, v_i(max.), for a specific consumer's v_i neighborhood, that consumer usually will not purchase the higher v_i. If producers can convince consumers to change their upper bounds on v_i, then acceptance of higher v_i is possible. Clearly, advertising and social pressure may attract consumers to the higher v_{i3}^p. If producers eliminate production of older (lower) v_{i2}^p, such that consumers are left with only the higher v_i, then acceptance of v_{i3}^p may increase. Conversely, availability of substitutes and the inertia of

Figure 13.13 **Increase in Quality with p_i Constant**

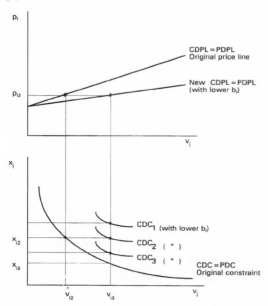

The nature of the Houthakker constraint in $v_i x_i$ space, the requirements of a decentralized budget M_i, combined with the requirements for consistency between $v_i x_i$ space and $v_i p_i$ price space, do not allow individual consumer demand curves, in $x_i p_i$ space, to shift outward in response to an increase in quality (i.e., to an increase in $\hat{v}_i^c$). It is interesting to investigate the conditions under which it is possible for individual consumer demand to increase or decrease in response to a change in v_i.

In Figure 13.13 we illustrate the phenomena behind individual consumer demand. Figure 13.13 combines information from Figures 13.11 and 13.12.[4] As shown, the price p_{i2} corresponds to the original price prior to the increase in quality (i.e., the increase from $\hat{v}_{i2}$ to $\hat{v}_{i3}$). To illustrate an increase in demand associated with an increase in quality, we proceed via two approaches: one, where price (p_i) is held constant, and the other, where quantity (x_i) is held constant.

In the first case, to hold p_i constant, we either reduce a_i or b_i, or some combination of both. Consistent with our earlier assumption that the price of the basic package remains fixed, we hold a_i constant and lower b_i. The magnitude of reduction in b_i will only be that which is sufficient to lower the CDPL = PDPL (the transaction surface) such that p_i remains unchanged for the new, higher $\hat{v}_{i3}$.

Examination of the bottom diagram in Figure 13.13 reveals the impact on quantity (x_i), which accompanies higher quality. Notice that along the original constraint the quantity, x_{i2}, is greater than the quantity x_{i3}, which is the new quantity corresponding to the higher variety, $\hat{v}_{i3}$. This result is obtained if the consumer remains on the original constraint.

Were we to combine the two diagrams of Figure 13.13 to create a demand curve in $x_i p_i$ space, as illustrated in Figure 13.5, we would have a demand curve that shifts to the left—that is, a decrease in individual consumer demand associated with an increase in quality. This result obtains because the consumer remains on the original budget constraint, and because we are examining the case of isoquality demand. If quality is allowed to vary along the demand curve (the case of variable-quality demand), then we cannot draw these conclusions.

The new isoquality demand curve derived from Figure 13.13 is isoquality at the higher level, $v_i = \hat{v}_{i3}$. The previous isoquality demand was set at the level $v_i = \hat{v}_{i2}$. The demand curve with higher quality is to the left of the lower isoquality curve. In other words, with price (p_i) constant, higher quality resulted in reduced demand. These results are counter to the common presumption that higher quality induces an increase in demand.

Examination of Figure 13.13 indicates that these results derive from the inverse relationship of quantity and quality along the Houthakker constraint. Recall from chapter 7, section 11, that the slope of the constraint is given by $dx_i/dv_i = -[(b_i M_i)/(a_i + b_i v_i)^2]$. Also, recall our previous discussion of the (a_i/b_i) ratio and its effect on convexity of the constraint, most notably that for "low" values of (a_i/b_i) the reduction in x_i, derived from an increase in v_i, will be greater for v_i values to the left of the focus point then for v_i values to the right of that point.

In the example just cited, the consumer operated along the original constraint. If, however, we allow change in b_i, that is, a reduction in b_i^c, such that p_{i2} remains unchanged, then the original constraint will shift upward, as explained earlier, and the impact on quantity may be quite different from that just described. Recall from chapter 7, section 11, $dx_i/db_i = -[(v_i M_i)/(a_i + b_i v_i)^2]$. In Figure 13.13 we have illustrated three possible shift patterns for the CDC. In all three cases (CDC$_1$, CDC$_2$, and CDC$_3$) the same size reduction in b_i applies. The three different CDCs represent three different magnitudes of shift associated with the same reduction in b_i. The impact of db_i on x_i will depend on the location of v_i with respect to the focus point, the magnitude of the ratio (a_i/b_i), and the size of the decentralized budget for the ith commodity, M_i.

In $x_i p_i$ space (see Figure 13.14) the implications corresponding to CDC$_1$, CDC$_2$, and CDC$_3$ are quite different. For CDC$_3$, the new isoquality demand curve, D(CDC$_3$), with v_i fixed at $\hat{v}_{i3}$, will be to the left of the original demand curve—that is, there will be a decrease in demand associated with higher quality. For CDC$_1$, the new isoquality demand curve, $D(\hat{v}_{i3}) = D(CDC_1)$, will be to the right of the original curve—that is, there will be an increase in demand associated with the increase in targeted v_i. And, for CDC$_2$ there will be no change in demand, no shift in the original

Figure 13.14 **Possible Demand Phenomena Under Increased v_i: First Case**

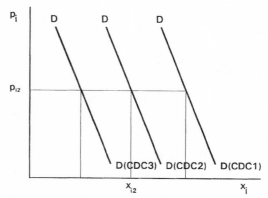

Demand shift patterns after an increase in quality.

demand curve, albeit that the level of quality has increased from $\hat{v}_{i2}$ to $\hat{v}_{i3}$. All three demand curves are illustrated in Figure 13.14.

The standard presumption that higher quality will induce an increase in demand requires, under conditions established by the new model, that isoquality demand on the part of individual consumers behave as demand curve D(CDC$_1$). As explained above, demand curve D(CDC$_1$) is one of three possibilities, and is by no means a foregone conclusion. As we will soon see, there exist strong arguments against the shift pattern illustrated by demand D(CDC$_1$). Before discussing that topic, however, it is useful to consider another approach to measure whether an increase in quality induces an increase in individual consumer demand.

Previously, to isolate the effect of higher quality on demand, we held the price p_i constant and examined the impact of a higher $\hat{v}_i$ on quantity x_i. Now we do just the reverse: We hold x_i constant and examine what happens to p_i. The presumption that higher quality will generate higher demand may now be measured by the effect of higher $\hat{v}_i$ on p_i. In Figure 13.15, which

Figure 13.15 **Increase in Quality with x_i Constant**

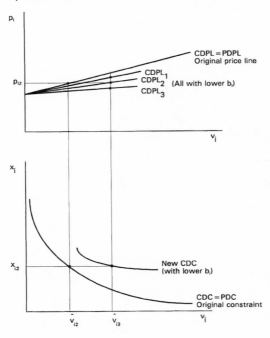

is essentially the same as Figure 13.13, we illustrate this procedure and identify the threshold values of interest.

As in Figure 13.13, in Figure 13.15 an individual consumer has initially targeted on $\hat{v}_{i2}$, along the original constraint where CDC = PDC. The quantity purchased is x_{i2}, and the price is p_{i2}, which is found along the original price line, CDPL = PDPL. As discussed previously, the higher targeted level of quality is $\hat{v}_{i3}$. Now, however, instead of p_{i2} fixed, we have x_{i2} fixed. To assure x_{i2} constant, either a_i and/or b_i must be adjusted such that x_{i2} remains unchanged. As before, we hold a_i constant and reduce b_i. Recall the requirements for transactions are $b_i^c \geq b_i^p$, given $a_i^c = a_i^p$, and that all transactions occur along the PDC and the PDPL (see also note 4).

As shown in Figure 13.15, it is assumed the reduction in b_i is such that x_{i2} remains constant. The new CDC reflects the lower

value for b_i^c. As we know from our previous discussion, reduction in b_i^c also affects the CDPL, and three possible consequences are illustrated by CDPL$_1$, CDPL$_2$, and CDPL$_3$. The standard presumption is that an increase in quality will induce an increase in demand. With quantity held constant, an increase in demand would be revealed by an increase in price, p_i. In Figure 13.15, therefore, we would expect the new transaction surface to be CDPL$_1$. If the change in b_i^c results in either CDPL$_2$ or CDPL$_3$, then the standard presumption is not realized.

As we explained earlier, shift patterns of the CDC depend on several factors, namely, the (a_i/b_i) ratio, the magnitude of M_i, and the value of $\hat{v}_i$. In particular, we noted that for a highly convex constraint, corresponding to a low (a_i/b_i) ratio, low values of $\hat{v}_i$ would result in significantly greater change in x_i for any given change in $\hat{v}_i$. In similar fashion, the change in b_i^c necessary to maintain x_{i2} constant will be less for low values of $\hat{v}_i$ than for high values of $\hat{v}_i$. Insofar as Figure 13.15 is concerned, these conditions mean that change in the CDPL will be influenced by convexity of the constraint and the location of $\hat{v}_i$. To obtain CDPL$_1$ (the standard presumption), a small reduction in b_i^c is required. A small reduction in b_i^c will be sufficient to maintain x_{i2} constant, if $\hat{v}_i$ is "low" in value and the constraint is highly convex. Otherwise, CDPL$_2$ or CDPL$_3$ may result.

In other words, the conditions necessary to obtain the standard presumption—that an increase in quality will generate an increase in demand—are numerous and complex. It should be noted, however, that our remarks apply to the case of individual consumer demand, not aggregated consumer demand.

As regards both Figures 13.13 and 13.15, it is important to recall that targeting on $\hat{v}_{i3}$ may involve the notion of a demand maintenance price. Recall that demand maintenance is defined as the reduction in price necessary to maintain the consumer at some specified level of quality. Heretofore, the price reduction has been a reduction in b_i. In Figure 13.13 the reduction in b_i^c was to assure both that p_{i2} remained constant and that the consumer remained at $\hat{v}_{i3}$. In Figure 13.15 the reduction in b_i^c was to assure that the consumer remain at $\hat{v}_{i3}$ and the previous quantity, x_{i2}.

In Figure 13.16 the results of Figure 13.15 are reflected in $x_i p_i$ space. As contrasted with Figure 13.14, the three demand curves reflect the three CDPLs. Note that demand curve $D(CDPL_1)$ gives the increase in demand expected under the standard presumption of the effect of higher quality on consumer demand. This demand curve corresponds to $D(CDC_1)$ in Figure 13.14. Demand curve $D(CDPL_3)$ corresponds to $D(CDC_3)$ in Figure 13.14 and represents a decrease in demand associated with higher quality. Both $D(CDPL_2)$ and $D(CDC_2)$ represent the case where there is no shift in demand associated with a change in quality.

6. Individual Consumer Demand Under a Decrease in Quality

To cover the topic of change in demand thoroughly, or demand shifts associated with change in the level of quality, we also consider the impact of a decrease in quality. We begin by assuming the consumer is initially at the quality level $v_i = \hat{v}_{i2}$. We assume now that the consumer decides to target on a lower level of quality—for example, on $\hat{v}_{i1}$. Under the standard presumption, when the level of quality declines, the demand curve should shift to the left (i.e., a decrease in demand). As before, we first examine this phenomenon by assuming the

Figure 13.16 **Possible Demand Phenomena Under Increased** v_i: **Second Case**

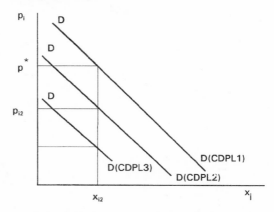

Demand-shift patterns after an increase in quality.

price of the ith commodity, p_i, remains constant, and then determine whether or not there is a decrease in quantity, x_i, when v_i is reduced from $\hat{v}_{i2}$ to $\hat{v}_{i1}$. In Figure 13.17 we provide two diagrams that are identical with those of Figure 13.13, except that in Figure 13.17 the level of quality has decreased. Note, however, that the price, p_i, remains constant.

As in the case of Figure 13.13 (only in reverse), if the consumer remains on the original constraint, the reduction in quality results in an increase in quantity. This result is not consistent with the standard presumption. To assure, however, that the price, p_i, remains constant, while v_i declines, the value of b_i must change. In this case, b_i must increase. In Figure 13.17 there are three new values of the CDC, each reflecting the same magnitude of increase in b_i^c. As before, the magnitude of shift in the new CDC is influenced by the (a_i/b_i) ratio, the location of the v_i with respect to the focus point of the hyperbolic constraint, and the magnitude of M_i. Note that CDC_1 is consistent with the standard presumption—that is, a decrease in quality

Figure 13.17 **Decrease in Quality with p_i Constant**

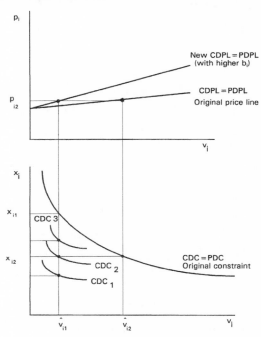

Figure 13.18 **Possible Demand Phenomena Under Decreased v_i: First Case**

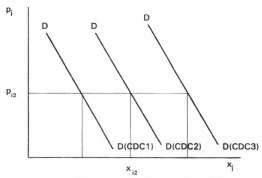

Demand-shift patterns after a decrease in quality.

results in a decrease in consumer demand. The CDC_3 indicates an increase in quantity as a result of a decrease in quality. And CDC_2 shows no change in x_i as a result of the decrease in v_i.

In Figure 13.18, which is comparable to Figure 13.14, we have translated the results of Figure 13.17 into x_ip_i space. Note, as before, the price, p_i, is constant. Also, as before, the demand curves are isoquality curves, where the level of quality is the same for each curve and is equal to $\hat{v}_{i1}$. In Figure 13.18 the price, p_i, and quantity, x_i, corresponding to the original level of quality, $\hat{v}_{i2}$, are represented by the price, p_{i2}, and quantity, x_{i2}—that is, the original demand curve corresponds to demand curve $D(CDC_2)$. The traditional presumption is that a decrease in quality will produce a decrease in consumer demand. These results are only demonstrated in demand curve $D(CDC_1)$. As demand curve $D(CDC_3)$ illustrates, there also exists the

possibility of an increase in demand corresponding to a decrease in quality.

As shown in Figure 13.17, the shift patterns of demand curves in Figure 13.18 arise from the shift patterns of the CDC in Figure 13.17. Shifts of the CDC result from the increase in b_i^c. For the same size increase in b_i^c, the magnitude of shift of each CDC depends, as before, on the magnitude of M_i, the (a_i/b_i) ratio, and on the location of v_i with respect to the focus point of the convex constraint.

Finally, as with Figures 13.15 and 13.16, we examine the shift pattern of demand curves when quantity, x_i, is held constant and quality is decreased. With quantity held constant, the standard presumption is that corresponding to a reduction in quality there will be a decrease in demand, and, therefore, a decrease in price, p_i. In Figure 13.19 we have constructed the v_ip_i and v_ix_i spaces necessary to illustrate this phenomenon. Note that Figure 13.19 is comparable to Figure 13.15. In Figure 13.15 there was an increase in targeted v_i. In Figure 13.19 $\hat{v}_i$ has decreased from $\hat{v}_{i2}$ to $\hat{v}_{i1}$.

The isoquality demand curves derived from Figure 13.19 are illustrated in Figure 13.20. Corresponding to each new CDPL in Figure 13.19 there is a demand curve in

Figure 13.19 **Decrease in Quality with x_i Constant**

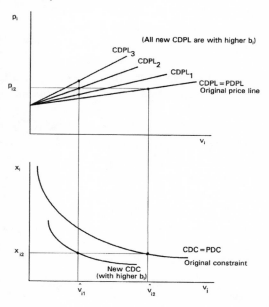

Figure 13.20 **Possible Demand Phenomena Under Decreased v_i: Second Case**

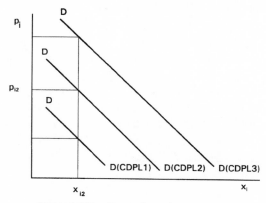

Demand-shift patterns after a decrease in quality.

Figure 13.20. Note that the original price, p_{i2}, and quantity, x_{i2}, pertain to the original quality level, $\hat{v}_{i2}$. In Figure 13.20 all three demand curves are isoquality at the same level of quality (i.e., $\hat{v}_{i1}$). Demand curve $D(CDPL_1)$ portrays what would happen under the standard presumption, namely, a decrease in quality results in decreased demand. Again, demand curve $D(CDPL_2)$ shows no change in demand after the decrease in v_i. Demand curve $D(CDPL_3)$ shows an increase in demand.

7. Necessary Conditions for an Increase in Individual Consumer Demand

A number of topics associated with shifts in isoquality demand need further clarification. Before we turn to those matters, however, we return to our earlier assertion that an increase in quality may not lead to an increase in demand.

In our earlier remarks regarding consumer behavior in $v_i x_i$ space, we assumed consumer income, M_i, reflected consumer decision making on a decentralized budget for the ith commodity. With few exceptions, we have generally assumed M_i constant. The assumption of unchanged M_i holds for our discussion of changes in quality and shifts of demand curves. In section 5 we identified three options for isoquality demand after a change in quality: an increase, a decrease, or no change in individual consumer demand. When we introduce the requirement that M_i remain constant, the likelihood of increased demand becomes small.

If we return to the case of an increase in $\hat{v}_i$ (i.e., from $\hat{v}_{i2}$ to $\hat{v}_{i3}$), we may now consider individual consumer expenditure on v_i. We calculate that expenditure by taking the product $p_{i2} x_{i2}$. We begin by assuming no previous saving exists out of the M_i budget—that is, $M_i = p_{i2} x_{i2}$, where $p_i = a_i + b_i v_i$. With this as background, we return to Figure 13.13 and consider the effect of expenditure constant and budgeted income constant. Note that expenditure need not always equal the budgeted income for the ith commodity, but always $p_{i2} x_{i2} \leq M_i$.

In Figure 13.13 three CDCs are identified as possible new constraints under a reduction in b_i^c. The different shift patterns for the three CDCs arise from different locations of $\hat{v}_i$ on the v_i axis, for different (a_i/b_i) ratios, and/or for different levels of fixed M_i. With M_i constant, it remains possible to generate the three CDCs and their corresponding three different demand curves in Figure 13.14. With expenditure on the initial variety constant, however, the outward shift of $D(CDC_1)$ becomes impossible. Demand curve $D(CDC_2)$ is possible; and, with saving permitted, demand curve $D(CDC_3)$ is likewise possible. Similarly, for a decrease in quality (see Figures 13.17 and 13.18), an increase in demand is impossible. In Figure 13.18, demand curve $D(CDC_2)$ is possible, and, with saving, demand curve $D(CDC_1)$ is possible. Demand curve $D(CDC_3)$ is not possible.

These results indicate that the standard presumption—that an increase in quality will induce an increase in consumer demand—must additionally presume that either individual consumers have experienced an increase in total income M_T, or that they have increased their budgeted income M_i (i.e., they have reduced their expenditures on other commodities), or that saving previously existed, either within M_T or M_i, or both. To increase demand for the ith commodity, which has experienced an increase in quality, it is necessary that one or more of these options exist and be adopted by consumers. In other words, an increase in demand must be supported by resources. Preference, without the support of budgeted funds in the M_i subbudget, is not sufficient to increase individual consumer demand.

As noted earlier, these results apply to individual consumer demand and not necessarily to aggregated consumer demand. There may be an increase in market demand for a commodity that has experienced an increase in quality, simply due to an increase in the number of consumers who are interested in the higher-quality variety—that is, the additional consumers are individuals who were not previously in the market for the ith commodity. It is also possible that consumers who were previously consuming many different lower-quality varieties are attracted to a single higher-quality v_i, and their combined purchases of the higher variety result in an outward shift of the market demand for the higher variety. More than likely, however, these new consumers will also have reduced expenditures on other commodities and/or drawn down savings.

As noted above, in the case of the individual consumer, it is possible to have an increase in demand if the consumer were to increase the budgeted funds for the ith commodity—that is, increase M_i, and/or if saving previously existed within the original budget, and those savings are now devoted to increasing the quantity, x_i, purchased as a result of the increase in quality. The requirement that increased individual demand be supported by either increased income or by a new allocation within decentralized budgets holds implications for other traditional assumptions of increased (individual) consumer demand (e.g., a change in consumer taste and other factors). As we will see in chapters 14 and 15, at the level of individual consumer demand, as derived from traditional $x_i x_j$ space, it may be impossible to discern the difference between a change in the level of quality and a change in consumer taste, or to distinguish between a change in quality and a change in the price p_i. These similarities raise questions regarding downward adjustment of price indices for improvements in quality. The definition and measurement of inflation also may be affected by these issues.

8. The Consumer Budget and Willingness-to-Pay

Earlier we examined consumer willingness-to-pay for a variety, $\hat{v}_i$. (See Figures 8.5, 8.6, 10.1 to 10.7, 11.1, 11.2, 12.6, 12.11, 13.11 to 13.13, 13.15, 13.17, 13.19, and related discussions.) At those junctures, we defined willingness-to-pay for $\hat{v}_i$ as either a change in quantity, x_i, or a change in p_i, or both. We retain those measures. Previously, we also discussed the concepts of a demand reservation and demand maintenance price. We explained the importance of a decentralized budget and introduced the symbol, M_i, to represent the amount of total consumer income, M_T, allocated (budgeted) to the ith commodity. We also discussed the concept of a basic package and its corresponding price, a_i. Generally, we have assumed a_i constant. In our discussion of producers we generally have assumed, $a_i^p = a_i^c$.

Throughout we have utilized b_i to stand for willingness-to-pay (WTP). We have identified three types of WTP. Of the three concepts, WTP(TK) is the most important, and is seen as either a subactivity nested within the other WTP concepts, or, as a stand-alone, independent decision-making activity. The symbol b_i was utilized to identify both consumer and producer decision making, where b_i^c represents consumer willingness-to-pay for a single variety or a range of v_i across a v_i neighborhood, and b_i^p represents producer estimates of consumer willingness-to-pay. Based on these concepts, we have been able to elaborate on the conditions necessary for transactions to occur between producers and consumers.

In chapter 9 we presented an algorithm for consumer decision making regarding b_i^c, which was based on consumer expectation of quality from some level of v_i, as well as on consumer consumption experience from the same. We assumed that learning was involved, some of which might involve pleasant surprise and/or disappointment. The b_i^c were assumed to have either stable period-one attractors (accuracy), higher-period attractors (vacillation

in decision making), or non-stable solutions (confusion). These results were assumed to affect the consumer-determined constraint (CDC), and to affect the consumer price strategy, or range of prices acceptable to the consumer, the CDPL, or consumer-determined price line. Producers were also assumed to go through a learning process as they endeavor to estimate consumers' b_i^c. The b_i^p influence the producer-determined constraint (PDC) and the PDPL (producer-determined price line), or range of prices offered by producers.

9. Neighborhoods and Individual Consumer Demand

To present the new model fully, as well as be able to expand upon earlier material, especially the demand reservation price (DRP) and demand maintenance price (DMP), we return to the concept of neighborhoods, both v_i and x_i neighborhoods, and include them in our discussion of individual consumer demand. We begin with the concept of a v_i neighborhood.

In chapter 8, section 4, we introduced the idea that an individual consumer might be interested in only a limited range of the varieties that exist within the ith commodity. Subsequently, we explained how incorporation of v_i neighborhoods could affect the consumer's constraint and preference map. We discuss now the impact of v_i neighborhoods on individual consumer demand. As mentioned earlier, this material has a bearing on the concepts of demand reservation and demand maintenance prices.

In our previous discussion of v_i neighborhoods we assumed the subset of v_i included within the neighborhood was of interest to the consumer because it served the consumer's self-image. We concluded that what was high or low quality to one consumer might not be similarly perceived by another. We also concluded that the ordering of v_i within the v_i neighborhood could be unique to each consumer. Also, similar to Ironmonger, we concluded that v_i outside the neighborhood, beyond either the upper or lower boundaries, might be ignored by the consumer. In other words, if a consumer is "offered" a variety of the ith commodity that is of higher quality than his or her v_i(max.), that variety might not be purchased. If the consumer has reached v_i(max.) for the ith commodity, any increase in total income, M_T, may either result in increased saving, or the consumer may increase the level of quality in some other commodity (e.g., purchase a higher v_j within the jth commodity, and so forth).

Similarly, for an individual consumer, varieties below his or her lower boundary, v_i(min.), might not be purchased. Under some circumstances, such as unemployment or a decrease in household income, the consumer might purchase v_i below v_i(min.). We assume, however, that it is more likely that the consumer will first reduce quality within a v_i neighborhood to v_i(min.), and then turn to other commodities and do likewise within each commodity $(j \neq i)$. In other words, we assume that consumers maintain their variety neighborhoods but reduce the level of quality to its lowest level within each neighborhood. This further implies, of course, that we assume the existence of neighborhoods within all commodities. (This assumption also imposes additional restrictions of separability across all other commodities associated with the ith commodity.)

Recall that earlier we distinguished between Duesenberry and Ironmonger on a related matter. Ironmonger assumed consumers with higher income were able to satisfy more "wants" than consumers with lower income. Duesenberry assumed that all consumers satisfy the same "wants," but that consumers with higher income satisfied their "wants" with higher-quality

products and services. Our approach is similar to that of Ironmonger. However, we combine both authors to some degree.

It is also possible that across the life cycle, individual consumers change their perspective and evaluation of individual v_i and/or of entire v_i neighborhoods. With regards to v_i neighborhoods, it is possible that consumers change the varieties included within a neighborhood, and/or they may change the ordering of v_i across a neighborhood. Under such circumstances, it is possible that v_i previously below v_i(min.) may become members of the neighborhood. In other words, v_i, previously deemed to be too low in quality, subsequently may become more highly regarded (evaluated) by the consumer and accepted within the neighborhood. Similar adjustments may occur for varieties above the upper boundary of the neighborhood.

Finally, it is possible for consumers to make mistakes, at least initially, in their evaluation of individual v_i. The b_i learning process discussed in chapter 9 is capable of explaining such mistakes and subsequent learning. Pleasant surprise, *acquired tastes*, disappointment, and other aspects of consumer decision making discussed at that juncture may apply here.

In addition to v_i neighborhoods, we assume consumers construct x_i neighborhoods. An x_i neighborhood has upper and lower boundaries, x_i(max.) and x_i(min.), similar to a v_i neighborhood. The existence of a maximum boundary on quantity presumes individual consumers will not increase quantity of the ith commodity beyond x_i(max.), even if the commodity price, p_i, falls and/or total consumer income, M_T, increases. In the fashion of Ironmonger and earlier classical economists (see chapters 2 and 6), we assume that once the maximum quantity, x_i(max.), has been reached, the consumer either increases quality, v_i, within the ith commodity, switches to greater expenditure on other commodities, or possibly saves excess funds within the M_i decentralized budget. Obviously, this form of decision making on the part of consumers places restrictions on the extent of diminishing marginal utility across any given x.

Insofar as a lower boundary on quantity is concerned, the existence of x_i(min.) implies that, regardless of the level of quality, individual consumers may have a quantity threshold requirement, which must be met in order for them to commence expenditure on the commodity. The minimum quantity may be $x_i = 1$, or some proportion less than one. We will assume x_i(min.) > 0 (i.e., that the lower boundary of the quantity neighborhood does not extend to the v_i axis; see our earlier remarks on the relationship of quantity and quality, chapter 4, section 3). It is also possible that x_i (max.) $= x_i$ (min.) (i.e., targeting on a specific level of quantity). The $x_i = 1$ case is probably the most likely example of this phenomenon.

10. The Consumer Window in Quality–Quantity Space

Figure 13.21 illustrates a v_ix_i space with v_i and x_i neighborhoods. The shaded area, where the two neighborhoods overlap, we will call a "window." For each consumer with v_i and x_i neighborhoods there exists a window. Each v_ix_i window may be unique to each consumer. It is possible, however, that social pressure and other factors could force similarity of windows across consumers, and/or that similarity of windows could arise for cohorts of consumers with similar socioeconomic-demographic characteristics.

Previously, in our discussion of transaction regions (see chapters 11 and 12) we indicated that in order for producers to carry out transactions with individual con-

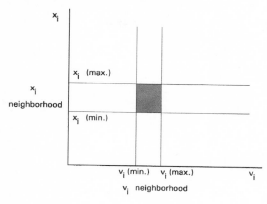

Figure 13.21 **Consumer Window in Quality-Quantity Space**

sumers, the following conditions must be met: $b_i^p \geq b_i^c$ such that $PDC \geq CDC$, $PDPL \leq CDPL$, and $\hat{v}_i^p = \hat{v}_i^c$. Generally, we have assumed $a_i^c = a_i^p$, and both constant and greater than zero. Given the existence of v_i neighborhoods for consumers, we have also assumed that in order to complete transactions with individual consumers, producers must provide varieties that fall within those neighborhoods. We described this activity as another dimension of the Waugh-Brems problem. Now, given overlapping x_i and v_i neighborhoods (i.e., given the existence of consumer windows), to carry out transactions with individual consumers, producers must have $PDC \geq CDC$ over at least some of the v_i and x_i ranges contained within those windows. An example of this condition is provided in Figure 13.22.

The region of possible transactions in Figure 13.22 is the area within the window, inclusive of the boundaries, and equal to or greater than the CDC. Recall that we assume transactions occur along or under the PDC; hence, that portion of the PDC that lies within the window and meets the above conditions identifies the transaction region in v_ix_i space. For a given commodity, if a producer does not have PDC that lie within the window of an individual con-

Figure 13.22 **Transactions in the Window**

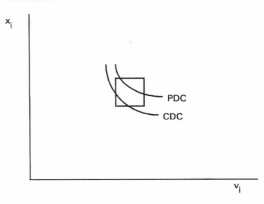

Figure 13.23 **Alternative Windows Along the Constraint: Low a_i/b_i Ratio**

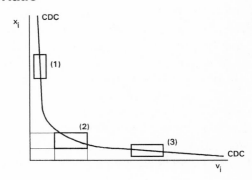

sumer, no transactions occur between that producer and consumer.

Along the PDC within the window, consumer decision making may consist of either utility maximization (NSUM) against the PDC, to identify the optimal combination of v_i and x_i, or the consumer may employ variety-specific targeting. Consumer targeting on v_i is assumed to be consistent with the boundaries of the window. The consumer might single-target, on either v_i or x_i, or the consumer might double-target. In order for transactions to occur, the PDC must meet the requirements of either single or double targets. In the case of a double target, the PDC must be on or above the double target while remaining within the window. If transactions occur below the PDC, yet within the window, savings may exist for the consumer. (Transactions below the PDC, however, will reveal to the producer a greater willingness-to-pay, or higher b_i^c, than previously estimated by the producer.)

As discussed earlier, slope and convexity of either CDC or PDC depend on the (a_i/b_i) ratio and on the location of $\hat{v}_i$, or the v_i neighborhood, along the v_i axis. In the case of consumer windows, slope and convexity of PDC and CDC, through the window, depend on location of the v_i

and x_i neighborhoods. Given low value of the (a_i/b_i) ratio, location of the window (along the v_i axis) to the left of the focus point will result in CDC and PDC with steep negative slope values. Location of windows to the right of the focus point will result in constraints, within the window, with flatter slopes. An illustration utilizing only the CDC is provided in Figure 13.23.

In the diagram, window (1) is an example of high negative slope value for a CDC. Window (3) illustrates a CDC with low negative slope. Window (2) is in an intermediate range and illustrates slope similar to that provided in Figure 13.22. For any single consumer, only one window is assumed to exist at any point in time. We continue our discussion of consumer windows based on the example provided in Figure 13.22 (i.e., a window in the intermediate range). Later, we will compare the results with windows (1) and (3).

As explained previously, for transactions to occur between an individual consumer and a producer, it is necessary that the PDC pass through the consumer's transaction region—that is, in the case of Figure 13.22, that the PDC rest on or above the CDC within the consumer window. We will assume that these conditions are met

Figure 13.24 **Single-Variety Targeting Within the Window**

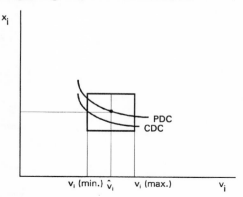

Figure 13.25 **The Window with Targeting in $v_i x_i$ and $v_i p_i$ Spaces**

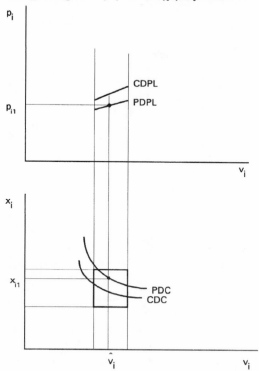

and, therefore, that transactions occur. Recall that transactions are assumed to occur along or under the PDC. We return now to our previous discussion of isoquality demand.

11. Consumer Windows and Iso-Quality Demand

In Figure 13.22, to generate an isoquality demand curve, we utilize the targeting approach and assume the consumer targets on a single v_i within the v_i neighborhood, between v_i(min.) and v_i(max.) inclusive. In this example we do not assume targeting on x_i. An illustration of variety-specific targeting is provided in Figure 13.24.

With v_i fixed at the targeted level, we proceed as previously explained to generate an isoquality demand curve for an individual consumer. Note, however, that corresponding to the boundaries of the window in $v_i x_i$ space, the CDPL in $v_i p_i$ space and the individual isoquality demand curve in $x_i p_i$ space become truncated. The truncations correspond to the v_i and x_i neighborhoods of the window. Figure 13.25 illustrates truncated CDPL, and corresponding PDPL under $b_i^p < b_i^c$ and accurate matching of neighborhoods by the producer. Figure 13.26 illustrates the effect

of a consumer window on individual consumer demand.

Recall from the discussion of Figure 13.5 that isoquality demand for an individual consumer was created by assuming a_i constant ($a_i^c = a_i^p$), and introducing variation in b_i^c. For transactions to occur, we assumed $b_i^p \leq b_i^c$ throughout. This implies that the producer adjusts b_i^p in response to consumer change in b_i^c. Thus, to produce Figure 13.26, we make similar assumptions, with the additional restriction that x_i remain on or within the boundaries of the x_i neighborhood. Further, note that the range of the transaction surface along the truncated PDPL establishes a truncated range for variation of p_i. The range of variation in x_i and p_i will depend on the range between x_i(min.) and x_i(max.) inclusive, and on the magnitude of shifts in the

Figure 13.26 Iso-Quality Demand and the Window: Simple Case

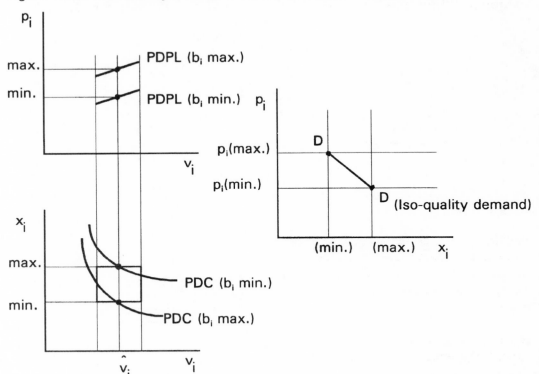

PDPL, that arise from change in b_i^p. Note that the minimum value for x_i (given $\hat{v}_i$) corresponds to the maximum value of p_i. Both x_i(min.) and p_i(max.) correspond to b_i^p(max.), and x_i(max.) and p_i(min.) correspond to b_i^p(min.). In Figure 13.26 we provide only the PDC and PDPL (along which transactions may occur), and assume throughout $b_i^p \leq b_i^c$, namely, PDC $\geq$ CDC and PDPL $\leq$ CDPL throughout. Note that the isoquality demand curve need not be linear, but should be monotonic decreasing.

12. An Increase in v_i Within the Consumer Window

With Figure 13.26 as reference, we return to our discussion of shift patterns in iso-quality demand. We commence by examining consumer behavior within the window in $v_i x_i$ space. We assume the consumer has made a decision to increase the level of targeted quality. We restrict the increase in $\hat{v}_i$ to be less than or equal to v_i(max.), the upper boundary on the v_i neighborhood. As before, the question remains: Will there be an increase in individual consumer demand as a result of an increase in quality?

We assume $b_i^c = b_i^p$, such that CDC = PDC, and we assume the b_i extend to the new, higher $\hat{v}_i$. Under this condition it is possible for the consumer to "reach" the new $\hat{v}_i$ under the previously existing b_i^c. No new evaluation of b_i^c is required. Given the downward slope of the constraint, however, use of the original b_i^c means attainment of the new, higher $\hat{v}_i$ will be accompanied by a reduction in quantity, x_i. This condition holds regardless of the window utilized in Figure 13.23. As mentioned previously, the rate of decline in x_i will vary depending on location of the window.

To examine shift patterns of the demand curve, we hold quantity constant. We hold quantity constant so as to examine the effects on price of an increase in quality. We assume $x_i = \hat{x}_i$, and that it lies within the range x_i(min.) to x_i(max.) inclusive.

When the consumer selects a higher level of quality, if he or she expects to continue to consume the same quantity as before the increase in $\hat{v}_i$, then the CDC must permit consumption at the intersection of the new $\hat{v}_i$ with the old $x_i = \hat{x}_i$, the targeted quantity in $v_i x_i$ space. As before, we continue to assume the PDC meets the condition $CDC \leq PDC$.

From the point of view of the CDC, attaining the intersection of $\hat{x}_i$ with the new $\hat{v}_i$ may be accomplished by either a reduction in b_i^c or by an increase in income budgeted to the ith commodity (i.e., an increase in M_i). From the point of view of the PDC, the condition may be similarly met by either a reduction in b_i^p or an increase in the producer's estimate of what consumers are willing to allocate to their M_i budgets.

From the point of view of the consumer, we assume that in order to increase the targeted level of quality within his or her window, while holding quantity constant, the consumer must link the decision of higher $\hat{v}_i$ to an increase in his or her decentralized budget for the ith commodity—that is, an increase in M_i by an amount sufficient to cover the intersection of $\hat{x}_i$ and the new $\hat{v}_i$. In other words, we assume that if the consumer is the source of the move to higher quality (i.e., the decision originates with the consumer), it is unreasonable to assume that he or she would correspondingly attain the higher $\hat{v}_i$ by reducing his or her willingness-to-pay for higher quality (i.e., reduce b_i^c). Of course, after consumption of the higher variety, and the consumption-learning experience, the consumer may reevaluate his or her assessment of b_i^c and subsequently reduce it.

As stated earlier, if the higher $\hat{v}_i$ falls within the consumer's v_i neighborhood, which reflects the consumer's ordering of v_i within that neighborhood, we assume the higher v_i is desired by the consumer. For v_i beyond v_i(max.), it is possible that the consumer does not desire such levels of quality, may in fact prefer to allocate more of his or her budget to some other commodity or commodities, and consequently would not want to increase M_i. Under such circumstances, the consumer may instead reduce b_i^c, indicating a lower willingness-to-pay for levels of quality higher than v_i(max.).

We make the assumption, therefore, that the decision to attain higher quality with constant quantity—where such decision originates with the consumer and lies within the consumer's window—must be accompanied by a simultaneous decision on the part of the consumer to increase the allocation of funds budgeted to the ith commodity. The consumer must increase the M_i subbudget. The accuracy of such budgetary decisions may be questionable and, therefore, it is further assumed that learning processes are involved as the consumer redistributes funds to M_i, in order to afford the higher v_i. In fact, all subbudget allocations most likely involve learning before accurate allocations of funds across subbudgets is attained.

For x_i fixed and with higher targeted v_i (both within the consumer's window), the shifts in PDC and CDC may be illustrated as in Figure 13.27. As explained above, the CDC shifts outward as a result of the consumer decision to increase M_i. The PDC may shift outward via one or both of the following: a reduction in b_i^p and/or an increase in the producer's estimate of consumer M_i.

From the point of view of the consumer, there exists the potential for the demand curve to shift outward in response to an

Figure 13.27 **An Increase in Quality Within the Window**

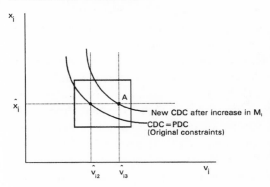

increase in quality. We draw this conclusion based on the requirement that quantity remained fixed (at $x_i = \hat{x}_i$) while v_i has increased, from $\hat{v}_{i2}$ to $\hat{v}_{i3}$. And, given $b_i^c \geq b_i^p > 0$ and constant, the price, p_i, will rise in price space along the PDPL. Examination of isoquality demand curves in $x_i p_i$ space would indicate that with quantity fixed and a higher price (p_i), there must be increased demand corresponding to the higher quality. The higher demand is possible, as contrasted with our earlier examples, owing to the increase in funds allocated by the consumer to the M_i budget.

13. Producer Behavior in the Window

From the point of view of the producer, the consumer's decision to change from $\hat{v}_{i2}$ to $\hat{v}_{i3}$ reveals no information regarding the value of b_i^c, nor does it reveal information regarding quantity, x_i. In fact, we assume these values, including the parameters of the consumer window, must be estimated and learned by the producer, based on data available regarding individual consumer characteristics and behavior, or on the characteristics and behavior of the consumer's cohort.

For starters, we assume that the producer takes the previous value of b_i^c, accurately estimated by the producer, and assumes it

remains unchanged. Given unchanged b_i^c, the producer would expect quantity to fall in response to the increase in quality. This expectation is based on the trade-off relationship of v_i to x_i along the constraint. Given producer knowledge of the CDPL, which is presumed with an accurate b_i^p (i.e., $b_i^p = b_i^c$), the producer would also expect transactions with the consumer to involve not only lower quantity but also, a higher price, p_i. These conclusions presume the producer does not know the consumer has targeted quantity at its previous level.

Once transactions commence, however, the producer would come to realize that the consumer has not reduced quantity. With a higher price, p_i, and no reduction in quantity, the producer would further realize that, to attain higher quality, the consumer must have allocated more resources to his or her budget for the ith commodity.

For our model, the implications of this behavior are that occasions may arise when the requirement of PDC $\geq$ CDC is violated, and yet transactions still occur. They now occur along the CDC; in this case, at the intersection of $\hat{x}_i$ and $\hat{v}_{i3}$ (point A) in Figure 13.27. We should note, parenthetically, that producers are assumed to be willing to let consumers spend more for any given v_i than was expected, or estimated, by producers. Occasions when CDC > PDC arise when consumers increase their decentralized budgets. Such behavior throws off the accuracy of producer estimates of M_i. However, as suggested earlier, producers will realize that consumer buying patterns have changed and they will adjust upward their estimates of M_i.

As discussed above, it is possible for the CDC to lie above the PDC in $v_i x_i$ space. We should note, however, that under these circumstances (where producer estimates of M_i are inaccurate) $b_i^c = b_i^p$ is still possible and, therefore, CDPL = PDPL is likewise possible. The discrepancy between PDC and CDC arises over the divergence between the consumer's actual M_i subbudget versus the producer's estimate of M_i. This difference, in turn, may create a divergence between demand expected by producers and the demand actually transacted.

In our earlier example, the demand expected by producers had an increase in p_i accompanied by a reduction in x_i, in $x_i p_i$ space. In other words, the new demand curve, corresponding to higher v_i, might not differ from the previous isoquality demand curve set at the previous (lower) level of quality (see sections 5 and 7 of this chapter). The demand that actually arises, however, as a result of greater funds allocated to the M_i subbudget, would be greater than the previous demand (at $v_i = \hat{v}_{i2}$). Producers, although initially surprised, would subsequently realize that higher consumer expenditure must have accompanied the increase in quality. With that information, producers would adjust upward their estimates of M_i.

14. Consumer and Producer Behavior Outside the Window

To this point we have assumed any change in the targeted variety, $\hat{v}_i$, remained within the consumer window. We have likewise assumed that quantity, x_i, remained within the window. Within any given individual consumer window we have further assumed that the ordering of v_i reflects individual consumer preferences, and that any decision to purchase higher quality originated with the consumer. We now go outside the window and examine consumer and producer decision making for v_i beyond v_i(max.).

At the outset it should be noted that the boundary for v_i(max.), for individual consumers, may be unknown to producers. We

assume individual consumers know their v_i(max.). For v_i beyond v_i(max.), we assume the decision to purchase $v_i > v_i$ (max.) rests with the consumer. We further assume the decision to "present" consumers with higher quality products and/or services originates with producers, and that, for reasons of profitability, market share, and/or to confuse consumers regarding increased prices, producers encourage consumers to purchase higher v_i.[5] As stated earlier, however, producers may not know whether higher v_i are beyond v_i(max.) for individual consumers.

We further assume that producers utilize advertising, possibly combined with reduced availability of lower v_i, to induce consumers to move up the quality axis (within any given commodity). The general presumption behind such behavior on the part of producers is that higher quality products and services are attractive to consumers, and that in order to maintain market share against other competitive firms, as well as to protect profit margins, producers must invent, produce, and/or otherwise introduce higher-quality products and services to consumers. Higher-quality products and services are, in fact, higher quality because they purportedly "better" address consumer needs (as understood and estimated by producers), and that producers address those needs to maintain or increase market share and profits. This form of behavior on the part of producers is also consistent with Duesenberry's hypothesis of the Demonstration Effect. There is also, of course, the old debate of whether producers seek to create new "needs" within consumers, and/or whether new products and services in themselves create new "needs." We will address some of these topics later.

Also, as introduced earlier in our discussion of the Waugh-Brems problem, it is possible for producers to perceive consumer needs inaccurately and thereby create products and/or services that are not desired by consumers, or which are not as desired by consumers as estimated by producers. Conversely, in some instances it may be necessary for producers to "educate" consumers as to the value of higher quality; this may be particularly true in fields such as medicine, legal services, and other professional services. Such "educational services" provided by producers may also apply to issues of product safety, as well as for products and services that are highly technical in nature, and so forth.

The topic of professional services, as well as the highly technical nature of some consumer products and services, introduces the principal-agent relationship and the need, on some occasions, for the producer to also "educate" the agent, who in turn, would "educate" the principal (the consumer). Given the increasingly technical nature of many products and professional services in modern economies, the Waugh-Brems problem may be more prevalent today than in the past.

15. The Introduction of v_i Outside the Window

In what follows we assume a producer has presented a single consumer with a product or service that lies beyond the upper bound of the consumer's window—that is, beyond v_i(max.). Three courses of action are possible.

First, after observing and "indirectly" evaluating the higher v_i, the consumer may decide against purchase. By "indirect evaluation" is meant whatever learning experience may be gained by the consumer without the actual purchase and consumption-learning experience discussed in chapters 7 through 9. In this evaluation process the consumer may rely upon information provided through advertising, by other con-

sumers regarding their consumption experience of the product or service, and/or possibly from a free trial experience afforded to the consumer by the producer. Without purchase of the higher v_i offered by the producer, however, the decision-making process stops at this point. The consumer remains within his or her window, possibly at the same (previously) targeted variety.

A second course of action might be expansion of the consumer's window to include the new, higher variety. The new v_i might become the new v_i(max.), or come to rest somewhere within the v_i ordering of the window—that is, at a position less than v_i(max.).

At this juncture, it is important to be clear as to the meaning of the word "new." The need for clarity derives from the need to distinguish "technological change," which introduces totally new products or services, that is, products or services that have not previously existed. In contrast, a product or service might be "new" to one consumer, but not "new" to another. We assume that products and services that arise through technological change, and hence have not previously existed for any consumer, are another issue apart from our discussion here. In the present context, any variety of a commodity that the consumer has not previously known will be defined as "new" to that consumer. The extent to which a consumer must be "unaware" of a variety in order for it to be "unknown," and therefore "new" to that consumer, is, in fact, an extremely subjective matter. Could the consumer, for example, have seen the new variety and still be considered to not know the product or service? Could the consumer have heard of the variety and still not know the product? Could the variety simply reside outside the consumer's window in order to classify it as unknown to the consumer? Variation in the observation and

Figure 13.28 An Increase in Quality Outside the Window

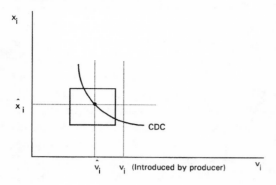

learning capacities of individual consumers comes into play in these cases.

A third course of action might be one in which the consumer initially purchases the new, higher variety, but subsequently discovers, through the consumption-learning process, that he or she is disappointed with the "higher" variety and reduces b_i^c, his or her willingness-to-pay for the higher v_i. In such cases, the consumer might discontinue purchase of the "higher" variety altogether and return to the window. What ultimately happens in these cases, however (i.e., what happens after consumer disappointment), may depend on subsequent decision making on the part of the producer.

If the higher variety is profitable (or projected to be profitable) to the producer and/or if it helps the producer maintain or gain market share, or if the producer believes that acceptability of the new variety will grow across time (e.g., become an acquired taste), and/or if the producer believes higher v_i now may result in even higher v_i later, and correspondingly result in higher market share later (a positive feedback loopy system capable of growing on itself), then we assume the producer would consider whatever means available to maintain sales of the newly introduced variety—that is, consider means to "encourage" con-

sumption of the higher v_i, even though the consumer has experienced disappointment upon initial consumption of that variety. One means available to the producer to accomplish this objective is to reduce b_i^p, which, of course, permits reduction of p_i. It is precisely this form of price reduction that we previously labeled the demand maintenance price (DMP). Under these circumstances we have a situation analogous to that illustrated in Figure 13.28.

In Figure 13.28 the producer has "introduced" the higher v_i and has been successful in getting the consumer to consume the new v_i at least once. In the third case discussed above, the consumer experienced disappointment as a result of his or her initial consumption-learning experience. At issue now is whether the consumer will continue to purchase and consume the higher v_i, which is beyond $v_i(\text{max.})$, or return to the window. Part of this decision turns on the producer's ability to compensate the disappointed consumer such that he or she continues to purchase and consume the higher v_i and subsequently expands his or her window to include that variety.

Given the consumer's experience of disappointment with the higher v_i, it does not seem reasonable that (without compensation) the consumer would expand the window to include the new variety. We further conclude that if the reduction in b_i^c and the associated upward shift of the CDC are of such magnitude that the increase in x_i exceeds $x_i(\text{max.})$, then for the new v_i the magnitude of disappointment is such that it may be impossible for the producer to adequately compensate the consumer, and under these conditions the consumer will simply return to the window.

If, on the other hand, the decline in b_i^c is such that x_i does not exceed $x_i(\text{max.})$, then it may be possible for the producer to adequately compensate the consumer such that he or she will continue to purchase and consume the new, higher variety. The process of compensation involves a decision on the part of the producer to reduce b_i^p such that $b_i^c \geq b_i^p$, while continuing to meet the requirement of $x_i \leq x_i(\text{max.})$. Given these conditions, the consumer may enlarge the window to include the new v_i. It is under these circumstances that the reduction in b_i^c and b_i^p produce what we have called a demand maintenance price (DMP). What is "maintained" is consumer purchase and consumption of the higher v_i.

The "compensation" granted to the consumer, to offset disappointment associated with the higher v_i, is an option to increase the quantity, x_i, of the ith commodity. And, this option to increase quantity comes at "no extra charge" to the consumer. (The reduction in p_i derived from lower b_i^p will be discussed shortly.) In other words, there is no requirement to change the decentralized budget, M_i, on the part of the consumer. Furthermore, consumer expenditure on the ith commodity, $p_i x_i$, which must be less than or equal to M_i, is assumed to remain constant or to decrease.[6] As we will see shortly, however, consumer expenditure on the higher v_i may increase later, if the consumer subsequently evaluates more highly the new variety and adjusts upward his or her b_i^c and $v_i(\text{max.})$. The consumer, in other words, has acquired a taste for the new, higher v_i.

The decision to compensate the consumer rests with the producer. Producers may not be aware of the magnitude of disappointment experienced by individual consumers, but if the projected volume of sales from higher quality products or services exceeds actual sales, some level of disappointment may be the explanation. In addition to increased advertising and other sales promotion activities, producers may reduce the price of higher quality products or services to increase their corresponding volume of sales and/or market share.

The closer the characteristics of the new (higher) variety are to those of previously purchased products or services within the v_i neighborhood—that is, the closer the new, higher v_i is to $v_i(\text{max.})$, the greater may be the acceptance of higher-quality varieties by the consumer. Similarly, the closer the prices of the higher quality items to the prices of previously purchased products or services, the greater may be the likelihood of transactions. There are issues of substitution involved here, between different levels of quality, and firms may discover that lower prices are a method to "lift" consumers to higher-quality products and services along a firm's product line. Under our assumption of constant a_i, the change in price, p_i, must arise from change (reduction) in b_i^p. The income and substitution effects associated with these price changes will be discussed in chapter 14.

Earlier we said the decision to compensate consumers rests with producers. Also, we stated that the consumer need not increase his or her expenditure on the ith commodity—that is, no increase in $p_i x_i$. In the presence of consumer disappointment, producers may select values of b_i^p such that the PDPL, along which transactions occur in $v_i p_i$ space, pivots downward and p_i either declines or possibly remains unchanged. Initially, the low value of b_i^p may be such that revenues fall for producers; however, if the strategy of firms is to raise expectations of quality on the part of consumers, the front-end cost of this strategy may be viewed as an investment. The reduction in b_i^p, accompanied by consumer "education" programs and other activities to "inform" consumers of the "greater value" of the higher v_i, may result in greater profits to producers in the long run.

We should note, however, that all of the above activities on the part of producers are only the "necessary" conditions to attract consumers to higher v_i. In our model we assume that unless higher-quality varieties fulfill consumer perceptions of quality, especially as these relate to self-image and to the subjective activities of consumption-evaluation, and unless the new varieties can be accommodated within the priorities of the consumer's decentralized budgets, the consumer may not purchase and consume the higher v_i introduced by the producer. Under such circumstances, the consumer would return to the window.

As regards the producer's decision to introduce higher v_i, an additional incentive for producers, over and above those already discussed, could be the relatively lower elasticity of demand corresponding to higher v_i. (See our earlier discussion of this topic in this chapter, section 3; see, also, equation (3), section 11 of chapter 7.) Recall from our discussion of the Houthakker constraint and the role played by the (a_i/b_i) ratio, that own-price elasticity of demand appears to be lower for v_i to the right of the focus point of the hyperbola (the constraint) than it is for v_i to the left of the focus point. More precisely, the quantity response (dx_i) for change in b_i (db_i) appears to be lower for v_i higher on the v_i axis than for v_i lower on that axis. Of course, (dx_i/db_i) does not equal $[(dx_i/x_i)/(dp_i/p_i)]$. Nevertheless, for low values of the (a_i/b_i) ratio, v_i lower on the v_i axis, or closer to the origin, have a greater x_i response to change in b_i than do higher v_i.

One explanation for this phenomenon may be that there are fewer substitutes among higher v_i than among lower v_i. The nature of technological change may be such that as knowledge accumulates, more substitutes become available; therefore, the longer a v_i exists, the greater the amount of time available to create substitutes, and hence the greater the likelihood that own-

price elasticity (for that level of v_i) will rise. Technological change that creates v_i that are new (or are "firsts") may, by definition, create v_i for which there are few, if any, substitutes, at least initially. If consumers demand the new v_i, for which there possibly exist no substitutes, the level of own-price elasticity correspondingly would be low. In any case, this is an empirical question that deserves investigation.

If our explanation of the process toward higher quality is correct, attracting consumers to higher v_i has the potential to generate greater revenue for producers. This conclusion, of course, presumes a positive relationship between price and revenue when own-price demand elasticity is low. Based on earlier conclusions drawn from our model, we would add that it is also necessary that consumers be willing to increase their M_i budgets.

The attraction toward higher v_i may also fit conveniently with beliefs in a concept of "progress" held by many consumers. The attraction of higher quality would also lend support to Duesenberry's hypothesis of the Demonstration Effect. In any case, the movement toward higher-quality varieties must be profitable to producers in order for them to be motivated to "lift" consumers up their v_i axes (expand their windows to higher v_i), and to convince consumers to increase their M_i subbudgets.

16. Varieties Beyond v_i(max.) and Individual Consumer Demand

In Figure 13.28, given that the producer can adequately compensate the consumer, such that the higher v_i is included in the consumer's window, how will change in the level of quality affect individual consumer demand in x_ip_i space? In an earlier example we assumed quantity, x_i, remained within the window, and that the price, p_i, corresponding to the new, higher v_i, was equal to or less than the price for the previously purchased v_i—that is, we assumed a demand maintenance price (DMP) strategy on the part of the producer. Given these conditions, the effect of higher quality on individual consumer demand may result in one of four outcomes.

First, recall that for higher v_i, we have assumed x_i (max.) $\geq \hat{x}_i$, where $\hat{x}_i$ is the previously purchased quantity, and the new p_i must be less than or equal to the previous p_i. In $x_i p_i$ space, the first possibility is that the new quantity and price are identical to the quantity and price of the earlier (lower) v_i. Under these conditions, after an increase in v_i there is no change in individual consumer demand, that is, the individual demand curve does not shift.

In our second case, if quantity remains constant (i.e., $x_i = \hat{x}_i$) and is accompanied by a decrease in price, then demand must decrease in the presence of the increase in v_i (i.e., a downward shift of the demand curve in $x_i p_i$ space). Unless, of course, elasticity of demand is zero, in which case there is either no change in demand after the increase in quality, or we have a variable-quality demand curve.

In the third case, if price, p_i, remains constant, while quantity increases—while remaining less than or equal to x_i(max.)—then demand would increase in response to the higher v_i (i.e., the standard presumption of an outward shift in demand as a result of an increase in quality). We should note, however, that in order to obtain this result, it is also necessary that the consumer increase M_i, which is contrary to our present assumptions, namely, that initially M_i remains constant.

And, finally, in the case of simultaneous change in price and quantity (i.e., if price falls and quantity rises) there is an indeterminate situation. We cannot discern between a change in demand versus a change (increase) in quantity demanded. In three of the four cases the magnitude of M_i is assumed constant.

In summary, the strategy of producers to "lift" consumers to higher v_i—a strategy that requires x_i to remain within the x_i neighborhood and p_i to be less than or equal to the previous p_i—cannot determine, a priori, whether there will be an increase in individual consumer demand in response to the introduction of higher quality.

At the level of interaction between an individual producer with an individual consumer, our model claims that if the consumer's decentralized subbudget, M_i, remains constant, producer revenue, generated by offering the consumer higher-quality varieties, will not increase. More specifically, producer revenue will not increase if individual consumer expenditure on the ith commodity, $p_i x_i \leq M_i$, does not increase.

If, however, the producer can convince the consumer to include the higher v_i within his or her window, then in subsequent time periods it is possible the consumer may increase M_i and $p_i x_i$. This behavior presumes that the consumer increases his or her willingness-to-pay, b_i^c, after gaining additional consumption experience with the higher v_i, and possibly acquiring a taste for that variety. In other words, it may be possible for a producer to offset an initial consumption experience that was "disappointing" to the consumer if additional consumption opportunities of the higher v_i are made available, at no additional cost, to the consumer.

Such behavior on the part of individual consumers is a form of preference reversal, and it presumes the existence of learning processes that are capable of influencing the structure of preferences; it also presumes that producers may affect these learning processes by affording consumers additional consumption opportunities. The additional experience must be sufficiently positive that it can offset or reverse the initial consumption experience that was negative, namely, disappointing. Within the repertoire of modern business "tools" there exist many psychological, sociological, and marketing strategies, in addition to pricing policies, that may be utilized by producers to encourage consumers to continue their consumption of higher v_i, even for $v_i > v_i$(max.) (i.e., beyond the consumer window).

For an individual producer to increase revenue from a higher-quality variety, it will be necessary to either attract new consumers to the higher v_i (either from the current population of ith commodity consumers, who do not currently consume the higher v_i, and/or from consumers outside of the ith commodity group), and/or be able to increase revenue from the higher v_i generated by consumers who currently purchase the higher v_i. To increase revenue from current consumers (those who currently purchase the higher v_i), it will be necessary to encourage them to increase their decentralized budgets and their expenditures for the ith commodity—that is, increase M_i and increase $p_i x_i$.

For the population of consumers who currently consume the higher v_i, if they choose to increase their M_i budgets and expenditures, then an outward shift in consumer demand for the higher v_i will occur. In this case, the isoquality (market) demand curve (fixed at the level of the higher v_i) shifts outward (in $x_i p_i$ space) relative to its previous position. The outward shift may also occur if other consumers of the ith commodity, but at lower v_i, commence purchases of the higher v_i, and/or if consumers from other commodities (e.g., commodity j) enter into the market for the ith commodity and also commence purchase of the higher v_i. However, if the number of consumers of the higher variety remains constant, and if they choose to hold constant their expenditures from their M_i budgets, there will be no increase in market demand for the higher variety.

When we expand to a market level of analysis, where many consumers and producers interact, it becomes more likely that an increase in v_i, across many consumers, where they all choose to target on the same higher v_i, will result in an outward shift in market demand for that variety. Correspondingly, we should expect to see some decrease in demand for those varieties abandoned as consumers switched to the higher variety. (Recall that we continue to assume that, at any given time period, consumers purchase only one variety of the commodity.)

Before elaborating further on market conditions and extension of our model to the demand for commodities, we consider next consumer and producer decision making when quality is reduced. We commence with a decrease in v_i such that the lower v_i remains within the consumer window.

17. A Decrease in Quality, the Consumer Window, and Individual Consumer Demand

Figure 13.29 illustrates consumer decision making when quality is decreased—for example, from v_i targeted on $\hat{v}_{i2}$ to the level at $\hat{v}_{i1}$. Similar to the case of an increase in quality (see Figure 13.27), the quantity target, $\hat{x}_i$, is retained so as to be able to discern shift patterns in individual consumer demand.

For the targeted variety to be reduced, the lower v_i must first exist, be known to exist by the consumer, and be the choice of the consumer. The decision to reduce quality within a commodity group is not the form of decision making usually attrib-

Figure 13.29 **A Decrease in Quality Within the Window**

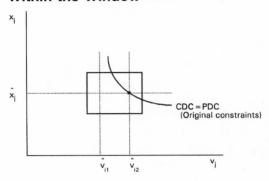

uted to consumers. One might ask: Why would a consumer ever choose to reduce quality? Under what set of circumstances might this type of decision occur?

The assumption that "more is preferred to less" may come into play here and imply a corollary assumption, namely, that "higher quality is preferred to lower quality." A limited review of the literature suggests that the corollary assumption is usually not explicit. As far as our model is concerned, the question remains as to why a presumably rational consumer would ever choose to reduce quality.

One rather straightforward explanation of this behavior might be that the consumer is forced to make this "choice," a type of "forced move," as in the game of chess. For example, unemployment, or any other reason for a reduction in household income, M_T, or wealth, might explain the choice to reduce quality.

Another reason to reduce quality might be to increase saving. Unlike the previous example, however, this choice usually is not a forced move. As discussed in earlier chapters of this text, the relationship of saving to quality needs further investigation. (Duesenberry is one of the few authors to suggest investigation of the quality-saving relationship.) Consumer decisions regarding saving underscore the

fact that consumer allocative decisions regarding subbudgeted expenditures, $p_i x_i \leq M_i$, are probably more directly related to choices regarding quality than is total household income, M_T. Nevertheless, there remains little doubt that total household income plays an important role in decisions to reduce quality. A reduction in income will likely force decisions to reallocate expenditures within and among the decentralized budgets of the household, and thereby possibly reduce the levels of quality within several commodities.

Similarly, the decision to increase household saving, especially if household income is constant, must be accompanied by decisions to reallocate expenditures within and among commodity groups, such that the levels of expenditure, and possibly quality, within some commodities are reduced. The reduction in expenditure from some decentralized budgets may result in leftover funds that might be assigned to saving. In the extreme case, a reduction in expenditure may totally eliminate some commodities (i.e., $x_i = 0$). In line with Ironmonger, however, we assume that rather than eliminate a commodity, the consumer will first reduce its level of quality to the lowest acceptable level (i.e., to $v_i(\text{min.})$), and in some cases the consumer may even reduce the lower boundary on his or her window—that is, a new lower $v_i(\text{min.})$. When v_i is less than $v_i(\text{min.})$ we have a case of the consumer reducing v_i such that it falls below the consumer's original window. We assume such cases are temporary and that the consumer will either return to the window as soon as possible, reduce the lower boundary of the window to match the new lower v_i, or possibly discontinue consumption of the ith commodity altogether (the extreme solution).

In addition to unemployment, reductions in income and/or wealth, and the decision to increase saving, there remain other explanations as to why the consumer might choose to reduce quality within any given commodity. For example, as the consumer grows older (advances through the life cycle), his or her consumption technology could change, which might change the magnitude of satisfaction derived from a given commodity, and, correspondingly, change the satisfaction derived from any variety within the commodity. Specifically, the level of quality targeted within the commodity could be affected by change in the consumer's consumption technology, such that the consumer would change the target—that is, in the present case, reduce $\hat{v}_i$. The consumer might even derive the same level of satisfaction from a lower v_i as was previously derived from a higher v_i, thanks to the change in consumption technology.

Change in consumption technology introduces issues of "efficiency" in consumption. In our model, given our emphasis on "quality" (from the point of view of the consumer), a change in consumption technology raises questions about the relationship of "quality" and "efficiency" in consumption. In our model, questions arise as to the relationship (and/or possible interaction effects) between the "consumption experience of *quality*" (from the point of view of the consumer's willingness-to-pay for some specific v_i) and "consumption *efficiency*," for example, the derivation of satisfaction (utility) from some variety of a commodity. In the world of variable quality, what does it mean to be "efficient" in consumption? Does "efficiency" mean accuracy in the consumer's estimation of b_i^c (see chapter 9), or is "efficiency" similar to Ironmonger's use of ω_{ij} in the consumer's consumption technology?[7] Furthermore, if both of these concepts are involved, what is the relationship between b_i^c and ω_{ij}?[8]

Because b_i^c measures the consumer's willingness-to-pay for some level of v_i, and ω_{ij}, according to Ironmonger, represents the level of satisfaction of the ith want derived from the jth commodity (which is Ironmonger's measure of quality), if we assume the consumer is not willing-to-pay more than he or she perceives to be the level of satisfaction, then we have the following relationship: $b_i^c \le \omega_{ij}$, which is analogous to the traditional condition that price be less than or equal to marginal benefit derived from the marginal unit along a demand curve. With some rearrangement of Ironmonger's terms, we have $(\Delta\omega_{ij}/\Delta x_j)$ = the marginal utility of the jth commodity, which under traditional theory would decrease as x_j increased. Given the condition, $b_i^c \le \omega_{ij}$, the above condition would require that b_i^c also decline as one moves downward along an isoquality demand curve. As discussed previously, we have already established this pattern of behavior of b_i^c along isoquality demand. If only one unit of quantity is purchased—our case of quantity targeting, where $\hat{x}_i = 1$—the notion of diminishing marginal utility is severely restricted. (See our earlier discussion of Knut Wicksell regarding the topics of quality and marginal utility, chapter 2, section 2.)

To return to the topic of change in consumption technology across the life cycle of a consumer, what may be "efficient" for a consumer at one stage in the life cycle might not be similarly efficient at another stage, and issues of quality more than likely influence (and complicate) these matters. As regards the role that self-image plays in the perception of quality, another interesting question is whether there exists interaction between change in self-image, across the life cycle, and change in consumption technology, as the consumer grows older and gains more experience, both personal information about himself or herself and "experience" from and about the consumption process. In other words, one of the driving forces behind change in a consumer's consumption technology, in addition to other forms of knowledge and experience, could be change (across time) in the consumer's self-image, both how the consumer perceives himself or herself and how the consumer wants to be perceived by others. Perception in the eyes of others, a form of mirror, may become less important with age. Additionally, consumer self-knowledge and self-confidence may be well established after years of consumption experience. Consumption signaling (e.g., of status) may, therefore, become less important with age.

If this is the case, that change in self-image contributes to change in consumption technology (and vice versa), then it is also possible that combined change in self-image and consumption technology influence the level of quality purchased and consumed (e.g., the v_i targeted within the ith commodity), as well as the ordering of varieties within a commodity group, the boundaries of neighborhoods and windows within individual commodities, the priorities assigned to different commodities across the set of all commodities purchased by the consumer, and the size of their corresponding decentralized budgets. In other words, in the world of consumer behavior under conditions of variable quality, the interaction of self-image and consumption technology could influence several dimensions of consumer decision making.

As stated earlier, change in self-image may alter the consumer's consumption technology such that the level of satisfaction previously derived from some targeted variety (e.g., $\hat{v}_{i2}$) declines. The decline could arise because the consumer has lost interest or reduced interest in that commodity, and the loss of interest derives

from change in the life cycle and change in self-image. Under such circumstances, the consumer might reduce the level of quality, say from $\hat{v}_{i2}$ to $\hat{v}_{i1}$. In fact, with the "lower" variety, $\hat{v}_{i1}$, the consumer might continue to obtain the same level of satisfaction as under the previously targeted variety, $\hat{v}_{i2}$. Furthermore, if the expenditure on $\hat{v}_{i1}$ is less than it was on $\hat{v}_{i2}$, this change in consumption would also allow increased saving, as expenditure could be reduced by targeting the lower v_i. The consumer could also decide to allocate some or all of the released funds to another commodity or commodities. It is also important to remember, however, that beyond some age threshold (e.g., age 65) income usually begins to decline, which may also contribute to reduction in v_i.

Our discussion of these issues introduces the prospect that some self-images may be more expensive (i.e., require higher M_T) than others. The inclusion of self-image in consumer theory opens the possibility of linkages to concepts of targeted life styles and their associated targeted incomes, both of which are probably influenced by self-image, as well as the idea that consumers might have targeted self-images, which could change with age.

Finally, to return to our earlier discussion of change in quality and shifts in consumer demand, we consider the case of reduced quality, as reflected in the change from $\hat{v}_{i2}$ to $\hat{v}_{i1}$. In our previous discussion of variable quality, we saw that an increase in quality ($\hat{v}_{i2}$ to $\hat{v}_{i3}$) could not assure an increase in individual consumer demand. A necessary condition for an increase in individual demand was that the consumer allocate additional funds to the ith decentralized budget. In addition, the consumer must increase expenditure out of that enlarged budget. In the case of a reduction in the level of quality, we find that there may not be a decrease in individual consumer demand unless the consumer likewise adjusts his or her decentralized budget, and expenditures $p_i x_i$, for the ith commodity. In this case, however, the consumer must shift excess funds $(M_i - p_i x_i)$ from the ith commodity budget (M_i) to other commodities $(j \neq i)$, and/or allocate excess funds to savings. In other words, there must be a decrease in expenditure for $\hat{v}_{i1}$, as compared with the previous expenditure on $\hat{v}_{i2}$, in order for there to be a decrease in individual consumer demand—in response to a decrease in quality.

We may now summarize our findings regarding change in quality and change in individual consumer demand. For either an increase in quality (movement from $\hat{v}_{i2}$ to $\hat{v}_{i3}$) or decrease in quality (movement from $\hat{v}_{i2}$ to $\hat{v}_{i1}$) the presumption of a corresponding increase or decrease in individual consumer demand cannot be established a priori. To establish the traditional presumption of higher demand for higher quality and lower demand for lower quality, it is necessary to include the following assumptions.

First, it must be assumed that higher quality induces consumers to allocate additional funds to higher quality products or services. Given M_T constant, however, this means that funds must be reduced for other commodities $(j \neq i)$, even though the quality levels of these other commodities might not change. In other words, other commodities $(j \neq i)$ may experience a decrease in demand if their levels of quality are to remain constant. Clearly there are cross-quality effects across commodities, much the same as cross-price effects and the much-studied issues of substitution and complementarity of commodities. These

are topics that also merit empirical investigation.

Second, for a reduction in the level of quality to induce a decrease in individual demand, it must be assumed that funds not expended on the lower level of quality (i.e., funds not expended on $\hat{v}_{i1}$ are free to be allocated to other commodities $(j \neq i)$, or to be saved. In other words, the consumer does not expend these funds on a larger quantity, x_i, of variety $\hat{v}_{i1}$. Specifically, we must assume that expenditure $p_i x_i$ on variety $\hat{v}_{i1}$ does not remain the same as the previous expenditure $p_i x_i$ on variety $\hat{v}_{i2}$. We assume expenditure on $\hat{v}_{i1}$ is less than it was on $\hat{v}_{i2}$. If targeting on quantity is assumed (e.g., $\hat{x}_i = 1$), then there can be no increase in quantity. The reduction in expenditure on $\hat{v}_{i1}$, therefore, must result in a downward shift in individual consumer demand. (Unless perfect inelasticity of demand is present.) This means that the reduction in quality initiates a reduction in the decentralized budget for the ith commodity, which, in turn, results in reduced expenditure (on, e.g., $\hat{v}_{i1}$) and a corresponding decrease in individual demand (again, unless perfect inelasticity is present.) Excess funds from the ith budget are assumed available either to expend on other commodities or to set aside as savings.

The expenditure of excess funds on other commodities $(j \neq i)$ could result in increased individual consumer demand for those commodities. As mentioned previously in the case of an increase in quality, cross-quality effects are generated through the reallocation of funds across the decentralized budgets of an individual consumer. Similarly, interaction between quality and saving may arise.

Chapter 14

Individual Consumer Demand from $x_i x_j$ Space

Interaction with the ith Commodity Producer

1. Variable Quality in $x_i x_j$ Space

Finally, it is useful to examine the concept of individual consumer demand for the ith commodity from the perspective of $x_i x_j$ space. As before, the level of quality of the ith commodity is assumed variable. The level of quality of the jth commodity is assumed constant. Likewise, the values of M_j and p_j are assumed constant. An illustration of $x_i x_j$ space with variable quality for the ith commodity was provided in Figure 8.3 of chapter 8. In Figure 14.1 we have modified Figure 8.3 by rearranging the x_i and v_i axes, and by introducing the assumption that v_i has no effect on x_j. In Figure 14.1 the values of M_i, a_i, and b_i are assumed constant.

To examine consumer behavior in $x_i x_j$ space, where the level of quality for x_j is held constant and quality is variable for x_i, we begin under the condition that no neighborhoods exist, neither for v_i nor for x_i. We reintroduce neighborhoods and their corresponding windows later in the chapter. For now we commence with the isoquality model, where the level of quality for ith commodity has been set at $v_i = \hat{v}_{i2}$. In Figure 14.2 we illustrate the case where $v_i = \hat{v}_{i2}$. In terms of $x_i x_j$ space, Figure 14.2 may be illustrated as shown in Figure 14.3.

Figure 14.1 **Variable Quality in $x_i x_j$ Space: Separability of v_i from x_j**

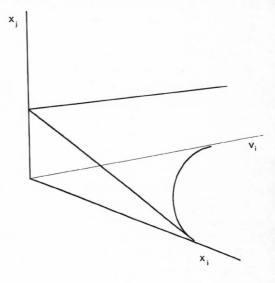

Before we introduce change in the level of v_i there are several aspects of Figure 14.3 requiring elaboration. First, Figure 14.3 represents a slice through Figure 14.2 at the level of quality, $v_i = \hat{v}_{i2}$. Note that the constraint in $x_i x_j$ space corresponds to the isoquality level, $v_i = \hat{v}_{i2}$.[1] Similarly, note that in Figure 14.3 the quantity of x_i and x_j correspond to quality level, $v_i = \hat{v}_{i2}$— that is, they are conditional on the level of isoquality, and they are designated by

Figure 14.2 **Iso-Quality at** v_{i2}

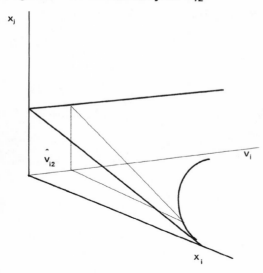

Figure 14.3 **Traditional Consumption Space: Quality at** v_{i2}

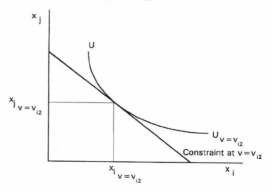

$x_{i_{v=vi2}}$ and $x_{j_{v=vi2}}$. Finally, note that the consumer preference map in $x_i x_j$ space also corresponds to the level of quality, $v_i = \hat{v}_{i2}$—that is, the preference map in $x_i x_j$ space is conditional on the level of quality from $v_i x_i x_j$ space and is indicated with a subscript, $U_{v=v_{i2}}$.[2]

We now elaborate further on the nature of preferences in quality–quantity consumption space.[3] In our previous discussion of consumer behavior in $v_i x_i$ space, we occasionally assumed targeting was employed in the selection of an individual variety or of a v_i neighborhood. From here on, until we reintroduce neighborhoods, we assume the consumer targets on a single variety. Later, we will link this assumption to recent work under the random utility model (RUM) and to other discrete choice models, and we will reintroduce v_i neighborhoods.[4]

In the present case, we assume the consumer has targeted on $\hat{v}_{i2}$. Under the assumption of single-variety targeting, we further assume that preferences in $v_i x_i$ space are lexicographic. In other words, we assume the consumer first targets on a level of quality (e.g., $\hat{v}_{i2}$) and then subsequently

maximizes quantity (x_i) of that variety.[5] In Figure 14.3 the consumer has targeted on $\hat{v}_{i2}$, and then, under lexicographic ordering, subsequently maximized preferences for the quantities of x_i and x_j (given $v_i = \hat{v}_{i2}$) by selecting the bundle, $\langle x_{i_{v=v_{i2}}}, x_{j_{v=v_{i2}}} \rangle$.

Once the level of quality has been selected (e.g., at v_{i2}), change in the price of the ith commodity, p_i, may proceed in the usual manner to create an isoquality demand schedule. All of the traditional operations regarding constrained optimization of utility, with corresponding substitution and income effects for dp_i, and so forth, apply. In addition, under conditions of constant quality, ordinary and compensated demands exist and obtain the same results as under the traditional homogeneity assumption.

We turn now to Figure 14.3 and examine what happens when the level of quality of the ith commodity is changed (again, under variety-specific targeting without windows). We begin by examining what happens when the level of quality is increased. An illustration is provided in Figure 14.4.[6]

In Figure 14.4 the level of quality has increased from to $\hat{v}_{i2}$ to $\hat{v}_{i3}$. The pivot of the constraint is inward toward the origin. The reason for the inward rotation of the constraint in $x_i x_j$ space lies in the nature of

Figure 14.4 **Consumption Space After an Increase in Quality**

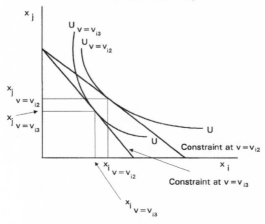

Figure 14.5 **Increase in Quality in $v_i x_i x_j$ Consumption Space**

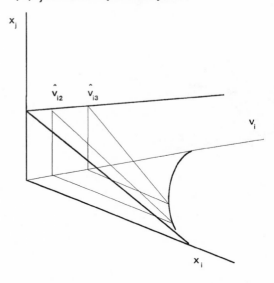

the Houthakker constraint in $v_i x_i x_j$ space. (We continue to assume M_i, M_j, p_j, a_i, and b_i constant.) An illustration of the change in quality from the perspective of $v_i x_i x_j$ space is provided in Figure 14.5. The two constraints are both identified in $x_i x_j$ space (Figure 14.4) with their corresponding levels of quality. As there has been no change in M_j, p_j, nor in v_j, the intercept on the x_j axis remains fixed. We further assume total consumer income, M_T, is constant, and that there is no change in the M_i subbudget.

In Figure 14.4, two levels of the consumer's preference map are identified. As shown, the two levels are $U_{v=v_{i2}}$ and $U_{v=v_{i3}}$, where, under lexicographic ordering, $U_{v=v_{i3}} > U_{v=v_{i2}}$. From the perspective of $x_i x_j$ space, these results are unusual; they are in conformity, however, with our model of consumer behavior in a 3-dimensional quality-quantity consumption space—that is, in $v_i x_i x_j$ space.

We should also note that in Figure 14.4 the quantities x_i and x_j have changed as a result of the change in quality. As illustrated, increase in quality of the ith commodity resulted in a reduction in quantity of both the ith and jth commodities. De-

pending on the nature of consumer preferences, these results need not always obtain. The fact that change in v_i has affected x_j occurs only if we relax our assumption of separability of the ith commodity in the map of consumer preferences. In our examination of $x_i x_j$ space, where we seek to identify the effects of variable quality, it becomes necessary at this juncture to relax our previous assumption of separability within preferences. The decrease in x_j as a result of higher v_i also requires that we relax our earlier assumption of decentralization of the ith commodity budget. The M_j subbudget, specifically expenditures on x_j, may now be affected by Δv_i. In the present case, given p_j and v_j constant, the increase in v_i results in a lower expenditure, $p_j x_j$, on the jth commodity. Resources have been taken from the jth commodity and allocated to the ith commodity.

2. Change in the Level of Quality in $x_i x_j$ Space

In the case of two different levels of quality in $x_i x_j$ space (e.g., $\hat{v}_{i2}$ and $\hat{v}_{i3}$), two sets of diagrams, each set containing an $x_i x_j$ consumption space and an $x_i p_i$ demand space, could be created, where one set corresponds to $v_i = \hat{v}_{i2}$ and the other to $v_i = \hat{v}_{i3}$. Each set could be used to produce an isoquality demand schedule corresponding to its targeted variety. (We will have more to say on this topic in chapter 15.)

Before comparing different levels of isoquality demand, however, there are several unusual aspects to $x_i x_j$ consumption space, under the assumption of variable quality, that must be examined. First of all, each constraint in Figure 14.4 is identified as an isoquality constraint, but where a different level of quality corresponds to each constraint. (Note that v_j is assumed constant, at the same level of quality, for both constraints.) Furthermore, based on the Houthakker constraint in $v_i x_i$ space, an increase in quality pivots the constraint inward toward the origin in $x_i x_j$ space, as illustrated in Figure 14.4. (See also Figure 14.5.) Additionally, under lexicographic ordering of the consumer preference map (ordered on quality over quantity), an increase in quality results in an indifference curve closer to the origin, but where $U_{v=v_{i3}} > U_{v=v_{i2}}$. As stated earlier, these results are unusual. Before we can proceed further with variable quality in $x_i x_j$ consumption space, we need to consider in more detail the Houthakker price system and constraint in $x_i x_j$ space.

3. Price of the *i*th Commodity: The Influence of Δv_i, Δb_i, and Δa_i

Review of the Houthakker price system, $p_i = a_i + b_i v_i$, reveals that pivoting of the constraint, as illustrated in Figure 14.4, could arise from three sources, either independently or in combination. As shown, the downward rotation of the constraint could arise from an increase in v_i, with a_i and b_i constant (the case illustrated in Fig-

Figure 14.6 **Influence of b_i on the Constraint in $x_i x_j$ Space**

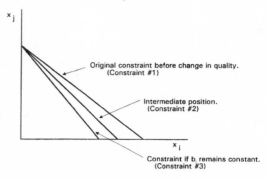

ure 14.4); from an increase in b_i, with a_i and v_i constant; or, from an increase in a_i, with b_i and v_i constant. As change in any of the three components of p_i can produce change in the commodity price, and change the slope of the constraint in $x_i x_j$ space, all three—Δa_i, Δb_i, and Δv_i—are essential to an understanding of consumer demand under variable quality.

First, in our model—where v_i represents a level of quality, and along the v_i axis the ordering of v_i represents the ranking of quality levels by an individual consumer—Δv_i is the only component of p_i that directly represents a change in quality. As such, it is only through change in v_i that we can examine the effects of variable quality on consumer demand, for example, only through Δv_i is it possible to examine whether an increase in quality generates an increase in individual consumer demand.

As noted above, p_i is also influenced by the values of the two parameters, a_i and b_i. We will consider first Δb_i. In Figure 14.6 the magnitude of Δv_i is the same as that in Figure 14.4, but different values of b_i^c are given. Throughout our previous discussion of Figure 14.4 we assumed b_i^c constant.

Two of the three constraints shown in Figure 14.6 are the same as the constraints in Figure 14.4. The outermost constraint in Figure 14.6, identified as the "original constraint,'' corresponds to the outermost constraint in Figure 14.4, where $v_i = \hat{v}_{i2}$. The innermost constraint in Figure 14.6 corresponds to the innermost constraint in Figure 14.4, where $v_i = \hat{v}_{i3}$. As before, the price of the jth commodity, as well as its level of quality, v_j, and subbudget, M_j, are assumed constant. The intercept on the x_j axis remains unchanged.

In Figure 14.6 we assume that the level of quality of the original constraint was initially set at $v_i = \hat{v}_{i2}$. When the targeted level of quality is increased from $\hat{v}_{i2}$ to $\hat{v}_{i3}$, the new position of the constraint in Figure 14.6 depends on the value of b_i^c. Recall from chapters 4 and 7 that the price of the ith commodity is given by $p_i = a_i + b_i v_i$, and, from the consumer's perspective, b_i^c represents consumer willingness-to-pay for a specific level of quality.

To illustrate the importance of b_i, we begin with the outermost constraint in Figure 14.6. We make the extreme assumption that the consumer's willingness-to-pay for the new, higher $\hat{v}_{i3}$ is of such a low magnitude that the constraint does not move! In terms of notation, we identify the consumer's willingness-to-pay for $\hat{v}_{i3}$ as $b_{\hat{v}_{i3}}^c$. The consumer's willingness-to-pay for $\hat{v}_{i2}$, the previous level of quality, is indicated by $b_{\hat{v}_{i2}}^c$. In other words, the consumer's b_i did not remain constant as the level of quality increased from $\hat{v}_{i2}$ to $\hat{v}_{i3}$. In this case, the change in b_i^c, or $\Delta b_i^c = b_{\hat{v}_{i3}}^c - b_{\hat{v}_{i2}}^c$, was such that the product $b_i^c v_i$ in the commodity price, $p_i = a_i + b_i^c v_i$, remained unchanged. The increase in v_i was exactly offset by the decrease in b_i^c such that $b_i^c v_i$ remained constant. Furthermore, given that a_i remains constant (which we continue to assume), it follows that we have no change in p_i (i.e., in p_i^c), arising from the change in v_i, and therefore no change in the ratio of commodity prices, (p_i / p_j). In $x_i x_j$ space, the position of the constraint at quality

level $\hat{v}_{i3}$ is the same position as at quality level $\hat{v}_{i2}$.

Corresponding to the innermost constraint of Figure 14.6, there is no change in consumer willingness-to-pay as quality increased from $\hat{v}_{i2}$ to $\hat{v}_{i3}$ (i.e., $b_{\hat{v}_{i2}}^c = b_{\hat{v}_{i3}}^c$). Under these circumstances, Δv_i has the same influence on Δp_i as previously existed under the original constraint (in Figure 14.4). In other words, given an increase in v_i, the degree of downward rotation of the constraint reflects the influence of both Δv_i and Δb_i^c. In fact, if $b_{\hat{v}_{i3}}^c > b_{\hat{v}_{i2}}^c$, for an increase in quality from $\hat{v}_{i2}$ to $\hat{v}_{i3}$, the downward rotation of the constraint would be greater than that illustrated in Figure 14.6.

Recall from our earlier discussion of willingness-to-pay in $v_i x_i$ space (i.e., the *special case*) that it is possible for v_i to remain constant, while change in b_i^c produces a change in the slope (and position) of the constraint in quality-quantity space. In $x_i x_j$ space, change in b_i^c also influences the slope of the constraint. (A discussion of CDC and PDC constraints in $x_i x_j$ space is presented in chapter 15.) Any change in b_i^c, as a consequence of its effect on the slope of the constraint in $x_i x_j$ space, also influences the magnitude of substitution and income effects, given that x_i and x_j are not perfect complements and given there is no targeting on quantity. As we shall see shortly, Δb_i^c may also influence shift phenomena for individual consumer demand.

Finally, in Figure 14.6 we have the intermediate case, where the constraint rests between the two previous constraints—that is, between the original constraint (Constraint #1) and the innermost constraint (Constraint #3). In the example provided (see the constraint labeled ''Intermediate position'') we assume $b_{\hat{v}_{i2}}^c > b_{\hat{v}_{i3}}^c$, but $b_{\hat{v}_{i3}}^c$ is not sufficiently low that we obtain the original, or outermost constraint. As explained previously, for smaller values of b_i^c (relative to the original value of b_i^c) the constraint pivots upward, and for larger values of b_i^c the constraint pivots downward.

Could there arise, however, the case where the consumer changed quality from $\hat{v}_{i2}$ to $\hat{v}_{i3}$, with preference ordering $\hat{v}_{i2} < \hat{v}_{i3}$, but where b_i^c changed, such that $b_{\hat{v}_{i2}}^c > b_{\hat{v}_{i3}}^c$? Such a hypothetical situation would indicate that the consumer had selected a higher level of quality but was willing to pay less for the higher quality than for the lower quality. The only circumstance where such a phenomenon might occur is when the higher variety, offered by producers, exceeds v_i(max.), the upper boundary on a consumer's v_i neighborhood. (To this point in our discussion of $x_i x_j$ space, however, we have excluded neighborhoods and windows.) Under these conditions, our previous discussion of a demand maintenance price (DMP) and reduced b_i^c would come into play.

Within the consumer's v_i neighborhood, however, where the v_i are ordered according to the consumer's evaluation, from lower v_i to higher v_i, it seems reasonable to assume that the consumer's corresponding b_i would be consistent with the v_i ordering (i.e., b_i^c is either constant or rising for higher v_i). Under such conditions the possibility that the constraint in $x_i x_j$ space would rotate upward for an increase in v_i is eliminated. We will assume, therefore, that within v_i neighborhoods the ordering of b_i^c is consistent with the ordering of v_i (i.e., for $\Delta v_i^c > 0$, within the v_i neighborhood, there is $\Delta b_i^c \geq 0$).

As discussed above, change in consumer willingness-to-pay, or Δb_i^c, may induce a change in p_i, with no change in the targeted level of quality. The downward rotation of the constraint (as shown, for example, in Figure 14.4) with v_i constant at $\hat{v}_{i2}$ could be accomplished via an increase in $b_{\hat{v}_{i2}}^c$—that is, by an increase in consumer willingness-

to-pay (WTP) for the same level of quality. Higher WTP(TK) could arise in our model as a result of change in consumer self-image, which could alter the expectation-experience process described in chapter 9 (i.e., change the folded function in $b_{it=k}^c$ phase space), or as a result of a newly acquired (or altered) taste for $\hat{v}_{i2}$, or from a change in the consumer's consumption technology as regards the use of $\hat{v}_{i2}$. Furthermore, all of these activities could be commingled.

Discussion of Δv_i and Δb_i introduces the subtle and complex issue of the relationship between a "change in quality" and a "change in taste." Some aspects of this relationship were presented in chapter 6 in the reviews of Fisher and Shell and of Ironmonger. It should be stated at the outset that it is difficult, and perhaps impossible, to distinguish clearly and consistently between the two concepts. Distinction between the two is important, however, inasmuch as price indices are frequently adjusted for change in quality, but rarely adjusted for change in consumer tastes.

In our model of consumer behavior at the retail level, we have argued that quality is in the eye of each individual consumer, hence subjective. Also, that quality is defined in terms of the ability of a product or service to serve the consumer's self-image (see chapter 9, section 3). We have argued that processes of perception, expectation, and the personal interpretation of consumption experience are involved in individual consumer assessment or evaluation of products and services purchased and consumed. We have assumed that the ranking of levels of quality within a commodity, the ordering of v_i along the v_i axis, and especially within a v_i neighborhood, also reflects individual consumer self-image and the subjective learning and evaluation processes described above.

Closely related to those learning and evaluation processes, which are associated with learning about "quality," is the phenomenon of learning and determining what an individual consumer would be willing-to-pay for different levels of quality (i.e., consumer determination of b_i^c). In the case where the consumer remains at $\hat{v}_{i2}$, but increases $b_{\hat{v}_{i2}}^c$, it could be argued that the change in $b_{\hat{v}_{i2}}^c$, among other factors, reflects a change in taste. Under this interpretation, the phenomenon called a "change in taste" could be defined as inclusive of a change in the willingness-to-pay for a specified level of quality.

On a related topic, change in quality could be viewed as arising from two sources: The consumer has changed from one targeted variety to another (the interpretation used in this text); or, the consumer has changed the ordering of varieties along the v_i axis. In the latter case, change in the ordering of v_i could also be interpreted as a change in tastes. (For an example in a similar vein, see Ironmonger on a change in the ordering of wants, which he defines as a change in tastes; see chapter 6, section 4 of the present text.) In our model heavy emphasis is placed on the relationship between quality and consumer self-image; however, in all likelihood, a change in tastes could also be brought about by a change in self-image. If self-image affects both the perception of quality and tastes, what is the relationship or interaction of quality and tastes? Does self-image first influence the perception of quality, and then subsequently, via the assessment of quality, influence tastes? In our model it is possible to argue that the perception of quality influences tastes, but interaction with other consumers could also influence tastes. In addition, interaction with other consumers probably influences self-image.

In Figure 14.4 we could assume that the impetus to increase quality from $\hat{v}_{i2}$ to $\hat{v}_{i3}$ came from a change in self-image of the individual consumer. For an individual consumer to change quality, however, it is not necessary, nor required, that there be a change in self-image. In fact, over the life cycle of an individual consumer, change in self-image may be an infrequent factor behind the decision to change quality. In other words, consumer decisions to change quality could occur under two different circumstances, namely, decisions to change quality could occur within the same self-image, and decisions to change quality could occur across a change in self-image. Heretofore, we have not been explicit regarding these phenomena.

Over periods of time wherein self-image remains constant, or does not change "significantly," we will assume v_i neighborhoods either remain unchanged or do not change "significantly." Within those neighborhoods the ordering of v_i is assumed not to change, or to experience only "minor" change. Similarly, any ordering of commodities is likewise assumed not to change "significantly." Significant change occurs in the ordering of v_i and/or in the ordering of commodities when there is a significant change in self-image.[7]

We will assume that most decisions to change quality occur under conditions of a stable or unchanged self-image. Change in quality under these conditions involves movement along a previously established ordering on the v_i axis, usually within a v_i neighborhood, and it involves change in subbudgets—for example, resources transferred from M_j to M_i, resources transferred from savings to M_i—or it involves an increase in total household income, M_T. Variety-specific targeting is assumed to apply in most cases, accompanied by an increase in the appropriate subbudget or in total household income, which allows targeting on higher varieties within a stable v_i neighborhood. And, as stated above, change in savings would also permit change in the level of quality targeted within any given commodity. It should be recalled that a change in the level of quality may also be in the downward direction.

Change in quality associated with a change in self-image might involve a re-ordering of v_i, usually within a v_i neighborhood (either enlarged or reduced in size), and/or possibly a reordering of commodities within the set of all commodities purchased with M_T. The b_i^c learning process explained in chapter 9 applies to decisions regarding quality in both cases (i.e., under stable self-image and changed self-image). Change in b_i^c when there is no change in the level of quality—for example, change in $b_{\hat{v}_{i1}}^c$ when the target has not changed (remains at $\hat{v}_{i1}$)—could arise owing to a change in self-image or for other reasons—for example, change in total income, change in tastes, change in consumption technology, and so forth.

Within the context of our model, however, we will argue that unless change in v_i orderings affects individual consumer demand schedules, and transactions with producers, such reorderings will not be revealed empirically. Change in an individual consumer's ordering of v_i along the v_i axis, or within a v_i neighborhood, will, therefore, remain unknown. Only those decisions regarding quality that are revealed through transactions will prove useful in identifying which variety is purchased and the corresponding price the consumer is willing-to-pay. In general, we assume that the reordering of v_i along the v_i axis is a phenomenon internal to the mind of the consumer and most likely is not revealed in the external world of markets. As explained in Appendix B, however, it may be possible to estimate a v_i ordering across a group, or cohort of similar consumers, based on aggregated market data. Knowledge of such orderings at the level of an individual consumer is probably impossible.

In our model we will define a reordering of v_i by an individual consumer, either along the v_i axis or within a v_i neighborhood, as precisely that: a reordering of varieties. A change in the ordering may in some sense reflect a change in quality of individual varieties as they are compared with one another. In our model, however, we limit the concept of a "change in quality" to a change in the level of quality purchased and consumed, not the ordering of varieties within the consumer's mind. We define, therefore, a change in quality to be a change in the variety purchased by an individual consumer; for example, the change from $\hat{v}_{i2}$ to $\hat{v}_{i3}$ in Figure 14.4.[8] This definition allows the generation of data related to a change in quality. Market data will indicate which varieties are purchased.

Similarly, we will narrowly define a change in tastes. We acknowledge that change in taste may involve issues other than quality. For matters that do involve quality, however, we will define a change in tastes as a change in the willingness-to-pay for a specific variety (e.g., $\Delta b_{\hat{v}_{i2}}^c$ for the targeted variety $\hat{v}_{i2}$). In other words, change in the perception and consumption experience of quality may have the same effects and be viewed as comparable to a change in consumer tastes. As we hope to show shortly, in some cases specific types of change in consumer preference maps may be utilized to differentiate change in tastes from change in quality.

Finally, although these definitions leave considerable room for overlap between the two concepts, some effort must be made to distinguish between a "change in quality" and a "change in taste." If no distinction can be made, then it seems unreasonable to adjust price indices for change in quality, but not for change in tastes. Unless the two concepts are distinguishable, in a manner that is consistent and measurable (i.e., based on available market data), it seems an argument could be made either to exclude both forms of change from adjustments to price indices or to include both in such adjustments.

The one remaining component of the Houthakker price system is a_i. In previous chapters we defined a_i as the price of the basic package, the value of x_i, Houthakker's definition of quantity. We have assumed that both consumers and producers could determine their corresponding values of the basic package, or a_i^c and a_i^p, respectively. We have generally assumed a_i constant and $a_i^c = a_i^p = \varphi > 0$. At this juncture we allow the introduction of additional factors that could influence the value of a_i. Specifically, we assume that other market phenomena, beyond those already considered under the topic of variable quality, could influence a_i. In other words, the price p_i can be influenced by phenomena beyond v_i and/or b_i, and the influence of these phenomena is captured in a_i. For example, in Figure 14.4 the downward rotation of the constraint, with v_i constant at $\hat{v}_{i2}$ and with constant $b_{\hat{v}_{i2}}^c$, could be accomplished by an increase in a_i, and the increase in a_i could arise owing to change in market forces associated with the ith commodity. With the expanded interpretation of a_i, we introduce additional notation. We define the basic package (BP) component of a_i as $a_{i(BP)}^c$ for consumers and $a_{i(BP)}^p$ for producers. The market forces' component of a_i we define as $a_{i(market)}$. The two components combined become $a_i^c = a_{i(BP)}^c + a_{i(market)}$ for consumers, and similarly for producers. We will have more to say on this topic after we

discuss the role of producers in $x_i x_j$ space and the interaction of consumers and producers in that space.

Given the existence of Δa_i, Δb_i, and Δv_i, the measurement of income and substitution effects, as well as the examination of shifts in demand under variable quality, have become more complicated. In Figure 14.4, for example, the downward rotation of the constraint, corresponding to an increase in p_i, may now be seen as arising from any one of four factors or various combinations thereof (e.g., $\Delta a_{i(BP)}^c$, $\Delta a_{i(market)}$, $\Delta b_{\hat{v}_i}$, and/or $\Delta \hat{v}_i$). The interaction of consumers and producers in markets also complicates the interpretation of Δp_i. Additionally, under these conditions, the theoretical and measurement issues associated with adjusting price indices for change in quality become more complicated.

4. Substitution and Income Effects Under Variable Quality

If we return now to Figure 14.4, we may examine in more detail the effects of variable quality.[9] After the change in quality from $\hat{v}_{i2}$ to $\hat{v}_{i3}$, along either indifference curve ($U_{v=v_{i2}}$ or $U_{v=v_{i3}}$) the substitution effect reveals an increase in quality of the ith commodity results in a decrease in quantity of that commodity, and an increase in quantity of the jth commodity. Such results always obtain, unless x_i and x_j are perfect complements, or if quantity targeting has been employed. In the discussion that follows, therefore, we assume x_i and x_j are not perfect complements, nor is there quantity targeting.

We now examine the differences between $U_{v=v_{i2}}$ and $U_{v=v_{i3}}$. Earlier in our discussion of targeting on v_i we explained the role that self-image is assumed to play in influencing consumer perception of the quality of a product or service. In our discussion of Figure 14.4 we stated that change in self-image could be assumed the reason for the change in quality from $\hat{v}_{i2}$ to $\hat{v}_{i3}$. Under this assumption, the self-image that generated the preference map corresponding to $\hat{v}_{i2}$ is assumed to have changed and is different from the self-image behind the preference map corresponding to $\hat{v}_{i3}$. As a consequence, although we are dealing with the same consumer, we have, as described earlier, two different self-images behind $U_{v=v_{i2}}$ and $U_{v=v_{i3}}$. This difficulty is not new; it was raised by Fisher and Shell. As far as demand theory is concerned, however, the significance of this issue is the question of which indifference curve to employ to assess the substitution effect— that is, do we employ the preference map generated by the "old" or by the "new" consumer?

In our model, consumer self-image is a factor in both substitution and income effects. In Figure 14.4, in assessing the income effect we are making a comparison across a single consumer who we assume has changed self-image, which is analogous to comparing the preferences of two different consumers. When considering the income effect, under Hicksian or compensating variation, we are confronted essentially with the same question as the choice between Laspeyres and Paasche indices. In our case, in $x_i x_j$ space, we are asking which set of parallel-shifted constraints to employ to identify the income effect associated with a change in quality. This is analogous to asking which set of preferences (i.e., associated with which self-image) to use as the base period: those of the old consumer or those of the new?

Note that if we select the preference map of the old consumer (i.e., in Figure 14.4 begin with tangency on $U_{v=v_{i2}}$ and parallel-shift the old constraint downward to the new indifference curve, $U_{v=v_{i3}}$), this is essentially the question: What does the old

consumer, with the old set of preferences based on the "old" self-image, *expect* by way of satisfaction from consumption at the new level of quality? In contrast, if we select the preference map of the new consumer (i.e., in Figure 14.4 begin with tangency on $U_{v=v_{i3}}$ and parallel-shift the new constraint back to the old indifference curve, $U_{v=v_{i2}}$), this is essentially the question: What does the new consumer, with the new set of preferences based on the new self-image, *experience* by way of a change in satisfaction in comparison with consumption at the old, or previous, level of quality?[10]

With the latter operation (which may be superior to the former, if one can assume memory is more accurate than expectation) there are obviously memory and learning processes involved between consumption on the isoquality constraint at $v_i = v_{i2}$ and consumption on isoquality constraint $v_i = v_{i3}$. The only available "invariant," however, across the two periods of consumption is the vehicle that carried these two sets of preference (i.e., the memory system of the consumer). Unfortunately, this is neither a reliable nor a consistent invariance operator. Human memory is notoriously flexible and capable of distortion. Memory, which is interpreted personal history, is where the self resides, and as such, memory represents the only means available to compare $U_{v=v_{i2}}$ and $U_{v=v_{i3}}$, moving across time from past to present.[11] (See also the discussion of expectation and experience in chapter 9.)

5. Is Change in Quality Analogous to a Change in Real Income?

Review of the two constraints in Figure 14.4 suggests that an increase in the level of quality, from $\hat{v}_{i2}$ to $\hat{v}_{i3}$, is analogous to an increase in the price of the ith commodity. Obviously the size of the feasible consumption set, measured in terms of x_i and x_j, has been reduced. Consistent with reduction in the feasible set in $x_i x_j$ space, it could be argued that real income of the consumer has been reduced. Given that there has been an increase in quality of the ith commodity, however, it is debatable whether real income has declined. Based on our model, it seems inappropriate to restrict the measurement of real income exclusively to a change in quantity.

Under the assumption of lexicographic ordering of quality on quantity, for example, we assume the consumer derives higher satisfaction along the constraint where $v_i = \hat{v}_{i3}$, albeit that quantity, x_i, may be lower (e.g., as shown in Figure 14.4). In this situation the consumer has a trade-off: higher quality for lower quantity. In standard consumer theory, the inward rotation of the constraint introduces no such trade-off; the consumer simply faces a reduction in the feasible set, which is defined only in terms of quantity. In the standard case, real income has declined. In our case, however, because we assume the consumer freely selects $\hat{v}_{i3}$ over $\hat{v}_{i2}$, even in the face of lower quantity (i.e., with prior knowledge that higher quality will be accompanied with lower quantity), it is unclear whether real income has declined. The consumer freely chose the bundle involving higher v_i and lower x_i. Compare $\hat{v}_{i2}$ with $\hat{v}_{i3}$ in Figure 14.5.

In Figure 14.4 the downward rotation of the constraint in $x_i x_j$ space, pivoting from the x_j axis, arose from an increase in quality, an increase in v_i. We may conclude that the behavior of the two constraints, pivoting from $v_i = \hat{v}_{i2}$ to $v_i = \hat{v}_{i3}$, is more than simply "analogous" to a price increase. According to the Houthakker model, where price of the ith commodity is given by $p_i = a_i + b_i v_i$, there is, accompanying any increase in v_i, a corresponding increase in p_i. A similar result obtains, but in reverse,

for a decrease in quality. In other words, the increase in v_i (from $\hat{v}_{i2}$ to $\hat{v}_{i3}$), given no change in a_i or b_i, will, under most circumstances, produce an increase in p_i. Recall from our discussion of the relationship of $v_i x_i$ space to $v_i p_i$ space that a change of v_i in $v_i x_i$ space results in a change of v_i in $v_i p_i$ space, and hence a change in p_i. These results hold given $b_i > 0$. With these relationships in mind, it may be argued that the income effect of a change in quality is more than simply analogous to a price change: A change in quality produces a change in price. From this perspective, then, the phenomenon of an income effect, traditionally associated with a change in price, also applies to a change in quality.

To state, however, that a change in quality is exactly equivalent to a price change is incorrect—at least to the extent one utilizes the Houthakker model. Under Houthakker, a change in quality is strictly equivalent to a change in the price of the commodity, if, and only if, $a_i = 0$ and $b_i = 1$—that is, if we restrict ourselves to Houthakker's *basic price system*. In our model we have dropped that requirement.

We see now that measurement of the income and substitution effects, associated with a change in quality, may differ depending on whether we utilize change in p_i or change in v_i. Furthermore, we see that measurement of v_i, independently of p_i, is essential to the exact measurement of any income and substitution effects that arise exclusively from a change in quality. Price data in itself is insufficient to the task— that is, without the basic price system, Δp_i will not accurately measure the effect of Δv_i. Variation in a_i and/or b_i further complicates the use of Δp_i as a measure of income and substitution effects that may arise from Δv_i.

The independent measurement of Δv_i is also important to the examination of shift phenomena of consumer demand schedules under variable quality. The same will be true for the measurement of demand shifts under change in a_i and/or b_i.

To illustrate, if we assume $0 < b_i^c < 1$ and $0 < a_i^c$, and if we assume that change in p_i can arise from forces other than a change in v_i (e.g., $\Delta a_{i(market)}$), then the change in p_i (which arises exclusively from change in v_i), will be less than the change in v_i (i.e., $\Delta p_i < \Delta v_i$, given $p_i = a_i + b_i v_i$ and $0 < b_i < 1$). However, we can state that, given $b_i > 0$, the change in p_i resulting from change in v_i will generate an income effect.

As discussed in section 3 of this chapter, recall that the value of b_i, $0 < b_i < 1$, will influence the degree of rotation of the constraint about the intercept on the x_j axis in Figure 14.4. In other words, the influence of Δv_i on Δp_i, and hence on the slope of the constraint in $x_i x_j$ space, depends on the value of b_i. We continue to assume, as before, $a_i^c = a_i^p = \phi > 0$, ϕ constant. Note, however, that Δa_i further complicates the use of Δp_i as a measure of the income effect generated by Δv_i. (Refer also to chapter 13, sections 3 and 4, for material on the importance of the (a_i/b_i) ratio to the configuration of the constraint in $v_i x_i x_j$ space.)

6. Is the Income Effect of a Change in Quality Normal or Inferior?

We turn now to the question of whether the income effect, derived from a change in quality, reveals varieties to be "normal" or "inferior." The reader is asked to recall the following: Change in quality is defined as a change in the variety purchased of the *i*th commodity; the quantity of the variety may change; and only one variety is purchased by the consumer at any moment in time.

As discussed above, if we assume change in v_i results in change in p_i, then an income effect may arise from Δv_i. (We assume here that a decrease [increase] in b_i sufficient to offset an increase [decrease] in v_i, such that the product $b_i v_i$ remains constant and $dp_i = 0$, does not occur.) Under these circumstances, whether the income effect is normal or inferior, depends on the configuration of the consumer preference map. For example, in Figure 14.4, if the downward rotation of the constraint, generated exclusively by an increase in v_i, results in an income effect operating in the opposite direction as the substitution effect, then the new targeted variety ($\hat{v}_{i3}$) is inferior. If the income effect operates in the same direction as the substitution effect, the variety $\hat{v}_{i3}$ is normal. Note that these results obtain even though $v_{i2} < v_{i3}$ along the v_i axis, or within a neighborhood nested on the v_i axis. The meaning of "normal" or "inferior" under these circumstances is understood solely in terms of the change in x_i. In other words, it is a technical phenomenon restricted to the traditional understanding of normal versus inferior when quality is constant and all change is restricted to change in quantity. As discussed earlier, the concepts of normal and inferior are not clearly defined under cases of variable quality (see chapter 8).

7. Double-Targeting and the Income Effect

We turn now to $x_i x_j$ and $x_i p_i$ spaces, and consider the income effect from the perspective of double-targeting, the case where the consumer targets on quality and on quantity. As before, we assume we can isolate Δv_i, where Δv_i represents the change from $\hat{v}_{i2}$ to $\hat{v}_{i3}$. We know from our previous discussion of $v_i x_i$ space that an increase in v_i, under conditions of quantity targeting (e.g., on $\hat{x}_i = 1$), requires an increase in the decentralized budget allocated to the *i*th commodity. Such a reallocation to M_i, given that M_T and saving remain constant, must result in reduced funds available to spend on other commodities (e.g., the *j*th commodity). Given these conditions, we may argue that the purchasing power of the consumer, defined strictly in terms of being able to purchase other commodities $j \neq i$, has been reduced as a result of an increase in the level of quality of the *i*th commodity (i.e., there has been a change in real income defined in terms of the quantities of other commodities, $j \neq i$). This is a more specific definition of real income.

Given the reduction in funds to spend on other commodities ($j \neq i$), we may inquire again as to whether a change in quality Δv_i can be utilized to determine whether specific varieties are normal or inferior. Under the case of double-targeting, however, it is impossible to determine whether any given variety is either normal or inferior. Given, as in traditional consumer theory, that the income effect is defined and measured by a change in quantity, under quantity-targeting, where by definition there is no change in quantity, there exists no means to measure an income effect (not at least for individual consumers).

As an example of targeting on x_i, when the v_i target has increased from $\hat{v}_{i2}$ to $\hat{v}_{i3}$, see Figure 14.7. In Figure 14.7 we have double-targeting, and we see there has been a change in the targeted level of quality from $\hat{v}_{i2}$ to $\hat{v}_{i3}$, while quantity has remained unchanged at its target, $x_i = \hat{x}_i$. The subscripts on $\hat{x}_i$ in Figure 14.7 indicate that the levels of quality, $\hat{v}_{i2}$ and $\hat{v}_{i3}$, both apply to the same targeted quantity, $\hat{x}_i$. The magnitude of increase in quality (from $\hat{v}_{i2}$ to $\hat{v}_{i3}$) is the same in Figure 14.7 as in Figure 14.4. (Figure 14.7 was constructed from Figure 14.4.)

Comparison of Figures 14.4 and 14.7 reveals the reduction in x_j is greater under targeting on x_i than when quantity-targeting

Figure 14.7 **Double-Targeting in $x_i x_j$ Space**

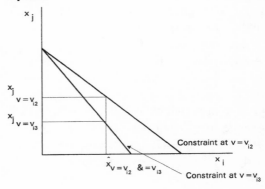

is not utilized. We should also note that under double-targeting there is no substitution effect in $x_i x_j$ space, as well as no income effect (as previously explained). Also, the traditional assumptions regarding convexity of indifference curves in $x_i x_j$ space no longer hold. Under double-targeting we have another application of lexicographic ordering; this time, in addition to an ordering of v_i on x_i, there is ordering of x_i on x_j. See, again, Ironmonger (chapter 6), for a similar concept of ordering (i.e., his case of the rank-ordering of wants).

We should note that the change in v_i illustrated in Figures 14.4 and 14.7 could have been larger or smaller than illustrated. In Figure 14.7, however, there is the requirement that x_i remain constant at $\hat{x}_i$. In reference to Figure 14.7, we further note that the position of the new constraint, corresponding to the higher v_i, not only reflects the change in v_i but also reflects the influence of b_i, specifically, b_i^c. Recall earlier we pointed out that the value of b_i, in conjunction with change in v_i, influences the magnitude of change in the slope of the constraint in $x_i x_j$ space. Earlier we also discussed how b_i influenced the constraint in $v_i x_i$ space. In both cases we continue to assume a_i constant.

Figure 14.8 **Income Compensation for Increase in v_i**

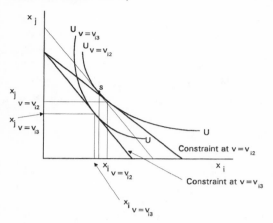

Figure 14.9 **Income Compensation Only to the ith Subbudget**

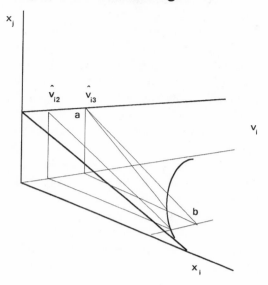

8. Additional Difficulties in Adjusting Price Indices for Variation in Quality

Given reduction in the feasible consumption set due to an increase in v_i, as portrayed in Figure 14.8, the increase in quality could be offset, or compensated, by an increase in income (that is, by an increase in M_T that is allocated to M_i and M_j) such that the consumer returns to the initial indifference curve, $U_{v=v_{i2}}$. (Note that this approach presumes that a decrease in the feasible set measured in the quantities x_i and x_j is not offset by an increase in v_i; i.e., real income is defined only in terms of quantity, exclusive of quality.) As shown in Figure 14.8 by the dotted constraint, the $\hat{v}_{i3}$ constraint is parallel shifted back to a point of tangency with the initial indifference curve at the point s. In the case of a parallel-shifted constraint, note that the increase in quality of the ith commodity requires a compensatory increase in income to the subbudgets of both x_i and x_j.

Contrarily, if the compensatory increase in income is restricted to an increase only in M_i, then the increase in M_i will restore the slope of the constraint (for $v_i = v_{i3}$) to its original position in $x_i x_j$ space. Figure

14.9 provides an illustration of a compensatory increase in M_i in $v_i x_i x_j$ space. Note that the increase in M_i has an effect on the constraint in $x_i x_j$ space analogous to a decrease in p_i (i.e., it returns the constraint to its original slope and position). In Figure 14.8, the M_i compensated constraint (at $\hat{v}_{i3}$) would overlay the original constraint (at $\hat{v}_{i2}$). The higher constraint at $\hat{v}_{i3}$ in $v_i x_i$ space (of Figure 14.9) is the constraint between points a and b, and reflects the increase in M_i.

Note that to compensate the consumer for an increase in v_i, an increase in M_i returns the consumer to the original constraint. As previously stated, the new constraint, corresponding to $v = \hat{v}_{i3}$, exactly overlays the original constraint. Unless the configuration of the preference map has changed, and given no change in b_i^c, the consumer would return to the original optimal solution, the original point of tangency in Figure 14.8, where previously $x_j = x_{jv=v_{i2}}$ and $x_i = x_{iv=v_{i2}}$. At the same tangency point, with the same quantity of x_i

and x_j, however, the consumer would be at the higher level of quality, $\hat{v}_{i3}$. These results suggest that the most accurate method of compensating for a change in the level of quality (if such a decision has been made) may be to compensate directly to the subbudget involved (e.g., to M_i). Given that subbudget compensatory allocation could be accomplished, change in quality of the ith commodity would not affect other commodities (e.g., not change the previous optimal solution for the jth commodity, nor affect consumers who did not purchase the ith commodity). In the absence of such accurate compensation, an increase in the level of quality of one commodity, compensated by an increase in M_T, will affect previous optimal solutions for other commodities, a form of substitution effect that arises from the M_T form of compensation. Reallocation between commodities by consumers introduces substitution effects derived from compensation of Δv_i and thereby reduces the accuracy of price indices adjusted for change in quality. A change in the quality of one commodity ripples out and affects other commodities. (See, however, the Fisher and Shell example involving the price of refrigerators and the price of ice cream, chapter 6, section 10.)[12]

In addition to change that occurs in the constraint, the change in quality from v_{i2} to v_{i3} (Figure 14.8) may involve change in the optimal solution on the preference map. The original optimization occurred on an indifference curve from the map of $U_{v=\hat{v}_{i2}}$. Tangency at the M_i-compensated solution involves an indifference curve from the map of $U_{v=\hat{v}_{i3}}$ (not shown in diagram), where under lexicographic ordering $U_{v=\hat{v}_{i3}} > U_{v=\hat{v}_{i2}}$, but where $U_{v=\hat{v}_{i3}}$ now overlaps $U_{v=\hat{v}_{i2}}$. What form of equivalency, if any, exists between the two maps? Given that quality has changed (increased in our present example), and

given that the consumer is not indifferent between $\hat{v}_{i2}$ and $\hat{v}_{i3}$, we have again the old problem of comparing preference maps across two consumers, but now with compensation restricted to M_i, there is no change in either x_i or x_j. Difficulties that arise due to intertemporal changes in both quality and the consumer (the phenomenon of a person stepping twice into a river) clearly apply to variable quality and the income effect.[13]

9. Change in Quality and Shifts in Individual Consumer Demand

In chapter 13 we examined various forms of change in quality and their effects on consumer demand schedules, or the shift pattern of individual consumer demand curves under a change in $\hat{v}_i$. Here we take up the topic again; however, we do so now from the perspective of $x_i x_j$ consumption space. Examination of shift phenomena based on consumer behavior in $x_i x_j$ space, especially the distinction of "change in quantity demanded" from "change in demand," involves many of the same difficulties previously encountered in $v_i x_i$ and $v_i p_i$ spaces. As stated earlier, assumptions of separability and decentralization have been relaxed, for we seek to investigate possible interactions between the ith and jth commodities under variable quality, Δv_i. Introduction of the jth commodity permits an additional source of funding for an increase in quality of the ith commodity. The possible confusion of "change in demand" with "change in quantity demanded" persists in $x_i x_j$ space, as it did in $v_i x_i$ and $x_i p_i$ spaces. It will be useful, therefore, to consider some other difficulties unique to the Houthakker price system.

Under traditional price theory, change in price of a product or service (e.g., Δp_i) initiates movement along a stationary demand curve (i.e., a change in quantity demanded). Change in other variables, such as change in the price of other products or services, change in consumer tastes and preferences, and/or change in consumer income, are assumed to produce shifts in consumer demand curves, or a change in demand. In Houthakker's price system, unfortunately, we have both types of price phenomena commingled. To examine shifts in individual consumer demand triggered by a change in the level of quality and to be able to distinguish such phenomena from movements along a demand curve, it is necessary to further examine $p_i = a_i + b_i v_i$.

Inasmuch as a change in quality is traditionally assumed to be a shift parameter behind consumer demand, we assume Δv_i has the "potential" to generate a change in demand, to bring about a shift in individual consumer demand. Note, however, that in Houthakker's single-variety case, p_i is the price of the variety. A change in the price of the variety is traditionally viewed as triggering a change in quantity demanded. Under the Houthakker price system, however, it is possible to have a change in quality, Δv_i, produce the change in p_i. In such cases, how does one distinguish between a change in demand and a change in the quantity demanded?

Similarly, b_i, which we have assumed to be a parameter that measures consumer willingness-to-pay, may be viewed as a shift parameter, reflecting either consumer perception of quality and/or tastes for quality. Yet b_i is also within p_i. As we have seen, change in b_i (with v_i constant) can produce a change in p_i. Here again, how does one distinguish between a shift in demand (that could arise with Δb_i) and movement along the demand curve (that would arise with Δp_i)?

In our model, where we permit consumer and producer determination of a_i and b_i, a_i has been expanded to consist of two components: $a_{i(BP)}$ and $a_{i(market)}$. Arguably, only $\Delta a_{i(market)}$ should be utilized to represent a change in quantity demanded, or movement along the demand curve. The component $a_{i(BP)}$ is related to issues of quality, specifically determination of the value of the basic package. Recall that the basic package is that "package" to which quality characteristics are added. Within the Houthakker price system, however, $\Delta a_{i(BP)}$ will trigger a change in p_i. As with the other components of p_i, there is again the need to distinguish between shift phenomena (that could arise with $\Delta a_{i(BP)}$) and change in the quantity demanded (that would arise with Δp_i). The study of shift patterns generated by variable quality is obviously more complicated under the Houthakker price system than under traditional price theory.

In our examination of variable quality and its effects on consumer demand, we will adopt the convention, consistent with traditional price theory, that change in quality and/or change in tastes are parameters that have the "potential" to shift individual consumer demand curves. In our model there exist three components associated with variable quality, namely, Δv_i, Δb_i, and $\Delta a_{i(BP)}$. As discussed previously, Δb_i may also reflect a change in consumer tastes. Consistent with our focus on consumer behavior, we will initially restrict our analysis to the following components of Δp_i: $\Delta \hat{v}_i^c$, Δb_i^c, and $\Delta a_{i(BP)}^c$, all of which influence Δp_i^c. Later, we will examine the role of producers and their interaction with consumers in $x_i x_j$ consumption space and in demand space. We examine now the impact of each component of the Houthakker price system on individual consumer demand. We begin with an increase in quality, or $\Delta v_i^c > 0$, as illustrated in Figure 14.4.

10. Δv_i^c and Individual Consumer Demand

In Figure 14.4 the level of quality has increased from $\hat{v}_{i2}$ to $\hat{v}_{i3}$. We assume b_i^c remains constant. As discussed previously, given $0 < b_i^c < 1$, the magnitude of the change in price, Δp_i^c, will be less than the magnitude of change in quality, or $\Delta p_i^c < \Delta \hat{v}_i^c$. Only in the case of $b_i^c = 1$ (and $a_i = 0$), the basic price system, do we have $\Delta p_i^c = \Delta v_i^c$. Given our assumption that $\Delta \hat{v}_i^c$ holds only the potential to change (shift) consumer demand, we must conclude that, without further examination (e.g., where we control for p_i or for x_i), we are unable to determine whether Δp_i^c corresponds to a change in quantity demanded or to a change in demand. Even though the distinction between a "change in quantity demanded" and "change in demand," both associated with change in p_i^c, could be assumed to turn on whether Δp_i^c arose from change in one of the aforementioned (potential) shift parameters, or from change in $a_{i(market)}$, we do not have enough information to determine whether there has been a change in demand due to a change in quality. We may assume, however, that Δv_i^c has changed the isoquality status of the demand curve, even if there is no change in demand—that is, the demand curve may retain its previous position and slope, but the demand curve changes from isoquality level $\hat{v}_{i2}$ to level $\hat{v}_{i3}$.

To demonstrate some of the difficulties with the Houthakker price system, we provide the following example. Under the traditional presumption, an increase in quality should result in an increase in individual consumer demand. For the change in quality portrayed in Figure 14.4, however, the Houthakker price system does not necessarily produce these results. The price of the ith commodity, p_i, has increased, but correspondingly quantity, x_i, has decreased.

Given these results, it is difficult to determine whether there has been a change in demand or a decrease in the quantity demanded. The price-quantity relationship (increased p_i, decreased x_i) corresponds to movement along a stationary demand curve, a decrease in quantity demanded. Given our assumption that Δv_i^c is a (potential) shift parameter, however, we could conclude that the stationary demand curve has nevertheless changed its isoquality status. In other words, the demand curve may have the same slope and position as before, but the level of quality is now higher (i.e., at the level of variety $\hat{v}_{i3}$). An alternative explanation would be that the demand curve represents variable-quality, instead of isoquality demand—that is, both $\hat{v}_{i2}^c$ and $\hat{v}_{i3}^c$ are present on the same demand curve, but at different values of p_i and x_i.

To assist in the determination of whether $\Delta \hat{v}_i^c$ has resulted in a change in quantity demanded or in a change in demand, it is useful to return to our earlier discussion of willingness-to-pay. Specifically, it is useful to examine Figure 10.2 (see also chapter 8, section 3 and chapter 10, sections 1, 2, 6, 10, 11, 13–15). The price consumption path illustrated in Figure 14.4 corresponds to path (2) in Figure 10.2. In the case of path (2), it was assumed that the "reach" of the previously existing b_i^c extended to the higher level of quality. There was no need to adjust b_i^c, which is consistent with our assumption that b_i^c is constant in Figure 14.4.

Path (2) in Figure 10.2 shows a decrease in quantity, x_i, corresponding to the increase in v_i. Also, recall from chapter 13 the importance of the (a_i/b_i) ratio in determining the magnitude of change in x_i associated with change in v_i (see chapter 13, sections 4–6, 8–13 and Figure 13.23). In chapter 13 we found that without an increase in resources allocated to the M_i subbudget, there could be no increase in con-

Figure 14.10 **Effect of Targeting on** x_j **Under an Increase in** v_i

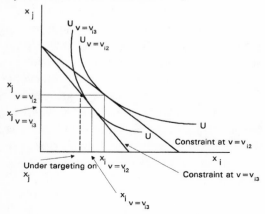

sumer demand under an increase in quality. Recall that a decrease in demand, or no change in demand, could occur, but an increase in demand, associated with an increase in quality, could occur only if the M_i budget was enlarged. These results applied to $v_i x_i$ and $x_i p_i$ spaces. In $x_i x_j$ space we confront the same issue, but the situation is further complicated now by the possibility that resources may be drawn from the *j*th commodity and placed in the M_i subbudget. The assumptions of separability and decentralization that applied to $v_i x_i$ space have been relaxed and do not apply to our discussion of $x_i x_j$ and $x_i p_i$ spaces.

We also learned from our analysis of $v_i x_i$ space that the degree of downward rotation of the constraint in $x_i x_j$ space, even with b_i constant, depends on the value of the (a_i / b_i) ratio and the location of Δv_i on the v_i axis (e.g., whether Δv_i is at the "high" end or "low" end of the v_i axis). In all cases, however, under the separability and decentralization assumptions we applied to $v_i x_i$ space, we found that in order to obtain an increase in demand, corresponding to an increase in quality, it was necessary to increase the level of funding of the commodity experiencing the increase in quality. Similarly, in $x_i x_j$ space,

when we examine behavior of an individual consumer, we find that without an increase in resources, there can be no increase in individual consumer demand. Now, however, these matters are complicated by the possibility that the additional funds may be drawn from either a decrease in x_j and/or a decrease in v_j.

As illustrated in Figure 14.4, the increase in quality of the *i*th commodity has imposed the cost of a reduction in both x_i and x_j. In the case of x_j, a portion of funds previously allocated to the *j*th commodity is now allocated to the *i*th commodity. If there had existed quantity (and quality) targeting on the *j*th commodity—for example, at the previous quantity $x_j = \hat{x}_{j_{v=v_{i2}}}$—then the magnitude of reduction in x_i would have been greater—that is, at the intersection of the targeted x_j with the v_{i3} constraint. (See x_i under x_j targeting in Figure 14.10.)[14] As suggested above, it is also possible that higher quality of the *i*th commodity results in lower quality of the *j*th commodity, either with or without quantity-targeting on x_j. Quantity-targeting on x_j would result in a greater reduction in v_j than the case where no such targeting occurs. Higher v_i can also result in reductions in both v_j and x_j.

11. Δv_i^c and Self-Image

To continue our discussion of the change in quality in Figure 14.4, recall that previously we introduced two phenomena capable of influencing consumer preferences. Based on the assumption that consumer perception of self influences consumer perception of quality (of the products and services purchased and consumed), we refined the application of the self-image concept by introducing two categories: the case where self-image remains essentially unchanged (stable), and the case where there has been a "significant" change in image. The latter phenomenon was assumed to occur infrequently over the life cycle of an individual consumer.

We have assumed that most decisions to change quality occur under a stable image, and that under such circumstances the ordering of v_i remains essentially unchanged. (The introduction of new varieties by producers, however, may alter such orderings.) Under a stable image, it may be assumed that change in the level of quality occurs primarily because there has been a change in income that allows the consumer to improve, or upgrade, the level of quality within commodities. Under a change in self-image, in contrast, we have assumed a reordering of v_i may occur, as well as a reordering of commodities.

In our discussion of Figure 14.4 we have heretofore assumed the consumer experienced a change in self-image and, as a consequence, chose $\hat{v}_{i3}$ over $\hat{v}_{i2}$. In Figure 14.4 we now examine variable quality under both cases: the case of a change in image and the case of a stable image.

Under a change in self-image, two preference maps are assumed to exist, one corresponding to the initial consumer image and a second corresponding to a subsequent image. Each preference map is assumed to be a set of well-ordered preferences over $x_i x_j$ space that are complete and provide a covering of the entire space. The preference map corresponding to the initial consumer is identified by $U_{v=v_{i2}}$ and the map for the subsequent consumer by $U_{v=v_{i3}}$. As shown in Figure 14.4, the new preference map, corresponding to the targeted variety, $\hat{v}_{i3}$, attains a bundle of quantities, $\langle x_{i_{v=v_{i3}}}, x_{j_{v=v_{i3}}} \rangle$, which is less than the corresponding bundle of quantities for the initial preference map, $U_{v=v_{i2}}$. This result is consistent with lexicographic ordering of v_i over x_i.

As mentioned earlier, Figure 14.4 may also be utilized to examine the case of variable quality under conditions of a stable, or unchanged, self-image. Given the consumption path illustrated in Figure 14.4, however, the results under a stable-image hypothesis are no different from those previously encountered under the variable-image hypothesis. No shift pattern in consumer demand may be confirmed in either case. The only presumed difference between the two cases is the assumption that the v_i ordering may have changed from the first preference map to the second preference map under the variable-image hypothesis. As the ordering of v_i is assumed to be unique to each consumer, the change in ordering may not be discernible from market data (even on an individual consumer), at least under the circumstances portrayed in Figure 14.4. As we shall see later, there may exist some circumstances, however, where the distinction between the two hypotheses of self-image is important.

A modified version of Figure 14.4 is presented below as Figure 14.11. In Figure 14.11 the increase in quality, from the targeted value of $\hat{v}_{i2}$ to the targeted value of $\hat{v}_{i3}$, is the same increase as illustrated in Figure 14.4. The two constraints, corresponding to the two levels of quality, are identified. Consumer income, M_T, is assumed constant.

As discussed earlier, the decision to change quality, from $\hat{v}_{i2}$ to $\hat{v}_{i3}$, may occur under conditions of a change in self-image or under conditions of an unchanged image. We begin our discussion of Figure 14.11 under conditions of the changed-image hypothesis.

Recall that change in self-image, within a single consumer, may be interpreted as comparable to comparing two different consumers. The two indifference curves illustrated in Figure 14.11 are assumed, therefore, to be drawn from two different preference maps: $\hat{v}_{i2}$ belongs to the prefer-

Figure 14.11 **Change in Level of Iso-Quality for Both the Constraint and the Preference Map**

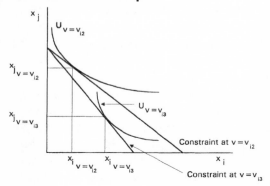

ence map of an earlier self-image, and $\hat{v}_{i3}$ belongs to the preference map of a subsequent self-image. Each preference map is assumed to be a set of indifference curves covering $x_i x_j$ consumption space.

As illustrated in Figure 14.11, under the second self-image a higher v_i has been targeted and has resulted in a higher quantity x_i than under the previous level of quality (i.e., $x_{i_{v_{i3}}} > x_{i_{v_{i2}}}$). (By way of contrast, note the reduction in x_i in Figure 14.4.) Under the Houthakker price system, $p_i = a_i + b_i v_i$, with a_i and b_i constant, an increase in v_i will produce an increase in p_i. The constraint in Figure 14.11, therefore, will rotate downward as illustrated. In $p_i x_i$ space there is, corresponding to the increase in v_i (from $\hat{v}_{i2}$ to $\hat{v}_{i3}$), an increase in p_i and an increase in x_i (from $x_{i_{v_{i2}}}$ to $x_{i_{v_{i3}}}$). These results suggest there may have been an increase in individual consumer demand as a result of the increase in quality (i.e., that isoquality demand $D^c_{\hat{v}_{i3}}$ may be greater than isoquality demand $D^c_{\hat{v}_{i2}}$). As discussed earlier, however, short of control on p_i (and comparison of x_i under variable v_i), or control on x_i (and comparison of p_i under variable v_i), we cannot confirm or deny the existence of a change in demand. Nevertheless, as stated previ-

ously, we may assume the status of iso-quality demand has changed from $\hat{v}_{i2}$ to $\hat{v}_{i3}$.

Consistent with our previous discussion of higher quality and individual consumer demand, in Figure 14.11 we observe that there is an increase in resources devoted to the ith commodity. The increased resources come from the jth commodity (i.e., from the reduction in x_j from $x_{j_{v_{i2}}}$ to $x_{j_{v_{i3}}}$). Note that had the consumer wished to remain at the previous quantity of the jth commodity (i.e., at $x_{j_{v_{i2}}}$), then some other means to increase the M_i subbudget would be required—for example, a reduction in v_j, a reduction in savings, a reduction in expenditure on some other commodity, $(h \neq j)$ and $(h \neq i)$, and so forth.

Finally, note that the solution on $U_{v=v_{i3}}$, the preference map corresponding to the new image, implies (under traditional theory) that the higher quality, $\hat{v}_{i3}$, is an inferior good. If real income is measured exclusively in terms of quantity, there has been a decline in real income associated with an increase in quality of the ith commodity. The decrease in real income has been accompanied, however, by an increase in quantity of the higher variety. As has been mentioned previously, variable quality introduces interesting questions regarding the measurement of real income, as well as the meaning of "normal" and "inferior."

In Figure 14.11 we may also examine $\Delta \hat{v}_i^c$ under the stable-image hypothesis. Here, the preference map is assumed not to have changed, in contrast to the two-preference-map assumption under the variable-image hypothesis. In addition, no reordering of v_i is assumed to have occurred. As shown in Figure 14.11, however, the single preference map is non-symmetric, skewed toward x_j. The issue of inferiority of the higher variety remains, as in the case of the variable-image hypothesis.

Figure 14.12 **A Change in Tastes**

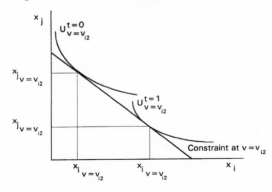

In the case of stable image, parallel-shifted constraints between the two indifference curves, $U_{v=v_{i2}}$ and $U_{v=v_{i3}}$, drawn from a consumer who has not experienced a "significant" change in self-image, may arguably be a stronger foundation for measurement of the income effect than a similar comparison of indifference curves drawn from a consumer who has changed image and correspondingly generated two different sets of preference maps. The consistency of preferences across time (in the stable-image case) would help reduce the amount of noise from confounding factors—as in the case of variable-image and two sets of preferences. These matters may prove useful in application of a *representative consumer* for assessing the effects of variable quality.

12. Δv_i^c and Change in Quality Versus Change in Tastes

The last issue we will address in our consideration of the Δv_i^c component of the Houthakker price system is the distinction between a change in quality and a change in consumer tastes. In Figure 14.12 the constraint has not changed. There has been no change in consumer income, M_T, or in the M_i and M_j subbudgets. There has been no change in any of the components of the Houthakker price, $p_i^c = a_i^c + b_i^c v_i^c$, nor has there been any change in price or quality

of x_j (i.e., all components of $p_j = a_j + b_j v_j$ are assumed constant). The intercept on the x_j axis remains constant. The constraint in Figure 14.12 is isoquality at the quality level, $v = \hat{v}_{i2}$, everywhere on the constraint. The consumer preference map is targeted on the variety, $\hat{v}_{i2}$, as is indicated by $U_{v=\hat{v}_{i2}}$.

Note that two preference maps are present in Figure 14.12: a map identified as $U_{v=v_{i2}}^{t=0}$, corresponding to an early time period; and $U_{v=v_{i2}}^{t=1}$, corresponding to a subsequent time period. The earlier preference map has been replaced by the newer map. Under the newer preference map the quantity preferred of the ith commodity has increased, albeit that the level of quality of the ith commodity, both in the preference map and constraint, has not changed. Under this set of circumstances, where quality is constant, we may conclude that a change in tastes brought about the increase in quantity, x_i. Contrast of Figures 14.12 and 14.11 may be used to characterize, or explain in part, the difference between a "change in quality" and a "change in tastes."[15]

13. Δb_i^c and Individual Consumer Demand: The Case of an Increase in Quality

The topic of change in tastes is a useful juncture to introduce another component of the Houthakker price system, the parameter b_i^c. Recall we have assumed b_i^c measures consumer willingness-to-pay for some specified level of quality, a specified variety (e.g., $\hat{v}_{i2}$). In earlier chapters we studied how Δb_i^c could affect the constraint in $v_i x_i$ space, and in this chapter we have examined how it affects the constraint in $x_i x_j$ space (see section 3). Earlier we also pointed out that Δb_i^c, as a parameter associated with variable quality, could be involved in shifts in individual consumer de-

Figure 14.13 **Increase in v$_i$ and in b$_i$**

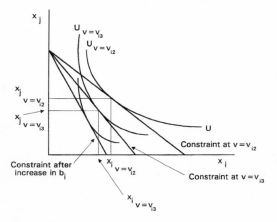

mand. In addition, we have suggested the possibility that perception of quality could be influenced by consumer tastes, and vice versa. In what follows, we first examine the role of b_i^c as a parameter that measures willingness-to-pay for a specified level of quality. Subsequently, we examine any role it might play in change of tastes.

In Figure 14.4 we earlier assumed b_i^c was constant. We now examine the case where quality has increased from $\hat{v}_{i2}$ to $\hat{v}_{i3}$, but b_i^c is not constant. Consistent with our earlier assumption that b_i^c either remains constant or increases, whenever the level of quality is increased, we now assume b_i^c has increased as quality rose from $\hat{v}_{i2}$ to $\hat{v}_{i3}$ (i.e., $b_{vi3}^c > b_{vi2}^c$). Under such an assumption, downward rotation of the constraint in $x_i x_j$ space will be greater than previously illustrated in Figure 14.4 (see our previous discussion of Figure 14.6 in section 3). Given the configuration of the preference map illustrated in Figure 14.4, the magnitude of reduction in x_i will be greater under the higher b_i^c than under a constant b_i^c. (See Figure 14.13.) This phenomenon is consistent with path (1) in Figure 10.2 of chapter 10. The reduction of quantity, x_i, is also consistent with the interpretation of the higher variety, $\hat{v}_{i3}$, as income normal.

Given the higher price, p_i^c, due to both

higher quality and greater willingness-to-pay, and given the decrease in quantity, x_i, we are again confronted with the difficulty of discerning whether there has been a change in demand or a decrease in quantity demanded. Given the availability of resources drawn from either a reduction in x_j and/or reduction in v_j, it is possible to have an increase in demand for the *i*th commodity. Again, without additional information, it is impossible to determine a priori what has happened to individual consumer demand under the combination of $\Delta v_i^c > 0$ and $\Delta b_i^c > 0$.

Change in b_i^c may also be used to explain the other paths in Figure 10.2 and to relate those paths to behavior in $x_i x_j$ and $x_i p_i$ spaces. As before, our focus in this section is the impact of Δb_i^c on individual consumer demand.

Path (3) of Figure 10.2 corresponds to the case of quantity-targeting under an increase in quality. Quantity-targeting— for example, the case of $\hat{x}_i = 1$—is particularly useful for distinguishing between change in demand versus change in quantity demanded. Path (3) permits control of quantity, $\hat{x}_i$, under variable quality, Δv_i^c, while permitting various patterns of price behavior, Δp_i^c. At this juncture, however, it is important to note that path (3) may be followed under two quite different sets of circumstances. Discussion of these options involves neighborhoods.

In the initial case of path (3), as described in chapter 10, the consumer was presented with a higher level of quality and found that he or she was not willing to pay as much for the higher v_i as for a previously consumed lower quality. In this case, b_i^c fell as quality went up. Given the existence of a v_i neighborhood, the higher v_i may be assumed to exceed v_i(max.), the upper bound on the neighborhood. This case represented our first

Figure 14.14 **Increase in v_i Offset by Decrease in b_i: Under Quantity-Targeting**

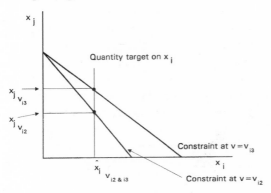

Figure 14.15 **Demand Phenomena Where Higher v_i Is Offset by Reduced b_i**

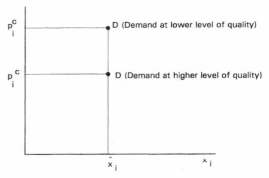

example of a demand maintenance price (DMP). When the higher v_i exceeds v_i(max.), we assumed that, for the consumer to purchase the higher v_i, it was necessary that the price, p_i, be equal to or lower than the price of the previously consumed (lower) level of quality. A relatively lower b_i^c would indicate the consumer is not willing-to-pay the same price for the higher variety as for the previous lower variety. A demand maintenance price, a lower p_i, must be offered to the consumer so as to encourage purchase and consumption of the higher v_i. Under path (3), the quantity purchased of the higher v_i remains the same as with the lower v_i (see chapter 10, sections 11–14). In terms of Houthakker's price system, the reduction in b_i^c more than offsets the increase in v_i, such that there is a decrease in the price, p_i^c. In the present case, $a_i^c > 0$ and is assumed constant.[16]

In terms of $x_i x_j$ space, this form of behavior on the part of the consumer requires that the constraint rotate upward, pivoting at the x_j intercept, as illustrated in Figure 14.14. The higher constraint corresponds to the higher level of quality. Note that under quantity-targeting, a decrease in b_i^c, with corresponding decrease in p_i^c, means it is

possible for the consumer to increase expenditure on x_j.

The reduction in price, p_i^c, combined with quantity-targeting, $\hat{x}_{vi2 = vi3}$, means that in $x_i p_i$ space, either demand is perfectly inelastic or there has been a decrease in demand. If demand is perfectly inelastic, we may assume it remains, nonetheless, isoquality at the higher v_i, $\hat{v}_{i3}$. (Otherwise, the two points are on a variable-quality, perfectly inelastic demand curve.) See Figure 14.15 for an example of this type of decrease in demand in $x_i p_i$ space. The demand dots of Figure 14.15 may represent points on two different negatively sloped demand curves, or may represent two different levels of point demand.

The second case of quantity-targeting under variable quality involves an entirely different set of assumptions regarding the processes behind path (3). In this case, we assume the consumer remains within his or her v_i neighborhood and has targeted a higher level of quality therein. Now, however, b_i^c either remains constant or increases in value. The quantity target remains as before (e.g., at $\hat{x}_i = 1$).

Under this scenario, instead of following paths (1) or (2), which would occur with an increase in b_i^c or with constant b_i^c, respectively, the consumer allocates increased resources to the M_i subbudget, ei-

Figure 14.16 **Increase in v_i with Constant b_i**

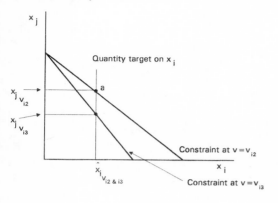

Figure 14.17 **Increase in v_i and in b_i: Under Quantity-Targeting**

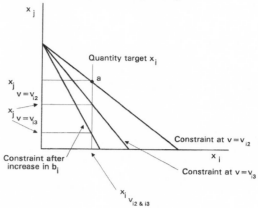

ther by drawing funds from some other commodity $h \neq i$, from savings, and/or from an increase in total household income, M_T. Path (3) is possible owing to the effect of increased funds on the constraint in $v_i x_i$ space. Specifically, the constraint shifts outward sufficient to fulfill both targets: attainment of $\hat{x}_i = 1$ at the higher targeted variety, $\hat{v}_{i3}^c$. In other words, this version of path (3) occurs not from a decrease in b_i^c (the case of a demand maintenance price) but from an increase in the M_i subbudget. We will call this the income-augmented approach. This behavior reflects a consumer choice to acquire a higher level of quality and a willingness to support this choice with increased funding to the appropriate subbudget. This is a quite different form of behavior from that behind the demand maintenance price. As we will see shortly, however, when the motives of producers are introduced, these two types of behavior may be connected.

In $x_i x_j$ space, under the second case, the constraint initially pivots downward toward the origin, similar to Figures 14.4 or 14.13. The downward rotation is due to the increase in p_i^c (derived from the increase in v_i, from $\hat{v}_{i2}$ to $\hat{v}_{i3}$), possibly accompanied by an increase in b_i^c (Figure 14.13). In both cases, however, there is quantity-targeting.

Under either the case where b_i^c remains constant or is increased in value, M_i is increased sufficiently such that the constraint in $x_i x_j$ space returns to its original position. At its original position, however, it is now at the higher level of quality, $\hat{v}_{i3}^c$. The case where b_i^c remains constant may be illustrated as in Figure 14.16.

The case where b_i^c has increased may be illustrated as in Figure 14.17. Comparison of Figures 14.16 and 14.17 reveals that an increase in b_i^c (Figure 14.17) results in a greater reduction in x_j than otherwise (Figure 14.16). In similar fashion, an increase in b_i^c requires a greater allocation of funds to the M_i subbudget than otherwise. This behavior on the part of consumers is of particular interest to producers and has a bearing on their (producers') willingness to offer a low demand maintenance price (DMP). As we shall see, there may be long-term payoffs to the initial offer of a DMP.

After the consumer has allocated sufficient funds to the M_i subbudget, the constraints in Figures 14.16 and 14.17 return to their original positions (i.e., rotate upward from their x_j intercepts until they overlay the original constraint). With targeting first of v_i, and then subsequently on

Figure 14.18 **Demand Under an Increase in v_i and in M_i(b_i Constant)**

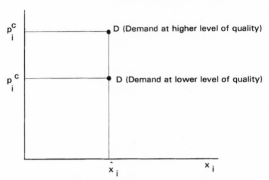

The Income-Augmented Approach (with constant b_i)

x_i (i.e., under lexicographic ordering of v_i on x_i, and then x_i on x_j), the bundle with higher v_i is preferred. Subsequently, given the targeted level of v_i (and the targeted x_i), the bundle with higher x_j is preferred. In Figures 14.16 and 14.17, the bundles with the greatest quantity of x_j, which correspond to points a on the original constraints, are the preferred bundles. Recall that after the increase in funding to the corresponding M_i subbudgets, the original constraints become the final constraints, but at the higher level of quality, $\hat{v}_{i3}^c$.

In x_ip_i space, the second case regarding path (3), which we have called the income-augmented approach, may be illustrated as in Figure 14.18. Figure 14.18 corresponds to the conditions portrayed in Figure 14.16 (i.e., the case where b_i^c remains constant).

In the case where b_i^c has increased in value, the value of p_i^c is higher than in the case where b_i^c remains constant. Figure 14.17 illustrated the case in x_ix_j space where, concurrent with the increase in quality, there was an increase in b_i^c. Under this version of the income-augmented approach to path (3), (from Figure 10.2), the magnitude of increase in the M_i subbudget is greater than in the b_i^c constant case. Similarly, as stated above, by $p_i^c = a_i^c + b_i^c v_i^c$, for the same magnitude of increase in v_i^c,

but with higher b_i^c, the value of p_i^c is higher than before. These results reflect the importance to producers of increased b_i^c on the part of consumers, and the potential higher revenue to producers when consumers acquire a taste for higher-level varieties. The strategy of a DMP may be utilized to "expose" consumers to higher varieties (i.e., those varieties in excess of individual consumer v_i neighborhoods).

In x_ip_i space the quantity target is assumed to be the same in this case as under b_i^c constant. The price, p_i^c, however, is higher. We may conclude, therefore, that the increase in demand associated with higher quality is greater when there is an increase in consumer willingness-to-pay than when b_i^c remains constant. Consumer expenditure on the ith commodity will increase in both cases, but a higher M_i subbudget will be required in the case where b_i^c rose. In terms of a diagram comparable to Figure 14.18, the demand dot corresponding to the higher level of quality will be higher in x_ip_i space than that illustrated in Figure 14.18. Likewise, the price, p_i^c, corresponding to that higher demand, will be higher.

These results are consistent with our findings in chapter 13, namely that higher demand on the part of an individual consumer requires greater funding, drawn either from other commodities, $j \neq i$, from savings, and/or from an increase in total household income, M_T. The justification for adjusting price indices for higher prices derivative of improved quality seems weak in light of these results. Any increase in individual consumer demand requires an increase in resources. Only the case of higher household income, higher M_T, appears capable of contributing to inflation. All other sources of increase in individual consumer demand for individual commodities do not appear to be inflationary, nor to deserve compensatory adjustments to income.

The last example we will examine regarding higher quality and Δb_i^c corresponds to path (4) of Figure 10.2. Recall from chapter 10, path (4) represents essentially the same phenomenon as path (3)—a lower willingness-to-pay for a higher level of quality—but where there is no targeting on quantity—that is, no $\hat{x}_i$ exists for path (4). In the case of path (4), as with the first version of path (3), we assume the higher v_i, $\hat{v}_{i3}$, exceeds the boundary, v_i(max.), of the individual consumer's v_i neighborhood. The magnitude of reduction in b_i^c is greater, however, under path (4) than under path (3). The DMP associated with path (4), correspondingly, is lower than under path (3). The magnitude of reduction in p_i^c is greater, and the magnitude of increase in x_i is greater for path (4) than for path (3).

Unfortunately, because there is no quantity-target corresponding to path (4), in $x_i p_i$ space we are again confronted with an inability to distinguish between a change in demand and an increase in quantity demanded. We should note, however, that if the individual consumer acquires a taste for the bundle at the terminus of path (4)—the bundle involving $\hat{v}_{i3}$ and higher x_i—and should the *acquired taste* become manifest through a higher value for b_i^c, then the possibility exists for producers to raise the price, p_i^p, and induce the consumer to raise the *i*th commodity subbudget, M_i. It is precisely in this manner that a DMP may be utilized to modify the upper boundary of a consumer's v_i neighborhood and thereby increase producer revenues from the sale of higher varieties.[17]

Of particular interest to our study, however, is the effect of this phenomenon on individual consumer demand in $x_i p_i$ space. If the consumer accepts (targets) the bundle at the end of path (4), we again have a case of double-targeting. If, subsequent to acquiring a taste for the new bundle, the consumer raises b_i^c, which would result in

Figure 14.19 **Change in Demand Under Constant v_i and x_i (with Increase in b_i)**

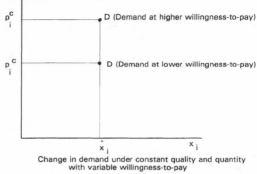

Change in demand under constant quality and quantity with variable willingness-to-pay

higher p_i^c (and probably in higher p_i^p), there would be an increase in individual consumer demand. In this case, however, the level of quality of the bundle remains constant (i.e., at $\hat{v}_{i3}$). Because quantity, x_i, also remains constant, it is possible to examine demand shift patterns under a change (increase) in consumer willingness-to-pay. Whether there is a subsequent increase in the consumer's M_i subbudget depends on whether producers learn of the higher b_i^c, and then raise p_i^p. In any case, with quantity constant and an increase in p_i^c, unless demand is perfectly inelastic, there must be an increase in demand. Figure 14.19 provides an example of these results.

The phenomenon of variable b_i^c, while quality remains constant, returns us to the matter of a change in consumer tastes and the role of b_i^c. An example of this behavior can be found in Figure 10.1. It is also illustrated in the movement from m to m' in Figure 10.3.

Earlier we discussed a set of conditions wherein it is possible to distinguish a change in consumer tastes from a change in quality. (See Figure 14.12 and associated discussion.) At that time, however, we also alluded to the fact that other conditions exist wherein it is difficult, and perhaps impossible, to distinguish between these two phenomena. A possible commingling of change in tastes and change in quality exists within b_i^c.

In Figure 10.3, the movement from the point m to m' corresponds to an increase in b_i^c. The level of quality remains constant at some specified variety (i.e., at $\hat{v}_{i2}$ in the case of Figure 10.3). This behavior is similar (though not identical) to that just described in Figure 14.19, where the consumer acquired a taste for the bundle at the terminus of path (4), in Figure 10.2, and subsequently increased b_i^c. In the case of path (4), double-targeting subsequently arose (i.e., both quantity and quality became fixed), but in Figure 10.3 the movement from m to m' involves a reduction in quantity. Quality is constant in both cases.

Earlier in this chapter (see section 3) we discussed the assumption that b_i^c reflects an individual consumer's perception of, and consumption experience from, some specified level of quality, some targeted variety. These processes were assumed to occur under the *special case*, which involved WTP(TK). Self-image of the consumer was assumed to play a major role in influencing the consumer's perception of quality. In section 3 we also pointed out, however, that tastes could be influenced by self-image, and hence also influence the value of b_i^c. In other words, it may be impossible to isolate the influence of quality on b_i^c from the influence of taste on b_i^c. Self-perception is mostly likely involved in both activities. The one case where we can clearly distinguish between change in quality and change in taste was discussed in association with Figure 14.12. In this instance, both v_i^c and b_i^c remained constant. The change in taste was clearly discernible; it was revealed by a change in the preference map, and only in the preference map.

There are some differences, however, between the phenomenon of Figure 14.19

and the movement between m to m' in Figure 10.3. As stated earlier, quantity, x_i, is reduced via the path from m to m', but under the double-targeting involved in Figure 14.19 there is no reduction in x_i. The rise in b_i^c, however, imposes a cost on the individual consumer in both cases. Essentially, the difference is in the method of payment. If a higher willingness-to-pay (WTP) is detected by producers, consumers manifesting the higher WTP will pay higher prices (assuming market segmentation). The higher prices may come in the form of a reduction in quantity—that is, a reduction in x_i as a result of higher b_i^c (and consequent higher p_i^c and p_i^p). This is the case corresponding to the path from m to m' in Figure 10.3. In the case of higher b_i^c under double-targeting, the consumer will pay in the form of allocating more resources to the ith commodity subbudget, M_i. These resources might come from reductions in quantity and/or quality of other commodities, $j \neq i$, reduced savings, or from an increase in M_T that is allocated to M_i. In terms of producers and market phenomena, whether the rise in b_i^c came from a change in the perception of quality, or from a change in consumer tastes, may not be a matter of great importance, except possibly in terms of market research and the motivation to encourage consumers to repeat this form of behavior.

14. Δb_i^c and Individual Consumer Demand: The Case of a Decrease in Quality

The last issue we will address regarding Δb_i^c and individual consumer demand is the effect of a decrease in quality, a reduction in $\hat{v}_i$. In chapter 10, section 15, and in chapter 13, section 17, the topic of a decrease in quality was discussed in terms of $v_i x_i$ space. We now address this phenomenon from the perspective of $x_i x_j$ consumption space and $x_i p_i$ demand space. In chapter 10, Figure 10.7 illustrates four paths toward lower quality. In chapter 10 each path was discussed in terms of willingness-to-pay; specifically, in terms of willingness-to-accept-payment-to-relinquish. We now consider each path, not only in terms of b_i^c, but also in terms of budgetary decisions regarding M_i and the magnitude of saving. Each path will also be examined in terms of its influence on individual consumer demand. We begin with path (3).

Along path (3) of Figure 10.7 the consumer remains on the original constraint; therefore, b_i^c is constant. It is assumed that b_i^c remains accurate for the lower level of quality, that b_i^c "reaches" to the lower variety (e.g., to $\hat{v}_{i1}$). In essence, path (3) of Figure 10.7 is analogous to path (2) of Figure 10.2. The value of b_i^c is constant in both cases: for an increase in quality for path (2) of Figure 10.2, and for a decrease in quality for path (3) of Figure 10.7.

In $x_i x_j$ space, reduction of v_i results in an upward rotation of the constraint, pivoting at the x_j intercept. With b_i^c constant, the reduction in p_i^c is attributable exclusively to Δv_i^c, the reduction in $\hat{v}_i^c$. As before, analyses of substitution and income effects only address the magnitude of change in quantity demanded, likewise the issues of whether a reduction in quality is "normal" or "inferior." The traditional presumption, however, would suggest that under a reduction in quality there would be a reduction in x_i—that is, for reduction in v_i (that leads to reduction in p_i), quality is an inferior good.

In $x_i p_i$ space, path (3) corresponds to a reduction in p_i^c (given $b_i^c > 0$) and an increase in x_i (given the nature of the Houthakker constraint in $v_i x_i$ space). Unfortunately, these are the same indeterminate results we encountered under an increase in quality. As before, unless we can establish (control for) either a constant price, p_i, or a constant quantity, x_i, based on the information we have a priori, we are unable to distinguish between a change in demand or an increase in quantity demanded. In the case of path (3), without controls for either price or quantity we cannot discern whether the reduction in quality has resulted in a shift in individual consumer demand or a movement along the demand curve. Path (3) in itself cannot confirm or deny that a decrease in quality results in a decrease in individual consumer demand.

Path (4) of Figure 10.7 also corresponds to a reduction in quality, but in this case there has also been a reduction in b_i^c. We assume in this case, however, that $b_i^c > 0$ still holds. Path (4) is consistent with our earlier assumption that (at least within v_i neighborhoods) for an increase in v_i, b_i^c either remains constant or increases in value (see section 3). The corollary to this assumption is that for a decrease in v_i, b_i^c either remains constant or decreases in value—that is, for $\Delta v_i^c < 0$ within the v_i neighborhood, there is $\Delta b_i^c \leq 0$. Paths (3) and (4) are both consistent with this assumption. In $x_i x_j$ space, there is an upward rotation of the constraint, pivoting at the x_j intercept. In contrast to path (3), however, owing to the reduction in b_i^c, the upward rotation is greater under path (4) than under path (3). (The magnitude of reduction in v_i is assumed to be the same for all paths identified in Figure 10.7.) All of the same issues regarding substitution and income effects discussed previously apply to path (4).

In $x_i p_i$ space we are again confronted with an inability to discern whether the reduction in quality resulted in a change in individual consumer demand or an increase in quantity demanded. We know there are a decrease in price and an increase in quantity, but based on that information alone it is impossible to discern what has occurred in demand space. Again, there is no theoretical support either to justify or deny the standard presumption of a decrease in demand corresponding to a reduction in the level of quality.

In the case of path (2), from Figure 10.7, we have again the useful situation of targeting by the consumer on a specified quantity of the ith commodity. To attain path (2), the consumer targets on the same quantity as at the point m on the original constraint. In order to pursue this path, the consumer must either increase b_i^c and/or decrease the M_i subbudget. An increase in b_i^c violates our assumption regarding the ordering of v_i and Δb_i^c within a v_i neighborhood.[18] To be consistent, therefore, we must conclude that either the lower v_i is outside the v_i neighborhood, or that the consumer does not increase b_i^c. In the case where b_i^c remains constant, path (2) is attained via a reduction in the M_i subbudget.

With the exception of some of our earlier comments regarding change in consumption technology (e.g., over the life cycle of a consumer), it would appear reasonable to assume that most consumers are not willing to pay more for lower levels of quality (i.e., attain path (2) via an increase in b_i^c). It seems far more likely that consumers follow path (2) either by choosing to reduce the M_i subbudget, or because they have been forced to do so, possibly owing to a reduction in total household income, M_T, brought on by unemployment, by downsizing, by divorce, and so forth.

In $x_i x_j$ space, path (2) involves double-targeting, first on the lower quality, $\hat{v}_{i1}$, and then on quantity, $\hat{x}_i$. If we assume b_i^c constant, the constraint in $x_i x_j$ space would initially rotate upward as before, owing to the effect of lower v_i on p_i (i.e., p_i is decreased). When the M_i subbudget is reduced, however, the constraint in $x_i x_j$ space rotates downward, pivoting at the x_j intercept. The degree of downward rotation depends on the magnitude of reduction in M_i. Given constant a_i^c, b_i^c, and targeting on $\hat{x}_i$, reduction in v_i^c results in reduction in p_i^c, and hence in reduced expenditure on the ith commodity, $p_i^c \hat{x}_i$. Unless we assume saving from the M_i subbudget, the reduction in expenditure would equal the reduction in M_i, by $M_i = p_i^c \hat{x}_i$. Recall that change in M_i rotates the constraint in $x_i x_j$ space, instead of parallel-shifting the constraint, as explained previously. After the decrease in M_i, the constraint in $x_i x_j$ space returns to its original position. The new isoquality constraint is now, however, at the lower level of quality, $\hat{v}_{i1}$. From our earlier discussion of double-targeting recall that there are no substitution or income effects under double-targeting. Because the constraint does not move in $x_i x_j$ space, under double-targeting there is no change in either x_i or in x_j. The new bundle in $x_i x_j$ space involves the lower v_i, a constant x_i, and unchanged x_j.

In $x_i p_i$ space, under double-targeting there is no change in x_i, albeit that there is a decrease in p_i. If we rule out perfectly inelastic demand, there is a decrease in individual consumer demand corresponding to a decrease in quality. Recall from our previous discussion (see Figure 14.18), under double-targeting, demand becomes a point in $x_i p_i$ space. Point demand is lower at the targeted quantity after the decrease in quality and decrease in M_i.

Another interpretation of path (2) of Figure 10.7 is that this path is initiated by a reduction in household income, M_T. Under this approach, reduction in M_T forces a reduction in M_i, while the consumer retains the previous quantity target, $\hat{x}_i$. Quality is reduced to the level dictated by reduction in the M_i subbudget. In other words, quality is no longer targeted; instead, the subbudget is targeted. Quality is reduced to that level of v_i^c allowed by the reduced budget and targeted quantity, presumably within the consumer's v_i neighborhood.

In the case of path (1) of Figure 10.7, as with path (2), one of two explanations is possible. Either the consumer has increased b_i^c, or there has been a reduction in the M_i subbudget. To be consistent with the assumption regarding ordering of v_i^c and b_i^c within v_i neighborhoods, we assume that if b_i^c is increased, the lower quality variety is outside the v_i neighborhood. As in the case of path (2), however, we assume that for most consumers, path (1) is attained via a reduction in M_i. The reduction in M_i corresponding to path (1) is greater than that corresponding to path (2). Likewise, if b_i^c is increased in value, it is higher for path (1) than for path (2). Note that via either approach ($\Delta M_i < 0$ or $\Delta b_i^c > 0$) there is a reduction in quantity, x_i, unlike the situation of path (2). We examine only the case where M_i is reduced.[19] For this case we assume that b_i^c is constant and the decrease in M_i is sufficient to produce path (1).

In $x_i x_j$ space, given $p_i^c = a_i^c + b_i^c v_i^c$ with a_i^c and b_i^c constant, decrease in v_i^c results in a lower p_i^c. Conversely, the constraint rotates upward, pivoting at the x_j intercept. The decrease in M_i is sufficient that quantity is lower than at point m in Figure 10.7 (i.e., a reduction in x_i). In $x_i x_j$ space, therefore, the reduction in M_i rotates the constraint downward sufficient that the new constraint is closer to the origin than before the reduction in v_i.

From the perspective of $x_i p_i$ space, barring the existence of positive sloped demand, a decrease in price, p_i^c, accompanied by a decrease in quantity, x_i, suggests there has been a reduction in demand (i.e., a downward shift in an individual consumer demand curve). The decrease in demand is accomplished, under this interpretation of path (1), via a reduction in the M_i subbudget. As explained previously, a de-

crease in household income, M_T, may be the driving force behind the reduction in M_i, and subsequent decrease in quality. The decrease in quality, in this case, results in a decrease in individual consumer demand. These results are consistent with the traditional presumption that a decrease in quality will produce a decrease in consumer demand.

15. Δa_i^c and Individual Consumer Demand

The last component of the Houthakker price system we examine is the effect of Δa_i^c on consumer demand. Recall that a_i may be divided into two subcomponents. From the point of view of the consumer, we have $a_i^c = a_{i(BP)}^c + a_{i(market)}$. Earlier we argued that, as regards variable quality, only the subcomponent $a_{i(BP)}^c$ should be included in an examination of the effects of Δa_i on individual consumer demand. Recall that $a_{i(BP)}$ is the price of the basic package under a basic package approach to variable quality (see section 3).

In the Houthakker price system an increase in the price of the basic package is a shift parameter for the price line in $v_i p_i$ space, either the CDPL or the PDPL (see chapter 7, section 8, and chapter 12, sections 1–3). In other words, with no change in b_i^c (willingness-to-pay), nor change in the level of quality, v_i^c, an increase (decrease) in $a_{i(BP)}^c$ will increase (decrease) p_i^c along the CDPL (consumer-determined price line). Recall that the CDPL reveals what an individual consumer considers an acceptable price for various combinations of quantity and quality. In addition, change in $a_{i(BP)}^c$ will change p_i^c, and thus change the constraint in $x_i x_j$ space. As with any other factor that produces Δp_i^c, there may be income and substitution effects associated with $\Delta a_{i(BP)}^c$. As with the other components of the Houthakker price system, $\Delta a^c_{i(BP)}$ may also affect individual consumer demand in $x_i p_i$ space.

Recall from our previous discussion of the basic package that it is conceivable that the basic package is relative for each consumer and that $\Delta a^c_{i(BP)}$ may be connected to the consumer's v_i neighborhood (see chapter 12, sections 2 and 3). With the introduction of v_i neighborhoods, the possibility arose of freestanding a_i versus a_i connected to neighborhoods, specifically connected to v_i(min.) of the v_i neighborhood. Also, recall that within v_i neighborhoods the v_i are rank-ordered according to the perception and preferences of an individual consumer.

If we accept that $a^c_{i(BP)}$ corresponds to v_i(min.) of an individual consumer's v_i neighborhood, then within $v_i p_i$ space a new subspace may be created corresponding to the v_i neighborhood, and is illustrated as in Figure 14.20. If within the new subspace we introduce a 45° line, which might be defined as the *basic price system* corresponding to the subspace, then we may define the value of the basic package as $a^c_{i(BP)} = 0$, where, as before, the basic price is $a_i = 0$, $b_i = 1$. Clearly, in the full $v_i p_i$ space, $a^c_{i(BP)} > 0$.

Across the full range of the v_i axis in a complete $v_i p_i$ space there may exist many $v_i p_i$ subspaces, from those with neighborhoods at the lower end of the v_i range to those with neighborhoods at the upper end. The possibility exists that as household income, M_T, rises, the v_i neighborhoods shift from the lower end of the v_i spectrum to the upper end. For each such v_i neighborhood and corresponding $v_i p_i$ subspace, the value of the basic package may vary. A reasonable hypothesis is that for higher v_i neighborhoods the corresponding v_i value of $a^c_{i(BP)}$ is higher than for lower neighborhoods.[20] An implication of this hypothesis is that the basic package should be adjusted for different income groups—that is, dif-

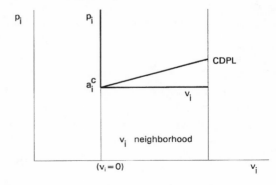

Figure 14.20 **When a_i Becomes the Price of v_i(min.)**

ferent basic packages correspond, for example, to the poor, the middle class, and the wealthy. The notion that the basic package extends across the entire breadth of quality variation of a commodity becomes less reasonable as the range of variable quality is enlarged. Corresponding to the possibility that different basic packages exist for different income groups is the possibility that different price (p_i) values of $a^c_{i(BP)}$ correspond to the different packages. A reasonable assumption is that a_i is lower in p_i value for a_i lower on the v_i axis—that is, the a_i connected to v_i(min.) of lower v_i neighborhoods is lower in p_i value than a_i connected to v_i(min.) of higher v_i neighborhoods. Figure 14.21 provides an illustration of three v_i neighborhoods and their corresponding $v_i p_i$ subspaces within the complete $v_i p_i$ space for the ith commodity.

The lines in Figure 14.21 representing the 45° lines correspond to each subspace. The v_i(min.) of the v_i neighborhoods of each subspace have been identified, as have the p_i values of $a^c_{i(BP)}$ for each subspace. Note that although we have assumed $a^c_{i(BP)} = 0$ in each $v_i p_i$ subspace, in the complete $v_i p_i$ space for the ith commodity, $a^c_{i(BP)} > 0$ for each subspace. Further, the $a^c_{i(BP)}$ are of ascending value corresponding to higher v_i neighborhoods. The solid lines in each subspace are the CDPL. The CDPL

Figure 14.21 **Neighborhoods Corresponding to Income Groups**

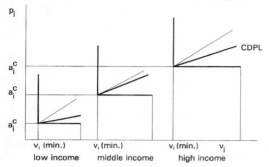

Figure 14.22 **Varieties Not on the CDPL**

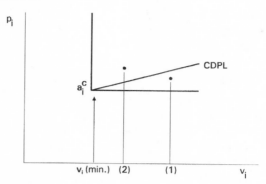

of the highest v_i neighborhood has been labeled. The assumption that higher v_i neighborhoods correspond to higher incomes is represented by the income categories illustrated.

The value of a_i in each of these subspaces could correspond to the basic price of the varieties included within each v_i neighborhood. The basic price would represent the price of the basic package in each neighborhood. Under this approach, in addition to all of the material previously discussed regarding consumer behavior within (and without) a single v_i neighborhood, we now see that as household income grows (declines) it is possible that the consumer rises (descends) from one v_i neighborhood to another. All of the material previously presented regarding $\Delta \hat{v}_i$, Δb_i^c, ΔM_i, and so on, may now apply, as well, to each $v_i p_i$ subspace.

16. Variety Prices

Finally, as regards the actual measure of v_i, previously we indicated that v_i could be an index identifying each variety. We can now return to Houthakker's original definition (i.e., that v_i is the price of the variety). We accept this definition as long as the price utilized to identify each variety is not necessarily the price paid by the consumer for the variety. Manufacturer Suggested Retail Price (MSRP), for example, might serve as the price, as long as there is room for the consumer to negotiate the final transacted price (even under take-it-or-leave-it pricing policies). If the consumer accepts the price offer of the producer (e.g., accepts the MSRP), then essentially we have $b_i^c = 1$, the basic price system. We now see, however, that as applied to each subspace, $a_i = 0$ is relative, as illustrated in Figure 14.21. In order for the basic price system of each subspace to correspond to the basic price system of the complete $v_i p_i$ space of the *i*th commodity, shift parameters, or transformations, need to be applied to each subspace.

Consistent with the assumption that within a v_i neighborhood the ordering of v_i is unique to each individual consumer, while at the same time allowing the price of each variety to serve as the index, we must allow that within each individual $v_i p_i$ subspace it is possible that the price p_i, corresponding to some specific v_i, does not lie on the CDPL. An illustration is provided in Figure 14.22, in which two varieties are identified that do not have prices on the CDPL. The variety identified as (2) has a price, p_i, that would correspond to a higher ranking in the ordering of v_i within the neighborhood—an original ranking possibly estimated by producers. The variety identified as (1) has a price, p_i, that would place it lower in the neighborhood. The actual position of both varieties, however, corresponds to an ordering based on an individual consumer's assessment of the varieties.

As shown, variety (2) would not be purchased by the consumer. Variety (1), on the other hand, because it meets the requirement to lie on or beneath the CDPL, could be purchased (see chapter 12). It is also possible that a point that does not lie on the CDPL—for example, the point corresponding to variety (2)—becomes a line segment, instead of a point, off the CDPL. The requirement to be on or beneath the CDPL, however, applies to line segments, as well as to points, in a $v_i p_i$ subspace. To the extent that producer assessment of consumer preferences is accurate (consumer cohort by cohort), the number of points off the CDPL will be diminished, and the ordering of v_i within v_i neighborhoods will correspond to the ordering of variety prices, v_i^p, provided by producers. This is another aspect of the Waugh-Brems problem.

17. Δa_i^c and the Constraint

In $v_i x_i$ space the value of a_i affects the position and convexity of the constraint. From $(dx_i/da_i) = [(-M)/(a_i + b_i v_i)^2] < 0$, for any specified (constant) v_i, the value of x_i is reduced as a_i is increased. Furthermore, from our previous study of the effect of the (a_i/b_i) ratio on the constraint, an increase in a_i reduces the degree of convexity of the constraint. As shown previously, the location of v_i also influences the magnitude of change in x_i derived from change in a_i. We can generally conclude, therefore, that for a specified value of v_i, quantity of the ith commodity will decrease as a_i is increased.

In $x_i x_j$ space, under the Houthakker price system, an increase in a_i ($a_{i(BP)}^c$) results in an increase in p_i (p_i^c), and the constraint rotates downward toward the origin, pivoting at the x_j intercept. Depending on the nature of the preference map, and/or whether quantity-targeting has been utilized, there may be a change in x_i and/or x_j. All of the traditional findings regarding substitution and income effects, normal versus inferior, and so forth, apply here. If targeting on x_i has been employed, then our previous remarks on double-targeting—on v_i and x_i—also apply.

Since we have assumed the basic package to be part of variable quality, the question remains, however, as to whether there is a change in quantity demanded or a change in demand associated with $\Delta a_{i(BP)}^c$. In $v_i p_i$ space, for constant v_i, we saw that higher $a_{i(BP)}^c$ results in higher p_i. In $v_i x_i$ space, for constant v_i, higher $a_{i(BP)}^c$ results in lower x_i. Again, there is the question of whether $\Delta a_{i(BP)}^c$ produces movement along an isoquality demand curve or in a shift of the curve.

If we assume quantity-targeting, $\hat{x}_i$ (i.e., if we control for quantity), we can discern whether there has been a change in demand as a result of a change in $a_{i(BP)}^c$. Because we are addressing the effects of $\Delta a_{i(BP)}^c$, we assume v_i^c and b_i^c are constant. Under x_i targeting, however, we must allow the M_i subbudget to be variable (see our earlier discussion of Δb_i^c). Recall that under double-targeting—on both v_i and x_i—there are no substitution or income effects. Under these conditions, as the price of the basic package ($a_{i(BP)}^c$) increases, p_i^c increases. Quantity, $\hat{x}_i^c$, and quality, $\hat{v}_i^c$, remain constant. The reduction in x_i, otherwise required by the increase in a_i, is offset by an increase in M_i sufficient to attain the quantity target, $\hat{x}_i$.

In $x_i p_i$ space, quantity remains constant while the price, p_i, has increased as a result of higher $a^c_{i(BP)}$. Recall that double-targeting produces point demand in $x_i p_i$ space. In the present case, however, there is no change in quality from one demand point to another (i.e., the points are isoquality). We conclude, therefore, that point demand is higher after the increase in $a^c_{i(BP)}$ (i.e., there is an increase in individual consumer demand as a result of a higher evaluation of the basic package). These results hold for any of the $v_i p_i$ subspaces illustrated in Figure 14.21.

18. $\Delta a_{i(market)}$ and Individual Consumer Demand

The second subcomponent of a_i is $a_{i(market)}$. This is the same component for both consumers and producers. As explained earlier, this component reflects all other forces affecting p_i, other than those factors involved with quality of the *i*th commodity. To examine the effects of $\Delta a_{i(market)}$, we assume all of the following are constant: $\hat{v}_i$, b^c_i, and $a^c_{i(BP)}$. To control for shift phenomena that might otherwise arise, we also assume M_i constant.

From $p^c_i = a^c_i + b^c_i v^c_i$ and $a^c_i = a^c_{i(BP)} + a_{i(market)}$, and the constancy assumptions described above, an increase (decrease) in $a_{i(market)}$ will result in an increase (decrease) in p^c_i. Furthermore, given no targeting on x_i, and given that the income effect does not exactly offset the substitution effect in $x_i x_j$ space, an increase in p^c_i will result in a reduction in x_i. In other words, $\Delta a_{i(market)}$ may be assumed to be the primary source of a change in quantity demanded—that is, movement along an isoquality demand curve.

As should be obvious from our earlier discussion of Δv_i, Δb^c_i, and $\Delta a^c_{i(BP)}$, however, a change in quantity demanded could also arise from change in any of these components of the Houthakker price system. Likewise, it is possible for other phenom-

ena to produce a change in demand other than a change in quality or change in income. In other words, $\Delta a_{i(market)}$ could create a change in demand, as well as a change in quantity demanded.

In the case of $\Delta a_{i(market)}$, if there is quantity-targeting, an increase (decrease) in $a_{i(market)}$, supported by an adequate change in M_i, will produce an increase (decrease) in demand, similar to all of the other cases previously examined. In the case of $\Delta a_{i(market)}$, however, there is by definition no change in any of the quality components of the *i*th commodity. The corresponding change in demand, therefore, could not be attributed to variable quality.

Except in the case of quantity-targeting, it is essentially impossible to discern, a priori, when a change has occurred in demand associated with any of the above manifestations of variable quality, either for an increase or decrease in demand. Empirical studies, supported with adequate controls for either quantity or price, are necessary to distinguish between shifts of demand and movements along an isoquality demand curve. In such studies it is also necessary to control for the level of quality so as to assure that the demand being analyzed is isoquality and not variable-quality demand.

Note that as regards $\Delta a_{i(market)}$ under quantity-targeting, change in $a_{i(market)}$ accompanied by parametric change in $\hat{x}^c_i$ may be utilized to reveal patterns of discrete choice in $x_i x_j$ space and patterns of point demand across $x_i p_i$ space. Furthermore, in the absence of statistical controls, we will assume $\Delta a_{i(market)}$ is the primary force behind a change in quantity demanded. Under this assumption, variation in $a_{i(market)}$ (without quantity-targeting) may be utilized, as in traditional price theory, to trace out an isoquality demand curve. Along such a curve we assume constant v^c_i and constant $a^c_{i(BP)}$. In addition, within a v_i neighborhood corresponding to such an isoquality demand curve, we would have b_i^c constant.

Constant willingness-to-pay along an individual consumer demand curve, however, is counter to traditional microeconomic theory. Higher magnitudes of willingness-to-pay are usually assumed to correspond to higher prices on the curve. It should be noted, however, that in the case of variable quality we have argued that b_i^c represents willingness-to-pay only with respect to the quality dimensions of a product or service. There are likely many other aspects of willingness-to-pay besides those associated with quality. Nevertheless, in the model we have developed, for individual consumer demand across a v_i neighborhood, we assume constant b_i^c along the demand curve.

From the Houthakker price system it is possible to create the traditional isoquality demand curve with variable willingness-to-pay. For such demand we commence by assuming v_i^c constant. We further assume both components of a_i^c constant. As in the case of traditional demand theory (ordinary demand), we also assume income, M_T, is constant. In this case, however, we further assume the funds allocated to the M_i sub-budget are constant. With these restrictions in place, the only source of variation in p_i^c is Δb_i^c. Obviously, quantity, x_i, remains variable.

From $M_i = p_i^c x_i$, or $M_i = (a_i^c + b_i^c \hat{v}_i)x_i$, combined with the above assumptions of constancy, an increase in p_i^c, derived from an increase in b_i^c (the only variable component of p_i^c), must result in a reduction in x_i. In $x_i p_i$ space these results are consistent with a change in quantity demanded. (Recall, however, our previous remarks regarding the inherent difficulty in the Houthakker price system to distinguish between shifts of demand and movements along demand.) In the present case, Δb_i^c produced Δp_i^c, or, for example, higher values of p_i^c correspond to higher willingness-to-pay. These results are consistent with traditional theory.

In the case of quantity-targeting with variable b_i^c, if income, M_i, is allowed to vary, it is possible to make another comparison with traditional theory, specifically between ordinary demand and compensated demand. Previously, we discussed the case of quantity-targeting, with constant a_i and v_i, but variable M_i and b_i. This case involved double-targeting and resulted in point demand. We were able to show an increase in demand corresponding to an increase in b_i^c (see Figure 14.19). At that juncture we indicated that there was either a change in demand or demand was perfectly inelastic. We assumed there was a change in demand. We may now use this information to illustrate ordinary versus compensated demand under the case of variable b_i^c. In the case of variable b_i^c and constant M_i, we have the case just discussed of variable willingness-to-pay along an isoquality demand curve—assuming we can establish the existence of a change in quantity demanded. These results would be consistent with ordinary demand.

In the case of variable b_i^c and variable M_i (i.e., the double-targeting case), we have a change in income sufficient that the consumer can continue to purchase the same quantity, x_i, that is, a Slutsky form of compensated demand, or equivalent variation. (See our earlier discussion of these topics under variable quality and consumer surplus in chapter 8.) Although perfect inelasticity of demand is involved, these results are consistent with compensated demand. As in traditional theory, ordinary demand has greater own-price elasticity than has (perfectly inelastic) compensated demand (see Nicholson 1985).

Although we have used Δb_i^c as the variable component within the Houthakker price system to illustrate issues involving change in demand versus change in quantity demanded, as explained earlier, $\Delta a^c_{i(BP)}$ or $\Delta a_{i(market)}$ would equally serve the purpose. We emphasized b^c_i, however, owing to its importance in willingness-to-pay and traditional concepts of consumer demand. The other component of p^c_i, variable quality or Δv^c_i, may also be utilized; however, in this case the analysis turns to one involving variable-quality demand. Given the difficulties involved in any empirical analysis of isoquality demand, the ability to examine the effects of variable-quality demand may prove useful. If statistical analyses involve "mixed" levels of quality, theoretical differences between isoquality and variable-quality demand may prove useful in discerning whether the empirical results conform to iso- or variable-quality.

In fact, some of the difficulties we have encountered in distinguishing between change in demand and change in quantity demanded go to the intent of the Houthakker approach. In our model we have consistently utilized the one-variety version of his model, whereas his price system was designed to address purchases of several varieties of the *i*th commodity. The multiple-variety version of his model involves variable-quality demand for the *i*th commodity. As regards some of the differences between our single-variety model and a multiple-variety model, the nature of substitution is more severe in our isoquality model than in the variable-quality model. In both versions there exists substitution between varieties within the *i*th commodity and substitution across commodities. The intracommodity form of substitution is essentially binary under the single-variety version of the Houthakker model. Substitution of one variety for another reduces the quantity of the former variety to zero. This might be labeled "severe substitution."

In the intercommodity form of substitution, under most circumstances, neither

commodity is reduced to zero quantity. This is the more traditional form of substitution. In Houthakker's multiple-variety version of the model both intra- and inter-commodity substitution are of the nonbinary type (i.e., both forms of substitution resemble traditional, non-zero quantity, substitution). As pointed out by Waugh, however, there is probably more substitution within a commodity than across commodities, and this behavior would apply as well to Houthakker's multiple-variety model. In our model, emphasis is placed on discrete choice, usually at the level of $\hat{x}_i = 1$, which seems appropriate for those items that constitute a large portion of a household's budget. (The purchase of groceries, and similar items of small percentage of household income, fit more appropriately in Houthakker's multiple-variety version of the *i*th commodity.) Under the single-variety restriction, however, intra-commodity substitution is of the severe form.

Only at the level of the representative consumer (based on cohorts of consumers with similar socioeconomic-demographic characteristics)[21] would the traditional form of substitution apply in our model. These distinctions in the magnitude of substitution at the intracommodity (single-variety) level may prove useful in empirical work involving "mixed" isoquality and variable-quality demand data and the need to distinguish between the two.[22]

19. Truncated Demand and Windows in $x_i x_j$ Space

To this juncture, most of our discussion of individual consumer demand in $x_i x_j$ space has involved consumer decision making without neighborhoods or windows. The introduction of neighborhoods, either for quality or for quantity, and the introduction of windows, place additional restrictions on

Figure 14.23 **An x_i Neighborhood in $x_i x_j$ Consumption Space**

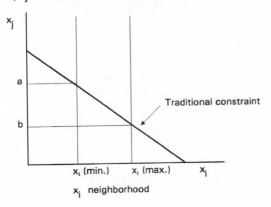

x_i neighborhood

Figure 14.24 **A Truncated Constraint in $x_i x_j$ Space**

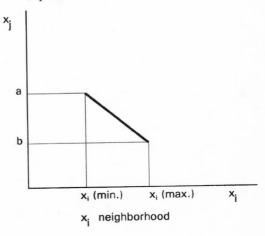

x_i neighborhood

individual consumer demand. We consider now the issue of neighborhoods and windows in $x_i x_j$ and $x_i p_i$ spaces. For a review of neighborhoods and windows, see the following: chapter 8, section 4; chapter 10, sections 2 through 9, and 14; chapter 11, sections 1 and 2; chapter 12, sections 2 through 5; and chapter 13, sections 10 through 17.

From our earlier assumption that a v_i neighborhood could exist along the v_i axis, we concluded that the constraint in $v_i x_i$ space was truncated and corresponded to the v_i neighborhood. Similarly, for x_i neighborhoods, we assumed the constraint corresponded to the range along the x_i axis that constituted the x_i neighborhood. A v_i neighborhood meant that in $v_i p_i$ space there was a limitation on the range of acceptable prices to an individual consumer. The combination of v_i and x_i neighborhoods creates a window in $v_i x_i$ space. The existence of upper and lower bounds on both v_i and x_i neighborhoods places restrictions on the variation of quality and quantity as producers interact with individual consumers in $v_i x_i$ space. As we will show, similar restrictions now apply in $x_i x_j$ space.

Figure 13.26 of chapter 13 provides an example of the restrictions on price and quantity that result from upper and lower

bounds on v_i and x_i neighborhoods. The existence of an x_i neighborhood in $x_i x_j$ space may be illustrated as in Figure 14.23.

As shown, an x_i neighborhood reduces the feasible range of the constraint. As explained previously, the consumer preference map is assumed restricted to the boundaries of neighborhoods.[23] On the x_i axis, therefore, utility maximization is restricted to the range between x_i(min.) and x_i(max.) inclusive, the lower and upper bounds on the quantity neighborhood. Interestingly, the restrictions on x_i also impose restrictions on consumer decision making regarding x_j.[24] Utility maximization may not occur along those portions of the constraint below x_i(min.) nor above x_i(max.). Furthermore, x_j may not exceed point (a) on the x_j axis, nor may it fall below point (b). The existence of an x_i neighborhood has, in effect, reduced the constraint in $x_i x_j$ space to a truncated region, as shown in Figure 14.24.

In similar fashion, the restriction imposed by a v_i neighborhood on the CDPL in $v_i p_i$ space restricts the amount of variation of p_i^c in $x_i x_j$ space. As always, the slope of the constraint in $x_i x_j$ space is the ratio of prices, p_i^c / p_j^c. The effect of v_i and x_i

Figure 14.25 **A Further Application of the Consumer Window**

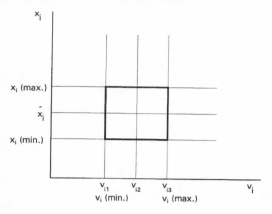

neighborhoods, therefore, is to restrict the amount of variation of x_i and p_i in $x_i p_i$ space, and ultimately to produce truncated individual consumer demand curves. This result was identified earlier in chapter 13. We see now, however, that the existence of neighborhoods within one commodity may produce truncated demand for other commodities. The rank-order of commodities, possibly according to an Ironmonger ordering of wants, may affect consumer decision making regarding subbudgets and may generate a cascading pattern of demands, from commodities of highest to lowest priority.

All of the material we have previously discussed regarding the effects of $\Delta \hat{v}_i^c$, Δb_i^c, $\Delta a_{i(BP)}^c$, and $\Delta a_{i(market)}$ on Δp_i^c, and on the slope of the constraint in $x_i x_j$ space, must now be considered within the context of truncated constraints and truncated individual demand curves. Similarly, all of the material previously discussed regarding v_i neighborhoods, change in quality, and shift patterns of individual consumer demand must be considered in terms of truncated demand. Under some circumstances the results will be the same as would occur with traditional (full-length) isoquality demand. The conditions associated with a

consumer window, however, provide a picture of individual consumer demand that is quite different from the traditional version.

20. The Consumer Window and Individual Consumer Demand

Combined with the previous material on consumer windows (see chapter 13, sections 10–17), and the material from this chapter on the role of $\Delta a_{i(market)}$ and change in quantity demanded, we are now prepared to present an enlarged version of the effects of variable quality on individual consumer demand. The concept of a consumer window in $v_i x_i$ space provides the foundation for the expanded version of consumer demand, and, in conjunction with $v_i p_i$ space, is extremely important to an understanding of the material that follows. We begin with a consumer window as illustrated in Figure 14.25.

In Figure 14.25 three levels of quality have been identified, from the lowest level of quality in the v_i neighborhood to the highest level. An intermediate level of quality, v_{i2}, has also been identified. Corresponding to the quantity neighborhood, the values of the highest and lowest values of x_i for the x_i neighborhood have also been identified, as well as an intermediate quantity target, $\hat{x}_i$. Recall that in $v_i x_i$ space, an increase in a_i results in a decrease in x_i (i.e., the constraint becomes more linear and moves closer to the origin). Also, recall that both the location of v_i on the v_i axis and the value of the ratio (a_i / b_i) influence the magnitude of change in x_i for any given change in a_i. For now, we assume M_i is constant, as well as b_i^c and the dimensions of the v_i and x_i neighborhoods.

In addition to $v_i x_i$ consumption space, it is important to recall the nature of the Houthakker price system in $v_i p_i$ space. Figure 14.26 provides an illustration of $v_i p_i$

Figure 14.26 **Alternative CDPL for Alternative Values of** a_i

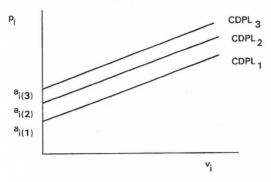

Figure 14.27 **The Effect of Increased** a_i **in** $x_i x_j$ **Space**

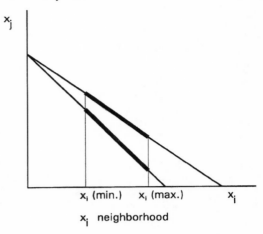

x_j neighborhood

space with variable $a_{i(market)}$. Three values of $a_{i(market)}$ are shown.

Corresponding to the three values of $a_{i(market)}$ there are three price lines (the CDPL), reflecting three alternative ranges of acceptable prices to an individual consumer. Recall that the value of a_i determines the intercept of the price line in $v_i p_i$ space. Also, recall that $a_i^c = a_{i(BP)}^c + a_{i(market)}$, and that b_i determines the slope of the price line. In Figure 14.26 the b_i^c are all constant, greater than zero, and equal in value. The higher CDPL correspond to higher values of $a_{i(market)}$ exclusively (i.e., as a_i increases, the CDPL shifts upward).

In $x_i x_j$ space we assume that M_T, M_i, p_j, and M_j are constant. In the $x_i x_j$ version of consumption space, an increase in $a_{i(market)}$ increases p_i^c and rotates the constraint downward, pivoting at the x_j intercept. An illustration is provided in Figure 14.27. The x_i neighborhood in $x_i x_j$ space corresponds to the x_i neighborhood in $v_i x_i$ space—that is, the range and boundaries of the two x_i neighborhoods are identical. Unless there is quantity-targeting on x_i, the preference map of the consumer in $x_i x_j$ space will determine the change in x_i derived from the increase in p_i^c (which results from the increase in $a_{i(market)}$).[25]

In the example that follows, assume that quality is constant at the level of v_{i1}—that

is, at v_i(min.) within the v_i neighborhood. Also, assume M_T, p_j, M_j, M_i, $a_{i(BP)}^c$, and b_i^c are constant. Finally, assume the consumer remains within the x_i neighborhood. We commence by assuming that there is an increase in $a_{i(market)}$. Recall that we have assumed the principal driving force behind a change in quantity demanded is $\Delta a_{i(market)}$. In terms of Figure 14.25, assume that the consumer is initially at the bundle corresponding to v_i(min.) and x_i(max.) (i.e., at the northwest corner of the window). In terms of Figure 14.26, assume the initial value of a_i is a_{i1}. Further, assume that the increase in a_i is represented by the change from a_{i1} to a_{i2}. In terms of Figure 14.27, assume that the increase in p_i arises solely from the increase in $a_{i(market)}$. We further assume that the preference map of the individual consumer is well-behaved, that the income effect does not offset the substitution effect, and that optimal solutions are found on the truncated constraints identified in Figure 14.27 by bold line segments.

Given all of the above, in $x_i p_i$ space the increase in $a_{i(market)}$ results in a decrease in x_i. Since we have restricted the change in $a_{i(market)}$ to the values of a_{i1} and a_{i2} (in Figure 14.26), we have two points, or point

Figure 14.28 Point Demand Under Variable a_i

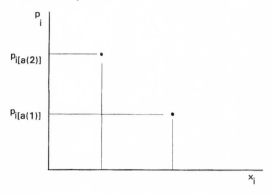

Figure 14.29 Continuous Demand Under Continuous Change in a_i

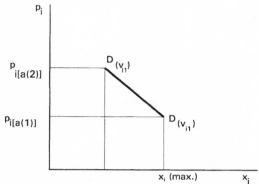

demand, in $x_i p_i$ space. The point corresponding to a_{i2} will have a lower quantity than that corresponding to a_{i1} (see Figure 14.28). If we allow continuous change in $a_{i(market)}$, for example, from a_{i1} to a_{i2} inclusive, and if we assume convexity, continuity and completeness of preferences in $x_i x_j$ space, then in $x_i p_i$ space we have a continuous demand curve from the point corresponding to a_{i2} down to the point corresponding to a_{i1}. This would represent the traditional downward-sloping isoquality demand curve. (See Figure 14.29.) Recall that both in the case of point and continuous demand only a single, individual consumer is involved. In the case of continuous demand, the magnitude of own-price elasticity depends, as in the traditional model, on consumer preferences, specifically on substitution and income effects. The demand curve illustrated in Figure 14.29 may have the full range of slope values from perfectly vertical to horizontal.

It should be understood that the establishment of continuous downward-sloping individual consumer demand curves could have also been accomplished without the use of $x_i x_j$ space (e.g., as was done previously in chapter 13). The use strictly of $v_i x_i$, $v_i p_i$, and $x_i p_i$ spaces, however, does not permit a determination of slope nor

of own-price elasticity. Cross-commodity issues (e.g., between the ith and jth commodities) are also precluded. The establishment of continuous downward-sloping demand without $x_i x_j$ space is illustrated in Figure 14.30. The level of isoquality is $v_i = v_{i1}$. In Figure 14.30, as long as it is possible to have continuous variation in $a_{i(market)}$ (in $v_i p_i$ space) and continuous variation in x_i (in $v_i x_i$ space), then in $x_i p_i$ space it is possible to have continuous variation in p_i and in x_i. The relationship of p_i to x_i is inverse. It is, therefore, possible to generate a continuous downward-sloping isoquality demand curve in $x_i p_i$ space. As stated before, the level of quality is v_{i1}.

Both in the approach that utilizes $x_i x_j$ space, and the approach that does not, it is possible to change $a_{i(market)}$ sufficiently such that quantity varies the entire range of the x_i neighborhood. In the discussion that follows, we assume that the magnitude of variation in $a_{i(market)}$ is such that the change in x_i covers the entire range of the x_i neighborhood—that is, from x_i(min.) to x_i(max.) inclusive.

Before we examine variation of x_i across the entire x_i neighborhood, we examine variation of v_i across the entire range of the v_i neighborhood, inclusive of v_i(min.) and v_i(max.). We will utilize the quantity target

Figure 14.30 **Generation of Iso-Quality Demand Without Use of $x_i x_j$ Consumption Space**

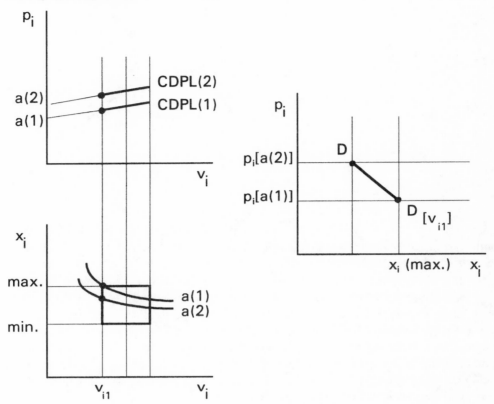

$\hat{x}_i$, of Figure 14.25, to accomplish this objective.

In $v_i x_i$ space we assume the consumer begins at v_{i1}, the lower boundary of the v_i neighborhood. Given quantity-targeting at $\hat{x}_i$, the consumer begins at the bundle $\langle v_{i1}, \hat{x}_i \rangle$—that is, at the intersection of v_i(min.) and $\hat{x}_i$ in Figure 14.25. Consistent with our previous work on attaining higher levels of quality, we assume the consumer can continuously increase the M_i subbudget, either through drawing resources from other commodities, from savings, and/or from an increase in M_T. Through the continuous increase in M_i the consumer effectively moves along the horizontal line perpendicular to $\hat{x}_i$, from the lowest value of v_i to the highest value within the neighborhood.

The increase in M_i, with a_i and b_i constant, shifts the constraint outward and upward in $v_i x_i$ space, effectively moving across the v_i neighborhood at the quantity level $\hat{x}_i$. With a_i, b_i, and x_i constant, a continuous increase in p_i (due to the increase in v_i), and a continuous increase in M_i, will result in point demand in $x_i p_i$ space. Each point corresponds to a level of quality, where higher v_i correspond to higher p_i. Given the assumptions of continuity, there is a continuous demand curve in $x_i p_i$ space; however, it represents variable-quality demand. Each point on the vertical demand curve corresponds to a different level of quality. An illustration is provided in Figure 14.31.

Figure 14.31 **Variable-Quality Continuous Demand Under Quantity-Targeting**

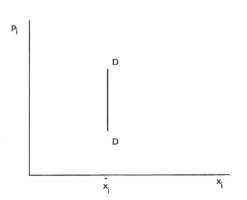

Figure 14.32 **Variable-Quality Point Demand Under Quantity-Targeting**

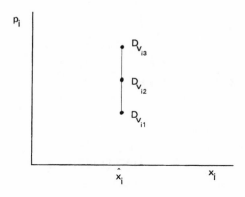

An illustration, where point demand is highlighted, is given in Figure 14.32. Higher points correspond to higher quality—that is, higher prices, p_i, correspond to higher v_i. In Figure 14.32 three levels of point demand are identified; they correspond to the v_i neighborhood presented in Figure 14.25. The lowest level of point demand, $D_{v_{i1}}$, corresponds to the lower boundary of the neighborhood, v_i(min.). The highest level of point demand, $D_{v_{i3}}$, represents the upper boundary on the neighborhood, v_i(max.). $D_{v_{i2}}$ corresponds to an intermediate value within the v_i neighborhood.

If we now introduce in $x_i p_i$ space the full range of the x_i neighborhood (as shown in Figure 14.25), combined with the v_i neighborhood, as introduced above, we have in demand space the phenomenon portrayed in Figure 14.33. Note that in this diagram the large dots identify the point demands previously illustrated in Figure 14.32. The three point demands were based on the assumption of quantity-targeting at the quantity $\hat{x}_i$. In Figure 14.29 we illustrated a single isoquality demand curve at the level of quality v_{i1}, the lowest level of quality in the v_i neighborhood. As explained at that time, the demand curve did not necessarily ex-

tend the full length of the x_i neighborhood. We indicated, however, that with adequate variation in a_i, specifically $\Delta a_{i(market)}$, the isoquality demand curve (at the level v_{i1}) could cover the entire breadth of the quantity neighborhood.

In Figure 14.33 three isoquality continuous demand curves are illustrated. As shown, the three levels of demand represent v_i(min.), v_i(max.), and an intermediate level of quality, v_{i2}. All three curves cover the entire length of the quantity neighborhood, but do not extend beyond the x_i neighborhood. Likewise, the highest and lowest demand curves do not extend beyond the v_i neighborhood. In effect, the existence of v_i and x_i neighborhoods, which create a consumer window in $v_i x_i$ consumption space, also results in a type of window in $x_i p_i$ space, what might be called a "demand window." The dimensions of the demand window depend on the size of the v_i and x_i neighborhoods, and on the magnitude of own-price elasticity of demand for the isoquality curves within the window.

Recall that movement along a single isoquality demand curve was obtained via change in $a_{i(market)}$, the variable within the Houthakker price system that we have assumed is the primary force for a change in quantity demanded. Recall that an increase in the level of quality was assumed to require an increase in income, specifically an increase in M_i.

Alternatively, a decrease in quality requires a decrease in M_i, either allocated to savings or to some other commodity. Within the demand window illustrated in Figure 14.33, therefore, we assume movement along the quantity axis is derived from a change in $a_{i(market)}$. Vertical movement within the demand window, on the other hand, is assumed to arise from a change in M_i. Although only three demand curves, of various levels of isoquality, are identified in the demand window of Figure 14.33, we assume the space is continuous and complete. Further, we assume that most individual consumers, most of the time, prefer to remain within their demand windows. Recall, however, our previous discussion of producer efforts to "lift" consumers beyond the upper bounds of their v_i neighborhoods. Also, the demand window reduces to a single vertical variable-quality demand curve under quantity-targeting (see Figure 14.31). Especially important under quantity-targeting is the case of $\hat{x}_i = 1$. Expensive consumer items, such as a home, fall into this category.

With the background of Figure 14.33 it is useful to reexamine the effects of Δv_i^c, Δb_i^c, as well as $\Delta a_{i(BP)}^c$. Previously, we made reference to the difficulty in distinguishing between a change in demand versus a change in quantity demanded. We have assumed that $\Delta a_{i(market)}$ is the primary force behind a change in quantity demanded, and that changes in the other components of the Houthakker price system, if accompanied by a change in M_i, are the forces behind change in demand.

We reexamine first the effects of Δv_i^c. Previously, we assumed that an increase in v_i^c, within the v_i neighborhood, was accom-

Figure 14.33 **A Demand Window in** $x_i p_i$ **Space**

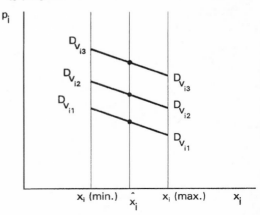

panied by an increase in M_i. This was the procedure behind Figure 14.32. In that exercise, quantity-targeting was also employed (i.e., at $\hat{x}_i$). We now drop quantity-targeting and the assumption of a change in M_i. We commence with an increase in v_i^c. We assume no change in b_i^c nor in any subcomponent of a_i^c. In terms of $v_i x_i$ space, this is analogous to path (2) of Figure 10.2. The increase in v_i^c results in a decrease in x_i in $v_i x_i$ space, and an increase in p_i^c in $v_i p_i$ space. In $x_i x_j$ space, the effect of higher p_i is a downward rotation of the constraint, pivoting at the x_j intercept. The decrease in x_i in $v_i x_i$ space requires that the income effect not offset the substitution effect in $x_i x_j$ space. In $x_i p_i$ space, as illustrated in Figure 14.33, the increase in p_i accompanied by a decrease in x_i corresponds to movement from, for example, D_{vi1} to D_{vi2}, where the value of x_i is lower on D_{vi2} than on D_{vi1}. If we assume no shifts in isoquality demand curves, the increase in v_i^c is analogous to a variable-quality demand curve that intersects D_{vi1} and D_{vi2}. (See Figure 14.34.) We may now view such a phenomenon as either a change in quantity demanded along a variable-quality demand curve, or, alternatively, as a locus of point demands, where each point is a different level of iso-

Figure 14.34 **A Demand Window Illustrating Iso-Quality and Variable-Quality Demands**

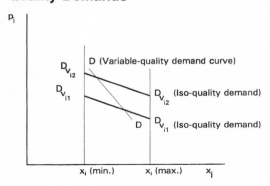

Figure 14.35 **Demand Windows Corresponding to Different Income Groups**

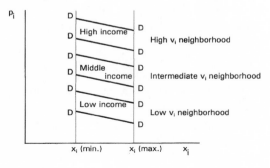

quality demand. (See Figures 14.31 and 14.32.) Under the second interpretation, there would be change in demand (i.e., change in isoquality point demand) as one moves across the variable-quality curve. This relationship may prove useful in empirical studies involving variable quality, and in efforts to isolate shifts in demand versus change in quantity demanded under conditions of variable quality.

As regards a reexamination of Δb_i^c, within the context of a demand window such as Figure 14.33, recall that change in b_i^c could produce a change in demand (if accompanied by a change in M_i) or change in quantity demanded (if unaccompanied by change in M_i). We now assume v_i^c and a_i^c are constant (e.g., $v_i^c = v_{i2}^c$). We assume an increase in $b_{v i2}^c$, that is, an increase in the individual consumer's willingness-to-pay for the quality level v_{i2}. We also assume M_i constant. In $v_i x_i$ space, the increase in $b_{v i2}^c$ is comparable to the path from m to m' in Figure 10.3. There is a reduction in x_i. In $v_i p_i$ space there is an increase in p_i^c derived from the increase in $b_{v i2}^c$, with constant v_i and a_i. In $x_i x_j$ space the higher p_i rotates the constraint downward, pivoting at the x_j intercept. Unless the income effect is negative and exactly offsets the substitution effect, there is a reduction x_i in $x_i x_j$ space. In

$x_i p_i$ space, as there is no change in M_i, the increase in $b_{v i2}^c$ cannot produce an increase in demand (see chapters 10 and 13). The increase in $b_{v i2}^c$, with resultant increase in p_i and reduction in x_i, is restricted to a decrease in quantity demanded. In a demand window, analogous to that in Figure 14.33, the increase in $b_{v i2}^c$ results in a northwest movement along the isoquality demand curve $D_{v i2}$.

The results just obtained for Δb_i^c also apply to $\Delta a_{i(BP)}^c$, the individual consumer's willingness-to-pay for the basic package. If M_i, v_i^c, and b_i^c are constant, $\Delta a_{i(BP)}^c$ must result in a change in quantity demanded along a given isoquality demand curve.

We return now to Figure 14.33 and examine the implications of some other aspects of variable quality. Previously, in our discussion of $v_i p_i$ subspaces and v_i neighborhoods in general (see, e.g., section 15 above), we alluded to the possibility that basic packages, v_i neighborhoods, and $v_i p_i$ subspaces could be different for different income groups. Those potential differences now surface as potentially different demand windows in $x_i p_i$ space. In what follows, we will assume there are three different categories of income: low, intermediate, and high.

On the assumption that quantity neighborhoods may be quite similar across income groups, while v_i neighborhoods likely range from low to high across low to high incomes, in $x_i p_i$ space we hypothesize that demand windows might be arrayed as shown in Figure 14.35.

For individual consumers there remains, however, the possibility that x_i and v_i neighborhoods may be larger or smaller than those illustrated in Figure 14.35. For items that constitute a high percentage of household income, the quantity target might be quite small. The case of $\hat{x}_i = 1$ seems appropriate in such cases. The stacking of v_i neighborhoods, from low to high, as illustrated in Figure 14.35, would likely continue, even in the case of $\hat{x}_i = 1$.

Finally, as was done earlier in $v_i x_i$ and $v_i p_i$ spaces, there remains the task of explaining consumer-producer interaction in $x_i x_j$ and $x_i p_i$ spaces. In our model, however, consumer-producer interaction becomes more complicated. As we shall see in the next chapter, in $x_i x_j$ space the individual consumer must now interact with both the ith commodity and jth commodity producers. We turn now to that objective.

Chapter 15

Individual Consumer Demand from $x_i x_j$ Space

Consumer Interaction with the ith and jth Commodity Producers

1. Interaction Between Consumers and Producers

As explained earlier, given $a_i^p = a_i^c$, and given accurate estimates by producers of consumer M_i subbudgets and of consumer v_i and x_i neighborhoods, transactions between consumers and producers occur in $v_i x_i$ space when $b_i^c \geq b_i^p$ and PDC $\geq$ CDC (see chapter 11). In $v_i p_i$ space transactions occur along the PDPL (*producer-determined price line*) where PDPL $\leq$ CDPL (*consumer-determined price line*; see chapter 12). We now examine consumer-producer interaction in $x_i x_j$ consumption space. In this chapter we expand interaction to include both the ith and jth commodity producers. The consumer in $x_i x_j$ space continues, as before, to be a single consumer. As explained earlier, our individual consumer is not the statistical average consumer, nor that cohort of consumers otherwise known as the *representative consumer*.

Comparable to producer behavior in $v_i x_i$ space, in $x_i x_j$ space we assume there exists a separate constraint generated by the producer. The constraint represents producer decision making, specifically the values

$p_i^p = a_i^p + b_i^p v_i^p$ and $a_i^p = a_{i(BP)}^p + a_{i(market)}$. Recall that in $v_i x_i$ space there were two separate constraints: the CDC (consumer-determined constraint, based on $M_i^c = p_i^c x_i^c = (a_i^c + b_i^c v_i^c) x_i^c$) and the PDC (producer-determined constraint, based on $M_i^p = p_i^p x_i^p = (a_i^p + b_i^p v_i^p) x_i^p$). The p-superscripts represent producer estimates of corresponding consumer variables. In $x_i x_j$ space we retain the same labels for both constraints, but we represent the PDC with a bolder line than that used to represent the consumer-determined constraint (CDC).

Figure 15.1 provides an example of PDC and CDC. The CDC presented are identical (i.e., have the same b_i^c values, and so forth) as those of Figure 14.6. As illustrated in Figure 15.1, the value of b_i^p is such that it is less than all values of b_i^c represented by the three CDCs. As a result, the PDC lies above all of the CDCs. Initially, we assume a_i for both producer and consumer are identical and greater than zero (i.e., $a_i^c = a_i^p > 0$). We also assume that the producer of the jth commodity has accurately estimated p_j^c and M_j^c (i.e., $p_j^p = p_j^c$ and $M_j^p = M_j^c$). Recall that for an individual consumer only one CDC is opera-

Figure 15.1 **Introduction of PDC into** $x_i x_j$ **Space**

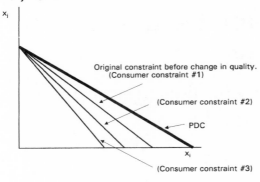

tive at a point in time. As shown, the consumer may choose from any of the b_i^c of Figure 15.1, or other values of b_i^c. As long as $b_i^c \geq b_i^p$, transactions may occur between this consumer and producer. Should the b_i^c fall and/or the b_i^p rise, a boundary will be reached wherein, given no change in $M_i^p = M_i^c$, transactions would cease.

Previously, in $v_i x_i$ space, we assumed that in order for transactions to occur it was necessary that the PDC rest on or above the CDC. This condition held when we examined only one commodity (e.g., the ith commodity). In chapter 14 we introduced $x_i x_j$ space, yet continued to focus primarily on the ith commodity. In this chapter we examine more closely the consequences of introducing a second commodity. In $x_i x_j$ space, the constraints (PDC and CDC) are both influenced by the prices, levels of quality, and subbudgets of the two commodities. Under these conditions the previous requirement of PDC $\geq$ CDC must be modified.

In $x_i x_j$ consumption space, for transactions to occur between an individual consumer and an individual producer of the ith commodity, it is necessary that $p_i^c \geq p_i^p$. Similarly, for transactions to occur between an individual consumer and a producer of the jth commodity, it is necessary that $p_j^c \geq p_j^p$. As we will see shortly,

these modifications permit occasions when the CDC rests above the PDC, yet transactions may still occur. For now, we assume producers are accurate regarding consumer subbudgets (i.e., $M_i^p = M_i^c$, $M_j^p = M_j^c$).

Recall our earlier assumption that profit motivates producers to accurately estimate consumer willingness-to-pay (both for $a_{i(BP)}^c$ and b_i^c), and to accurately estimate consumer incomes and subbudgets.[1] In other words, as regards the ith commodity, producers are assumed to seek the conditions: $b_i^p = b_i^c$, $a_{i(BP)}^p = a_{i(BP)}^c$, and $M_i^p = M_i^c$. In $x_i x_j$ space, if producers are accurate, the PDC will overlay the CDC throughout the space. We also assume that producers are generally aware, or quickly learn, of any variety-targeting behavior on the part of consumers, such that $\hat{v}_i^p = \hat{v}_i^c$, or that producers accurately target consumer v_i neighborhoods.

Note that if $b_i^c > b_i^p$, the consumer is willing to pay more for some specified bundle of v_i and x_i than he or she is required to pay (i.e., consumer surplus exists). We assume producers seek to eliminate consumer surplus as, for example, in the case of a first-degree price-discriminating monopoly. In our model, consumer surplus may be viewed as a form of savings—for example, a portion of M_i that may be allocated to the purchase of other commodities, $j \neq i$, or simply retained as savings. We assume it is beneficial to consumers to hide the magnitude of their willingness-to-pay. Gaming behaviors, hunter-prey models from biology, free-rider strategies, and so forth, are assumed to exist between consumers and producers.

In Figure 15.1 we assume producers of the jth commodity accurately estimate $p_j^c = a_j^c + b_j^c v_j^c$ and M_j^c, such that $p_j^p = p_j^c$ and $M_j^p = M_j^c$, and there is a single intercept on the x_j axis. (This is essentially the case examined earlier in chapter 14.)

Figure 15.2 **Intersection of PDC and CDC: Case I**

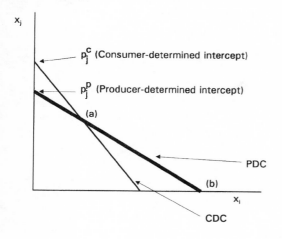

Figure 15.3 **Intersection of PDC and CDC: Case II**

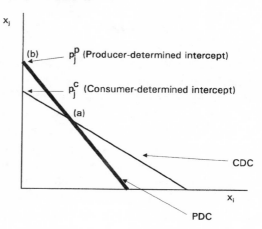

Just as in the case of producers of the ith commodity, it is possible for producers of the jth commodity to inaccurately estimate any or all of the components of $M_j^c = p_j^c x_j^c = (a_j^c + b_j^c v_j^c)x_j^c$. As in the case of producers of the ith commodity, the p-superscript on variables represents producer estimates of the corresponding consumer variables. If producers of the jth commodity are inaccurate, we may have $p_j^p \neq p_j^c$ and/or $M_j^p \neq M_j^c$, and two intercept values exist on the x_j axis. For now, we assume $M_j^p = M_j^c$ on the part of jth commodity producers. The value of p_j^c represents an acceptable per-unit price to the consumer,[2] for some specified level of quality, v_j, of the jth commodity. The value of p_j^p represents the producer's estimate of that price. In $x_i x_j$ space, given $M_j^p = M_j^c$, if $p_j^p > p_j^c$, then the producer intercept on the x_j axis is closer to the origin than the consumer intercept.[3]

Recall that previously if the PDC of an individual producer was beneath the CDC of an individual consumer, no transactions would occur between that producer and consumer, at least over the relevant range. This condition applies to $v_i x_i$ space. In $x_i x_j$ space, however, depending on the value of the x_i

and x_j intercepts, there may be circumstances where the PDC lies below the CDC and transactions still occur. Two examples of inaccuracy on the part of producers, and the effect of inaccuracy on x_i and x_j intercepts, are provided in Figures 15.2 and 15.3.

Note that in Figure 15.2 transactions involving the ith commodity are possible everywhere along the PDC, even though to the left of the intersection of constraints the PDC lies below the CDC. Transactions are possible because everywhere along the PDC the condition $p_i^c \geq p_i^p$ is met.[4] In Figure 15.2, however, there are no transactions involving the jth commodity (i.e., the condition $p_j^c \geq p_j^p$ is not met).

The reverse of the situation illustrated in Figure 15.2 may also occur. These conditions arise if $p_i^p > p_i^c$ and $p_j^p < p_j^c$. As shown in Figure 15.3, a different intersection of constraints exists. In this case, owing to $p_i^c < p_i^p$, no transactions occur between the individual consumer and the ith commodity producer. However, by $p_j^c > p_j^p$, transactions may occur everywhere along the PDC between the consumer and the jth commodity producer.

We should note that if the PDC is everywhere below the CDC (i.e., if $p_i^c < p_i^p$ and

$p_j^c < p_j^p$), no transactions occur between producers and the individual consumer. This result requires that neither commodity have an intercept where PDC = CDC at the intercept.

As can be seen in Figures 15.2 and 15.3, decision making in $x_i x_j$ space may involve two different producers—the ith commodity and jth commodity producers—each of whom interacts with the same individual consumer. Both producers must estimate consumer willingness-to-pay, the size of subbudgets, desired level of quality, and so forth. As will be shown through the remainder of this chapter, decision making on the part of the jth commodity producer, who interacts with an individual consumer, may affect transactions between that consumer and the producer of the ith commodity. The ith commodity producer may likewise affect transactions between a single consumer and the jth commodity producer. In addition to price and subbudgets, change in the level of quality (e.g., Δv_j) may affect the ith commodity producer, and vice versa. In what follows, in order to simplify the material, we will initially examine consumer-producer interaction under the conditions portrayed in Figure 15.1.

In Figure 15.4 we have slightly modified Figure 15.1. We have provided only one CDC. The PDC remains as before. Both CDC and PDC have the same intercept on the x_j axis, signifying accuracy on the part of the jth commodity producer (i.e., $p_j^p = p_j^c$ and $M_j^p = M_j^c$). In $x_i x_j$ space, we assume both constraints are isoquality and that the ith commodity producer has been accurate regarding the level of quality. We assume $v_i = v_{i2}$, and based on the assumption of accuracy, $v_{i2}^p = v_{i2}^c$. Note that in $x_i x_j$ space the constraints, both PDC and CDC, are also influenced by the level of quality of the jth commodity—that is, the isoquality assumption regarding the constraint must

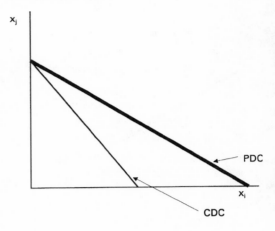

Figure 15.4 **Inaccuracy by the _i_th Producer: Underestimation of Consumer WTP**

now involve two levels of quality: $\hat{v}_i$ for the ith commodity and $\hat{v}_j$ for the jth commodity.

In the present case we do not assume the existence of v_i nor x_i neighborhoods. We assume all components of p_i^c and p_i^p are constant, except $a_{i(market)}$. We assume that the ith commodity producer has underestimated $b_{v_{i2}}^c$, such that $b_{v_{i2}}^p < b_{v_{i2}}^c$ and therefore $p_{v_{i2}}^p < p_{v_{i2}}^c$. The underestimation of $b_{v_{i2}}^c$ is the sole reason for the PDC to rest above the CDC. We assume the producer has accurately estimated the M_i subbudget (i.e., $M_i^p = M_i^c$).

As explained in chapter 14, we assume variation in $a_{i(market)}$ generates change in quantity demanded for the ith commodity. From $x_i x_j$ consumption space we may now produce an individual consumer isoquality demand curve in $x_i p_i$ space. The level of isoquality is v_{i2}. We assume (for now) that within the consumer preference map the ith and jth commodities are substitutable. Recall from chapter 14 that the substitution effect may arise from a change in the level of quality. In terms of $x_i x_j$ space, therefore, Δv_j may affect isoquality demand for the ith commodity. The individual consumer preference map in $x_i x_j$ space, through income and substitution effects, will influence the slope and own-price elasticity of individual isoquality demand.

Note that, as in traditional consumer theory, optimization occurs at tangencies of indifference curves (from the preference map) with alternative positions of the constraint (based on alternative values of $a_{i(market)}$). We assume a single preference map exists in $x_i x_j$ space over the time period of optimization, and that b_i^p and b_i^c are stable. In our model, however, there are two constraints (the PDC and CDC), which may be different and exist simultaneously. We assume it is possible for an individual consumer to optimize against each constraint separately. We assume market transactions and consumer interaction with producers involve optimization against the PDC. Optimization involving consumer perception of quality and individual willingness-to-pay occurs against the CDC. We assume that market data is generated from transactions along the PDC. The CDC reflects optimization within the mind of the consumer. These two processes of optimization need not agree. If producers are accurate, however, in their estimation of consumer decision making as regards the components of the Houthakker constraint, there will be agreement between the two forms of optimization.

In the present example (Figure 15.4), where the two constraints (PDC and CDC) are identical except for $b_{v_{i2}}^p < b_{v_{i2}}^c$, the change in $a_{i(market)}$ rotates the constraints in similar fashion, yet the constraints remain apart by $b_{v_{i2}}^p < b_{v_{i2}}^c$. In traditional consumer theory, at a single point of optimization (tangency) of indifference curve against constraint, we have $(MU_i/p_i) = (MU_j/p_j)$. In our model the process of optimization has become more complicated.

First of all, in our model the traditional optimization results described above still

hold (i.e., $(MU_i/p_i) = (MU_j/p_j)$). Now, however, such results may be seen as incomplete, and possibly misleading. For example, as illustrated by the PDC and CDC in Figure 15.4, for any specified quantity, x_i, the slope of the CDC is higher than the slope of the PDC. If the value of x_i along the x_i axis corresponds to the optimal solution on the PDC (the point of tangency of indifference curve with PDC), at that quantity the ratio of prices along the CDC is greater than the ratio of prices along the PDC. In other words, there is $(p_i/p_j) = (MU_i/MU_j)$ at the optimal value of x_i on the PDC, but $(p_i/p_j) > (MU_i/MU_j)$ at the same value of x_i on the CDC. If the CDC were parallel-shifted to the point of tangency between PDC and the indifference curve, the CDC would intersect the indifference curve at the point of tangency (i.e., the CDC is steeper than the PDC at the optimal value of x_i).

Under traditional consumer theory the condition $(p_i/p_j) > (MU_i/MU_j)$ would indicate that the consumer could attain higher satisfaction via a reduction in x_i and an increase in x_j. In our model, however, if the producer accurately knew $b_{v_{i2}}^c$, the price, p_i^p, would rise, the PDC would pivot downward until it overlay the CDC, and the consumer would likely experience (under well-behaved preferences) a reduction in x_i and a reduction in x_j.

As regards Figure 15.4, with PDC above CDC, this condition exists because the producer has inaccurately estimated consumer willingness-to-pay for the variety, v_{i2} (i.e., because $b_{v_{i2}}^p < b_{v_{i2}}^c$). As we will see shortly in our discussion of individual consumer demand, there is no incentive on the part of the consumer to accurately reveal his or her willingness-to-pay for v_{i2}, nor for any other level of quality. Producer ignorance may, at times, be beneficial to consumers.

In addition to the case of inaccurate b_i^p, there exists the possibility of inaccurate

Figure 15.5 **Quantity-Targeting Under Producer Inaccuracy**

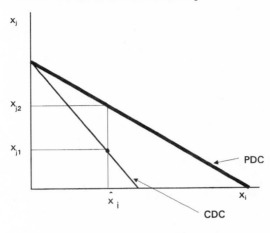

$a_{i(BP)}^p$. Recall that $a_{i(market)}$ is the same for both producer and consumer. Also, recall that $a_{i(BP)}^c$ represents the consumer's willingness-to-pay for the basic package, and $a_{i(BP)}^p$ represents the producer's estimate of $a_{i(BP)}^c$. As in the case of b_i^p, producers may under- or overestimate $a_{i(BP)}^c$. If $a_{i(BP)}^p <$ $a_{i(BP)}^c$, and if the producer is accurate regarding all other components of p_i^c, then we have $p_i^p < p_i^c$, or the PDC rests above the CDC, as before. All of the same issues and results previously discussed regarding the case of $b_i^p < b_i^c$ now apply as well to the case where $a_{i(BP)}^p < a_{i(BP)}^c$.

Finally, analogous to the conditions illustrated in Figures 15.2 and 15.3, it is possible to have various combinations of $b_i^p \neq b_i^c$ and $a_{i(BP)}^p \neq a_{i(BP)}^c$ such that the PDC intersects the CDC in $v_i x_i$ space. Such results affect transactions in $x_i x_j$ space.

We return now to Figure 15.4 and examine the effect of the conditions portrayed there on individual consumer isoquality demand in $x_i p_i$ space. For simplicity, we commence with the case of quantity-targeting in $x_i x_j$ space. Subsequently, we expand to the full range of variation in x_i (i.e., the FCSUM case; see chapter 10, section 3). We assume $v_i = v_{i2}$ for both PDC and

CDC. As before, we assume the only difference between PDC and CDC is $b_{v_{i2}}^p <$ $b_{v_{i2}}^c$. Quantity-targeting on $\hat{x}_i$ is illustrated in Figure 15.5.

As before, $p_i^c > p_i^p$, such that the PDC is above the CDC, and the feasible consumption set is larger under the PDC than under the CDC. In this case, which involves double-targeting (i.e., on $\hat{v}_{i2}$ and on $\hat{x}_i$), the consumer obtains $\hat{x}_i$ quantity of the ith commodity, at the level of quality $\hat{v}_{i2}$, and x_{j2} quantity of the jth commodity. (Transactions are possible between the individual consumer and the jth commodity producer by $p_j^c = p_j^p$, which meets the condition $p_j^c \geq p_j^p$.)[5] Note that had the ith commodity producer accurately estimated $b_{\hat{v}_{i2}}^c$, such that $b_{\hat{v}_{i2}}^p = b_{\hat{v}_{i2}}^c$, the consumer would receive $\hat{x}_i$, $\hat{v}_{i2}$ and only x_{j1} quantity of the jth commodity. With $b_{\hat{v}_{i2}}^p = b_{\hat{v}_{i2}}^c$, and a_i constant and equal for both consumer and producer, the producer constraint would rotate downward and overlay the consumer constraint. Inaccuracy on the part of the ith commodity producer, in this case, benefits not only the consumer but also the jth commodity producer.

As illustrated, with $b_{\hat{v}_{i2}}^p < b_{\hat{v}_{i2}}^c$ the consumer gains by the distance between x_{j2} and x_{j1}. Or, as we have assumed throughout, the consumer may save the funds equivalent to the value of the additional x_j—that is, the consumer may monetize the consumer surplus (possibly through the resale of excess x_j). The savings would represent funds allocated to the subbudget for the ith commodity, M_i, based on the consumer's willingness-to-pay for $\hat{x}_i$ quantity at $\hat{v}_{i2}$ level of quality, but which the consumer did not have to spend owing to the inaccuracy of the producer's estimate of $b_{\hat{v}_{i2}}^c$. Had the producer been accurate, there would be no excess funds in the consumer's M_i budget.

If we construct demand schedules based on the conditions portrayed in Figure 15.5,

Figure 15.6 **Point Demand Under Producer Inaccuracy**

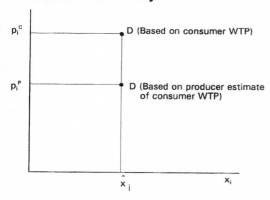

we obtain in $x_i p_i$ space two isoquality demand dots, or point demand, as illustrated in Figure 15.6. Each point corresponds to the same level of quality (i.e., both are at $\hat{v}_{i2}$). The higher of the two point demands indicates consumer willingness-to-pay for the bundle $\langle \hat{v}_{i2}, \hat{x}_i \rangle$. The lower of the two points represents the producer's (inaccurate) estimate of consumer willingness-to-pay for the same bundle. We designate each point demand as: $D^c_{\hat{v}_{i2}\hat{x}_i}$, for the consumer, and $D^p_{\hat{v}_{i2}\hat{x}_i}$, for the producer. In Figure 15.6 the two demands diverge owing to the difference, $b^c_{\hat{v}_{i2}} > b^p_{\hat{v}_{i2}}$. As shown in $x_i p_i$ space, the consumer's higher willingness-to-pay translates to a p^c_i higher than that estimated by the producer. We assume the consumer would rather pay the lower of the two prices, and hence has a motive to hide b^c_i and p^c_i. Obviously, if the producer knew b^c_i, $D^p_{\hat{v}_{i2}\hat{x}_i}$ would approach and attain $D^c_{\hat{v}_{i2}\hat{x}_i}$, and eliminate consumer surplus.

Once we drop the assumption of quantity-targeting in $x_i x_j$ space, and assume $\Delta a_{i(market)}$ generates change in quantity demanded of the ith commodity, we may produce continuous isoquality demand curves in $x_i p_i$ space. Given the difference between PDC and CDC in our example (i.e., $b^p_{v_{i2}} < b^c_{v_{i2}}$), we assume utility maximization

(FCSUM) may occur along the PDC, and separately along the CDC. In both cases, we assume the change in price, either Δp^p_i in the case of the PDC, or Δp^c_i in the case of the CDC, arises exclusively from $\Delta a_{i(market)}$. We further assume the configuration of the consumer preference map is the same under either optimization against the PDC or against the CDC. Unless otherwise stated, we assume the substitution effect is not offset by the income effect (i.e., we preclude Giffen effects). In fact, in most instances we assume the preference map is homogeneous.

Given a continuous increase in p^p_i, derived from the increase in $a_{i(market)}$, the PDC will rotate downward in $x_i x_j$ space, pivoting at the x_j intercept. Given that preferences are well-behaved as described above, the price-consumption path (for the PDC) will exhibit a reduction in quantity, x_i. In $x_i p_i$ space, therefore, an inverse relationship will arise between p^p_i and x_i. In similar fashion, an increase in p^c_i in $x_i x_j$ space will rotate the CDC downward and produce a reduction in x_i, and establish an inverse relationship between p^c_i and x_i in $x_i p_i$ space. For any given value of $a_{i(market)}$, by $b^p_{v_{i2}} < b^c_{v_{i2}}$, there is $p^p_i < p^c_i$ and $x^c_i < x^p_i$. In fact, the price-consumption path generated by the PDC is precisely the same path as that generated by the CDC (since we assume the preference map remains the same under both processes of optimization). There will be a single isoquality demand curve generated from both the PDC and CDC. For any value of $a_{i(market)}$, however, the point on the demand curve is different for the CDC than for the PDC. As described above, for any given $a_{i(market)}$, under the CDC process of optimization there is a higher price, p^c_i, and lower quantity, x^c_i, than the corresponding values for the PDC. The level of quality along the single isoquality demand curve is v_{i2}. Figure 15.7 provides an illustration of this type of demand.

Figure 15.7 **Iso-Quality Demand for the *i*th Commodity Derived from Figure 15.4**

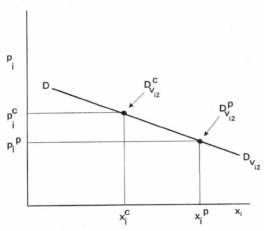

Figure 15.8 **Producer Attempts to Reduce Inaccuracy**

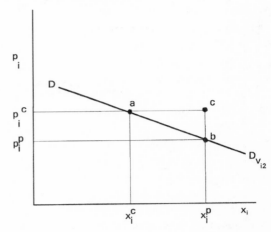

In Figure 15.7, the point on the demand curve corresponding to the CDC, the bundle $\langle x_i^c, p_i^c \rangle$, we will label as $D_{v_{i2}}^c$. The corresponding point for the PDC, the bundle $\langle x_i^p, p_i^p \rangle$, we label as $D_{v_{i2}}^p$. Note that the consumer is willing to pay a higher price and receive a lower quantity than the bundle offered by the producer. This situation exists solely due to inaccuracy on the part of the producer (i.e., $b_i^p < b_i^c$). Had there been accuracy on the part of the producer, there would be $b_i^p = b_i^c$, $p_i^p = p_i^c$, and $D_{v_{i2}}^p = D_{v_{i2}}^c$. The point corresponding to $D_{v_{i2}}^p$ would approach the point $D_{v_{i2}}^c$ on the demand curve in Figure 15.7. With knowledge of these two points, it is debatable, however, whether the producer would increase p_i^p. Depending on own-price elasticity of demand and the revenue generated at the lower price, the producer is assumed to choose that price which would render the higher revenue. If the consumer were willing to remain at x_i^p, for example, then charging a higher price (a higher p_i^p) would increase revenue to the producer.

In Figure 15.8 we illustrate this last strategy. Note that in Figure 15.8 the individual consumer is willing to be at point

(a), paying the higher price, $p_i^c > p_i^p$, and receiving the lower quantity, $x_i^c < x_i^p$. The consumer, however, is at point (b), paying only the price offered by the producer, p_i^p, and receiving the quantity, x_i^p. Given the consumer's willingness to pay the higher price, p_i^c, for a lower quantity, x_i^c, the producer may try to increase p_i^p to the value of p_i^c, while offering the consumer the quantity x_i^p—that is, encourage the consumer to move from point (b) to point (c). Whether the consumer accepts the offer (possibly because the quantity x_i^p is tied to the price p_i^c) may depend on how the offer is framed in the mind of the consumer; namely, does the consumer compare the bundle at point (b) with the bundle at point (c), or does the consumer compare the bundle at point (a) with the bundle at point (c)?[6]

In a comparison of what the consumer is willing to pay for x_i^c, the point (c) is superior to point (a). In a comparison of what the consumer receives at point (b), movement from point (b) to point (c) involves a greater expenditure at (c) than at (b). Point (b), therefore, would be preferable. The strategy on the part of the producer may be to eliminate the option of point (b) and only offer point (a) or (c), where quantity is tied to price. Under these circumstances, the individual consumer would likely choose point (c), unless the quantity x_i^p exceeds the upper boundary on a quantity neighborhood. (Recall that we have dropped the assumption of neighborhoods in this portion of the chapter.)

With knowledge of the consumer's willingness-to-pay, the producer may induce movement by the consumer from point (b) to point (c). If this strategy is successful across a range of prices along the demand curve in Figure 15.8, then we may conclude that for this individual consumer the original isoquality demand curve has shifted outward, reflecting the consumer's higher willingness-to-pay. If the strategy is not successful, then the producer (with knowledge of the consumer's higher willingness-to-pay) simply moves the point (b) to the point (a).[7] The demand curve does not shift. Under the first case, there is a change in demand. Under the second case, there is a change in quantity demanded. Note that in the first case, the individual consumer must be willing to increase his or her M_i subbudget for there to be movement from point (b) to point (c). This result is consistent with our earlier finding that an increase in demand occurs only if there is an increase in resources to the corresponding subbudget.

Recall from our earlier discussion of the two constraints in Figure 15.4, when the producer accurately estimates all components of the Houthakker price, we have $p_i^p = p_i^c$. In our present example, when the producer accurately estimates b_i^c, we have $b_i^p = b_i^c$, which gives $p_i^p = p_i^c$. With accuracy, the PDC pivots downward until it overlays the CDC. (In Figure 15.8, this result would have point (b) approach and attain point (a).) If, after accuracy, the individual consumer is willing to increase resources to the M_i subbudget, the single

constraint (where PDC = CDC) rotates outward, pivoting at the x_j intercept, until it comes to rest at the original position of the (formerly inaccurate) PDC. Under well-behaved preferences, this new optimal solution would involve a lower quantity than at point (c). The outward shift in demand would be less than illustrated in Figure 15.8. There would, however, exist an increase in demand. The greater shift discussed earlier reflects the value of bundling or tying prices and quantities. It is another example of demand maintenance.

We return now to Figure 15.4 and consider interaction between the individual consumer and the jth commodity producer. Recall the price condition for transactions is $p_j^c \geq p_j^p$. The single intercept on the x_j axis meets this requirement (i.e., $p_j^c = p_j^p$). To examine the price-consumption path for change in $p_j^c = p_j^p$, we utilize $\Delta a_{j(market)}$. We assume an increase in $a_{j(market)}$. As before, we assume preferences are well-behaved, and that optimal solutions (tangencies) on the PDC and CDC are obtained under the same map of preferences. With the increase in $a_{j(market)}$, both the PDC and CDC pivot at their corresponding x_i intercepts. As shown in Figure 15.4, the intercept of the PDC is higher on the x_i axis than the intercept for the CDC.

Under well-behaved preferences, for the same value of $a_{j(market)}$, the optimal quantity derived from the CDC is less than the optimal quantity derived from the PDC (i.e., $x_j^c < x_j^p$). These results are obtained albeit that the price of the jth commodity is identical for PDC and CDC. In $x_j p_j$ demand space, therefore, we have the conditions illustrated in Figure 15.9.

The unusual result of $x_j^c < x_j^p$, given $p_j^c = p_j^p$, arises from the individual consumer's greater willingness-to-pay for the ith commodity, that is, greater willingness-to-pay than estimated by the ith commodity producer. Had the ith commodity producer

Figure 15.9 **Effects of *i*th Producer Inaccuracy on the *j*th Producer**

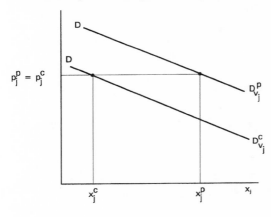

accurately estimated p_i^c, the PDC of Figure 15.4 would overlay the CDC, and in terms of transactions with the *j*th commodity producer, we would have x_j^p approach x_j^c until $x_j^c = x_j^p$. Under the conditions of $p_i^c > p_i^p$ in Figure 15.4, it is possible that the consumer saves unused resources of the M_i subbudget and allocates them to some other commodity (e.g., $h \neq i$ and $h \neq j$). This is another example of how decision making on the part of one producer may affect circumstances for another producer.

Under the circumstances illustrated in Figure 15.9, it is possible that transactions occur between the individual consumer and the *j*th commodity producer. For transactions to occur, it is necessary that the *j*th commodity producer not tie price and quantity. In other words, it is necessary that the producer allow the consumer to purchase the lower quantity at x_j^c. If the producer ties quantity and price such that the price p_j^p (in Figure 15.9) is bundled with the quantity x_j^p, then most likely no transactions occur.[8] The consumer has not allocated sufficient resources to the *j*th commodity to make such an expenditure. If, however, the consumer allocates the excess funds in the *i*th commodity subbudget to the *j*th subbudget (i.e., does not allocate

them to the *h*th commodity), then the consumer could purchase the larger quantity, x_j^p. If, on the other hand, the *i*th commodity producer became aware of the inaccuracy of, for example, $b_i^p < b_i^c$, and adjusted p_i^p such that $p_i^p = p_i^c$, then the consumer could not afford the bundle at x_j^p. The demand curves in Figure 15.9 would come together, with $D_{v_j}^p$ shifting downward toward and becoming equal to $D_{v_j}^c$.

Given $D_{v_j}^c < D_{v_j}^p$, as shown in Figure 15.9, if the *j*th commodity producer allows the consumer to purchase less than estimated by $D_{v_j}^p$, then some inaccuracy in estimating consumer demand is revealed. The difficulty, as illustrated by this example, is in determining wherein lies the inaccuracy. The producer of the *j*th commodity could incorrectly conclude that p_j^p was overestimated. Also, included in circumstances such as those illustrated in Figure 15.9 is the possibility that the consumer has priority ordering of commodities, and, for example, ranks the *i*th and/or the *h*th commodity(s) higher than the *j*th commodity. Under such circumstances, conditions surrounding the *i*th commodity (surpluses within the M_i subbudget) may affect (negatively) the *j*th commodity.

There remain the two cases where PDC and CDC intersect in $x_i x_j$ space. Figures 15.2 and 15.3 illustrate this condition. In the case of intersections of PDC and CDC, as explained earlier, the PDC may rest below the CDC and transactions continue to be possible. As far as individual producers are concerned, if the condition $p^p \leq p^c$ is met, transactions may occur. In Figure 15.2, for example, as regards the *i*th commodity, over the entire range of the PDC, transactions are possible between the individual consumer and the *i*th commodity producer. By the requirement $p_j^c \geq p_j^p$, however, no transactions occur with the *j*th commodity producer.[9] Under such circumstances, it is assumed the consumer will search out other producers of the jth commodity that offer "better" prices (i.e., producers who meet the condition: $p_j^c \geq p_j^p$).

In $x_i p_i$ space the conditions of Figure 15.2 give results that are different from those illustrated in Figure 15.7. Different intercept values on the x_j axis, the result of $p_j^p > p_j^c$, generate price-consumption paths from the PDC and CDC that are not identical—given our assumption that the same preference map applies to both processes of optimization. The degree of divergence between the two paths depends on the magnitude of the substitution effect and on the location of the price-consumption paths with regards to the point of intersection of the two constraints.

For the same value of $a_{i(market)}$ (which we continue to utilize to produce change in prices p_i^p and p_i^c), and given well-behaved preferences, the optimal quantity derived from the CDC will be less than the optimal quantity derived from the PDC, if the two paths are to the right of the intersection of constraints. Under these conditions, for any given value of $a_{i(market)}$, we continue to have $p_i^c > p_i^p$, and tangency solutions where $x_i^c < x_i^p$. Along the two price-consumption paths in $x_i x_j$ space, for any given value of x_i, there will exist unequal prices. Specifically, for any given x_i, we have $p_i^c > p_i^p$. Consequently, in $x_i p_i$ space we may conclude that for price-consumption paths to the right of the intersection of constraints in Figure 15.2, there is $D_{v_i}^c > D_{v_i}^p$. An illustration is provided in Figure 15.10. As before, we continue to assume that the level of quality, v_i, is the same along the PDC and CDC, and, therefore, the level of quality is the same along both demand curves in Figure 15.10.

For price-consumption paths to the left of the point of intersection (specifically, where both paths are to the left of the intersection), for the same value of $a_{i(market)}$,

Figure 15.10 **Demand Conditions for ith Commodity Derived from Figure 15.2**

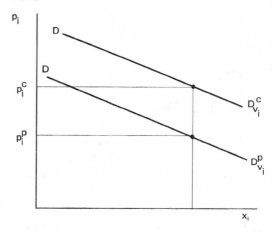

and given well-behaved preferences, the optimal quantity derived from the PDC will be less than the optimal quantity derived from the CDC. Under these conditions, for any given value of $a_{i(market)}$, we continue to have $p_i^c > p_i^p$, but tangency solutions where $x_i^c > x_i^p$. As before, for an increase in $a_{i(market)}$ there is an increase in both p_i^c and p_i^p. Along the two price-consumption paths in $x_i x_j$ space, however, for any given value of x_i, there remains $p_i^c > p_i^p$. In $x_i p_i$ space, therefore, the results are the same as for paths to the right of the intersection of constraints (see Figure 15.10).

Note that unless the ith and jth commodities are perfect complements in the preference map, it is not possible to obtain optimal solutions at the point of intersection of PDC and CDC. It is conceivable, however, given the "right" configuration of the preference map, for one price-consumption path to be to the right of the intersection (in Figure 15.2 this would be the path corresponding to optimization along the PDC) and the other path to be to the left of the intersection (in Figure 15.2 this would correspond to the CDC). Under such circumstances, again with well-

Figure 15.11 **Inaccuracy of the *j*th Producer: Underestimation of Consumer WTP**

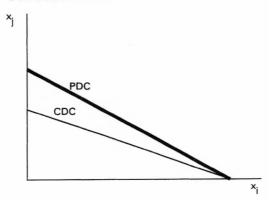

Figure 15.12 **Inaccuracy of the *j*th Producer: Overestimation of Consumer WTP**

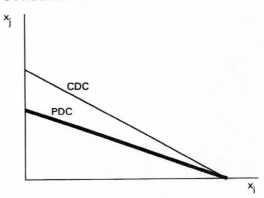

behaved preferences, the results would be similar to those already presented (i.e., $x_i^c < x_i^p$ and $p_i^c > p_i^p$). In $x_i p_i$ space we would have, again, demand conditions similar to those presented in Figure 15.10.

Finally, as regards the conditions portrayed in Figure 15.10, we assume that inasmuch as no transactions occur with the *j*th commodity producer, the consumer will seek producers of the *j*th commodity who offer prices such that transactions may occur. If consumers are successful in their search for such producers, the conditions presented in Figure 15.2 will not endure. Figure 15.2 may convert to Figure 15.4, or become an $x_i x_j$ space where the CDC lies everywhere beneath the PDC. Note that the condition, $p_j^c \geq p_j^p$, may be met either by a reduction in p_j^p or an increase in p_j^c. Adjustments in the consumer's M_j^c subbudget and/or change in the producer's estimate, M_j^p, may also facilitate transactions between the individual consumer and the *j*th commodity producer.

We turn now to the conditions illustrated in Figure 15.3. Recall that in this diagram we have $p_i^p > p_i^c$ and $p_j^p < p_j^c$. We have also assumed accuracy in estimation of both subbudgets (i.e., $M_i^p = M_i^c$ and $M_j^p = M_j^c$). Under these conditions, transactions occur

between the individual consumer and the *j*th commodity producer, but no transactions occur with the *i*th commodity producer. The analysis of price-consumption paths in Figure 15.3 is essentially the same as was performed regarding Figure 15.2. In terms of $x_i p_i$ demand space, the results are analogous to those illustrated in Figure 15.10. As in the case of Figure 15.2, we assume the consumer will search for those producers of the *i*th commodity with whom he or she may successfully have transactions—that is, the consumer (and possibly the producer or producers) will seek to find a way to meet the condition: $p_i^c \geq p_i^p$. Adjustments in subbudgets are also possible.

In addition to the conditions portrayed and described in Figures 15.2 through 15.4, we need to consider situations such as those illustrated in Figures 15.11 through 15.13.

Figure 15.11 is essentially the same as Figure 15.4. Transactions may occur with both the *i*th and *j*th commodity producers. The results obtained from Figure 15.4 apply to Figure 15.11, except that the producers are switched, as are the demand spaces. Figure 15.12, on the other hand, is new.

Figure 15.13 **Inaccuracy of the ith Producer: Overestimation of Consumer WTP**

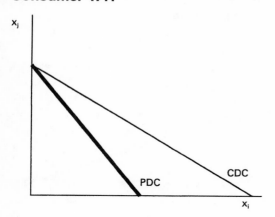

Figure 15.14 **Demand Conditions for the ith Commodity Derived from Figure 15.12**

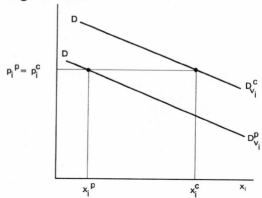

In Figure 15.12, transactions occur with the ith commodity producer, due to $p_i^p \geq p_i^c$, but not with the jth commodity producer, due to $p_j^p > p_j^c$. Insofar as transactions with the ith commodity producer are concerned, the results are analogous to those obtained for the jth commodity producer in Figure 15.4, except that in $x_i p_i$ demand space the demand curve derived from the PDC rests below the demand curve derived from the CDC. These results are illustrated in Figure 15.14. (Compare these results with those in Figure 15.9.) As regards the jth commodity producer (in Figure 15.12), the circumstances are similar to those illustrated in Figure 15.2.

Finally, as regards Figure 15.13, comparison of this figure with Figure 15.12 reveals that it is simply the reverse of Figure 15.12. All of the findings regarding Figure 15.12 are applicable to Figure 15.13, with rearrangement of axes and terms in demand space.

In general, we assume that given adequate time for the consumer to discover alternative producers, and given learning on the part of both consumers and producers, adjustments will be made by consumers and producers in all prices and subbudgets

such that the PDC and CDC will tend to approach each other. This conclusion, however, does not deny the possibility that, at any given time, considerable divergence could exist between the two constraints. When the constraints overlap (i.e., PDC = CDC) in $x_i x_j$ space, the traditional solutions $(p_i/p_j) = (MU_i/MU_j)$ and $(MU_i/p_i) = (MU_j/p_j)$ apply. As we have seen, however, in Figures 15.2 through 15.4, and 15.11 through 15.13, these results need not always obtain, nor be the only solutions. Ample possibilities exist for optimal solutions on the PDC (e.g., the optimal value of x_i) to correspond to $(p_i/p_j) > (MU_i/MU_j)$ for the same value of x_i on the CDC (see Figure 15.4), or to correspond to $(p_i/p_j) < (MU_i/MU_j)$ for the same value of x_i on the CDC (see Figure 15.11).

2. Two Definitions of Individual Consumer Demand and the Measurement of Consumer Surplus

As regards individual consumer isoquality demand curves derived above from the various configurations of $x_i x_j$ space, we make the following distinctions. The demand curve derived from optimization against the CDC will be identified as the "true"

Figure 15.15 **Consumer Surplus Under Demand Conditions Derived from Figure 15.2**

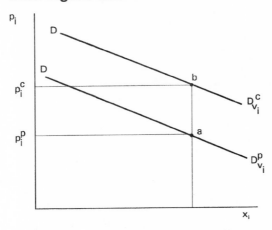

demand of an individual consumer. We label such demand D_v^c, where v may have the subscript i, j, and so on. The "true" demand, like the CDC, is based on individual consumer perception and decision making regarding all of the variables in the Houthakker constraint (i.e., it is based on $M_i^c = p_i^c x_i^c = [(a_{i(BP)}^c + a_{i(market)}) + b_i^c v_i^c] x_i^c)$.

The demand curve derived from optimization against the PDC will be identified as the "estimated" or "revealed" demand. We label this form of demand D_v^p, where again the subscript on v may be i, j, and so on. The "estimated" or "revealed" demand, like the PDC, is based on individual producer estimates of the consumer variables described above—that is, the p-superscripts in $M_i^p = p_i^p x_i^p = [(a_{i(BP)}^p + a_{i(market)}) + b_i^p v_i^p] x_i^p$ represent producer estimates of the corresponding consumer variables. The title, "revealed" demand, is intended to represent information regarding willingness-to-pay that the consumer has revealed, or was willing to reveal. For the most part, we will identify D_v^p as the producer "estimated" demand. Finally, as should be obvious, the possibility of $D_v^p \neq D_v^c$ exists and introduces additional

complications in the estimation of consumer demand and in the measurement of consumer surplus (see Appendix B).

Under our model of variable quality in consumer theory, the definition of consumer surplus must be modified, and the measurement of the surplus becomes more difficult. We return to Figure 15.10 to illustrate some of the unusual aspects of consumer surplus under our model. (Figure 15.14 could also be utilized for this purpose.) Figure 15.10 is reproduced as Figure 15.15.

Under traditional consumer theory, consumer surplus would consist of the area under the demand curve identified as $D_{v_i}^p$ and above the price p_i^p. That is, consumer surplus is the area bounded from above by the demand $D_{v_i}^p$ out to the point (a), and bounded from below by the price p_i^p out to the point (a). Under the demand conditions portrayed in Figure 15.15, however, our model suggests that consumer surplus is larger than that found under traditional theory.

In our model, given that the CDC reflects an individual consumer's perception and consumption experience of the quality level v_i, the demand curve derived from the CDC is argued to be the accurate measure of individual consumer willingness-to-pay. This demand is labeled $D_{v_i}^c$, and identified as the "true" demand. Under the conditions of Figure 15.15, for every value of x_i, the consumer's true willingness-to-pay is greater than that estimated by the producer, hence $D_{v_i}^c > D_{v_i}^p$ everywhere in $x_i p_i$ space. If we measure consumer surplus on the basis of the "true" demand, $D_{v_i}^c$, the surplus is larger than on the basis of the "estimated" demand, $D_{v_i}^p$. Under our model the area of consumer surplus is the area under the demand curve labeled $D_{v_i}^c$ out to point (b), down to point (a), and above the price p_i^p. The surplus is bounded from above by $D_{v_i}^c$ out to point (b), bounded from below

Figure 15.16 Consumer Surplus Under Demand Conditions Derived from Figure 15.4

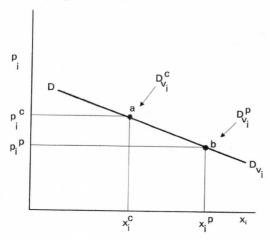

(b) corresponds to the PDC (i.e., it reflects producer estimates of consumer willingness-to-pay). Here, as before, there is inaccuracy, either in the form of $b_i^p < b_i^c$ and/or $a_{i(BP)}^p < a_{i(BP)}^c$. At the point (b), consumer surplus is the area under the demand curve and above the price p_i^p. If the producer had accurately estimated consumer willingness-to-pay, the producer could raise the price such that p_i^p approaches and attains the position of the price p_i^c. The point (b), corresponding to $D_{v_i}^p$, would approach the point (a), corresponding to $D_{v_i}^c$. The size of consumer surplus, for this individual consumer, would be reduced. The addition to consumer surplus, which arises due to underestimation of consumer willingness-to-pay, is the area bounded from above by the price p_i^c to the point (a) and bounded from below by the price p_i^p to the point (b). We should note that the decision on the part of the producer to raise the price p_i^p depends on elasticity of demand and the alternative revenues at point (b) versus point (a).

Finally, there is the demand relationship illustrated in Figure 15.9. This was an example involving the jth commodity, but similar results are possible for the ith commodity. Recall that in the discussion surrounding Figure 15.9 we explained that if the producer tied price and quantity, no transactions would occur. In other words, if the producer forced the consumer to purchase according to the producer's estimated demand, instead of from the "true" demand of the individual consumer, no transactions would arise between this producer and consumer. Given only the option to purchase the bundle on $D_{v_j}^p$, it was assumed the consumer would decline, and possibly pursue negotiations with other producers of the jth commodity. In cases where there are no transactions, there is no consumer surplus.

In Figure 15.9, however, if the consumer were allowed to purchase according to the

by the price p_i^p out to the point (a), and bounded by the line segment between points (a) and (b). The addition to consumer surplus is the area between the two demand curves out to the points (a) and (b). Recall that the difference between the two demands could arise from either $b_i^c > b_i^p$ and/or $a_{i(BP)}^c > a_{i(BP)}^p$. We continue to assume accuracy in the estimation of sub-budgets. Producer inaccuracy in the estimation of subbudgets, however, may also contribute to underestimation of consumer surplus.

In our examination of consumer surplus, we turn now to a different set of demand conditions. In Figure 15.7, recall that the configuration of PDC and CDC results in a single demand curve. Under these conditions, however, we again find that the magnitude of consumer surplus depends on the degree of inaccuracy on the part of producers. Figure 15.7 is reproduced as Figure 15.16, where the points (a) and (b) correspond to $D_{v_i}^c$ and $D_{v_i}^p$, respectively.

Recall that we assume, in the absence of an x_i neighborhood, that the consumer would prefer the price-quantity bundle at the point (b) over that at the point (a). Point

$D_{v_j}^c$ (i.e., purchase the quantity x_j^c), then transactions are possible. Under such circumstances, consumer surplus would exist. The size of the surplus would be the area under the $D_{v_j}^c$ and above the price $p_j^p = p_j^c$. In this case, the size of the surplus is smaller under the $D_{v_j}^c$ than under the $D_{v_j}^p$. Also, note that in this case, if transactions occur at all, they occur along the $D_{v_j}^c$, not on the $D_{v_j}^p$. If individual consumers are allowed to make transactions on their D_v^c, their demand is revealed. In the situation portrayed in Figure 15.9, however, the difference between $D_{v_j}^c$ and $D_{v_j}^p$ did not arise owing to inaccuracy on the part of the jth commodity producer; it arose owing to inaccuracy by the ith commodity producer. In this case, the jth commodity producer could be forced to reduce the price p_j^p to compensate for an estimation error on the part of the ith commodity producer.

The circumstances illustrated in Figure 15.9 also identify some potential difficulties in the statistical estimation of consumer demand. Under the conditions portrayed in Figure 15.9, if producers tie quantity to price, then estimation of demand will reveal the level of demand our model labels as $D_{v_j}^p$. If producers do not tie quantity and price (e.g., the example of an old-fashioned hardware store in note 8), then a different level of demand could be discovered. In our model, under the conditions of Figure 15.9, the second type of demand would be $D_{v_j}^c$. Recall that we assume transactions might not occur, or a fewer number would occur, if the consumer is forced to purchase off the $D_{v_j}^p$. In other words, the manner in which items are packaged (i.e., the case of $\hat{x}_j^p > 1$) may introduce bias into the sampling and estimation of some forms of consumer demand. In the present example there likely would be underestimation of consumer demand.

In general, we will make the simplifying assumption that, under the circumstances illustrated in Figure 15.9, transactions do not occur between an individual consumer and producer. In other words, to avoid the issues associated with packaging, we assume that transactions (usually) occur under the conditions $D_v^c \geq D_v^p$. Consistent with our previous assumptions regarding learning on the part of producers, we also assume that across time there is a tendency for producer accuracy to improve and that D_v^p approaches D_v^c. We assume the goal of producers is to have $D_v^p = D_v^c$. As we saw earlier in our discussion of $x_i x_j$ space, producer accuracy also tends to the condition PDC = CDC. When producers are accurate, the magnitude of consumer surplus is reduced.

3. Consumer-Producer Interaction, Neighborhoods, and Truncated Individual Consumer Demand

In sections 1 and 2 we discussed conditions that must be met for transactions to occur between an individual consumer and an individual producer. These conditions apply to consumer-producer interaction in $x_i x_j$ consumption space. As we have seen, conditions encountered in $x_i x_j$ space place restrictions on the generation of isoquality demand in $x_i p_i$ space and/or in $x_j p_j$ space. We also discussed two manifestations of individual consumer isoquality demand: the "true" demand—which reflects consumer expectation, consumption experience, willingness-to-pay, and subbudgets—which we label D_v^c; and the "estimated" demand—which reflects producer estimates of consumer willingness-to-pay, magnitude of consumer subbudgets, and so forth. This second demand we label D_v^p.

In all of the material we have covered so far regarding consumer-producer inter-

Figure 15.17 **PDC, CDC, and the Quantity Neighborhood**

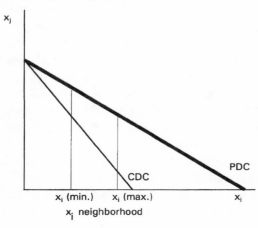

truncated constraint (CDC) in $x_i x_j$ space. Truncation of the constraint and preference map, both in $v_i x_i$ and $x_i x_j$ spaces, converts the utility optimization process from FCSUM to Neighborhood Simple Utility Maximization, or NSUM.

In addition, we found that a window in $v_i x_i$ consumption space creates another form of a window in $x_i p_i$ demand space. The task before us now is to examine the effects of a consumer window in $v_i x_i$ space on producer decision making in $x_i x_j$ space and in $x_i p_i$ space. In sections 1 and 2 of this chapter we examined producer-consumer interaction in $x_i x_j$ space without consumer windows. In this section we examine, first, the effect of a consumer window in $v_i x_i$ space on consumer-producer interaction in $x_i x_j$ space, and then follow that with an examination of consumer-producer interaction under a window in $x_i p_i$ demand space.

With Figure 15.4 we were able to study the conditions under which consumer-producer interaction (i.e., transactions) were possible everywhere along the PDC. In chapter 14, section 19 we studied the impact of x_i neighborhoods on the length of the CDC in $x_i x_j$ space (see Figures 14.23 and 14.24). We now introduce an x_i neighborhood in Figure 15.4. A hypothetical case is presented in Figure 15.17. In Figure 15.17 we assume $M_i^p = M_i^c$, $p_i^p < p_i^c$, and accuracy on the part of the jth commodity producer.

Although it is possible that the entire length of the PDC is present in $x_i x_j$ space, the effective range of the PDC (i.e., the range over which transactions may occur with an individual consumer) is now reduced to the range of the x_i neighborhood. In Figure 15.17 the CDC is essentially reduced to the range between x_i(min.) and x_i(max.) inclusive, as shown in Figure 15.18.

action, we have assumed there were no neighborhoods, neither for v_i nor for x_i. As a result, we have generally assumed the process of constrained optimization was Full Constraint Simple Utility Maximization, or FCSUM. With a few exceptions, we have assumed no targeting behavior by the consumer.

In this section we reintroduce neighborhoods and consider the interaction of consumer and producer under the conditions of consumer windows. The existence of a window (e.g., in $v_i x_i$ space) places restrictions on the range of variation of x_i and x_j in $x_i x_j$ space. A window in $v_i x_i$ space also places restrictions on the range of variation of v_i. As explained in chapter 14, the combination of restrictions on x_i and v_i creates a demand window in $x_i p_i$ space. We turn now to the nature of consumer-producer interaction under these conditions.

In chapter 14 we discussed the implications of a consumer window in $v_i x_i$ space. We found that a window corresponds to a truncated preference map and a truncated constraint (specifically, a truncated CDC) in $v_i x_i$ space, and is also reflected in a truncated preference map and

Figure 15.18 **Truncation of the CDC in $x_i x_j$ Space**

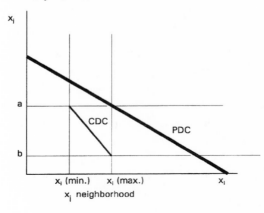

One implication of an x_i neighborhood in $x_i x_j$ space is that truncation of the CDC affects the effective range for transactions with the jth commodity producer, whatever that commodity might be. The consumer is assumed free to select the commodity to match with the ith commodity.[10] In Figure 15.18, transactions between the consumer and a single producer of the ith commodity occur only within the range x_i(min.) and x_i(max.) inclusive. Transactions occur on the PDC.

From our previous discussion of the conditions illustrated in Figure 15.4, we learned that these conditions result in a single isoquality demand curve in $x_i p_i$ space (see Figure 15.7 and associated discussion). Recall that for the same value of $a_{i(market)}$, the optimal bundle of price and quantity derived from the CDC corresponds to a higher price, p_i^c, and lower quantity, x_i^c, on the single demand curve, than the optimal bundle derived from the PDC (see the price-quantity bundles illustrated in Figure 15.7). On the single demand curve the point corresponding to $D_{v_i}^c$ will rest higher on the curve than the point $D_{v_i}^p$.

From our discussion of Figure 14.27 (see chapter 14, section 20), recall that an

increase in p_i^c pivots downward the CDC. The effective range for transactions, however, remains within the x_i neighborhood, inclusive of the boundaries. In Figure 15.18 we assume, as stated above, that change in $a_{i(market)}$ is the source of change in both p_i^c and p_i^p. An increase in $a_{i(market)}$ pivots downward both the PDC and the CDC. As the CDC swings downward it ultimately sweeps across the full range of the x_i neighborhood, from x_i(max.) to x_i(min.). At a sufficiently high value of p_i^c, the CDC will fall below x_i(min.). At that high p_i^c price it is no longer possible to generate demand, $D_{v_i}^c$, from the CDC (i.e., due to $x_i^c < x_i$(min.)). It is possible, however, to continue generating demand from the PDC (i.e., the producer-estimated demand, $D_{v_i}^p$).

Similar to the price-consumption path of the CDC, when the value of p_i^p is sufficiently high, the PDC will also sweep across the full range of the x_i neighborhood. When x_i^p falls below x_i(min.), it likewise becomes impossible to generate further demand from the PDC (i.e., the $D_{v_i}^p$ terminates at the price where $x_i^p < x_i$(min.)). Note that this price will be the same price off either the CDC or the PDC. Finally, note that both for the CDC and PDC, low values for p_i^c and p_i^p will not eliminate the corresponding constraints from the x_i neighborhood—that is, there is no price sufficiently low such that it forces the consumer beyond the upper bound of the neighborhood. Figure 15.19 illustrates the isoquality demand curve in $x_i p_i$ space derived from the $x_i x_j$ space of Figure 15.18. In Figure 15.19 the two values, $D_{v_i}^c$ and $D_{v_i}^p$, represent two different points on the single demand curve generated by a single value of $a_{i(market)}$.

In terms of the $x_i x_j$ space illustrated in Figure 15.18, we have only considered the effect of the x_i neighborhood on the ith commodity. We need to consider briefly the impact of that neighborhood on the jth

Figure 15.19 **Truncated Iso-Quality Demand Derived from Figure 15.18**

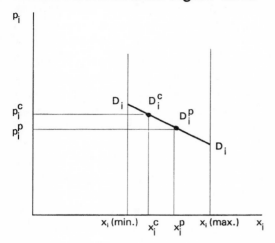

Figure 15.20 **Quantity Neighborhood Under Demand Conditions of Figure 15.10**

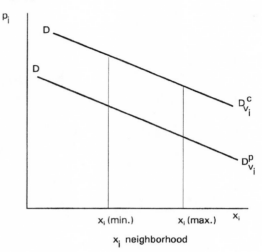

commodity. Review of our earlier discussion of the constraints in Figure 15.4 reveals that such an arrangement of constraints results in the demand conditions illustrated in Figure 15.9.

In section 1 we decided that the likelihood of transactions under such demand conditions was small. We subsequently introduced an additional requirement regarding transactions. To avoid complications arising from quantity-packaging—that is, when producers link or bundle price to a quantity greater than one, $\hat{x}_j^p > 1$—we introduced an additional requirement. The additional requirement was as follows: For transactions to occur in demand space, the demand relationship must be $D_v^c \geq D_v^p$. We conclude, therefore, that under the arrangement of constraints shown in Figure 15.4, transactions do not occur between the consumer and the jth commodity producer. It follows, then, that the existence of an x_i neighborhood in the $x_i x_j$ space of Figure 15.4 is of no consequence regarding the jth commodity. We assume, however, as mentioned earlier, that the consumer seeks out other jth commodity producers with whom transactions are possible.

We consider next the demand conditions illustrated in Figure 15.10. Recall that these conditions were derived from Figure 15.2. In Figure 15.20 we have reconstructed Figure 15.10 and introduced an x_i neighborhood. As with Figure 15.18, the existence of an x_i neighborhood in $x_i x_j$ space affects both the ith and jth commodities. An example of Figure 15.2 with x_i neighborhood is provided in Figure 15.21.

In Figure 15.21 the x_i neighborhood includes the intersection of constraints. As discussed earlier, however, the position of price-consumption paths relative to the point of intersection does not change the demand relationship illustrated in Figure 15.20. As explained in the case of Figure 15.4, at sufficiently high prices, p_i^c and p_i^p, the x_i intercepts of the CDC and PDC will sweep across the x_i neighborhood and eventually fall below x_i(min.). Similarly, for continuous increase in $a_{i(market)}$, which generates continuous increase in p_i^c and p_i^p, the intersection of constraints (the point a) moves across the x_i neighborhood toward the x_j axis.[11] Under all of these circumstances, however, the relationship of $D_{v_i}^c$ to

Figure 15.21 **Introduction of a Quantity Neighborhood in Figure 15.2**

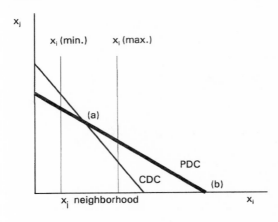

$D_{v_i}^p$ remains as illustrated in Figure 15.20 (i.e., at every level of quantity x_i, there is $D_{v_i}^c \geq D_{v_i}^p$). Transactions occur between the individual consumer and the ith commodity producer. Consumer willingness-to-pay is greater than or equal to that estimated by the producer.

There remain the situations in $x_i x_j$ consumption space illustrated by Figures 15.3, 15.11, 15.12, and 15.13. The results applicable to Figure 15.3 are essentially the same as those just explained for Figure 15.2, except that transactions occur with the jth commodity producer. The $x_j p_j$ demand space derived from Figure 15.3 would be similar to that of Figure 15.10, with the change of subscripts, i to j. Introduction of an x_j neighborhood would be analogous to that provided in Figure 15.20 for the ith commodity.

As regards Figures 15.11 through 15.13, many of the results already obtained from previous diagrams apply. Figure 15.11 is essentially the same as Figure 15.4, except that transactions occur with the jth commodity producer. Figure 15.7, with modification of subscripts, illustrates the demand space. The introduction of an x_j neighborhood gives results similar to those already obtained for Figure 15.4. The demand space derived from Figure 15.12 is illustrated in Figure 15.14. The introduction of an x_i neighborhood is similar to that shown in Figure 15.20. Finally, as explained previously, Figure 15.13 is the reverse of Figure 15.12, and all of the results obtained for Figure 15.12 are applicable to Figure 15.13, only in reverse (i.e., rearranging the axes and subscripts from i to j).

Given the conditions necessary for transactions to occur, we may summarize the above results for demand space. The conditions for transactions to occur between an individual consumer and either the ith or jth commodity producer can be illustrated in just two diagrams—Figure 15.7 or Figure 15.10. In both cases we assume the producer has accurately estimated the level of quality (i.e., $\hat{v}_i^p = \hat{v}_i^c$ or $\hat{v}_j^p = \hat{v}_j^c$). These results are the same either with or without quantity neighborhoods (i.e., with or without truncated demand).

Finally, we should note that the existence of a quantity neighborhood allows the more restricted version of a neighborhood (i.e., the case where a specific level of quantity is targeted). We have frequently used the example $\hat{x}_i = 1$. The same options are available for the jth commodity. As explained earlier, the existence of quantity-targeting results in point demand (if there is also targeting on the level of quality), or it results in a band of quality levels (if a v_i neighborhood is utilized). See Figures 14.31 and 14.32 for illustrations of this form of demand.

4. Demand Windows and Consumer-Producer Interaction

As discussed earlier, the existence of a consumer window in $v_i x_i$ space derives from the existence of x_i and v_i neighborhoods. In chapter 14, section 20, particularly the ma-

Figure 15.22 **Interaction of Producer-Estimated Iso-Quality Demand with Consumer Iso-Quality Demand**

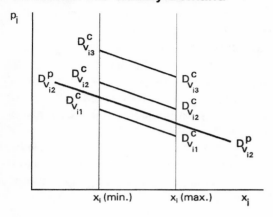

terial surrounding Figure 14.33, we examined how the existence of v_i and x_i neighborhoods creates a window in $x_i p_i$ demand space. The nature of demand windows across levels of consumer income, M_T, was also discussed earlier and illustrated in Figure 14.35. We are now prepared to discuss the interaction of an individual consumer and producer when demand windows exist in $x_i p_i$ space.

Previously, in discussing the relationship of $D^p_{v_i}$ to $D^c_{v_i}$, where both demands were at the same level of isoquality (e.g., at $\hat{v}^p_{i2} = \hat{v}^c_{i2}$), in order for transactions to occur in $x_i p_i$ space, we concluded that $D^p_{v_{i2}} \le D^c_{v_{i2}}$. The range of variation of x_i could be the entire length of the x_i axis, could be restricted to an x_i neighborhood, or there could be quantity-targeting (e.g., $\hat{x}_i = 1$). In all cases, the requirement $D^p_{v_{i2}} \le D^c_{v_{i2}}$ applies. In the case of a demand window, such as that illustrated in Figure 14.33, the requirement $D^p_{v_i} \le D^c_{v_i}$ applies to any level of isoquality within the window. As shown in Figure 14.33, for any given v_i (e.g., $\hat{v}_{i2}$), the demand generated from the PDC for that level of quality (i.e., $D^p_{v_{i2}}$) must rest on or below the demand generated from the CDC (i.e.,

$D^c_{v_{i2}}$). An illustration is provided in Figure 15.22.

As shown, the demand curve, $D^p_{v_{i2}}$, meets the requirement for transactions with the single consumer who generated the demand curve $D^c_{v_{i2}}$. The demand $D^p_{v_{i2}}$ could exactly overlay the true demand, $D^c_{v_{i2}}$, and transactions occur. When $D^p_{v_{i2}} = D^c_{v_{i2}}$, we assume accuracy on the part of the producer. When $D^p_{v_{i2}} < D^c_{v_{i2}}$, we assume the consumer would prefer to pay the lower price, $p^p_{v_{i2}}$, for any given quantity within the x_i neighborhood, rather than pay the price $p^c_{v_{i2}}$. The price $p^p_{v_{i2}}$ is taken from the "estimated" demand curve, $D^p_{v_{i2}}$. The price $p^c_{v_{i2}}$ is taken from the "true" demand curve, $D^c_{v_{i2}}$. Given $D^p_{v_{i2}} \le D^c_{v_{i2}}$, the consumer faces $p^p_{v_{i2}} \le p^c_{v_{i2}}$, and we assume that, whenever possible, the consumer would prefer to pay the lower price.

In Figure 15.22, if the demand $D^p_{v_{i2}}$ overlays a demand curve of a lower level of quality (e.g., $D^c_{v_{i1.5}}$), for the same price and quantity, it is assumed that within the demand window the individual consumer would prefer the higher quality (i.e., prefer $D^p_{v_{i2}}$ over $D^c_{v_{i1.5}}$). In essence then, within the window the ordering of v_i, offered by the producer, would approach the ordering of v_i generated by the consumer. In all cases, however, for any specified level of v_i, the estimated demand, $D^p_{v_i}$, must be on or below the true demand, $D^c_{v_i}$. The conclusions we have drawn for truncated demand also hold for point demand.

For any individual producer of the ith commodity it is possible that the producer also has a demand window in $x_i p_i$ space. For any given commodity, it is unlikely that a single producer will cover the entire range of varieties that constitute, for example, the ith commodity. In the case of the ith commodity, it is unlikely that a single producer would cover all of the varieties from v^-_i to v^+_i, to use Houthakker's notation (see chapter 4, section 2). It seems reasonable that a producer would cover a range of varieties, or have one or more v_i neighborhoods upon which the producer would focus or specialize. Given cost considerations, it likewise seems reasonable that single producers would have an upper bound on quantity, x_i, of the varieties they offer consumers. As far as an x_i neighborhood is concerned, the demand window of an individual producer would likely extend from zero to some x_i(max.).

Given the existence of demand windows for individual producers and individual consumers, for transactions to occur between any individual consumer and producer it is necessary that an intersection, or overlap, of the two windows exist. Within that region of overlap, the conditions for transactions described above (i.e., $D_{v_i}^p \leq D_{v_i}^c$) would apply.

It seems reasonable that producers would seek to maximize their number of overlapping windows with consumers. It also seems reasonable that some consumer windows would be more profitable than others. Producer windows that do not generate sufficient revenue would likely be either modified or discontinued entirely. With an increase in the number of consumers of the ith commodity, and in the number of producers of the ith commodity, the likelihood of transactions between consumers and producers would increase.[12]

5. The Rank-Ordering of Commodities

In $x_i x_j$ space, the existence of quantity- and quality-targeting implies the existence of priority across commodities, or the rank-ordering of commodities by individual consumers. Such ordering is manifest in the magnitude of, for example, $a_{i(BP)}^c$ and b_i^c, as well as in the magnitude of subbudgets (e.g., the magnitude of M_i^c as a percentage of M_T).

Previously, in our discussion of x_i neighborhoods within $x_i x_j$ space, we pointed out that the existence of an x_i neighborhood imposed restrictions on the range of variation in x_j. (See Figure 15.18 and associated discussion; see also chapter 14, sections 17 through 19.) The restriction on x_j becomes even more severe when quantity-targeting is utilized, for example, for the ith commodity. In this connection, we assume that if the individual consumer starts with a target on the ith commodity and then subsequently expands his or her decision making to include another commodity, the second commodity is restricted by decisions previously reached regarding the first commodity. In other words, because targeting on the ith commodity affects, for instance, the jth commodity, we assume that in a two-way comparison, the commodity targeted first is the higher rank-ordered commodity (e.g., the ith commodity has a higher priority to the individual consumer than the jth commodity).

We further assume that the process of rank-ordering across commodities begins with decision making regarding subbudgets. A reasonable assumption in this regard is that those commodities that constitute a high percentage of the total budget, M_T, are given a higher priority than those commodities that represent a low percentage of the M_T budget. In a manner similar to Ironmonger's ordering across wants, we assume that decision making cascades downward across commodities, from those representing the highest percentage of the total budget to those representing the lowest percentage. We further assume that targeting behavior reflects this same ordering—that is, that the commodity that constitutes the highest percentage of the total budget is the commodity that is targeted first, both in terms of level of quality and quantity. The degrees of free-

Figure 15.23 **The CDC Everywhere Below the PDC**

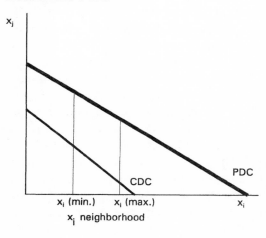

dom for decision making regarding the second commodity are more restricted than are those of the first commodity. In similar fashion, decisions regarding the second commodity place restrictions on the third commodity. The decisions may involve quality and quantity, or may involve just quality and not quantity, or vice versa.

We hypothesize that it is only in the case of commodities that represent a small percentage of M_T that restrictions regarding quality and quantity can be relaxed. In other words, the degree of substitution and the range of variation in a quantity neighborhood are assumed to be higher for commodities that are low in the rank-ordering of commodities. This approach is similar to that of earlier classical economists (see chapter 6, section 1). Note particularly the following quotation from Ironmonger:

> The idea that commodities may only indirectly produce utility through first satisfying some particular separate wants has been dropped from the theory of consumer behavior. In the development of the theory, the idea of separate wants—an intermediate stage between the dominant want, happiness, and the commodities consumed—has

been lost. . . . The idea that some, if not most, commodities have several uses . . . was not made an integral part of the theory and is still dismissed as relatively unimportant. . . . As originally developed, the law of diminishing marginal utility seems to have been a law of priority among wants . . . which states that the most important wants are satisfied before the least important. (Ironmonger 1972, pp. 11–12)

The application of lexicographic ordering of preferences seems appropriate for those commodities that hold high priority within the household budget. As explained earlier, the use of lexicographic preferences is consistent with the practice of targeting, either on the level of quality and/or on quantity (e.g., on $\hat{v}_i^c$ and/or on $\hat{x}_i^c$). Lexicographic ordering of preferences is also consistent with rank-ordering of commodities, at least in the upper range of the ordering. As suggested above, it may be only the lower-priority commodities that contain neighborhoods and where the NSUM process is utilized. In the world of variable quality, it seems unlikely that FCSUM is utilized often, if at all.

In the world of variable quality, discrete choice behavior (e.g., targeting and lexicographic ordering) on the part of consumers need not be seen as irrational. Considerable progress has been made in the field of discrete choice. Studies by Anderson, de Palma, and Thisse (Anderson et al. 1992) and Jean Tirole (1988), among others, have richly enhanced the theory of the firm, either as a discriminating monopolist or in an oligopolistic industry structure, where firms enter markets for products or services of variable quality.[13] In a related fashion, development of the random utility model, largely in the context of empirical work, has also lent support to the assumption of discrete choice behavior on the part of consumers (see note 7, chapter 9 and note 4, chapter 14).

Figure 15.24 **Truncated CDC and the Ranking of Commodities**

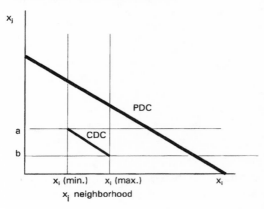

The rank-ordering of commodities permits us to examine another aspect of quantity-targeting. Earlier we pointed out that it was possible for the CDC to everywhere rest below the PDC. In $x_i x_j$ space this condition would arise if $p_i^c > p_i^p$ and $p_j^c > p_j^p$. An illustration is provided in Figure 15.23.

The existence of an x_i neighborhood, as explained above, affects the range of possible transactions with both the ith and jth commodity producers. An illustration is provided in Figure 15.24. See also Figure 15.18.

As shown in Figure 15.24, the x_i neighborhood reduces the range of transactions on the PDC for the ith commodity. The range on the PDC is between x_i(min.) to x_i(max.) inclusive. Note, however, that based on the truncated CDC of Figure 15.24, the effective range of transactions for the jth commodity is now reduced to the range between points (a) and (b) on the x_j axis. Caution must be exercised, however, not to conclude that the individual consumer conducts transactions along two separate segments of the PDC—that is, along the PDC between the points corresponding to x_i(min.) and x_i(max.) for the ith commodity, and along the PDC between

the points (a) and (b) for the jth commodity. Transactions could occur along either segment of the PDC, but not along both simultaneously. Transactions occur only along a single range, or segment, of the PDC.

Under the rank-ordering of commodities, that segment of the PDC in Figure 15.24 corresponding to the quantity-targeted commodity is the transaction surface. The other commodity is assumed to be of lower priority than the targeted commodity and is affected by decisions regarding the higher priority commodity. In $x_i x_j$ space this means that quantity-targeting on the ith commodity establishes the effective range for transactions on the PDC. In the case of Figure 15.24, NSUM would determine the optimal bundle of x_i and x_j within the range on the PDC between x_i(min.) and x_i(max.). The quantity of x_j would be determined from the bundle that corresponds to an optimum within the x_i neighborhood. Were the quantity neighborhood first established on the x_j axis, then the range between points (a) and (b) would determine the range for NSUM and the optimal quantity of x_j would determine the quantity of x_i.

In Figure 15.24, note that an optimum on the PDC, within the range of the x_i neighborhood, would correspond to a higher quantity of x_j than would be obtained by optimization along the truncated CDC. As explained previously regarding cases of this sort, this result is obtained whenever inaccuracy exists concerning consumer willingness-to-pay. In the case of Figure 15.24 there is inaccuracy regarding both the ith and jth commodities. Under these circumstances, we have assumed that the consumer may either retain the excess x_j or resell it to purchase a greater quantity (or higher quality) of some other commodity (e.g., of the hth commodity).

6. Vibrating Constraints and Individual Consumer Demand

In chapter 9 we described a Feigenbaum model for consumer decision making regarding the value of b_i^c. The model involved individual consumer perception and expectation of quality and consumption experience of quality. Until expectation became consistent with experience, it was possible for b_i^c to jump about in the manner of different period-attractors in the Feigenbaum model of attractors. Stable b_i^c were obtained when a period-one attractor was attained. Preference reversal could be characterized as a period-two attractor. We assumed under the Feigenbaum model that individual consumer perception and learning were capable of modifying the folded function in a b_{it}^c phase space, thereby changing the value of λ, and influencing the nature of the attractor. We also explained that in $v_i x_i$ space, for any level of v_i, if the consumer was not accurate regarding b_i^c, the constraint was not stable—that is, it could exhibit a pattern similar to that shown in Figure 10.4 (for different values of λ). We are now prepared to discuss this phenomenon as it applies to $x_i x_j$ space and to demand space.

Heretofore in our discussion of $x_i x_j$ space, we assumed the divergence of CDC and PDC arose from inaccuracy on the part of the producer (e.g., $b_i^p < b_i^c \Rightarrow p_i^p < p_i^c$). We generally assumed accuracy as regards subbudgets (i.e., $M_i^p = M_i^c$). Accuracy on the part of producers regarding the value of b_i^c presumes that the consumer has first reached stability regarding the value of b_{it}^c (i.e., $b_{it=k}^c = b_{it=k+1}^c$). Note that the same conditions apply to learning about $a_{i(BP)}^c$ and M_i^c. In the case of the CDC, if the consumer has not attained a stable value for b_{it}^c, then p_i^c is not stable. Given constant M_i^c, the intercept value for the CDC on the x_i axis will change for every value of b_{it}^c. If

we assume stability for all components of the Houthakker constraint as it applies to the jth commodity, there will exist a constant intercept of the CDC on the x_j axis. In $x_i x_j$ space, however, we will encounter a CDC that vibrates along the x_i axis, corresponding to the different values of b_{it}^c. If similar conditions also apply to the jth commodity (i.e., b_{jt}^c is not stable), then the CDC vibrates along both axes. Either with a single intercept that vibrates, or with vibration of both intercepts, the CDC will vibrate across $x_i x_j$ consumption space. The magnitude of vibration is most likely greater with instability of intercepts along both axes. (The same results would hold for hypersurfaces in higher-dimension consumption spaces.) The attainment of accuracy on the part of either the ith or jth commodity producers becomes much more unlikely under these circumstances.

In fact, when b_i^c is unstable, efforts on the part of individual producers to estimate accurately (or hone in on) the values of b_i^c and p_i^c may lead to instability of the PDC. Both constraints could vibrate simultaneously in $x_i x_j$ space. In other words, vibration in one constraint (the CDC) may initiate vibration in the other (the PDC), analogous to phase transitions in dynamic systems. Both constraints could become ergodic. It seems likely, however, that under such circumstances producers would eventually utilize some statistical average for the values of p_i^p and p_j^p. The size of the variance around such averages would likely be influenced by the magnitude of vibration of the CDC. The possibility for inaccuracy on the part of producers seems high under these circumstances. As before, inaccuracy could result in either consumer surplus or in the elimination of transactions.[14]

In demand space, the existence of vibrating constraints means that demand curves, either D_v^c and/or D_v^p, could also vibrate. This, in fact, may be the nature of consumer demand, not just an empirical artifact. All of the various forms of inaccuracy that can arise under the Houthakker constraint in $v_i x_i$ space (i.e., as regards the values of $a_{i(BP)}$, b_i, v_i, and/or M_i), combined with our model of Feigenbaum decision making, increase the likelihood of vibration in $x_i x_j$ and $x_i p_i$ spaces. As suggested earlier in this study, the nature of consumer behavior in the world of variable quality may be inherently stochastic.

7. Indeterminacy Revisited and Conclusions

We began part 2 in an effort to address a problem of indeterminacy in the Houthakker constraint. The problem arose regarding determination of values for b_i and a_i away from the basic price system (i.e., away from $a_i = 0$, $b_i = 1$). To address that difficulty we proposed two different interpretations of a_i and b_i: one according to the consumer and another according to the producer. In our model, indeterminacy is eliminated if, and only if, two conditions are met. First, consumers attain accuracy in their willingness-to-pay for the basic package (i.e., $a_{i(BP)}^c$ becomes stable), and they attain accuracy in their willingness-to-pay for quality improvements above the basic package (i.e., b_i^c becomes stable). Second, producers accurately estimate both forms of consumer willingness-to-pay. That is, producers accurately estimate consumer willingness-to-pay for the basic package and for quality improvements above the basic package (i.e., $a_{i(BP)}^p = a_{i(BP)}^c$ and $b_i^p = b_i^c$). In the introduction of our model we focused primarily on the process of attaining accuracy of b_i^c, both for the individual consumer and for the ith commodity producer. Attainment of accuracy regarding $a_{i(BP)}^c$ is equally important.

As the model unfolded, however, we learned that there exist additional factors that must be accurately estimated. The opportunities for inaccuracy include the level of quality, v_i, and the magnitude of subbudgets allocated by consumers to various commodities. These difficulties represent an expanded version of the Waugh-Brems problem discussed in part 1.

To focus on the determination of a_i and b_i, we generally assumed accuracy regarding subbudgets and the level of quality. We learned that determination of a_i and b_i requires transactions between individual consumers and individual producers. The model presents conditions that must be met for transactions to occur. These conditions apply to $v_i x_i$, $v_i p_i$, $x_i x_j$, and $x_i p_i$ spaces. The model, however, identifies circumstances wherein transactions may occur yet inaccuracy still exists on the part of producers. Consumers typically gain under such circumstances. In other words, transactions are a necessary condition to the elimination of indeterminacy, but they are not sufficient.

The model assumes that, across time, profit motives on the part of producers will tend to reduce, and occasionally eliminate, inaccuracy. Only under the conditions of accuracy, both on the part of consumers and producers, are the values of a_i and b_i determined. When accuracy is present, both for consumers and producers, the new model provides results similar to those of traditional consumer theory, at least for commodities not under lexicographic ordering. The condition of accuracy, however, will likely endure for brief periods of time, and may arise infrequently. In the meantime, the model assumes that processes of shopping, learning, and negotiation continue for individual consumers and individual producers.

In the process of eliminating indeterminacy, a new model of consumer theory has evolved. As described in part 2, under the new model several additional concepts and hypotheses have been developed. For example, the model posits that commodities are rank-ordered; that lexicographic ordering, targeting, and other discrete choice models more accurately reflect consumer decision making under conditions of variable quality; and that the traditional preference map applies only to commodities of low priority in household budgets.

Development of the new model involved construction of a Feigenbaum model of consumer decision making. The algorithm opened the possibly that constraints in $v_i x_i$ and $x_i x_j$ spaces are dynamic. The model also posits that consumers utilize neighborhoods, both for quality and quantity, in their decision-making and shopping processes. The existence of neighborhoods results in "windows" in $v_i x_i$ consumption space and in $x_i p_i$ demand space. As a result, truncated demand arises frequently at the level of individual consumer demand.

Throughout development of the model, our focus has been the individual consumer, and the role of individual consumer decision making at the level of retail markets. Emphasis on the individual has underscored the subjective nature of quality. At the level of the individual, we have argued that quality, like beauty, is in the eye of the beholder (i.e., in the eye of the individual consumer). The model, therefore, recommends a more limited use of the concept of a representative consumer. In fact, we argue that the representative consumer is, and always has been, essentially a statistical concept, an application of statistical sampling theory.

Given the heavy emphasis on the individualistic and subjective nature of quality, the new model of consumer theory argues that the sampling techniques utilized to investigate consumer behavior should be restricted to stratified-clustered samples drawn on numerous cohorts of consumers. In other words, there is no single "representative consumer," but rather a representative consumer for each cohort of consumers under examination. The tighter the stratification and clustering of characteristics of a cohort population, the greater is the ability to control for and study the effects of variable quality.

The model recommends that consumer theory be cohort based, instead of a general theory of the consumer. Consumers should be subdivided into cohorts based on, for example, age, sex, income, geographical location, level of education, occupation or profession, worldview, culture, religion, and so forth. Under conditions of variable quality, the application of a general theory of the consumer may lead to statistical results that obfuscate the impact of quality or generate mixed results. Our model identifies circumstances wherein such results could occur.

Consumer decision making regarding subbudgets within the total household budget receives increased importance. In fact, the model posits that the presumption that an increase in quality will generate an increase in individual consumer demand is inadequate. Unless higher quality is supported by an increase in budgetary resources, our model concludes there can be no increase in individual consumer demand. The model also hypothesizes that there may be a relationship between consumer decision making regarding the allocation (and reallocation) among subbudgets and consumer surplus. As in the case of learning from experience so as to accurately establish willingness-to-pay, consumers are assumed to learn from experience regarding the funds to allocate to subbudgets. A Feigenbaum phase space, involving expectation and experience, may be used to model consumer learning regarding accurate subbudgets.

Finally, our model raises some new questions regarding the justification and methodology used in adjusting price indices for change in quality. As regards the hedonic technique, our approach emphasizes the importance of Houthakker's varieties, and the manner in which characteristics cluster to form a variety. Perception of the bundled characteristics, which are in essence the variety, may be significant to consumers. In other words, not just the characteristics themselves, but the manner in which they are combined together, may determine consumer willingness-to-pay for different varieties of a commodity. Many applications of the hedonic technique, however, bypass varieties and go directly from characteristics to the commodity.

Based on the conclusion that subbudget reallocations are required in order to purchase higher quality, our model finds it difficult to justify downward adjustment of price indices for improvements in quality.

Such adjustments typically reflect producer perception of consumer choice—that is, such adjustments are a manifestation of the Waugh-Brems problem in the construction of price indices. In general, our recommendation would be to not adjust price indices for change in quality. If adjustments must be made, then it seems appropriate to make such adjustments both for improvements and reductions in quality. Furthermore, if such adjustments are to be made, then it seems appropriate to also adjust price indices for change in consumer tastes. As was pointed out in the development of our model, at the theoretical level it is impossible, except under special circumstances, to distinguish between a change in quality and a change in tastes.

Appendix A
The a_i/b_i Ratio and the Constraint

Convexity of the Houthakker constraint is given by Equation (2) of chapter 7: $(d^2x_i/dv_i^2) = [(2M_ib_i^2)/(a_i + b_iv_i)^3]$. For any given income, M_i, and specified values for v_i and b_i, higher values of a_i reduce convexity of the constraint (at specified levels of v_i). See Figure 13.9 for examples of the effect of variation in a_i. Note in Figure 13.9 that for higher values of a_i the constraint is falling to lower values of x_i along the x_i axis. (Under the MathCad Plus 5.0 program utilized to produce the diagrams in Figure 13.9, $g(v)$ represents x_i.)

For any given income, M_i, and for specified value of a_i, higher values of b_i increase the degree of convexity of the constraint. See Figures A.1 through A.8 of this appendix. (The same MathCad program was utilized for variation in b_i as was used for variation in a_i.)

The fact that high values of a_i correspond to low convexity of the constraint, while high values of b_i correspond to high convexity of the constraint, led to examination of the interaction of a_i and b_i and their combined effect on the constraint. Inasmuch as Houthakker defined a_i and b_i as prices, of quantity and quality, respectively, and the fact that the ratio of prices (e.g., p_i and p_j) typically determine the slope of the constraint in consumption space, examination of the ratio of a_i and b_i seemed appropriate.

Of particular interest was the configuration of the constraint for values of a_i and b_i under the *basic price system* (i.e., $a_i = 0$ and $b_i = 1$). The top left-hand diagram in Figure 13.9 illustrates the constraint under such prices. Subsequent diagrams of Figure 13.9 (proceeding from left to right, top to bottom) illustrate the effect of higher values of a_i, while all other initial values are held constant. For values of $(a_i/b_i) \approx 250$, or higher, the constraint "appears" linear. Use of a first derivative test throughout the range of the constraint, however, revealed that even for extremely high values of (a_i/b_i) (i.e., $(a_i/b_i) = 1,000,000$), the constraint only became piecewise linear. Typically, for high values of v_i the slope of the constraint began to decrease.

Similar tests were conducted for variable b_i, with constant a_i. See Figures A.1 through A.8 of this appendix. As explained earlier, for high values of b_i, convexity of the constraint was increased. As with a_i, however, the constraint only approached linearity for low values of b_i. Whether change arose from variation in a_i or b_i, for similar values of the (a_i/b_i) ratio, the constraint exhibited similar characteristics of convexity, position in v_ix_i space, and so forth. Variation in income, M_i, did not change convexity of the constraint (see Figures A.9 through A.13).

Given our definition of a_i as the price of the basic package, and b_i as the markup consumers are willing to pay for levels of quality above the basic package, the (a_i/b_i) ratio becomes, in effect, the ratio of quantity price to quality price. Interestingly, for the constraint to approach the linear constraint of traditional consumer theory, a_i must be large relative to b_i. Or, in other words, to approach the traditional iso-quality version of consumer theory, the markup for quality, b_i, must approach zero—that is, become insignificant in comparison with the quantity price, the price of the basic package. Also, in this regard, the level of income, M_i, plays no role in the distinction between the traditional iso-quality constraint and the variable-quality constraint.

Figures A.1–A.8 **For Any Given Income, M_i, and for Specified Value of a_i, Higher Values of b_i, Increase the Degree of Convexity of the Constraint**

Figure A.1

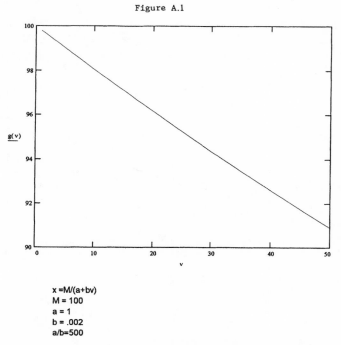

x =M/(a+bv)
M = 100
a = 1
b = .002
a/b=500

Figure A.2

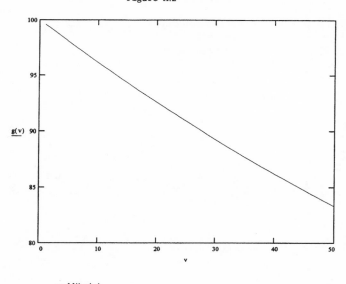

x =M/(a+bv)
M = 100
a = 1
b = .004
a/b=250

Figure A.3

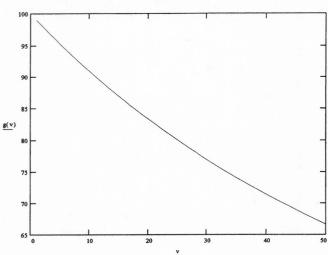

x =M/(a+bv)
M = 100
a = 1
b = .01
a/b=100

Figure A.4

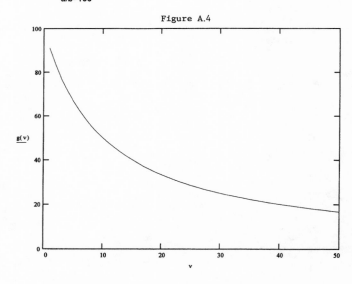

x =M/(a+bv)
M = 100
a = 1
b = .1
a/b=10

Figure A.5

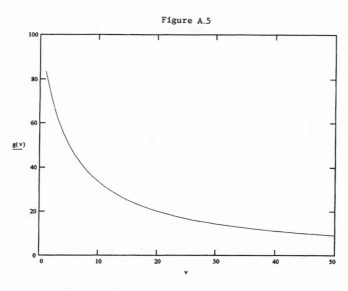

x =M/(a+bv)
M = 100
a = 1
b = .2
a/b=5

Figure A.6

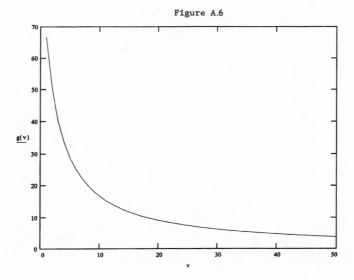

x =M/(a+bv)
M = 100
a = 1
b = .5
a/b=2

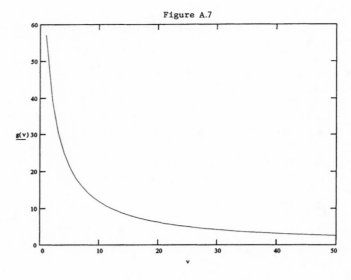

Figure A.7

x =M/(a+bv)
M = 100
a = 1
b = .75
a/b=1.333...

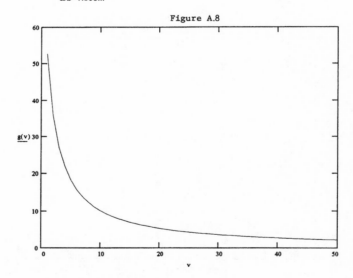

Figure A.8

x =M/(a+bv)
M = 100
a = 1
b = .9
a/b=1.111...

Figures A.9–A.13 **Variation in Income, M_i, Does Not Change Convexity of the Constraint**

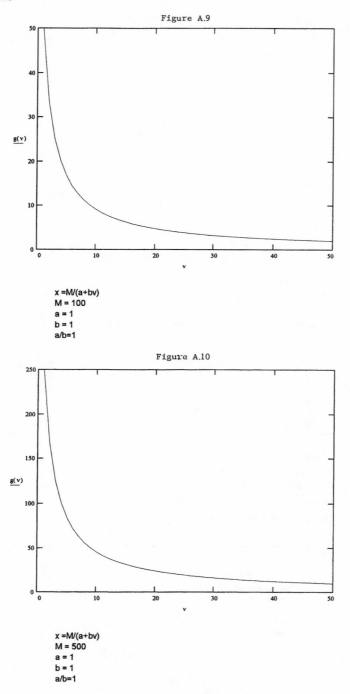

Figure A.9

$x = M/(a+bv)$
M = 100
a = 1
b = 1
a/b=1

Figure A.10

$x = M/(a+bv)$
M = 500
a = 1
b = 1
a/b=1

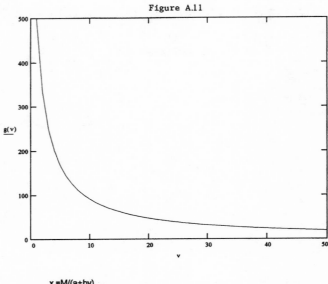

Figure A.11

x =M/(a+bv)
M = 1000
a = 1
b = 1
a/b=1

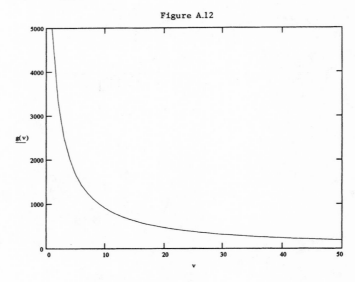

Figure A.12

x =M/(a+bv)
M = 10,000
a = 1
b = 1
a/b=1

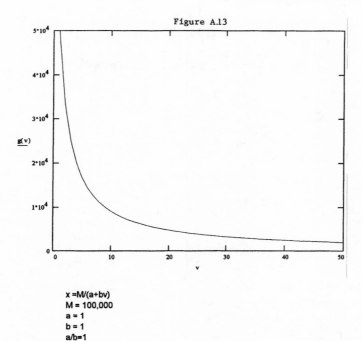

Figure A.13

x =M/(a+bv)
M = 100,000
a = 1
b = 1
a/b=1

Appendix B
Empirical Issues

1. Difficulties of Aggregation When Quality Is Variable

Development of this model of consumer behavior, under conditions of variable quality, has been restricted to the level of an individual consumer and to individual consumer demand. We turn now to issues of aggregation, specifically the aggregation of individual demand to obtain market demand. To do so, we assume, as in traditional theory, that it is possible to horizontally sum individual, isoquality demand curves. In our model, however, the aggregation of individual isoquality demand is complicated by several additional requirements. They are as follows:

1. The ranking of varieties within each consumer's v_i neighborhood may be unique to that consumer.
2. Consumers may be unfamiliar with varieties outside their v_i neighborhoods, and it takes consumption experience to gain familiarity and to evaluate varieties.
3. Consumers may have different size x_i neighborhoods.
4. Some consumers may target on a fixed quantity, and the quantity targets may differ across consumers.
5. The range of both x_i and v_i neighborhoods may vary from consumer to consumer.
6. Within any given commodity, each consumer may have a unique window in *quality-quantity* consumption space.
7. The (a_i/b_i) ratio may differ across consumers.
8. The existence of neighborhoods opens the possibility for truncated individual consumer demand curves, reflecting the limited range of variation in quantity and quality within a single commodity for individual consumers.
9. Each consumer is assumed to create his or her own isoquality demand for a single variety within the ith commodity.
10. It is not assumed that consumers necessarily create the same level of isoquality demand—that is, consumers need not target on the same v_i.

Throughout the study we have retained the assumption that only a single variety is purchased by any individual consumer at any given point in time. We have not considered the case of multiple-variety purchases by a single consumer.

The model allows consumer income to vary across the group of consumers of any given commodity. In our model, different levels of income and/or different (a_i/b_i) ratios may result in different elasticities of demand for the same variety, as well as different elasticities across varieties within the same commodity. Whether there is any relationship between the level of budgeted income, M_i, and each consumer's (a_i/b_i) ratio is an empirical issue that deserves investigation. Another empirical question is whether the markup over the basic package (i.e., b_i^c) increases as M_i increases.

A further complication is the assumption that consumer self-image influences consumer perception of quality and consumer willingness-to-pay for different levels of quality (i.e., the value of b_i^c). Individual consumer evaluation of the level of quality

278

of a specific variety, or of a neighborhood of varieties, will likely be unique. Additionally, such evaluations may vary across time for each consumer. The speed of learning from consumption experience may vary across consumers. The assumption that individual consumers determine the value of a_i^c requires investigation, as does identification of the "basic package" for each commodity. Investigation of these issues will require sophisticated experimental research designs, sampling and survey methods, questionnaire designs and interviewer training, and techniques of data collection, management, and analysis.

2. Aggregate Market Demand

We now address the process of aggregating individual consumer demand to obtain isoquality market demand. We begin by returning to $v_i x_i$, $v_i p_i$, and $x_i p_i$ spaces for an individual consumer, and, as previously explained, generate a single isoquality demand curve for the consumer. Recall from Figure 13.23 that windows can exist in many different regions along the constraint in $v_i x_i$ space. To examine the case where $\hat{x}_i = 1$, as well as other values for x_i, we modify Figure 13.23 slightly, as shown in Figure B.1.

In Figure B.1 the lines extending from each window toward the v_i axis are intended to depict enlarged neighborhoods for quantity, x_i. As shown, the lower bound on quantity has become x_i close to, but not equal to, the v_i axis (i.e., $x_i > 0$). Recall that the v_i axis is open (see chapter 4). To illustrate isoquality demand, it will be useful to allow consumers to select $x_i = 1$, or other targeted magnitudes of x_i.

Recall that ordering along the v_i axis is assumed unique to each consumer, hence not necessarily the same across consumers. The unique ordering of v_i is consistent with

Figure B.1 Alternative Windows Along the Constraint: Low a_i/b_i Ratio

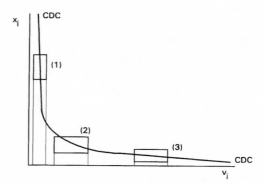

variability of individual consumer perception and consumption experience, which is assumed to occur for all consumers as they assess the quality of products and/or services they purchase. At this juncture, however, where we seek to aggregate individual consumer demand to obtain isoquality market demand, the uniqueness of v_i axes introduces difficulties not encountered in most consumer models.

In our model, variability of the v_i axes requires that we subdivide consumers into separate cohort groups, according to targeted v_i, and restrict the use of the representative consumer to stand for, or represent, one of these cohorts. In other words, we have a v_i-targeted, or isoquality representative consumer. In the world of variable quality, consumer behavior is more accurately assessed when analyzed in small groups. The concept of a representative consumer is essentially a statistical matter (a stratified-clustered sample), and, unless controlled, the introduction of variable quality contributes to enlarged variance around mean behavior as the size of the group is increased. Similarly, to aggregate consumers obtain isoquality market demand, the market must be subdivided according to targeted v_i cohorts of consumers. This process is explained as follows.

First, it is necessary to group consumers by the variety of the ith commodity they purchase. Recall that we retain the assumption that each consumer purchases only one variety of the commodity. If consumers purchase two or more varieties of the same commodity, we exclude them from the sample.[1] We assume budgeted incomes for the ith commodity remain constant for each consumer (i.e., M_i does not change during the period of study).

For illustrative purposes, we begin with the case of two consumers of the ith commodity. Previously we used $\hat{v}_i$ to represent the targeted variety of an individual consumer. In situations of two or more consumers, it becomes necessary to identify the targeted v_i of each consumer. For this purpose we introduce $\hat{v}_i^{c=n}$, where $n = 1,2,$ $\ldots N$, and N is the total number of consumers of the targeted variety. The symbol c represents a specific consumer, the cth consumer of the targeted variety.

Regarding $\hat{v}_i^{c=n}$, recall that our model links the e_{ih} of Henri Theil to individual varieties—that is, a variety may be viewed as a bundle of characteristics. Our model posits that the contents of the bundles, as well as the manner in which the e_{ih} are combined to form a bundle, are important to consumers. As we aggregate consumers by the varieties they purchase, we must be able to distinguish varieties that are "similar" from varieties that are "different." We must also recognize that some varieties may be quite similar, in terms of the composition of their characteristics (the e_{ih}), but that they might not be perfectly identical, either in how they bundle their characteristics or in the nature of those characteristics.

This, then, raises the question: When is the composition of e_{ih}, which are bundled to form varieties, sufficiently different that they must be classified as two different varieties? In other words, when are the two bundles of characteristics sufficiently different that their two corresponding varieties must be classified as different? This topic touches on Lancaster's issue of significant or "relevant" characteristics (see chapter 6, sections 6–8, particularly section 7). Earlier, we introduced the prospect that some e_{ih} may not be detectable by the consumer. Under such circumstances, although the characteristics within two bundles (i.e., two varieties) may be different, the difference might not be detectable to the consumer and therefore may not matter to the consumer. Under other circumstances, there could exist threshold values for characteristics, and if the e_{ih} do not meet or exceed the threshold values, they may not matter to the consumer.

Finally, the importance of characteristics, and the manner in which they are combined to form bundles, may be viewed differently by consumers versus producers, namely, the two groups may perceive the e_{ih} differently. This represents an aspect of the Waugh-Brems problem.

Recognition of the fact that products and services are rarely identical, not only in terms of perception but also in terms of technical specifications (e.g., issues of quality control), we must concede that there is the likelihood that varieties (as used in our model) may not be perfectly identical. Consequently, there may arise circumstances where two or more targeted varieties, for two or more consumers, only approximate being the same variety. Which is to say, two or more varieties may not be perfectly identical, albeit that their e_{ih} characteristics are approximately similar. This being the case, for empirical purposes we will accept the possibility that varieties included in isoquality demand may not be perfectly identical (i.e., they are only approximately identical). In terms of empirical work on isoquality demand, we assume, therefore, that all such varieties fall within some "acceptable variance" of the isoquality target, $\hat{v}_i$.

In other words, two or more consumers targeting on exactly the same variety may serve as a theoretical ideal, but, in fact, it may be difficult (if not impossible) to find two or more perfectly identical varieties. For empirical purposes we may have to accept, therefore, that the e_{ih} patterns of "similar" varieties cluster around an ideal pattern that serves as the measure of central tendency. This measure of central tendency may be classified as the "true" targeted variety along an isoquality demand schedule. In this sense, the true target is analogous to other measures of central tendency, and may be assumed to have a corresponding measure of variance, and other moments. We will identify the statistical measure of central tendency for a targeted variety by $\bar{v}_i$.

In the case of two consumers who have targeted on the same variety, we will identify the targeted variety by $\bar{v}_i^c$, where the first consumer is labeled $c = 1$ and the second as $c = 2$. For simplicity, we assume the two consumers have targeted on and purchased exactly identical varieties (i.e., the variance around the "true" targeted variety is zero).

We can now explain aggregation of individual isoquality demand schedules to obtain market demand. In the two-consumer case with theoretically identical v_i targets, we have essentially the same phenomenon encountered in horizontal summation of individual consumer demand under the assumption of homogeneous goods or services. Here, all demand is homogeneous at $\hat{v}_i$.

Although individual consumer demand may be truncated, the aggregation of consumer isoquality demand schedules in $x_i p_i$

space, to obtain a single aggregated demand schedule, is straightforward. As long as consumers target on the same variety, or $\bar{v}_i$ has acceptably small variance, as the number of consumers (N) is increased, the likelihood that market demand will be truncated is reduced.

It is important to recall that although all consumers in the case just described are targeting on the same variety, the v_i axis utilized by each consumer may be different, as well as any numbering system generated on each v_i axis. In other words, to identify the group of identical targeted varieties, it will be necessary to actually compare the varieties purchased, because the v_i numbering systems utilized by each consumer might be different. In this theoretically simple example, we assume that consumers can be aggregated by their corresponding targeted varieties, that the targeted varieties within a cohort group of consumers are identical varieties (or that the variance around $\bar{v}_i$ is acceptably small), and that demand schedules are aggregated only after the process of identifying targeted varieties has been completed. We further assume that all consumers who target on the selected variety are included in the aggregation process (i.e., no consumer who targets on $\hat{v}_i^{c=N}$ is left out of N).

3. Variety Ordering Under Market Demand

For constant (but not necessarily identical) levels of budgeted income, M_i, and for constant (but not necessarily identical) values of the (a_i / b_i) ratio, we may now proceed to generate market-demand schedules for targeted values of v_i. At this juncture, we assume that there are only two targeted varieties of the ith commodity, namely, $\hat{v}_{i1}$ and $\hat{v}_{i2}$. We assume that all consumers of variety v_{i1} have been identified and their individual demand schedules have been aggregated through horizontal summation to obtain the market-demand schedule for that variety. We likewise assume that consumers of variety v_{i2} have been identified and their individual demand schedules aggregated, in similar fashion, to obtain the market-demand schedule for variety v_{i2}.

Interestingly, once these market-demand schedules have been generated, it becomes possible to compare and rank-order the two varieties according to their corresponding market demands. In other words, at the level of an individual consumer, where each consumer creates his or her own v_i axis, it is impossible to compare consumers to determine which variety is preferred; however, with the creation of market-demand schedules, it is possible to make such comparisons and thereby obtain preference orderings. These are preference orderings across representative consumers (or across consumer cohorts), instead of across individual consumers. To illustrate this process of comparison, we begin with the two targeted varieties, $\hat{v}_{i1}$ and $\hat{v}_{i2}$.

Assume that the market demand schedules for these two varieties have been generated. We label the market demand for targeted variety $\hat{v}_{i1}$, as $D_{\hat{v}_{i1}}$, and the market demand for variety $\hat{v}_{i2}$, as $D_{\hat{v}_{i2}}$. To control for the possibility that there could be a different number of consumers behind each market demand schedule, we divide each demand schedule by some specified number of consumers such that we obtain market-demand per unit of population (e.g., per 10,000 population of consumers).

Next, across the total population of consumers—that is, across the total combined number of consumers obtained from the sum of both market-demand schedules—we group consumers by their socio-economic-demographic (SED) characteristics. Do not, however, include income as one of the characteristics. Identify the largest group of consumers with similar SED characteristics (again, except for income). Ignore the rest of consumers who do not belong to this group. From the group of consumers with similar SED characteristics, split the group into two cohorts: those consumers who purchased variety $\hat{v}_{i1}$ and those who purchased $\hat{v}_{i2}$. Examine average consumer income, $\overline{M}_T$, for each of the two cohorts.

Along the lines of revealed preference, adopt the null hypothesis that if income, $\overline{M}_T$, is higher for one cohort than for another, whichever of the two varieties is predominately purchased[2] by the higher income group (given that there is a statistically significant difference in $\overline{M}_T$ between the two groups), that variety is revealed as preferred. The higher income group, with similar SED characteristics to the lower income group, could chose to purchase either variety, but being able to choose between the two, the higher income group revealed its preference by the variety purchased (e.g., $\hat{v}_{i2} \geq \hat{v}_{i1}$). Note, however, that in the comparison just described we have implicitly assumed quality is a "normal" good (see our earlier discussion of this matter, chapter 8, section 2).

Notes

Notes to Chapter 2

1. See Diewert 1990, p. 234. See also, Sidgwick 1901, pp. 72–73.
2. See Diewert 1990, pp. 234–35.
3. See Hirsch 1963, p. 164.
4. See particularly his remarks on "grades" of labor (Marshall 1916, pp. 217–18).
5. Brems may be correct so far as "product" quality is concerned.
Earlier work on quality variation was oriented, for the most part, to input quality.
6. See Benner and Gabriel 1927; Corbett 1926; Davis, Waugh, and McCarthy 1927; Heddon and Cherniak 1924; Kroeck 1928; Kuhrt 1926–27; Waugh 1923; Working 1925.
7. If one does not assume commodity groupings within which products vary through differentiation, then one has essentially the homogeneous goods assumption where all products are unique, that is, each differentiated product is a commodity and the number of differentiated products in each commodity set is one, and we have again the homogeneous goods assumption for each commodity (= product).
8. See Brems 1951, 1957, 1959. In the interim between Chamberlin and Brems numerous other contributions were made to monopolistic competition. Many of these dealt with location theory and advertising and are only tangentially related to our subject here. Note that many of these authors were Danish economists. The list below is by no means complete. See the following: Barfod 1937, Barfod 1944–45, Copeland 1940, Enke 1941, Hotelling 1929, Isard 1949, Lerner and Singer 1937, Pedersen 1939, Robinson 1933, Zeuthen 1968 and Zeuthen (1935).
9. In the early development of a theory of variable quality the terminology employed was sometimes unclear or with multiple meaning. As we shall see later, although there have been improvements in this regard, the problem remains. Later, we hope to show that there is a fundamental reason for this situation, and that it is probably unavoidable.
10. For additional perspectives on this matter, see Theil and Suhm 1981, pp. 77–91. Note, especially, the following:

> The approaches of the two previous paragraphs, based respectively on the average price paid for a composite good and on the income elasticities of all n goods, are both behavioral in the sense that they do not involve an outside value judgment on what is "good" for the consumer. This is in contrast to the approach implicit in the hedonic price index theory, which may be viewed as claiming that "a powerful big car is good for you" (Theil and Suhm 1981, p. 78).

11. Also note that Abbott's use of activities and constellation of wants can be utilized to create a concept of derived demand for products or services similar to the Lancaster model.

Notes to Chapter 3

1. This topic is addressed, in part, through the use of separability in the utility function and decentralization of the consumer budget. A more thorough analysis requires recursive function theory as applied to the nesting of subsets (each one potentially infinite) within the set identified as the commodity.
2. On the subjects of vertical and horizontal quality, see chapter 2, section 6, and Abbott 1953, pp. 828–29.
3. It is interesting that in the constant-quality competitive model, the non-price-tied units-of-measure of the good are assumed not to vary; consequently, the priced unit-of-measure of the isoquality good captures all change in the good (i.e., only quantity is allowed to vary).

Notes to Chapter 4

1. Recall our earlier discussion of quantity when we reviewed the work of Henri Theil. See chapter 3, section 7.

2. It should be noted at this juncture that it is useful to define a commodity as a set that is itself a collection of subsets. Under such an approach the set-theoretic notion of the power-set axiom may be applied—that is, for any set C, there is a set whose members are exactly the subsets of C. Here we may use the notation P(C), the power set of C, which means the collection of all subsets of C. Note the word "subsets" is appropriate terminology as any "variety" of a commodity may be viewed as a set of "quality elements." In fact, each such subset may itself be viewed as a power set nested within a higher-level power set. Additionally, it is important to note that Houthakker's use of a_i, as described above, wherein we can identify a quantity unit of measure, allows us to index the subsets, and furthermore to rank the subsets. (The price of each variety v_i is such a ranking. There are problems of subjectivity, however, in the ordering of varieties to form a commodity set. We will discuss some of these problems later.) Houthakker's methodology does not establish rules for membership in C (i.e., he provides no entrance requirements for membership to the power set). Similarly, his v_i^- and v_i^+ provide at best fuzzy boundaries to the set. Finally, the notion of nested power sets suggests application of recursive function or computability theory, and the prospect that this line of thought may ultimately lead to the implications encountered in Kurt Godel's Incompleteness Theorem (Godel). See Winrich 1984.

3. The economic meaning of $a_i \leq 0$ is clearly not in keeping with traditional micro theory, especially as the author defines a_i to be "the quantity price," and that it "is identical with the price of a good in customary theory." However, also note that under the basic price system, the author allows $a_i = 0$. Also, note that the spanning of price space and the introduction of quality prices as subcomponents of the overall total commodity price, p_i, was a totally new analytical methodology attributable to Houthakker. The case for $a_i < 0$ suggests (among other possible interpretations) that, across time (i.e., through intertemporal changes of preference) the quality level of the original numeraire variety has become sufficiently low, in comparison with other higher-quality varieties, that consumers no longer buy it, even at a zero price. $a_i < 0$ suggests that if the variety is available (produced), the consumer must be paid to take it. This situation could arise from disutility associated with embarrassment of purchasing and consuming an old-fashioned variety, and so forth. Obviously, such a variety will not be in existence very long as producer profit motives typically will not endure $a_i < 0$ for any extended time. Also, on the disappearance of varieties, see Hofsten 1952, pp. 49–64, 92–110, 119–22, and Sidgwick 1901, pp. 72–77.

4. Houthakker's original model did not address the problem of trade-offs between e_{ih}; for example, between miles-per-hour and miles-per-gallon in the mix of quality characteristics of an automobile. A more thorough analysis of this topic, in terms of contemporary methods, would require a discussion of orderings in a set-theoretic context, and, more appropriately, the application of lattice theory to the arrangements of the e_{ih} within variety subsets and the overall commodity set. A problem alluded to earlier (see note 2) is the set of all sets problem, addressed by Godel. We encounter the problem again here. The ability of the v_i to reflect trade-off relationships between the e_{ih} must rest with the functional structure that maps e_{ih} to v_i. Obviously, weighting must be introduced in the process.

Notes to Chapter 6

1. Earlier the author introduced the limiting assumption to do away with "common" satisfaction, namely, "where commodities are capable of satisfying more than one want, it will be assumed that these are cases of joint satisfaction" (Ironmonger 1972, p. 20).

2. The use of ordinal utility, along with individual consumer ranking of wants, limits comparisons across individuals, although the number of satisfied wants may provide the basis for a subjective comparison of consumers.

3. In his efforts to provide numerical examples, Ironmonger selected objective values reflecting physical characteristics of the commodities analyzed (e.g., calories, vitamins, protein, driving-time of automobiles, and so forth).

4. To obtain a more complete picture of the evolution of Lancaster's thought, there is no substitute for a thorough review of chapters 7 through 9 of his text and comparison of those chapters with his basic model in part 1 (Lancaster 1971).

5. The use of the word "aims" instead of "wants" is a semantic exercise. The general meaning of the two terms is in harmony with the work by Ironmonger, Duesenberry, Abbott, Jevons, Menger, and others. Note that Lancaster's statement regarding "conceptual redundancy" ultimately turns on

acceptance of the positivist or structuralist philosophical concept of the study of humanity (i.e., Hume versus Kant). See Stent 1975, pp. 1052–57.

6. See also Theil's more recent comment: "The approaches of the two previous paragraphs, based respectively on the average price paid for a composite good and on the income elasticities of all n goods, are both behavioral in the sense that they do not involve an outside value judgment on what is 'good' for the consumer. This is in contrast to the approach implicit in the hedonic price index theory, which may be viewed as claiming that 'a powerful big car is good for you' " (Theil and Suhm 1981, p. 78). For more information on the hedonic technique, see also Bartick 1987; Cowling and Cubbin 1970; and Epple 1987.

7. Recall that Fisher and Shell criticized the use of indices that compare utility levels instead of constraint loci (Fisher and Shell 1971, pp. 18–23).

8. See Fisher and Shell 1971, pp. 21–22 and note 7 (from their text), for a similar conclusion regarding the effects of a change in tastes.

9. Hendler suggests that consumers are not indifferent to the manner in which characteristics are mixed to arrive at a given proportion of characteristics within a good or service. In other words, within their utility functions, consumers assign different weights to the same combination of characteristics according to the manner (or path) via which the characteristics are mixed (e.g., the utility from one cold and one very hot steak does not equal the utility from two warm steaks). He indicates that linear combinations of goods in characteristics space will lead to inappropriate conclusions, because "Each indifference curve is meaningful only when each point on the curve is achieved by a single process. Any point on the same indifference curve may reflect a different level of utility if obtained through a linear combination rather than a single process" (Hendler 1975, p. 199). Unless more information is available on the consumer's utility function, Lancaster's efficiency frontier is reduced to rays or points in characteristics space. On the same topic, see also Roth 1987, pp. 57–75, and especially note 2, p. 71. Roth also raises interesting questions regarding non-singularity of Lancaster's **B** matrix. See Roth 1987, pp. 60–61.

10. A careful reading of Muellbauer reveals that he has assumed Houthakker's v_i to be a characteristic instead of a price. The reader is asked to recall our earlier discussion of different interpretations of the meaning of v_i. See chapter 4. More coverage of this material is provided in chapter 7.

11. Note that, "If consumers adjust fully, then shadow prices in utility terms should reflect these market shadow prices if the latter exist" (Muellbauer 1974, p. 992). Both the existence and the extent of consumer ignorance are critical issues.

Notes to Chapter 7

1. Under the equilibrium condition of $p_i = v_i$, $v_i = 0$ is not allowed. Because Houthakker restricts $(a_i + b_i v_i) > 0$, given $p_i = (a_i + b_i v_i)$, then $p_i > 0$ is required. Houthakker also restricts b_i to $b_i > 0$. In order to obtain an intercept of Houthakker's constraint on the x_i axis in $v_i x_i$ space (i.e., in order to obtain $x_i = (M / a_i)$), it is necessary to have the product $b_i v_i = 0$. By the requirement that $b_i > 0$, it is necessary that $v_i = 0$ so as to have $b_i v_i = 0$. By the equilibrium condition, $p_i = v_i$, and by the requirement, $p_i > 0$, it is impossible to obtain $v_i = 0$, and hence it is impossible to establish an intercept of the constraint on the x_i axis. Muellbauer utilized an intercept on the x_i axis in his discussion of Houthakker. See his Figure 5, p. 991, in Muellbauer 1974. This result is only possible if he has assumed there is no requirement that $p_i = v_i$, which is to say that Muellbauer appears to have assumed that the Houthakker model can operate away from the basic price system.

2. See also Muellbauer's discussion of shadow prices and consumer utility (chapter 6).

3. With reference to this topic, see the discussion of Leontief's fixed proportions utility function in Blackorby et al. 1978.

4. Aggregation on an isoquality measure of quantity is, in some respects, similar to the composite commodity issue first presented by J.R. Hicks. See Hicks 1946, pp. 312–13, and Diewert 1993.

5. On the concepts of separability and strict separability, as well as the various forms of decentralizability and the problems of aggregation, see Blackorby et al. 1978. Also note that as regards decentralization of commodity i in the consumer's budget, we are assuming that the consumer can accurately project the expenditure $(p_i x_i)$ associated with this decentralized component of his or her budget. More will be provided later on the role of expectation and experience as regards the topics of price and quantity in decentralized budgets.

6. With the exception of Lancaster-Ironmonger type models, where, in characteristics space, consumer perception can influence the constraint. In these and other models, however, the authors have not focused on the issue of inseparability of the consumer from the constraint, nor on its implications.

7. Related to the inseparability problem we are discussing here are recent developments in game theory, dynamic programming, stochastic control theory (with feedback and active learning), dynamic gaming, as well as developments in hierarchical and self-reference systems, neural networks, and self-organizing systems.

8. One of the difficulties in the Houthakker formulation of a quality-quantity model is that ultimately he must assume that the consumer has the ability to see through prices to the underlying quality of each variety (see, among others, Scitovsky 1944–45), and that a complete ordering can be established by the consumer over the full range of variable quality from v_i^- to v_i^+ (in order that comparisons can be made by the consumer across varieties). Seeing through prices to the underlying quality of a product or service is an act of perception.

9. There is an important question here: In selecting the weights a_i and b_i, can the consumer perceive the quality of a separate variety (a ''targeted'' variety) of the commodity, or must the consumer perceive the entire range of the commodity set? (Are issues of positional goods involved in this process of evaluation?) As an additional possibility, might the consumer perceive just a segment of the range from v_i^- to v_i^+, or a neighborhood around some targeted v_i? Recall that $b_i = (dp_i/dv_i)$, which, with b_i constant, applies to price change across all varieties from v_i^- to v_i^+. This issue opens the question of whether the quality-augmenting function should be linear, or some other specification. Human processes of focusing and filtering come into play here, as do models of decision making based on decomposition, sequential or recursive nesting, and so forth.

10. Note that the *special case* could occur frequently if consumers employ habit in their consumption patterns, namely, the habit of always consuming the same variety, $\hat{v}_i$. This type of decision is efficient in the sense of holding down search and information costs, and in the sense of holding down the anxiety conceivably associated with guessing at the initial value of b_i, and then going through the subsequent learning process. The guessing and learning process would be associated with each new variety consumed; therefore, it might be simpler, less costly, and with less anxiety of the unknown, for the consumer to remain with a specific variety. In this sense, habit can be viewed as rational behavior for consumers in the world of variable quality. Duesenberry's demonstration effect, however, would argue that there is always social pressure to upgrade the level of quality.

11. Note that in contrast to habit (see note 10 above), the consumer who seeks to avoid boredom may not exhibit behavior as modeled in the special case. The boredom avoidance consumption pattern would, in all likelihood, reveal frequent consumption of different varieties of the commodity. Besides boredom avoidance, the desire for ''higher'' standards of consumption, possibly in line with Duesenberry's hypothesis, might also contribute to the consumption patterns we shall discuss under the *general case*.

12. The extent of truncation would depend on steepness of the learning curve of an individual consumer, or speed of learning.

13. Note that from equation (1) we can take $(\partial x_i^2)/(\partial v_i \partial b_i)$, a measure of the effect of db_i on the convexity of the constraint. For this we have:

$$\frac{\partial^2 x_i}{\partial v_i \partial b_i} = -\frac{M_i(a_i^2 + 2a_i b_i v_i + 2b_i^2 v_i^2) + M_i(2a_i b_i v_i + 4b_i^2 v_i^2)}{a_i^4 + 4a_i^3 b_i v_i + 8a_i^2 b_i^2 v_i^2 + 8a_i b_i^3 v_i^3 + 4b_i^4 v_i^4} < 0 \tag{1.1}$$

Inasmuch as we have assumed a_i fixed, the effect of db_i on the convexity of the constraint is influenced by the value of v_i in the neighborhood of db_i. We will have more to say on this topic in subsequent chapters of part 2.

14. A ''change in the perception of v_i'' is understood to mean a change in the personal value of v_i as reflected in the weight b_i. The ''value of v_i'' is the personal perception of that value by the consumer.

Notes to Chapter 8

1. Willig argued that either *compensating variation* or *equivalent variation* gives similar results in terms of consumer surplus (Willig 1976). More recently, as a result of further consideration of psychological phenomena (Prospect Theory, etc.), these results have been questioned. See Kahneman and Tversky 1979; Thaler 1980; Tversky and Kahneman 1981; Knetsch and Sinden 1984, among others.

2. Note that this insertion illustrates how p_i serves as a price aggregator in the Houthakker model and is essentially a variation on the Hicksian concept of a composite commodity. A number of issues, still to be addressed, have to do with the consistency of assumptions underlying this type of aggregation process, the nature of the utility function, decentralization of the budget, and whether we are dealing with symmetric or nonsymmetric separability.

3. Muellbauer makes no reference to these conditions and assumes that an x_i intercept is established at M/a_i whenever $v_i = 0$. See chapter 6 and Muellbauer 1974, pp. 990–92.

4. Following Willig, instead of Maurice et al. 1982.

5. If time is not introduced, then we have a difficulty similar to that alluded to by Wicksell (see chapter 2). The problem is how to incorporate rising quality (v_i) with diminishing marginal utility. As v_i goes up, should not the consumer's willingness-to-pay increase, or at least not decrease? How does one rectify a downward-sloping curve in quality-price space—specifically, the downward-sloping curves in $v_i b_i$ space of Figure 8.4?

6. These statements imply that consumer perception applies not only to b_i, but also to estimated or projected decentralized budgets. Furthermore, there exists the possibility of interaction between projected budgets, or expenditure on commodity i, and the consumer's selection of $\hat{v}_i$. In all likelihood, there exists an expectation-experience loop associated with these processes.

7. Although not shown in Figure 8.5, convexity of the constraint is also affected. The constraint becomes more convex to the origin.

8. Impulse buying requires further explanation, but can be addressed, in part, in our model.

9. On "wants" and the related concept of "interests," see Penz 1986.

10. The old statement "What the budget will allow" may now be modified to "What the consumer wants the budget to allow." This later statement applies to decision making regarding the targeted variety. Other decentralized (sub) budgets could, of course, be in conflict and create trade-off decisions for the consumer. Such trade-offs between projected subbudget allocations represent a somewhat different manifestation of substitution.

11. See Blackorby et al. 1978 for more on the subjective aspects of the decentralized budget process.

12. This could be stated: The nature of the constraint is perceived by the consumer, and, consequently, exists for the consumer in the manner in which it is perceived. Furthermore, for each consumer the constraint would likely be unique.

13. We are here assuming the b_i selected for the neighborhood around $\hat{v}_i$ is the same b_i extended across the entire constraint.

14. The length of time b_i remains stationary, and whether, in fact, it ever becomes stationary, is influenced by a number of factors: for example, the introduction of new varieties, especially in or near the $\hat{v}_i$ neighborhood; a change in consumer income; a change in this or other decentralized budgets; and not least of all, a change in the consumer—for example, a change in age, education, a major geographical relocation, a change in the workplace, a change in peer group and/or friendships and/or neighbors, and so forth. Any of these phenomena could change individual consumer perception of $\hat{v}_i$.

15. Of course, consumer exhaustion—from the time and pecuniary costs of learning about $\hat{v}_i$ and adjusting b_i—may result in the consumer simply accepting the current period's variety-price relationship, $(\hat{v}_i, p_i)$, even though the b_i weight is "inaccurate." Under such circumstances, consumer exhaustion may result in consumer submission to the b_i established by producers, and in that state of mind simply accept producers' assessment of b_i for $\hat{v}_i$ as what the consumer would be willing to pay.

16. See also Heiner 1985a, 1985b, 1985c, 1986; Knez et al. 1985; Bookstaber and Langsam 1985; Garrison 1985; Wilde et al. 1985; and March 1978.

17. On intentional behavior and intentional systems, see Ackoff and Emery 1972; Boden 1972; Changeux and Connes 1995; Dennett 1978, 1981, 1991; Fodor 1975; Kernberg 1982; Quine 1953; Searle 1983; Waterman and Hayes-Roth 1978. See also Gregory 1987, pp. 383–86. Note especially the following material from Changeux and Connes 1995, pp. 143–46:

> CONNES: The concept of conditioning, an important concept in the theory of probability, may be applicable in this context. To define an intention . . . I think one has to identify it with an evaluation function that serves to estimate at any given moment how far one stands from the goal one wishes to reach . . . [;] let's suppose that we have this function at our disposal. . . . Physicists have come up with a very good idea . . . the stationary phase principle . . . [;] it has great flexibility, which physicists exploit all the time using Feynman's path integral.

> CHANGEUX: It amounts almost to a selection mechanism, then, doesn't it?

> CONNES: Yes, but unfortunately only on the assumption that the evaluation function has already been constructed. . . . A correlation must exist, it seems to me, between the evaluation function and the frustration, or pleasure, that one feels when one gets nearer to solving a problem. But I don't know exactly how to define it. . . .

> CHANGEUX: . . . It's also possible to imagine a circuit looped back on itself, that involves the limbic system as a function of desire. Imagine the brain generates a hypothesis that has "pleasure" written all over it, and that this serves as a guide and shows the way to a solution—which, however, may or may not turn out to be as pleasurable as anticipated.

In Changeux and Connes 1995, pp. 173–78, chapter 6, the section titled "A Self-Evaluating Machine That Can Suffer" provides additional material on the same topic.

18. In this portion of the text, where we are discussing consumer perception and action (or potential action), we assume no gaming, deception, or free-rider behavior on the part of the consumer. This is to say, we assume the consumer is internally honest with himself or herself. We continue to assume, however, that learning is involved in discovering one's willingness-to-pay.

19. For a good discussion of a related concept, as well as the consumer activity of "guessing," see Cohen and Axelrod 1984.

20. As explained earlier, to this point we have only addressed the special case, or equivalent variation.

21. For additional information on related concepts of willingness-to-pay, see Knetsch and Sinden 1984; Hanemann 1991; Thomas Brown 1994; Boyce, et al. 1992, as well as the growing literature in the general field of willingness-to-pay. See also Alberini 1995; Benhabib and Day 1981; Cooper and Loomis 1992; Cyert and DeGroot 1975; Huang et al. 1997; Flores and Carson 1997; Frykblom 1997; Kahneman and Tversky 1982a, 1984; March 1978; Nickerson 1995; and Shipley 1975.

Notes to Chapter 9

1. Closure of the loop will permit expectation to be a function of experience (i.e., experience from a previous time period).

2. See Hofstadter 1981. My first exposure to strange attractors was through Douglas Hofstadter. For additional comments on the subject, see his *Metamagical Themas,* Hofstadter 1985. For additional sources on nonlinear dynamics and strange attractors, see Arrowsmith and Place 1990; Casti 1979, 1994; Cohen and Stewart 1994; Collet and Eckmann 1980; Diamond 1976; Feigenbaum 1981; Guckenheimer 1973a, 1973b; Kadanoff 1983; Kellert 1993; Li and Yorke 1975; Lorenz 1963; May 1976; Metropolis et al. 1967, 1973; Morse 1925, 1931; Myrberg 1958, 1963; Nicolis and Prigogine 1977, 1989; Prigogine 1980; Prigogine and Stengers 1984; Ruelle 1989a, 1989b, 1991; Schwenk 1976; Shaw 1981; Smale 1967; Thom 1975; and Whitney 1955. In economic applications, see Barnett et al. 1989; Benhabib 1992; Benhabib and Day 1980, 1981, 1982; Day 1967, 1970, 1981, 1983; Shipley 1975; Smale 1973, 1974a, 1974b, 1974c, 1974d; and Stutzer 1980.

3. For more on the relationship of expectation and experience, see Riedl 1984. The setting for Riedl is evolutionary biology and the role of expectation and experience in the evolution of intelligent life. Also from the field of biology, see Eigen 1971; Eigen and Schuster 1977, 1978a, 1978b. For additional reading on expectation and experience, see J.A. Anderson, et al. 1977; Benhabib and Day 1981; Changeux and Connes 1995; Cohen and Axelrod 1984; Cyert and DeGroot 1975; Day 1970, 1975; Day and Kennedy 1970; Elster 1979; Festinger 1957; Goldsmith 1991; Greenfield 1995; Grossberg 1980, 1981; Harth 1982, 1993; Kahneman and Tversky 1979, 1982a, 1982b, 1984; Kauffman 1993; Kelso 1995; Minsky 1985; Ornstein 1993; Rosenzweig et al. 1972; Shipley 1975; Sutton and Barto 1981; Thaler 1980; and Tversky and Kahneman 1981.

4. Some authors have subsequently discovered that not only is the location of the seed unimportant, but that, except for certain topological properties, the nature of the function also does not matter.

5. Our previous single-fixed-point solution was a one-period attractor.

6. The value for λ_c is drawn from Hofstadter's example. It is a variation on work done by Mitchell Feigenbaum and what has come to be known as "Feigenbaum's number," or 4.66920160910299097. . . . See Feigenbaum 1981.

7. In subsequent chapters we introduce more information on consumer decision making. Lexicographic ordering and discrete choice are combined with more traditional models. As we shall see then, the Feigenbaum decision-making model introduced here fits quite consistently with random utility models of a *representative consumer.* The model should also prove useful for more general applications of Bayesian processes. The capacity of the Feigenbaum model to become ergodic relates well, only in reverse, with Bayesian methods, and it provides theoretical support for the random utility approach. The Feigenbaum model developed in this chapter may also prove useful to Changeux and Connes in their work with an evaluation function. See note 17 from chapter 8, and Changeux and Connex 1995, pp. 143–46. Note their need to identify a measure of distance from accuracy and how our b_{it} suggests a method to assess, at least, the change between $(b_{it=k})$ and $(b_{it=k+1})$. For our model, accuracy is attained when $(b_{it=k}) = (b_{it=k+1})$.

8. It could be that there are two forms of accuracy. First, where the consumer's initial guessed value of b_i is always at the intersection of the curve with the 45° line. Second, there is no curve other than the 45° line and the consumer's initial b_i is always $(b_{it=k}) = (b_{it=k+1})$. For this second form of accuracy, all such initial values of b_i would be stable (there is no path away from the seed value), so

once picked there would be no movement, and there is no need to look further for an optimal solution. Note, however, that the point could be anywhere on the 45° line and the consumer's expectation would be perceived as accurately satisfied by experience. The constraint in $v_i x_i$ space would remain stable for the initial value of b_i.

9. It is important to remember that we assume experience must be perceived and interpreted by each consumer. In this sense, each consumer creates his or her own individual "reality" or interpreted experience. This form of reality is individualistic, subjective, and dynamic; it changes across time within the "same" individual. Our model does not accept the assumption that reality, or consumption experience, is absolute, universal, or static. Except within the context of the representative consumer, which is essentially a statistical sampling issue, we do not accept the homogeneous consumer, or iso-human model of human beings. Experience, consumption or otherwise, is assumed to be unique to each person. It is assumed that no two people ever consume, in the same manner, the same good or service; nor do they receive the same "satisfaction" from the same good or service. Each consumer's consumption technology is assumed to be unique. It is further assumed that until individual consumer b_i stabilizes, if ever, no individual consumer experiences the same act of consumption twice. The act of consumption and the experience and interpretation of that act are unique to each consumer and within the same consumer may vary across time and place. (See Fisher and Shell and their discussion of the Chinese proverb: A person never steps twice in the same river.)

The importance of this distinction, between absolute and subjective-individual reality, will be further developed in this and subsequent chapters. Part of the distinction is also reflected in our earlier discussion of human wants. (See chapter 6.) At that juncture, we highlighted the difference between a universal reality regarding attributes or characteristics—Lancaster's **B** matrix—and a more subjective, individual reality—Ironmonger's **W** matrix.

10. The constrained optimum solution for a consumer in traditional consumption space, with preference map and constraint, implies both purchase-transaction and the act of consumption. For some goods and services the act of purchase may be separate from the act of consumption. Willingness-to-pay focuses on payment in the transaction-purchase stage. The learning process associated with consumption of v_i and evaluation of b_i involves the act of consumption. To keep our analysis simple, we assume that purchase and consumption are simultaneous—that is, we assume a very small or zero time interval between purchase and consumption.

11. On rent-seeking, although within different contexts, see Buchanan 1980.

12. For more information on concepts of the Self, see Masterson 1985. Note, also, the following definitions:

> *Self-image.* "The image an individual has of himself at a particular time and in a specific situation. It consists of his body image and the mental representation of his state at the time. This image may be conscious or unconscious, realistic or distorted...."

> *Self Representation.* "A more enduring schema than self-image, constructed by the ego out of the multitude of realistic and distorted self images which an individual has had at different times. It represents the person as he consciously and unconsciously perceives himself and may be dormant or active...." (Masterson 1985, pp. 20–21).

13. On object relations see Jacobson 1964; Kernberg 1982; Kohut 1971, 1977; Masterson 1985; Rinsley 1982. For other works on the concept of Self and related issues, see Dennett 1991; Edelman 1987, 1989; Elster 1986; Ey 1978; Gardner 1983, 1985; Goldsmith 1991; Greenfield 1995; Harth 1982, 1993; Hofstadter 1979; Hofstadter and Dennett 1981; Horowitz and Zilber 1983; Kelso 1995; Mahler and McDevitt 1982; Minsky 1985; Ornstein 1993; Popper and Eccles 1977; Restak 1994; Rose 1992; Rosenfield 1988. For recent work on the concept of a rational self, see Rubinstein 1998.

Notes to Chapter 10

1. We should point out, however, that change from $\hat{v}_i$ at m (in Figure 10.1) to the v_i corresponding to path (1) could also arise from a new targeting process on the original constraint (i.e., b_i does not change; instead, the consumer targets a different point on the original constraint).

2. This is a form of lexicographic ordering that has previously (implicitly) existed in the homogeneous goods case. We discuss such orderings in more detail later in chapter 15.

3. Duesenberry's Demonstration Effect hypothesis may also contribute to this process of gathering information (shopping) prior to the purchase of higher v_i.

4. A neighborhood is defined in terms of a range along the v_i axis. An accurate b_i may apply to only a specific targeted variety, $\hat{v}_i$, or to the neighborhood that surrounds that $\hat{v}_i$. In the introductory

material of part 2 we previously assumed that an accurate b_i could also extend the entire length of the constraint in $v_i x_i$ space. With the introduction of neighborhoods, unless stated otherwise, we no longer assume that b_i extends the full length of the constraint.

5. For more on the disparity between expectation and experience, see Cohen and Axelrod 1984. The following quotes are of particular interest. Note that they build on the principle that "surprise" is "the main driver of adaptation," or, in our context, learning:

> The first of these is essentially the principle that the utility function adapts not to experience itself, but to the difference between experienced and expected utility. In effect, the adaptation of the function is to the errors of the cognitive system: today's intrinsic utilities are in part the result of yesterday's misunderstandings of the world. (Cohen and Axelrod 1984, p. 40)

> Our results show that when beliefs are misspecified, controlled preference change can actually be adaptive. By allowing *pleasant* and *unpleasant surprises* to guide changes in utility, a decision maker can actually achieve better performance on both the original and revised utility functions. (Cohen and Axelrod 1984, p. 39)

> An individual need not realize that he or she is coming to like things that are associated with pleasant surprises—but the resulting change in the utility function can still be adaptive. (Cohen and Axelrod 1984, p. 39) [Note that *acquired taste*, e.g., for Scotch, may easily fall under this explanation.]

For more information on "surprise" in another context, and the role of disappointment, see Cohen and Axelrod 1984, pp. 31, 34. For more on adaptive utility, see Cyert and DeGroot 1975. In a related area, see Shipley 1975. On the psychophysical aspects and other brain activities associated with positive and negative surprise, see Duncan-Johnson and Donchin 1977.

6. This manner of utility behavior, or construction of the preference map by the consumer, is an example of invariance. In fact, the activity of targeting or focusing requires invariance, or is in itself a form of invariance. For more information on the process of focusing, see "Focusing and Filtering" in Hofstadter 1979, pp. 657–59. In related areas, consider "Copies and Sameness" in Hofstadter 1979, pp. 146–49; "Recursive Structures and Processes," in Hofstadter 1979, pp. 127–52; "Templates and Sameness-Detectors," Hofstadter 1979, pp. 650–51; also, "Conceptual Skeletons and Conceptual Mapping," "Multiple Representation," and "Forced Matching" all in Hofstadter 1979, pp. 668–72. Related to the concept of focusing, in the field of psychology, is pattern recognition, signal detection, and search theory. Also from the field of psychology, the process of "framing" is related to the process of focusing; see, e.g., Tversky and Kahneman 1981; Thaler 1980; Kahneman and Tversky 1979, 1982b. From information theory, the process of focusing is related to filtering, editing, and pattern recognition. See, e.g., Pierce 1980 and Fukunaga 1990.

7. It is conceivable that similar concepts of separability and decentralization could be employed to establish the independence of a v_i neighborhood. Within such a neighborhood, substitution of v_i (exclusively between v_i within the neighborhood) could be embedded. Here the concept of boundaries to the neighborhood is analogous to our previous discussion of boundaries on the v_i that constitute the ith commodity.

8. The form of budgeting required here must be anticipated or planned budgeting, which is another case of guessing, that is, the decentralized budget for $\hat{v}_i$ is guessed to be of a magnitude that, if accurate, adequately covers expenditures on $\hat{v}_i$ and does not affect other v_i, and does not have leftover funds (unless saving is allowed). Our previous application of attractors could be applied to this budgeting process as well, since accuracy is likely to be attained only after iterative adjustment of the budget. The same statement applies to all other uses of separability and decentralization—for example, of commodity i out of $x_i x_j x_h$ space, and so forth.

9. If we are concerned about strict decentralization, then, in addition, we would not allow variation in expenditure on the other v_i to affect $\hat{v}_i$.

10. In the Houthakker single-variety model this presents no problem per se, as only one variety is purchased; however, where the consumer may purchase multiple varieties, this phenomenon becomes important.

11. Obviously, our discussion here is not in agreement with the typical preference relation of acyclic ordering. (See Schofield 1984, p. 24, on such orderings.) We have, at several junctures in this text, questioned the extent of "rationality" in human decision making. This is another of those junctures. Without the basic package, against which the consumer could make comparisons, it is argued that the consumer may become confused and, as a result, occasionally fall, possibly unawares, into a cyclical ordering pattern. It should be recalled that via the mathematics of period-two and higher attractors,

consumer decision making may exhibit cyclical, or even chaotic, patterns. (See Kenneth Arrow 1963 on cyclical voting patterns. For a contemporary view on rationality assumptions, see Rubinstein 1998).

12. The weighting process of the e_{ih} implies the existence of an invariant over the e_{ih}. The invariant serves as an aggregator that combines and rank orders bundles of e_{ih}. The bundles of e_{ih} are called varieties. The process of aggregation over an invariant is another example of nesting or recursion, and it underscores the need for separability in our functional structure. In the case of the v_i axis, the axis must be assumed separable over all quality characteristics in e_{ih} space.

13. An alternative and more strict requirement is that, within any v_i neighborhood, the consumer must be able to order the v_i on the basic package. This requirement, in turn, may lead to the requirement of separability and nesting of neighborhoods within neighborhoods, and so forth. We alluded to this difficulty earlier in our discussion of targeting of v_i within the utility function. Both of these topics suggest, as well, fractal analysis of the structure of preferences and constraints in quality-quantity space.

14. The possibility of chaotic decision making under democratic voting procedures, especially in coalitional models of government, suggests some interesting applications of nonlinear dynamic modeling.

15. For more material on various forms of willingness-to-pay, see note 21 of chapter 8.

Notes to Chapter 11

1. On the Waugh-Brems problem, see chapter 2. On a related topic, see Benassy 1986 on non-Walrasian transactions involving the short sides of demand and supply.

2. The purpose of this portion of the text is not to discuss profit maximizing behavior on the part of producers, but rather to identify conditions under which transactions occur, and that reduce the likelihood of the Waugh-Brems problem.

3. Across time, it is assumed that learning will occur for individual producers as they study periodic market analyses and adjust their b_i^p. Such learning may result in an adjustment of the folded function in expectation-experience phase space for individual producers. As individual producers become more accurate in their estimates of consumers b_i^c, the fold in the folded function may change such that it reduces higher-period attractors toward a single-period attractor (accuracy). In their drive to maximize transactions, it is as though the producers b_i^p are seeking, or approaching, the consumers b_i^c. Such behavior is analogous to hunter-prey phenomena, the b_i^p honing in on the b_i^c. Numerous models in mathematical biology might prove useful in explaining this form of behavior. This phenomenon is another example of adaptive behavior.

Notes to Chapter 13

1. A rough estimate of an (a_i/b_i) value sufficiently high to produce an approximately linear constraint in $v_i x_i$ space is $(a_i/b_i) \geq 250$. For more information on the (a_i/b_i) ratio and the constraint in $v_i x_i$ space, see Appendix A.

2. At this juncture, we continue to utilize preference maps with convex indifference curves. Later, we examine the assumptions of substitutability across commodities. In our model, occasions may arise where commodities are not substitutable, although substitution within a commodity, across varieties, may exist. Under other circumstances, substitution across some commodities may occur.

3. See Appendix A for information on M_i and convexity of the constraint.

4. In sections 5 and 6 of chapter 13 we assume that producers quickly adjust to change in consumer willingness-to-pay (i.e., that Δb_i^p quickly adjusts to Δb_i^c, such that $b_i^p = b_i^c$ and PDC = CDC). In Figure 13.13, and subsequent diagrams in these two sections, we assume all PDC = CDC unless noted otherwise.

5. For information and historical examples on the producer strategy to introduce higher quality in order to confuse consumers regarding higher prices, see Hofsten 1952, particularly chapter 3. See also the following: "When the producer wants to increase the price, he prefers to do it in such a way that he issues a new model, which may be only slightly different from the old one. It is not surprising that the producer finds this procedure preferable to increasing the price of the old product" (Hofsten 1952, p. 53).

6. Remember our model is focused on Houthakker's single-variety case.

7. See chapter 6, sections 1-5, 8, and 10. For additional perspectives on this topic and related material, see Fisher and Shell 1971.

8. Also, recall the Fisher and Shell discussion of BTUs, efficiency and quality. See chapter 6.

Notes to Chapter 14

1. As we will see later, the constraint may also be influenced by the level of quality of the jth commodity, v_j. Presently, we assume v_j constant.

2. The same as indicated in note 1 regarding the constraint, the preference map in $x_i x_j$ space may also be influenced by the level of quality of the jth commodity, v_j. These matters will be discussed later in this chapter and in chapter 15.

3. As regards the nature of the consumer preference map, see also note 2 from chapter 13.

4. On random utility, see Bockstael et al. 1984, 1987, 1989; Hanemann, 1982; Kaoru, 1988, 1995; and Kaoru et al. 1995.

5. Under this form of lexicographic ordering, the bundle of $v_i x_i$ that has the higher v_i (within a v_i neighborhood) is the preferred bundle, regardless of the corresponding quantity of the bundle.

6. Both in Figures 14.3 and 14.4 we continue with the usual assumptions of convexity and continuity of the preference map. (See earlier reference to this topic in note 2 of chapter 13.) To this juncture we have not adequately addressed the issue of substitutability of commodities. In chapter 15 we discuss consumer interaction with the ith and jth commodity producers. In that chapter we address the prospect of a rank-ordering of commodities, similar to Ironmonger's treatment of "wants," and we present situations where substitution of commodities is severely restricted, or possibly nonexistent. Lexicographic ordering will apply in these cases. There are other situations, however, where limited substitution across commodities may exist. We cover these issues in chapter 15.

7. One implication of our model of variable quality and consumer behavior is that it might be possible to examine a consumer's self-image via analysis of purchase patterns.

8. We may not know what drives the change in quality. Additional research by psychologists, marketing research specialists, and others, may be able to identify the nature of the phenomena involved. Our hypothesis is that, at the level of retail purchases, self-image is a significant factor in such decision making.

9. For earlier work on variable quality and the Slutsky equation, see Peterson 1976. For more recent work utilizing the Slutsky approach, see Golden 1995. In our model the distinction between income and substitution effects via the Slutsky approach is limited by the frequent use of targeting, neighborhoods, and lexicographic ordering.

10. The relationship of these two preference maps may be viewed as another expectation-experience loop. It is a loop, however, with a potentially long time interval between the expectation and the experience, and then the return loop for reformulation of the expectation. Memory becomes an important factor in establishing the loop (pattern recognition across time) and in the learning processes involved in adjusting subsequent expectation.

11. As a general recommendation, the new consumer with U_{v3} is a better manifestation of current preferences and hence going from a tangency on U_{v3} back to U_{v2} is superior. The use of lexicographic preference orderings suggests this approach as well. For the approach of the representative consumer, history of previous buying patterns (historically revealed preference) would have to serve as a form of collective memory for the cohort. For the representative consumer, the analog to memory involves linking of consumption patterns across time, similar to the linking approach used when new products are introduced in price indices. (See, e.g., Griliches 1990, Triplett 1983, 1990; Hofsten 1952.)

12. Finally, note that the increase in M_i, used to compensate for higher v_i, may be less than the increase in M_T required to parallel shift outward the constraint in Figure 14.8. Accurate compensation to a subbudget (e.g., to M_i) may be less costly than compensation to the overall household budget, M_T. Furthermore, depending on differences in the configuration of preference maps U_{v2} and U_{v3}, the direct subbudget form of compensation could reduce, or potentially eliminate, substitution and income effects.

13. These issues also apply to any application of a representative consumer. Recall our earlier recommendation to use a representative consumer for each consumer cohort, where the cohorts are broken out according to targeted v_i, or narrow v_i neighborhoods. In our effort to assess the income effect, comparisons must be made of aggregated preferences across two different representative consumers. The statistical methods suggested in Appendix B apply here.

14. In Figures 14.4 and 14.10 we assume $a^c_{i(BP)}$, $a_{i(market)}$, and b^c_i are constant.

15. From an empirical perspective, what is required is the ability to control for levels of quality, and then partition the remaining variance. The partition would be between consumer income and other non-taste-related factors, on the one hand, from factors that could reflect tastes. Under such an approach it is also possible that some "change in taste" phenomena remain in the unexplained variance (i.e., in the error term).

16. Note that if the decrease in b^c_i just offsets the increase in v_i, then there is no change in p_i, and

no change in the constraint in $x_i x_j$ space. If the decrease in b_i^c is less than the increase in v_i, then there is an increase in p_i and the constraint rotates downward in $x_i x_j$ space.

17. Comparison of expenditure on the previous (lower) variety with expenditure on the higher variety is necessary to determine whether there has been an increase in expenditure on the ith commodity corresponding to the higher variety.

18. In order to pursue path (2), the increase in b_i^c must exactly offset the decrease in v_i such that x_i and p_i remain constant. By $M_i = p_i x_i$, given both p_i and x_i constant, M_i is constant.

19. Under the increase in b_i^c approach to path (1), the magnitude of increase in b_i^c is greater than the decrease in v_i, thus, p_i is increased. Correspondingly, the reduction in x_i, combined with the increase in p_i, introduces the possibility of a change in quantity demanded.

20. It seems unlikely that the poor would be able to purchase the same varieties as, for example, the rich.

21. See Appendix B.

22. The difficulties of change in demand versus change in quantity demanded are not likely going to be resolved under the Houthakker price system. It is for these reasons that we recommend statistical controls to identify isoquality, and to discern shifts in isoquality demand versus movement along a variable-quality demand.

23. See our earlier discussion of NSUN in chapter 10, section 3.

24. "... the restrictions on x_i also impose restrictions on consumer decision making regarding x_j" (whatever the consumer selects to be the jth commodity). This aspect of consumer decision making reflects the importance of how the consumer frames the comparison of commodities (i.e., how the consumer selects the commodities to place in $x_i x_j$ space). The comparison of commodities may also reveal an ordering of commodities by the consumer.

25. As before, we continue to assume substitution between commodities is possible. Later, we will introduce restrictions on such substitution.

Notes to Chapter 15

1. Consumer subbudgets may be estimated on the basis of percentage of household disposable income, M_T. Socioeconomic-demographic characteristics of consumers also influence the percentages corresponding to different subbudget categories.

2. The price, p_j^c, "represents an acceptable price to the consumer" (i.e., it is drawn from the CDPL in $v_j p_j$ space).

3. Note that in terms of the ith commodity intercept, $p_i^p > p_i^c$ (given $M_i^p = M_i^c$) is equivalent to $M_i^p < M_i^c$ (given $p_i^p = p_i^c$).

4. Given $M_i^p = M_i^c$, and given the CDC intercept on the x_i axis lies closer to the origin than the intercept of the PDC, requires $p_i^c > p_i^p$.

5. As we will see later, under the conditions illustrated in Figures 15.4 or 15.5, transactions usually do not occur with the jth commodity producer.

6. On the importance of "framing," see, among others, Tversky and Kahneman 1981, Kahneman and Tversky 1984, and Thaler 1980.

7. Assuming revenue rises for the producer in the movement from (b) to (a).

8. Examples of bundling of price and quantity are frequently encountered in hardware stores, where a quantity greater than one is packaged in a sealed container and the consumer must purchase the container. Under such circumstances, the consumer's option is basically take-it-or-leave-it. In some "old-fashioned" hardware stores, on the other hand, items are placed in bins and the consumer may choose how many he or she wants to purchase. Under the situation described in the main text (Figure 15.9), it is possible that transactions would increase in frequency if consumers were given the options, for example, offered by "old-fashioned" hardware stores versus the more limited options available in "modern" hardware stores.

Arguments regarding technological change and repackaging, which use the analogy of adding more widgets to the package, would be affected by the circumstances portrayed in Figure 15.9. As illustrated in Figure 15.9, the consumer may not desire the additional widgets in the package. Adjustments of price indices based on the additional widgets in the package are essentially a cost approach, where firms assume consumers desire the additional widgets in the package. (This is another manifestation of the Waugh-Brems problem.) Under such an assumption, justification is given for downward adjustment in price indices. This may be appropriate for producer cost indices, but may be misleading for consumer-oriented indices. Market transactions reflecting the influence of consumer decision making would be appropriate for consumer-oriented price indices. In such indices it is not a forgone conclusion that the index should be adjusted downward owing to the additional widgets derived from technological change.

9. Given the assumption of accuracy regarding estimation of subbudgets (i.e., $M_j^p = M_j^c$), the intercepts reflect the price values: $p_j^p > p_j^c$.

10. See Figure 14.24 for a similar situation; however, prior to consideration of consumer-producer interaction.

11. For Figure 15.21, and in $x_i x_j$ space in general, we have $M_T \geq M_i + M_j = p_i x_i + p_j x_j$. Along the PDC (e.g., in Figure 15.21) we have $x_j = [(M_i + M_j)/p_j^p] - (p_i^p/p_j^p)x_i$, and for the CDC we have $x_j = [(M_i + M_j)/p_j^c] - (p_i^c/p_j^c)x_i$. At the point of intersection in Figure 15.21, i.e., at point (a), the values of x_j are identical; therefore, we have $[(M_i + M_j)/p_j^p] - (p_i^p/p_j^p)x_i = [(M_i + M_j)/p_j^c] - (p_i^c/p_j^c)x_i$, which with rearrangement of terms becomes: $x_i = \{[(M_i + M_j)/p_j^c] - [(M_i + M_j)/p_j^p]\}\{(p_j^c p_j^p)/[(p_i^c p_j^p) - (p_i^p p_j^c)]\}$. In Figure 15.21, the values of p_j^c and p_j^p are such that $p_j^p > p_j^c$; therefore, the value of the first bracketed expression { } is positive. We will symbolize the first bracketed expression, $\{[(M_i + M_j)/p_j^c] - [(M_i + M_j)/p_j^p]\}$, as $\{\alpha\}$, and we have $\{\alpha\} > 0$. The numerator in the second bracketed expression, $\{(p_j^c p_j^p)/[(p_i^c p_j^p) - (p_i^p p_j^c)]\}$, or $(p_j^c p_j^p)$, is constant and positive. We symbolize $(p_j^c p_j^p)$ as (β), and $(\beta) > 0$. The denominator in the second bracketed expression, $[(p_i^c p_j^p) - (p_i^p p_j^c)]$, is positive, owing to the slope of the CDC, p_i^c/p_j^c, being greater than the slope of the PDC, p_i^p/p_j^p. The expression, $[(p_i^c p_j^p) - (p_i^p p_j^c)]$ was derived from a rearrangement of $[(p_i^c p_j^c) - (p_i^p p_j^p)]$ such that we obtain $\{[(p_i^c p_j^p)/(p_j^c p_j^p)] - [(p_i^p p_j^c)/(p_i^c p_j^p)]\}$. As explained above, (p_i^c/p_j^c) is the slope of the CDC and (p_i^p/p_j^p) is the slope of the PDC. Under the conditions of Figure 15.21, we have $(p_i^c/p_j^c) > (p_i^p/p_j^p)$. Recall that p_j^p and p_j^c are assumed constant and $p_j^p > p_j^c$. Also, recall $p_i^c = a_i^c + b_i^c v_i^c$ and $p_i^p = a_i^p + b_i^p v_i^p$, where $p_i^c > p_i^p$ due to $b_i^c > b_i^p$. Most important to the behavior of the intersection point in Figure 15.21, point (a), the value of $a_{i(market)}$ is in the denominator of the second bracketed expression. Given an increase in $a_{i(market)}$, there is an increase in both p_i^c and p_i^p, and the value of x_i must decrease. The value of x_i is the value x_i at point (a).

12. In markets for the ith commodity, the increased likelihood of transactions (between consumers and producers) would facilitate the generation of market demand curves, for various levels of isoquality. See Appendix B.

13. For more information on discrete choice and related topics, see Anderson, de Palma, and Thisse 1992, Tirole 1988, and Anderson, de Palma, and Nesterov 1995. For more information specifically regarding discrete choice and consumer theory, see also Ben-Akiva and Lerman 1985, and Hensher and Johnson 1981.

14. If we assume a relationship exists between b_i^c and the level of satisfaction a consumer derives from a variety (of the commodity), then it is possible that the learning process regarding b_i^c (or other components of the CDC) reflect, and/or possibly influence, the preference map. Vibration may also apply, then, to the map. As in traditional consumer theory, we assume only a monotonic transformation applies to the quantity of the variety and the level of satisfaction. Recall, however, that there are a number of differences between our approach to consumer theory and the traditional version. Most importantly, the use of lexicographic preferences, among the high-priority commodities, places restrictions on the map.

Notes for Appendix B

1. These consumers may be studied as a separate group, which is then subdivided into cohorts according to their ranking of multiple varieties. As before, this is essentially a sampling issue, but caution must be exercised in these cases that the representative sample size remain sufficiently large to be statistically significant. This approach would place any consumer who purchases two or more varieties during the period of study into two or more separate consumer cohorts, one cohort for each type of variety purchased.

2. By "predominately purchased" is meant: The mean number of purchases for one variety is (statistically) significantly higher than the mean number of purchases of the other variety, both taken from the higher-income group.

References

Abbott, Lawrence. 1953. "Vertical Equilibrium Under Pure Quality Competition." *American Economic Review* 43, no. 5, pt. 1: 826–45.

———. 1955. *Quality and Competition.* New York: Columbia University Press.

Ackoff, Russell L., and Fred E. Emery. 1972. *On Purposeful Systems.* Chicago: Aldine-Atherton.

Adelman, Irma, and Zvi Griliches. 1961. "On an Index of Quality Change." *Journal of the American Statistical Association* 56: 535–48.

Alberini, Anna. 1995. "Testing Willingness-to-Pay Models of Discrete Choice Contingent Valuation Survey Data." *Land Economics* 71, no. 1: 83–96.

Anderson, J.A., J.W. Silverstein, S.A. Ritz, and R.S. Jones. 1977. "Distinctive Features, Categorical Perception, and Probability Learning: Some Applications of a Neural Model." *Psychological Review* 84: 413–51.

Anderson, Simon P., Andre de Palma, and Jacques-Francois Thisse. 1992. *Discrete Choice Theory of Product Differentiation.* Cambridge, MA: MIT Press.

Anderson, Simon P., Andre de Palma, and Yurii Nesterov. 1995. "Oligopolistic Competition and the Optimal Provision of Products." *Econometrica* 63, no. 6: 1281–1301.

Arrow, Kenneth J. 1963. *Social Choice and Individual Values.* 2d ed. New York: Wiley.

Arrowsmith, D.K., and C.M. Place. 1990. *An Introduction to Dynamical Systems.* Cambridge, UK: Cambridge University Press.

Barfod, Borge. 1937. *Reklamen i teoretisk-okonomisk Belysning.* Copenhagen: Schonbergshe Forlag.

———. 1944–45. "En Note om teoretisk Tolkning af Reklamen." *Nordisk Tidsskrift for Teknisk Okonomi.*

Barnett, William A. 1981. *Consumer Demand and Labor Supply: Goods, Monetary Assets, and Time.* Amsterdam: North-Holland.

Barnett, William A., John Geweke, and Karl Shell, eds. 1989. *Economic Complexity: Chaos, Sunspots, Bubbles, and Nonlinearity.* Proceedings of the Fourth International Symposium in Economic Theory and Econometrics. Cambridge, UK: Cambridge University Press.

Bartik, Timothy J. 1987. "The Estimation of Demand Parameters in Hedonic Price Models." *Journal of Political Economy* 95, no. 1: 81–88.

Becker, Gary. 1964. *Human Capital.* New York: NBER.

———. 1965. "A Theory of the Allocation of Time." *Economic Journal* 75, no. 299: 493–516.

Ben-Akiva, Moshe, and Steven R. Lerman. 1985. *Discrete Choice Analysis: Theory and Application to Travel Demand.* Cambridge, MA: MIT Press.

Benassy, Jean-Pascal. 1986. *Macroeconomics: An Introduction to the Non-Walrasian Approach.* Orlando, FL: Academic Press.

Benhabib, Jess, ed. 1992. *Cycles and Chaos in Economic Equilibrium.* Princeton, NJ: Princeton University Press.

Benhabib, Jess, and Richard H. Day. 1980. "Erratic Accumulation." *Economic Letters* 6: 113–17.

———. 1981. "Rational Choice and Erratic Behavior." *Review of Economic Studies* 48: 459–71.

———. 1982. "A Characterization of Erratic Dynamics in the Overlapping Generations Model." *Journal of Economic Dynamics and Control* 4: 37–55.

Benner, Claude L., and Harry G. Gabriel. 1927. "Marketing of Delaware Eggs." *Bulletin,* Delaware Agricultural Experiment Station, no. 150.

Berndt, Ernst R., and Jack E. Triplett, eds. 1990. *Fifty Years of Economic Measurement: The Jubilee of the Conference on Research in Income and Wealth.* Chicago: University of Chicago Press.

Blackorby, Charles, Daniel Primont, and Robert R. Russell. 1978. *Duality, Separability, and Functional Structure: Theory and Economic Applications.* New York: North-Holland.

Bockstael, N.E., W.M. Hanemann, and I.E. Strand. 1984. "Measuring the Benefits of Water Quality Improvements Using Recreation Demand Models." Vol. II. Prepared for the Office of Policy Analysis, U.S. Environmental Protection Agency. Washington, DC.

Bockstael, N.E., W.M. Hanemann, and C.L. Kling. 1987. "Estimating the Value of Water Quality Improvements in a Recreation Demand Framework." *Water Resources Research* 23: 951–60.

Bockstael, N.E., K.E. McConnell, and I.E. Strand. 1989. "A Random Utility Model for Sportfishing: Some Preliminary Results for Florida." *Marine Resource Economics* 6: 245–60.

Boden, Margaret A. 1972. *Purposive Explanation in Psychology.* Cambridge, MA: Cambridge University Press.

Bookstaber, Richard, and Joseph Langsam. 1985. "Predictable Behavior: Comment." *American Economic Review* 75, no. 3: 571–75.

Boyce, Rebecca R., Thomas C. Brown, Gary H. McClelland, George L. Peterson, and William D. Schulze. 1992. "An Experimental Examination of Intrinsic Values as a Source of the WTA-WTP Disparity." *American Economic Review* 82, no. 5: 366–74.

Brems, Hans. 1948. "The Interdependence of Quality Variations, Selling Effort and Price." *Quarterly Journal of Economics* 62: 418–40.

———. 1951. *Product Equilibrium Under Monopolistic Competition.* Cambridge, MA: Harvard University Press.

———. 1952. "Employment, Prices and Monopolistic Competition." *Review of Economics and Statistics* 24, no. 4: 314–25.

———. 1957. "Input-Output Coefficients as Measures of Product Quality." *American Economic Review* 47, no. 1: 105–18.

———. 1959. *Output, Employment, Capital and Growth.* New York: Harper.

Brown, James N., and Harvey S. Rosen. 1982. "On the Estimation of Structural Hedonic Price Models." *Econometrica* 50, no. 3: 765–68.

Brown, Thomas C. 1994. "Experiments on the Difference Between Willingness to Pay and Willingness to Accept: Comment." *Land Economics* 70, no. 4: 520–23.

Buchanan, James M. 1980. "Rent Seeking and Profit Seeking." In *Toward a Theory of the Rent-Seeking Society,* ed. James M. Buchanan, Robert D. Tollison, and Gordon Tullock. College Station: Texas A&M University Press.

Butler, Richard J. 1984. "The Effect of Education on Wages—Hedonic Makes Selectivity Bias (Sort of) Simpler." *Economic Inquiry* 22: 109–20.

Cagan, Phillip. 1965. "Measuring Quality Changes and the Purchasing Power of Money: An Exploratory Study of Automobiles." *National Banking Review* 3: 217–36.

Caldwell, Bruce J. 1982. *Beyond Positivism: Economic Methodology in the Twentieth Century.* London: George Allen & Unwin.

Casti, John L. 1979. *Connectivity, Complexity, and Catastrophe in Large-Scale Systems.* New York: Wiley.

———. 1994. *Complexification.* New York: HarperCollins.

Carver, Thomas N. 1921. *Principles of National Economy.* New York: Ginn.

Chamberlin, Edward. 1933. *The Theory of Monopolistic Competition.* Cambridge, MA: Harvard University Press.

———. 1953. "The Product as an Economic Variable." *Quarterly Journal of Economics* 67, no. 1: 1–29.

Changeux, Jean-Pierre, and Alain Connes. 1995. *Conversations on Mind, Matter, and Mathematics.* Princeton, NJ: Princeton University Press.

Cohen, Jack, and Ian Stewart. 1994. *The Collapse of Chaos: Discovering Simplicity in a Complex World.* New York: Viking.

Cohen, Michael D., and Robert Axelrod. 1984. "Coping with Complexity: The Adaptive Value of Changing Utility." *American Economic Review* 74, no. 1: 30–42.

Collet, Pierre, and Jean-Pierre Eckmann. 1980. *Iterated Maps on the Interval as Dynamical Systems.* Boston: Birkhauser.

Coombs, Clyde H., Robyn M. Dawes, and Amos Tversky. 1970. *Mathematical Psychology.* Englewood Cliffs, NJ: Prentice-Hall.

Cooper, Joseph, and John Loomis. 1992. "Sensitivity of Willingness-to-Pay Estimates to Bid Design in Dichotomous Choice Contingent Valuation Models." *Land Economics* 68, no. 2: 211–25.

Copeland, Morris A. 1940. "Competing Products and Monopolistic Competition." *Quarterly Journal of Economics* 55: 1–35.

Corbett, Roger B. 1926. "Concerning Wholesale Market Preferences for Fruits and Vegetables in Providence, R.I." *Bulletin.* Rhode Island Agricultural Experiment Station. no. 206.

Court, Andrew. 1939. "Hedonic Price Indexes with Automotive Examples." In *The Dynamics of Automobile Demand.* New York: General Motors Corp., pp. 99–117.

Cowling, Keith, and John Cubbin. 1970. "Price, Quality and Advertising Competition: An Econometric Investigation of the U.K. Car Market." Department of Economics, St. Louis: Washington University (mimeographed).

Cowling, Keith, John Cubbin, and A.J. Rayner. 1970. "Price, Quality, and Market Share." *Journal of Political Economy* 78: 1292–1309.

Cressman, Ross. 1992. *The Stability Concept of Evolutionary Game Theory. A Dynamic Approach.* Berlin: Springer-Verlag.

Cross, John G. 1983. *A Theory of Adaptive Economic Behavior.* Cambridge, U.K.: Cambridge University Press.

Cyert, Richard M., and Morriss H. DeGroot. 1975. "Adptive Utility." In *Adaptive Economic Models,* ed. Richard H. Day and Theodore Groves. New York: Academic Press.

Davies, H.B. 1972. "The Consumer's Choice Among Qualities of Goods." Fels discussion paper 25, University of Pennsylvania.

Davis, I.G., F.V. Waugh, and Harold McCarthy. 1927. "The Connecticut Apple Industry." *Bulletin.* Connecticut Agricultural Experiment Station. no. 145.

Day, R.H. 1967. "A Microeconomic Model of Business Growth, Decay and Cycles." *Unternehmensforschung* 2, no. 1: 1–20.

Day, Richard H. 1970. "Rational Choice and Economic Behavior." *Theory and Decision* 1: 229–51.

———. 1975. "Adaptive Processes and Economic Theory." *Adaptive Economic Models,* ed. Richard H. Day and Theodore Groves. New York: Academic Press.

———. 1981. "Unstable Economic Systems." *Economic Notes* 10, no. 3: 3–15.

————. 1983. "The Emergence of Chaos From Classical Economic Growth." *Quarterly Journal of Economics* 98, no. 2: 201–13.

Day, Richard H., and Peter E. Kennedy. 1970. "Recursive Decision Systems: An Existence Analysis." *Econometrica* 38, no. 5: 666–81.

Dean, C.R., and H.J. DePodwin. 1961. "Product Variation and Price Indexes: A Case Study of Electrical Apparatus." *Proceedings of the Business and Economic Statistics Section,* American Statistical Association, pp. 271–79.

Deaton, Angus. 1992. *Understanding Consumption.* Oxford: Clarendon Press.

Deaton, Angus, and John Muellbauer. 1980. *Economics and Consumer Behavior.* Cambridge, UK: Cambridge University Press.

Dennett, Daniel C. 1978. *Brainstorms: Philosophical Essays on Mind and Psychology.* Montgomery, VT: Bradford Books.

————. 1981. "Intentional Systems." In *Mind Design: Philosophy, Psychology, and Artificial Intelligence,* ed. John Haugeland. Cambridge, MA: MIT Press.

————. 1991. *Consciousness Explained.* Boston: Little, Brown.

DeVany, Arthur S., and Thomas R. Saving. 1983. "The Economics of Quality." *Journal of Political Economy* 91, no. 6: 979–1000.

Dhrymes, Phoebus. 1971. "Price and Quality Changes in Consumer Capital Goods: An Empirical Study." In *Price Indexes and Quality Change,* ed. Zvi Griliches. Cambridge, MA: Harvard University Press, pp. 88–149.

Diamond, Phil. 1976. "Chaotic Behavior of Systems of Difference Equations." *International Journal of Systems Science* 7, no. 8: 953–56.

Diewert, W. Erwin. 1990. "Comment." In *Fifty Years of Economic Measurement,* ed. Ernst R. Berndt and Jack E. Triplett. Chicago: University of Chicago Press, pp. 233–37.

————. 1993. "Hicks' Aggregation Theorem and the Existence of a Real Value Added Function." In *Essays in Index Number Theory* 1, ed. W.E. Diewert and A.O. Nakamura. New York: Elsevier Science Publications B.V.

Dorfman, Robert, and Peter Steiner. 1954. "Optimal Advertising and Optimal Quality." *American Economic Review* 44, no. 5: 826–36.

Dorfman, Robert, Paul Samuelson, and Robert Solow. 1958. *Linear Programming and Economic Analysis.* New York: McGraw-Hill.

Duesenberry, James S. 1949. *Income, Saving and the Theory of Consumer Behavior.* Cambridge, MA: Harvard University Press.

Duncan-Johnson, Connie C., and Emanual Donchin. 1977. "On Quantifying Surprise: The Variation of Event Related Potentials with Subjective Probability." *Psychophysiology* 14: 456–67.

Early, John F., and James H. Sinclair. 1983. "Quality Adjustment in the Producer Price Indexes." In *The U.S. National Income and Products Accounts: Selected Topics,* ed. Murray F. Foss. Chicago: University of Chicago Press.

Edelman, Gerald M. 1987. *Neural Darwinism. The Theory of Neuronal Group Selection.* New York: Basic Books.

————. 1989. *The Remembered Present. A Biological Theory of Consciousness.* New York: Basic Books.

Eigen, Manfred. 1971. "Self Organization of Matter and the Evolution of Biological Macromolecules." *Naturwissenschaften* 58: 465–528.

Eigen, Manfred, and Peter Schuster. 1977. "The Hypercycle: A Principle of Natural Self-Organization. Part A. Emergence of the Hypercycle." *Naturwissenschaften* 64: 541–65.

————. 1978a. "The Hypercycle: A Principle of Natural Self-Organization. Part B. The Abstract Hypercycle." *Naturwissenschaften* 65: 7–41.

————. 1978b. "The Hypercycle: A Principle of Natural Self-Organization. Part C. The Realistic Hypercycle." *Naturwissenschaften* 65: 341–69.

Elster, Jon. 1979. *Ulysses and the Sirens: Studies in Rationality and Irrationality.* Cambridge, U.K.: Cambridge University Press.

————, ed. 1986. *The Multiple Self.* Cambridge, U.K.: Cambridge University Press.

Ely, Richard T. 1923. *Outlines of Economics.* 4th rev. ed. New York: Macmillan.

Enke, Stephen. 1941. "Profit Maximization and Monopolistic Competition." *American Economic Review* 31, no. 2: 317–26.

Epple, Dennis. 1987. "Hedonic Prices and Implicit Markets: Estimating Demand and Supply Functions for Differentiated Products." *Journal of Political Economy* 95, no. 1: 59–80.

Ey, Henri. 1978. *Consciousness. A Phenomenological Study of Being Conscious and Becoming Conscious.* Bloomington: Indiana University Press.

Farquhar, L.E. 1964. *Ergodic Theory in Statistical Mechanics.* London: Interscience.

Feder, Jens. 1988. *Fractals.* New York: Plenum Press.

Feigenbaum, Mitchell. 1981. "Universal Behavior in Nonlinear Systems." *Los Alamos Science* 1, no. 1: 4–27.

Festinger, L. 1957. *A Theory of Cognitive Dissonance.* Stanford, CA: Stanford University Press.

Fettig, Lyle, 1963. "Adjusting Farm Tractor Prices for Quality Changes, 1950–1962." *Journal of Farm Economics* 45: 599–611.

Fisher, Franklin, Zvi Griliches, and Carl Kaysen. 1962. "The Costs of Automobile Model Changes since 1949." *Journal of Political Economy* 79: 433–51.

Fisher, Franklin, and Karl Shell. 1971. "Taste and Quality Change in the Pure Theory of the True Cost-of-Living Index." In *Price Indexes and Quality Change,* ed. Zvi Griliches. Cambridge, MA: Harvard University Press, pp. 16–54.

Flores, Nicholas E., and Richard T. Carson. 1997. "The Relationship between the Income Elasticities of Demand and Willingness to Pay." *Journal of Environmental Economics and Management* 33: 287–95.

Fodor, J. 1975. *The Language of Thought.* Scranton, PA: Crowell.

Frykblom, Peter. 1997. "Hypothetical Question Modes and Real Willingness to Pay." *Journal of Enviornmental Economics and Management* 34: 275–87.

Fukunaga, Keinosuke. 1990. *Introduction to Statistical Pattern Recognition.* 2d ed. Boston: Academic Press.

Gardner, Howard. 1983. *Frames of Mind: The Theory of Multiple Intelligences.* New York: Basic Books.

————. 1985. *The Mind's New Science. A History of the Cognitive Revolution.* New York: Basic Books.

Garrison, Roger W. 1985. "Predictable Behavior: Comment." *American Economic Review* 75, no. 3: 576–78.

Gavett, Thomas. 1967. "Quality and a Pure Price Index." *Monthly Labor Review* 90: 16–20.

Gibbons, Robert. 1992. *Game Theory for Applied Economists.* Princeton, NJ: Princeton University Press.

Godel, Kurt. 1965. "On Formally Undecidable Propositions of Principia Mathematica and Related Systems." In *The Undecidable: Basic Papers on Undecidable Propositions, Unsolvable Problems and Computable Functions,* ed. Martin Davis. New York: Raven Press.

Golden, Dan. 1995. "The Generalized Slutsky Equation and Trading Under Asymmetric Information." Working Paper. Presented at the Kenan-Flagler Business School Finance Area Workshop, University of North Carolina, Chapel Hill, July 19, 1995.

Goldman, S.M., and H. Uzawa. 1964. "A Note on Separability in Demand Analysis." *Econometrica* 32, no. 3: 387–98.

Goldsmith, Timothy H. 1991. *The Biological Roots of Human Nature. Forging Links between Evolution and Behavior.* New York: Oxford University Press.

Gordon, R.J. 1970. "Recent Developments in the Measurement of Price Indexes for Fixed Capital Goods." *Proceedings of the Business and Economics Statistics Section,* American Statistical Association.

Gorman, W.M. 1959. "Separability and Aggregation." *Econometrica* 27, no. 3: 469–81.

Greenfield, Susan A. 1995. *Journey to the Centers of the Mind. Toward a Science of Consciousness.* New York: W.H. Freeman.

Gregory, Richard L., ed. 1987. *The Oxford Companion to the Mind.* Oxford: Oxford University Press.

Grether, David M., and Charles R. Plott. 1979. "Economic Theory of Choice and the Preference Reversal Phenomenon." *American Economic Review* 69: 623–38.

Griliches, Zvi. 1964. "Notes on the Measurement of Price and Quality Changes." In *Models of Income Determination. Studies in Income and Wealth.* 28. Princeton, NJ: NBER, pp. 301–404.

———. 1967. "Hedonic Price Indexes Revisited: Some Notes on the State of the Art." *Proceedings of the Business and Economics Statistics Section,* American Statistical Association, pp. 324–32.

———. 1971. "Hedonic Price Indexes for Automobiles: An Econometric Analysis of Quality Change." In *Price Indexes and Quality Change,* ed. Zvi Griliches. Cambridge, MA: Harvard University Press.

———. 1990. "Hedonic Price Indexes and the Measurement of Capital and Productivity: Some Historical Reflections." In *Fifty Years of Economic Measurement,* ed. Ernst R. Berndt and Jack E. Triplett. Chicago: University of Chicago Press.

Grossberg, Stephen. 1980. "Biological Competition: Decision Rules, Pattern Formation, and Oscillations." *Proceedings of the National Academy of Sciences* 77: 2338–2342.

———. 1981. "Adaptive Resonance in Development, Perception, and Cognition." In *Mathematical Psychology and Psychophysiology,* ed. S. Grossberg. Providence, RI: American Mathematical Society.

Grossman, Sanford. 1975. "Equilibrium under Uncertainty and Bayesian Adaptive Control Theory." In *Adaptive Economic Models,* ed. Richard H. Day and Theodore Groves. New York: Academic Press.

Guckenheimer, J. 1973a. "Bifurcation and Catastrophe." In *Dynamical Systems,* ed. M.M. Peixoto. Proceedings International Symposium. New York: Academic Press.

———. 1973b. "Catastrophes and Partial Differential Equations." *Annales. Institut. Fourier* 23: 31–59.

Haken, Hermann. 1978. *Synergetics: An Introduction: Nonequilibrium Phase Transitions and Self-Organization in Physics, Chemistry and Biology.* New York: Springer-Verlag.

Hall, Robert. 1971. "The Measurement of Quality Change from Vintage Price Data." In *Price Indexes and Quality Change,* ed. Zvi Griliches. Cambridge: Harvard University Press, pp. 240–71.

Hall, Robert E. 1990. *The Rational Consumer: Theory and Evidence.* Cambridge, MA: MIT Press.

Hammond, P.J. 1976. "Endogenous Tastes and Stable Long-Run Choice." *Journal of Economic Theory* 13, no. 76: 329–40.

Hanemann, W.M. 1982. "Applied Welfare Analysis with Quantitative Response Models." California Experiment Station Working Paper no. 241.

Hanemann, W. Michael. 1991. "Willingness to Pay and Willingness to Accept: How Much Can They Differ?" *American Economic Review* 81, no. 3: 635–47.

Harth, Erich. 1982. *Windows on the Mind. Reflections on the Physical Basis of Consciousness.* New York: William Morrow.

———. 1993. *The Creative Loop. How the Brain Makes a Mind.* Reading, MA: Addison-Wesley.

Hebb, D.O. 1949. *Organization of Behavior.* New York: Wiley.

Heddon, Walter P., and N. Cherniak. 1924. "Measuring the Melon Market." Preliminary Report, U.S.D.A.

Heiner, Ronald A. 1983. "The Origin of Predictable Behavior." *American Economic Review* 73: 560–95.

———. 1985a. "Experimental Economics: Comment." *American Economic Review* 75: 260–63.

———. 1985b. "Origin of Predictable Behavior: Further Modeling and Applications." *American Economic Review,* Papers and Proceedings 75, no. 2: 391–96.

———. 1985c. "Predictable Behavior: Reply." *American Economic Review* 75, no. 3: 579–85.

———. 1986. "Uncertainty, Signal-Detection Experiments, and Modeling Behavior." In *Economics as a Process,* ed. Richard N. Langlois. New York: Cambridge University Press.

Hendler, Reuven. 1975. "Lancaster's New Approach to Consumer Demand and Its Limitations." *American Economic Review* 65, no. 1: 194–99.

Hensher, David A., and Lester W. Johnson. 1981. *Applied Discrete-Choice Modelling.* New York: Wiley.

Hicks, J.R. 1946. *Value and Capital.* 2d ed. Oxford: Clarendon.

Hirsch, Werner Z. 1963. "Quality of Government Services." In *Public Expenditure Decisions in the Urban Community,* ed. Schaller. Baltimore: Johns Hopkins University Press, pp. 163–79.

Hirshleifer, Jack. 1955. "The Exchange Between Quantity and Quality." *Quarterly Journal of Economics* 69, no. 4: 596–606.

Hofstadter, Douglas R. 1979. *Godel, Escher, Bach: An Eternal Golden Braid.* New York: Basic Books.

———. 1981. "Metamagical Themas: Strange Attractors, Mathematical Patterns Delicately Poised Between Order and Choas." *Scientific American* 245, no. 5: 22–43.

———. 1985. "Mathematical Chaos and Strange Attractors." In *Metamagical Themas: Questing for the Essence of Mind and Pattern,* ed. Douglas R. Hofstadter. New York: Basic Books.

———, and Daniel C. Dennett, eds. 1981. *The Mind's I: Fantasies and Reflections on Self and Soul.* New York: Basic Books.

Hofsten, Erland von. 1952. *Price Indexes and Quality Changes.* Stockholm: Boklorlaget Forum AB.

Horowitz, M., and N. Zilber. 1983. "Regressive Alterations in the Self Concept." *American Journal of Psychiatry* 140, no. 3: 284–89.

Hotelling, Harold. 1929. "Stability in Competition." *Economic Journal.*

———. 1932. "Edgeworth's Taxation Paradox and the Nature of Demand and Supply Functions." *Journal of Political Economy* 40, no. 5: 577–616.

Houthakker, Hendrick. 1951–52. "Compensated Changes in Quantities and Qualities Consumed." *Review of Economic Studies* 19(3), no. 50: 155–64.

Huang, Ju-Chin, Timothy C. Haab, and John C. Whitehead. 1997. "Willingness to Pay for Quality Improvements: Should Revealed and Stated Preference Data Be Combined?" *Journal of Environmental Economics and Management* 34: 240–55.

Ironmonger, D.S. 1972. *New Commodities and Consumer Behaviour.* London: Cambridge University Press.

Isard, W. 1949. "The General Theory of Location and Space-Economy." *Quarterly Journal of Economics* 63: 476–506.

Jacobson, E. 1964. *The Self and the Object World.* New York: International Universities Press.

Jantsch, Erich. 1980. *The Self-Organizing Universe: Scientific and Human Implications of the Emerging Paradigm of Evolution.* Oxford: Pergamon Press.

Jevons, William Stanley. 1871. *The Theory of Political Economy.* London: Macmillan. (See chapter 4, "Definition of a Market.")

Jordan, J.S. 1982. "The Generic Existence of Rational Expectations Equilibrium in the Higher Dimensional Case." *Journal of Economic Theory* 26: 224–43.

Kadanoff, Leo. 1983. "Roads to Chaos." *Physics Today* 36, no. 12: 46–53.

Kahn, Shulamit, and Kevin Lang. 1988. "Efficient Estimation of Structural Hedonic Systems." *International Economic Review* 29, no. 1: 157–66.

Kahneman, D., and Amos Tversky. 1979. "Prospect Theory: An Analysis of Decision Under Risk." *Econometrica* 47: 263–91.

Kahneman, D., P. Slovic, and A. Tversky, eds. 1982. *Judgment Under Uncertainty: Heuristics and Biases.* New York: Cambridge University Press.

Kahneman, Daniel, and Amos Tversky. 1982a. "Variants of Uncertainty." In *Judgment Under Uncertainty: Heuristics and Biases,* ed. D. Kahneman, et al. New York: Cambridge University Press.

Kahneman, D., and A. Tversky. 1982b. "The Psychology of Preferences." *Scientific American* 246: 160–74.

———. 1984. "Choices, Values, and Frames." *American Psychologist* 39: 341–50.

Kant, I. 1958. *Critique of Pure Reason.* New York: Random House.

Kaoru, Y. 1988. "A Discrete Choice Benefit Analysis of Marine Recreational Fishing: Does Site Definition Matter?" Unpublished memo, Marine Policy Center, Woods Hole, MA.

———. 1995. "Measuring Marine Recreation Benefits of Water Quality Improvements by the Nested Random Utility Model." *Resource and Energy Economics* 17(2): 119–36.

Kaoru, Y., V.K. Smith, and J.L. Liu. 1995. "Using Random Utility Models to Estimate the Recreational Value of Estuarine Resources." *American Journal of Agricultural Economics* 1: 141–51.

Kauffman, Stuart A. 1993. *The Origins of Order. Self–Organization and Selection in Evolution.* New York: Oxford University Press.

Kellert, Stephen H. 1993. *In the Wake Of Chaos. Unpredictable Order in Dynamical Systems.* Chicago: University of Chicago Press.

Kelso, J.A. Scott. 1995. *Dynamic Patterns. The Self–Organization of Brain and Behavior.* Cambridge, MA: Bradford Books.

Kernberg, O. 1982. "Self, Ego, Affects, Drives." *Journal of the American Psychoanalytic Association* 30: 893–917.

Kihlstrom, Richard. 1974. "A Bayesian Model of Demand for Information About Product Quality." *International Economic Review* 15, no. 1: 99–118.

Knetsch, Jack L., and J.A. Sinden. 1984. "Willingness to Pay and Compensation Demanded: Experimental Evidence of an Unexpected Disparity in Measures of Value." *Quarterly Journal of Economics* 99, no. 3: 507–21.

Knez, Peter, Vernon L. Smith, and Arlington W. Williams. 1985. "Individual Rationality, Market Rationality and Value Estimation." *American Economic Review,* Papers and Proceedings 75, no. 2: 397–402.

Kohut, H. 1971. *The Analysis of the Self.* New York: International Universities Press.

———. 1977. *The Restoration of the Self.* New York: International Universities Press.

Kravis, Irving, and Robert Lipsey. 1971. "International Price Comparisons by Regression Methods." In *Price Indexes and Quality Change,* ed. Zvi Griliches. Cambridge, MA: Harvard University Press, pp. 150–79.

Kroeck, Julius. 1928. *McIntosh Apple Study.* Massachusetts Department of Agriculture.

Kuhrt, W.S. 1926–27. "A Study of Farmer Elevator Operation in the Spring Wheat Area." Preliminary Report, U.S.D.A.

Kydland, Finn E., and Edward C. Prescott. 1977. "Rules Rather Than Discretion: The Inconsistency of Optimal Plans." *Journal of Political Economy* 85: 473–91.

Lancaster, Kelvin. 1966a. "A New Approach to Consumer Theory."*Journal of Political Economy* 74, no. 2: 132–57.

———. 1966b. "Change and Innovation in the Technology of Consumption." *American Economic Review,* Papers and Proceedings, 56, no. 2: 14–23.

———. 1971. *Consumer Demand. A New Approach.* New York: Columbia University Press.

———. 1975. "Socially Optimal Product Differentiation." *American Economic Review* 65, no. 4: 567–85.

Leland, Hayne E. 1977. "Quality Choice and Competition." *American Economic Review* 67, no. 2: 127–37.

Lerner, P.A., and H.W. Singer. 1937. "Some Notes on Duopoly and Spatial Competition." *Journal of Political Economy* 45, no. 2: 145–86.

Li, T.Y., and J.A. Yorke. 1975. "Period Three Implies Chaos." *American Mathematical Monthly* 82: 895–992.

Lipsey, Richard, and Gideon Rosenbluth. 1971. "A Contribution to the New Theory of Demand: A Rehabilitation of the Giffen Good." *Canadian Journal of Economics* 4, no. 2: 131–63.

Lorenz, Edward. 1963. "Deterministic, Non-periodic Flow." *Journal of Atmospheric Sciences* 82: 985–92.

Machlup, Fritz, and Una Mansfield. 1983. *The Study of Information.* New York: John Wiley.

Mahler, M., and J. McDevitt. 1982. "Thoughts on the Emergence of the Self with Particular Emphasis on the Body Self." *Journal of the American Psychoanalytic Association* 30: 827–47.

Mandelbrot, Benoit. 1977. *Fractals: Form, Chance and Dimension.* San Francisco: W.H. Freeman.

———. 1982. *The Fractal Geometry of Nature.* New York: W.H. Freeman.

Mandler, George. 1981. "The Structure of Value: Accounting for Taste." Center for Human Information Processing, Report 101, University of California–San Diego.

March, James G. 1978. "Bounded Rationality, Ambiguity, and the Engineering of Choice." *Bell Journal of Economics* 9, no. 2: 587–608.

Marshall, Alfred. 1916. *Principles of Economics.* 7th ed. London: Macmillan.

Mas-Colell, Andreu. 1975. "A Model of Equilibrium with Differentiated Commodities." *Journal of Mathematical Economics* 2: 263–95.

Masterson, James F. 1985. *The Real Self. A Developmental, Self, and Object Relations Approach.* New York: Brunner/Mazel.

Maurice, S. Charles, Owen R. Phillips, and C.E. Ferguson. 1982. *Economic Analysis: Theory and Application.* 4th ed. Homewood, IL: Irwin.

May, Robert M. 1976. "Simple Mathematical Models With Very Complicated Dynamics." *Nature* 261: 459–67.

McKenzie, Lionel. 1957. "Demand Theory Without a Utility Index." *Review of Economic Studies* 24: 185–89.

Mesarovic, Mihajlo D., Donald Macko, and Yasuhiko Takahara. 1970. *Theory of Hierarchical, Multi-Level Systems.* New York: Academic Press.

Metropolis, N., M.L. Stein, and P.R. Stein. 1967. *Numerische Mathematik* 10: 1–19.

———. 1973. *Journal of Combinatorial Theory* 15(A): 25–44.

Michael, Robert, and Gary Becker. 1973. "On the New Theory of Consumer Behavior." *Swedish Journal of Economics.*

Mills, Terence C. 1990. *Time Series Techniques for Economists.* Cambridge, UK: Cambridge University Press.

Minsky, Marvin. 1985. *The Society of Mind.* New York: Simon & Schuster.

Monod, Jacques. 1972. *Chance and Necessity.* New York: Random House.

Morishima, M. 1959. "The Problem of Intrinsic Complementarity and Separability of Goods." *Metroeconomica* 11: 188–202.

Morse, M. 1925. "Relations Between the Critical Points of a Real Function of *n* Independent Variables." *Transactions American Mathematical Society* 27: 345–96.

———. 1931. "The Critical Points of a Function of *n* Variables." *Transactions American Mathematical Society* 33: 72–91.

Muellbauer, John. 1974. "Household Production Theory, Quality, and the 'Hedonic Technique.' " *American Economic Review* 64, no. 6: 977–94.

Murray, J.D. 1993. *Mathematical Biology.* 2d corrected ed. Berlin: Springer-Verlag.

Muth, R.F. 1966. "Household Production and Consumer Demand Functions." *Econometrica* 34, no. 3: 699–708.

Myrberg, P.J. 1958. *Annales. Academiae Scientiarum Fennicae.* A.l. no. 259: 3–16.

———. 1963. *Annales. Academiae Scientiarum Fennicae.* A.l. no. 336/3: 3–18.

Neisser, Ulric. 1976. *Cognition and Reality.* San Francisco: W.H. Freeman.

Newhouse, Joseph P. 1970. "Toward a Theory of Nonprofit Institutions: An Economic Model of a Hospital." *American Economic Review* 60, no. 1: 64–74.

Nicholson, Walter. 1985. *Microeconomic Theory. Basic Principles and Extensions.* 3d ed. New York: Dryden Press.

Nickerson, Carol A. 1995. "Does Willingness to Pay Reflect the Purchase of Moral Satisfaction? A Reconsideration of Kahneman and Knetsch." *Journal of Environmental Economics and Management* 28: 126–33.

Nicolis, George, and Ilya Prigogine. 1977. *Self-Organization in Nonequilibrium Systems: From Dissipative Structures to Order Through Fluctuations.* New York: Wiley.

———. 1989. *Exploring Complexity.* New York: W.H. Freeman.

Ornstein, Robert. 1993. *The Roots of the Self.* New York: HarperCollins.

Pedersen, Winding. 1939. "Omkring den moderne Pristeori." *Saertryk af Nationalokonomisk Tidsskrift.*

Penz, G. Peter. 1986. *Consumer Sovereignty and Human Interests.* Cambridge, UK: Cambridge University Press.

Peterson, Jerrold M. 1976. "Product quality and the Slutsky equation." *Journal of Economics and Business* 29, no. 1: 53–58.

Pierce, John R. 1980. *An Introduction to Information Theory. Symbols, Signals and Noise.* 2d rev. ed. New York: Dover Publications.

Popper, Karl R., and John C. Eccles. 1977. *The Self and Its Brain.* New York: Springer International.

Popper, Karl R. 1979. *Objective Knowledge: An Evolutionary Approach.* Oxford: Oxford University Press.

Pratt, John W., David A. Wise, and Richard Zeckhauser. 1979. "Price Differences in Almost Competitive Markets." *Quarterly Journal of Economics* 93, no. 2: 189–211.

Prochiantz, Alain. 1989. *How the Brain Evolved.* New York: McGraw-Hill.

Prigogine, Ilya. 1980. *From Being to Becoming. Time and Complexity in the Physical Sciences.* San Francisco: W.H. Freeman.

Prigogine, Ilya, and Isabelle Stengers. 1984. *Order Out of Chaos. Man's New Dialogue With Nature.* Boulder, CO: New Science Library.

Quine, Willard van Orman. 1953. "The Problem of Meaning in Linguistics." In *From a Logical Point of View,* ed. Willard van Orman Quine. Cambridge, MA: Harvard University Press.

Restak, Richard M. 1994. *The Modular Brain.* New York: Macmillan.

Ricardo, David. 1969. *The Principles of Political Economy and Taxation.* New York: Dutton, pp. 35–36.

Riedl, Rupert. 1984. *Biology of Knowledge, The Evolutionary Basis of Reason.* New York: John Wiley.

Rinsley, D.B. 1982. *Borderline and Other Self Disorders: A Developmental-Object Relations Perspective.* New York: Jason Aronson.

Robinson, Joan. 1933. *The Economics of Imperfect Competition.* London: Macmillan.

Rose, Steven. 1992. *The Making of Memory. From Molecules to Mind.* New York: Anchor Books.

Rosen, Sherwin. 1974. "Hedonic Prices and Implicit Markets: Product Differentiation in Pure Competition." *Journal of Political Economy* 82, no. 1: 34–55.

Rosenfield, Israel. 1988. *The Invention of Memory.* New York: Basic Books.

Rosenzweig, M.R., E.L. Bennett, and M.C. Diamond. 1972. "Brain Changes in Response to Experience." *Scientific American* 226: 22–29.

Roth, Timothy P. 1987. *The Present State of Consumer Theory.* Lanham, MD: University Press of America.

Rubinstein, Ariel. 1998. *Modeling Bounded Rationality.* Cambridge, MA: MIT Press.

Ruelle, David. 1989a. *Chaotic Evolution and Strange Attractors. The Statistical Analysis of Time Series for Deterministic Nonlinear Systems.* Cambridge, UK: Cambridge University Press.

———. 1989b. *Elements of Differentiable Dynamics and Bifurcation Theory.* San Diego: Academic Press.

———. 1991. *Chance and Chaos.* Princeton, NJ: Princeton University Press.

Sato, Ryuzo. 1981. *Theory of Technical Change and Economic Invariance: Application of Lie Groups.* New York: Academic Press.

Saving, Thomas R. 1982. "Market Organization and Product Quality." *Southern Economic Journal* 48, no. 4: 855–67.

Schofield, Norman. 1984. *Mathematical Methods in Economics.* New York: New York University Press.

Schroeder, Manfred. 1991. *Fractals, Chaos, Power Laws.* New York: W.H. Freeman.

Schwartz, Alan, and Louis L. Wilde. 1985. "Product Quality and Imperfect Information." *Review of Economic Studies* 52: 251–62.

Schwenk, Theodor. 1976. *Sensitive Chaos.* New York: Schocken.

Scitovsky, Tibot. 1944–45. "Some Consequences of the Habit of Judging Quality by Price." *Review of Economic Studies*, 100–105.

Searle, J. 1983. *Intentionality: An Essay in the Philosophy of Mind.* Cambridge, MA: Cambridge University Press.

Shaw, Robert. 1981. "Strange Attractors, Chaotic Behavior, and Information Flow." *Z. Naturforsch* 36a: 80–112.

Shipley II, Frederic B. 1975. "Convergence of Adaptive Decisions." In *Adaptive Economic Models,* ed. Richard H. Day and Theodore Groves. New York: Academic Press.

Sidgwick, Henry. 1901. *The Principles of Political Economy.* 3d ed. London: Macmillan.

Simon, Herbert A. 1979. "Information Processing Models of Cognition." *Annual Review of Psychology* 30: 363–96.

Sinai, Ya G. 1977. *Introduction to Ergodic Theory.* Princeton, NJ: Princeton University Press.

Slovic, Paul, and Sarah Lichtenstein. 1983. "Preference Reversals: A Broader Perspective." *American Economic Review* 73: 596–605.

Smale, Steve. 1967. "Differentiable Dynamical Systems." *Bulletin of the American Mathematical Society* 73: 747–817.

———. 1973. "Global Analysis and Economics I: Pareto Optimum and a Generalization of Morse Theory." In *Dynamical Systems,* ed. M.M. Peixoto. New York: Academic Press.

———. 1974a. "Global Analysis and Economics IIA. Extension of a Theorem of Debreu." *Journal of Mathematical Economics* 1: 1–14.

————. 1974b. "Global Analysis and Economics III. Pareto Optima and Price Equilibria." *Journal of Mathematical Economics* 1: 107–17.

————. 1974c. "Global Analysis and Economics IV. Finiteness and Stability of Equilibria with General Consumption Sets and Production." *Journal of Mathematical Economics* 1: 119–27.

————. 1974d. "Global Analysis and Economics V. Pareto Theory with Constraints." *Journal of Mathematical Economics* 1: 213–21.

Smith, Adam. 1952. *Wealth of Nations.* The Great Books edition. Chicago: University of Chicago Press. (Original work published 1776.)

Stent, Gunther. 1975. "Limits to the Scientific Understanding of Man." *Science* 187, no. 4181: 1052–57.

Stigler, George J., and Gary S. Becker. 1977. "De Gustibus Non Est Disputandum." *American Economic Review* 67, no. 2: 76–90.

Stokey, Nancy L. 1986. "Learning-by-Doing and the Introduction of New Goods." Discussion Paper no. 699, The Center For Mathematical Studies In Economics And Management Science, Northwestern University, Evanston, IL.

Stone, Richard. 1956. *Quantity and Price Indexes in National Accounts.* Paris: Organization for European Economic Co–operation.

Strotz, Richard. 1957. "The Empirical Implications of a Utility Tree." *Econometrica* 25, no. 2: 269–80.

————. 1959. "The Utility Tree–A Correction and Further Appraisal." *Econometrica* 27, No 3: 482–88.

Stutzer, Michael J. 1980. "Chaotic Dynamics and Bifurcation in a Macro Model." *Journal of Economic Dynamics and Control* 2: 353–76.

Sutton, Richard S. and Andrew G. Barto. 1981. "Towards a Modern Theory of Adaptive Networks: Expectation and Prediction." *Psychological Review* 88: 135–70.

Sweeney, James L. 1974. "Quality, Commodity Hierarchies, and Housing Markets." *Econometrica* 42, no. 1: 147–67.

Thaler, Richard. 1980. "Toward a Positive Theory of Consumer Choice." *Journal of Economic Behavior and Organization* 1: 39–60.

Theil, Henri. 1951–52. "Qualities, Prices and Budget Enquiries." *Review of Economic Studies* 19(3), no. 50: 129–47.

Theil, Henri, and Frederick E. Suhm. 1981. *International Consumption Comparisons: A System-Wide Approach.* Amsterdam: North-Holland. Found in the series, Henri Theil and Herbert Glejser, eds., *Studies in Mathematical and Managerial Economics.* Amsterdam: North-Holland, Vol. 30.

Thom, R. 1975. *Structural Stability and Morphogenesis.* Reading, MA: W.A. Benjamin.

Thomas, Janet M. 1993. "The Implicit Market for Quality: An Hedonic Analysis." *Southern Economic Journal* 59, no. 4: 648–74.

Tirole, Jean. 1988. *The Theory of Industrial Organization.* Cambridge, MA: MIT Press.

Triplett, Jack. 1969. "Automobiles and Hedonic Quality Measurement." *Journal of Political Economy* 77: 408–17.

————. 1971. "The Theory of Hedonic Quality Measurement and Its Use in Price Indexes." Staff Report Paper no. 6, Bureau of Labor Statistics, U.S. Department of Labor. Washington, DC.

Triplett, Jack E. 1983. "Concepts of Quality in Input and Output Price Measures: A Resolution of the User-Value Resource-Cost Debate." In *The U.S. National Income and Product Accounts: Selected Topics,* ed. Murray F. Foss. Chicago: University of Chicago Press.

————. 1986. "The Economic Interpretation of Hedonic Methods." *Survey of Current Business* (January): 36–40.

———. 1990. "Hedonic Methods in Statistical Agency Environments: An Intellectual Biopsy." In *Fifty Years of Economic Measurement,* ed. Ernst R. Berndt and Jack E. Triplett. Chicago: University of Chicago Press.

Tversky, Amos, and Daniel Kahneman. 1981. "The Framing of Decisions and the Psychology of Choice." *Science* 211: 453–58.

Viscusi, W. Kip. 1985. "Are Individuals Bayesian Decision Makers?" *American Economic Review,* Papers and Proceedings. 75, no. 2: 381–85.

Wang, Paul P., and S.K. Chang. 1980. *Fuzzy Sets. Theory and Applications to Policy Analysis and Information Systems.* New York: Plenum.

Waterman, Donald A., and Frederick Hayes-Roth, eds. 1978. *Pattern-Directed Inference Systems.* New York: Academic Press.

Waugh, Frederick V. 1923. "Factors Influencing the Price of New Jersey Potatoes in the New York Market." Circular no. 66, New Jersey Department of Agriculture.

———. 1929. *Quality as a Determinant of Vegetable Prices.* New York: Ams Press.

Weibull, Jorgen W. 1995. *Evolutionary Game Theory.* Cambridge: MIT Press.

Whitney, H. 1955. "On Singularities of Mappings of Euclidean Spaces I, Mappings of the Plane into the Plane." *Annals of Mathematics* 62: 374–410.

Wicksell, Knut. 1934. *Lectures on Political Economy.* Vol. 1. London: Lund Humphries. (Original work published 1901.)

Wilde, Keith D., Allen D. LeBaron, and L. Dwight Israelsen. 1985. "Knowledge, Uncertainty, and Behavior." *American Economic Review,* Papers and Proceedings 75, no. 2: 403–8.

Willig, Robert D. 1976. "Consumer's Surplus Without Apology." *American Economic Review* 66, no. 4: 589–97.

Winrich, J. Steven. 1984. "Self-Reference and the Incomplete Structure of Neoclassical Economics." *Journal of Economic Issues* 18, no. 4: 987–1005.

Witte, Ann D., Howard J. Sumka, and Homer Erekson. 1979. "An Estimate of a Structural Hedonic Price Model of the Housing Market: An Application of Rosen's Theory of Implicit Markets." *Econometrica* 47, no. 5: 1151–73.

Wold, H., and L. Jureen. 1953. *Demand Analysis: A Study in Econometrics.* New York: Wiley.

Working, Holbrook. 1925. "Factors Affecting the Price of Minnesota Potatoes." *Bulletin.* no. 29. Minnesota Agricultural Experiment Station.

Zadeh, Lotfi A., King-Sun Fu, Kokicki Tanaka, and Masamichi Shimura, eds. 1975. *Fuzzy Sets and Their Applications to Cognitive and Decision Processes.* New York: Academic Press.

Zeeman, E.C., and C. Isuard. 1972. "Some Models from Catastrophe Theory." Conference on Models in Social Sciences. Edinburgh.

Zeeman, E.C. 1976. "Catastrophe Theory." *Scientific American* 234, no. 4: 65–83.

Zeuthen, F. 1968. *Problems of Monopoly and Economic Warfare.* New York: Kelley. (Translation of the original Danish published 1930.)

———. 1935. "Effect and Cost of Advertisement from a Theoretic Aspect." *Nordisk Tidsskrift for Teknisk Okonomi.*

Index

About the Author

William M. Wadman received his PhD. in economics from Claremont Graduate School in 1976. He has worked as a health economist with the California State Department of Health, and as a research scientist with the Center for Health Studies, Research Triangle Institute, North Carolina. He has also worked in Latin America, Africa, and Central Asia. He has taught at Pomona College and Western Illinois University and is currently at the University of North Carolina at Wilmington. In 1989 he worked in Chile as a Fulbright professor (lecturer). His research interests are variable quality, human decision making, comparative economic systems, and health care in developing nations.